THE PRINCIPLES
AND PRACTICE OF
FREEDOM OF SPEECH

Second Edition

Edited by
Haig A. Bosmajian
University of Washington

UNIVERSITY
PRESS OF
AMERICA

Lanham • New York • London

Copyright © 1983 by

University Press of America,™ Inc.

4720 Boston Way
Lanham, MD 20706

3 Henrietta Street
London WC2E 8LU England

Copyright © 1971 by

Houghton Mifflin Company, Boston

Library of Congress Cataloging in Publication Data

Main entry under title:

The Principles and practice of freedom of speech.

   Originally published: Boston : Houghton Mifflin,
[1971]
   1. Freedom of speech—United States. I. Bosmajian,
Haig A.
KF4772.A7P74   1983   342.73'0853   82-23739
ISBN 0-8191-2962-3 (pbk.)   347.302853

Contents

Part III Contemporary Essays on Freedom of Speech:
General Principles and Specific Issues

Introduction

Who in a society is to be silenced, who is to be prosecuted for his utterances, who is to be denied what we now refer to as freedom of speech — these questions have confronted almost all societies in the past twenty-five centuries. Men and women have been ostracized, persecuted, jailed, tortured, and executed for expressing their opinions and advocating doctrines which other men and women have judged to be offensive, immoral, subversive, or simply undesirable. In the fourth century B.C., Socrates, the Athenian gadfly, was tried and put to death for not worshipping the gods of the state and for corrupting the minds of the youth. In the fifteenth century, Savonarola had the works of Dante, Ovid, and Boccaccio burned in Italy, and then was himself tortured on the rack, forced to confess his heresy in criticizing papal corruptions and demanding church reforms, and hung on a cross and burned with all his writings, sermons, and pamphlets. In the sixteenth century, Joan of Arc was burned at the stake, and in Italy Pope Leo X ordered Martin Luther burned in effigy along with his books. In the seventeenth century, Galileo was required under threat of torture and imprisonment to promise that he would never again through speaking or writing spread the Copernican theory. In the eighteenth century, the Puritans were persecuted and in turn persecuted men of other faiths. In the nineteenth century, abolitionists were harassed, threatened with violence, beaten, and run out of town for their attempts to spread antislavery sentiments. And in the twentieth century, antiwar protesters and civil rights workers have been persecuted, beaten, and sent to jail for their demonstrations. Since the founding of the country, Americans have tried, too often with success, to suppress the expression of other Americans: Quakers, Jeffersonian Republicans, abolitionists, Jehovah's Witnesses, Mormons, socialists, anarchists, ministers, war protesters, labor leaders, pacifists, Nazis, Wobblies, teachers, students, and a host of others have been harassed, threatened, brought to trial, and imprisoned for propagating their beliefs.

Americans continue to try to silence other Americans. Students protesting the war in Viet Nam are prosecuted; ministers and laymen advising youth to resist the draft are jailed; speakers are banned from college campuses; symbolic protests of various kinds are "busted." And suppression will remain with us as long as there are men and women who question, challenge, and threaten the beliefs, doctrines, and dogma of other men. The usefulness of dissent is seldom recognized by those who are the objects of dissent; every effort is made to silence the dissenter, and little is done to safeguard his freedom of speech. Men who recognize that the persecution and imprisonment of the dissenters of the past were unreasonable and unjustified can at the same time not recognize as unreasonable and unjustified the persecution and imprisonment of their contemporaries. Somehow, men in positions of power can prosecute and imprison those who do not believe in the gods of the state or are suspected of corrupting the minds of the youth and at the same time deplore what the Athenians did to Socrates. The same men who attempt to justify the silencing of socialists, communists, or anarchists can condemn John Milton for denying free expression to the Catholics of his day, though they seemed as much a threat to Milton's society as the dissenters to ours. The same men who would admit that the Federalist persecution and imprisonment of the Jeffersonian Republicans was never justified by the circumstances of the late eighteenth century can somehow justify prosecuting those who dissent against contemporary administrations. The same men who look with amusement at the attempts to silence the nineteenth-century abolitionists can look with all seriousness on the jailing of twentieth-century civil rights demonstrators.

The local, state, and federal legislation proposed within the last two decades to ban speakers, restrict assembly, discourage free discussion, and restrict symbolic opposition to governmental policies would easily fill several thick volumes. Much of this proposed legislation has never been passed, but enough of it has become law to suppress Americans with divers views who take seriously Thomas Jefferson's advice that "if there be any among us who would wish to dissolve this Union or to change its republican form, let them stand undisturbed as monuments of the safety with which error of opinion may be tolerated where reason is left free to combat it." Too often we have relied on the courts to protect our freedom of speech, when we ourselves should have seen to it that suppressive measures were never legislated in the first place. We cannot always expect the courts to guard our freedom of speech from overzealous men who are afraid of freedom and attempt to restrict the expression of others. As Daniel Pollitt, Professor of Law, wrote in the December, 1967, *North Carolina Law Review:*

> Although the courts have held fast to democratic traditions, and in some instances have extended first amendment freedoms to new fields, the pressures of uncertainty and confusion have pushed other public agencies, and private citizens, to extreme action. Pacifists have been beaten by toughs, the Georgia legislature attempted to deny an elected seat to Julian Bond because of his antiwar expressions, high school students have been suspended for wearing black armbands in mourning for the Viet Nam dead.[1]

Professor Thomas I. Emerson has pointed out that "the American people have frequently been warned that they must not count too heavily upon the legal system for the preservation of democratic liberties." He quotes an incisive comment from Judge Learned Hand:

> I often wonder whether we do not rest our hopes too much upon constitutions, upon laws and upon courts. These are false hopes; believe me, these are false hopes. Liberty lies in the hearts of men and women; when it dies there, no constitution, no law, no court can save it; no constitution, no law, no court can even do much to help it. While it lies there it needs no constitution, no law, no court to save it.[2]

In the end, the breadth of freedom of speech is determined by the citizenry. Yet the natural tendency of Man the citizen is not only to attempt to eliminate unorthodox expression but also to refrain from expressing the unorthodox himself. As John Stuart Mill put it: "Who can compute what the world loses in the multitude of promising intellects combined with timid characters, who dare not follow out any bold, vigorous, independent train of thought, lest it should land them in something which would admit of being considered irreligious or immoral?" It is difficult enough to get men to think the unthinkable and to express the unthinkable without threatening them, directly or indirectly, with some type of penalty for the expression of those "un-

---

[1] Daniel Pollitt, "Free Speech for Mustangs and Mavericks," *North Carolina Law Review,* 46 (December, 1967), 39–40.

[2] Thomas I. Emerson, "Toward A General Theory of the First Amendment," *The Yale Law Journal,* 72 (April, 1963), 893.

thinkable" ideas. Of man's tendency to eliminate unorthodox expression, Professor Emerson has written:

> Most men have a strong inclination to suppress opposition even where
> differences in viewpoint are comparatively slight. But a system of free
> expression must be framed to withstand far greater stress. The test
> of any such system is not whether it tolerates minor deviations but
> whether it permits criticism of the fundamental beliefs and practices
> of the society. And in this area the drives to repress, both irrational
> and rational, tend to become overwhelming.[3]

An example of how far a representative of the citizenry will go in
an attempt to suppress criticism was reported in the May 6, 1967,
New York Times:

> Members of the House Armed Services Committee demanded today
> that the Justice Department disregard the First Amendment right of
> free speech and prosecute those who urged young men to defy the
> draft law. "Let's forget about the First Amendment," Representative
> F. Edward Hébert, Democrat of La., told Assistant Attorney General
> Fred M. Vinson, Jr. in a loud voice during hearings on the draft.

One Congressman wanted to know why Stokely Carmichael had
not been prosecuted for leading students at Hampton Institute in
chanting, "We ain't gonna go. Hell no." The Assistant Attorney
General replied that his department could not prosecute Mr. Carmichael because of the First Amendment, and he cited a decision
going back to Oliver Wendell Holmes that utterances were protected
by the First Amendment unless they constituted a "clear and present
danger" to the country. Congressman Hébert's reply revealed that he
was ready to deny First Amendment rights to more people than Mr.
Carmichael. "We have been made aware of that in the past year,"
Mr. Hébert replied. "How can the Carmichaels and Kings stand
before the American people and incite violation of the law while the
Justice Department stands idly by?" "No one," Mr. Vinson said,
"has been prosecuted because the department felt no one has violated
the law." Could the law be amended to "get around the First Amendment?" Mr. Hébert asked. "Any law that deals with utterances must
be read in the light of the First Amendment," Mr. Vinson said. Then

[3] *Ibid.,* 887.

Congressman Hébert said, "Let's forget about the First Amendment."

Realizing that we have been, are, and will be confronted with decisions about who should be allowed to communicate his beliefs in our society, what philosophical, legal, and "practical" bases do we have for making these decisions? Few people will say, "He should not be allowed to speak simply because I don't like what he says." They will usually try to dredge up some philosophical or legal argument to defend the suppression of speech, even though the arguments are quite superficial. Furthermore, individuals arguing against the suppression of speech too often present the weakest arguments for allowing free speech.

The purpose of this book is to bring to the student a variety of arguments which have been used to explain and defend freedom of speech. For instance, he will find the philosopher John Stuart Mill propounding the utility of free expression: to know truth, we must know error; heretical works should be read so that we can understand the heretic and see if our own ideas can withstand the collision with error; suppression of speech will not keep wise men from being wise or fools from being foolish; suppression discourages learning; the opinion which is suppressed may, for all we know, be the truth; if opinion held to be the "truth" is left unchallenged it may degenerate into dogma or prejudice. Reading utilitarian Mill on free expression will give the student a stronger base for judging later free-speech cases and issues, for he will find Supreme Court justices and free-speech scholars echoing in their decisions and essays the ideas of Mill.

This book contains some of the classic freedom-of-speech court cases and some of the tests used to determine who can or cannot speak, what can or cannot be said. The student will find in the cases and selected essays arguments for and against such tests as the "clear and present danger" test, the "bad tendency" test, the "balance of interest" test, and the "absolutist" test. He will also find that the freedom of speech guaranteed by the First Amendment has come to include more than "speaking" as we usually think of it. The courts have decided that civil rights demonstrations, under certain circumstances, are forms of expression protected by the First Amendment; some have looked on draft card burning as a form of expression protected by the First Amendment; others have had to decide whether burning the American flag is protected by the First Amendment; still others have had to decide whether a student can be reclassified from II-S to I-A for antiwar protests and activities.

The editor hopes that the combination of materials in this volume — philosophical essays, court cases, and analyses of contemporary issues — will enable the student to make sounder decisions about current and future problems in freedom of speech.

Haig A. Bosmajian

*　　*　　*

Since much of the discussion of freedom of speech in the United States hinges on the Supreme Court's interpretation of the First and Fourteenth Amendments to the Constitution, pertinent sections of both amendments are reprinted below.

Article I

Congress shall make no law respecting an establishment of religion, or prohibiting the free exercise thereof; or abridging the freedom of speech, or of the press; or the right of the people peaceably to assemble, and to petition the government for a redress of grievances.

Article XIV
Section 1

All persons born or naturalized in the United States, and subject to the jurisdiction thereof, are citizens of the United States and of the State wherein they reside. No State shall make or enforce any law which shall abridge the privileges or immunities of citizens of the United States; nor shall any State deprive any person of life, liberty or property, without due process of law; nor deny to any person within its jurisdiction the equal protection of the law.

Section 5

The Congress shall have power to enforce, by appropriate legislation, the provisions of this article.

PART

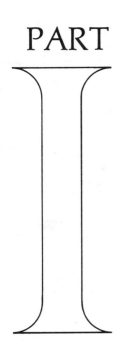

Freedom of Speech:
Antecedents and
Determinants

John Stuart Mill

The following selection is Chapter Two of John Stuart Mill's essay *On Liberty*, first published in 1859. Mill, the English utilitarian, argues the case for freedom of thought and expression on the grounds of social utility. In Chapter One of the essay Mill writes:

> It is proper to state that I forgo any advantage which could be derived to my argument from the idea of abstract right, as a thing independent of utility. I regard utility as the ultimate appeal on all ethical questions; but it must be utility in the largest sense, grounded on the permanent interests of man as a progressive being.

The object of his essay, he points out,

> . . . is to assert one very simple principle, as entitled to govern absolutely the dealings of society with the individual in the way of compulsion and control, whether the means used be physical force in the form of legal penalties, or the moral coercion of public opinion. That principle is, that the sole end for which mankind are warranted, individually or collectively, in interfering with the liberty of action of any of their number, is self-protection. That the only purpose for which power can be rightfully exercised over any member of a civilized community, against his will, is to prevent harm to others. His own good, either physical or moral, is not a sufficient warrant. He cannot rightfully be compelled to do or forbear because it will be better for him to do so, because it will make him happier, because, in the opinions of others, to do so would be wise, or even right. These are good reasons for remonstrating with him, or reasoning with him, or persuading him, or entreating him, but not for compelling him, or visiting him with any evil in case he do otherwise.

The reader of Chapter Two of *On Liberty* must also be aware that Mill's ideas and doctrine on freedom of thought and expression are "meant to apply only to human beings in the maturity of their faculties." Mill explains in Chapter One:

> We are not speaking of children, or of young persons below the age which the law may fix as that of manhood or womanhood. Those who are still in a state to require being taken care of by others, must be protected against their own actions as well as against external injury. For the same reason, we may leave out of consideration those backward states of society in which the race itself may be considered as in its non-age. The early difficulties in the way of spontaneous progress are so great, that there is seldom any choice of means for overcoming them; and a ruler full of the spirit of improvement is warranted in the use of any expedients that will attain an end, perhaps otherwise unattainable. Despotism is a legitimate mode of government in dealing with barbarians, provided the end be their improvement, and the means justified by actually effecting that end. Liberty, as a principle, has no application to any state of things anterior to the time when mankind have become capable of being improved by free and equal discussion.

The student should not allow these "exceptions" to detract from the fundamental arguments and doctrine of Mill, just as Milton's "exceptions" should not have detracted from his basic arguments and doctrine as presented in his "Areopagitica" (1644).

The universality and timelessness of *On Liberty* were predicted by Mill himself when he wrote in his autobiography that "the 'Liberty' is likely to survive longer than anything else that I have written." It has been translated into nearly all the living languages. It has been banned and burned by various totalitarian regimes. Albert W. Levi points out in *The Six Great Humanistic Essays of John Stuart Mill* that

> . . . In 1861 'On Liberty' was translated into Russian and became a thorn in the flesh of the Czar's secret police, but fifteen years later another Slav, Peter Karageorgevitch, later to become King of Serbia, painstakingly translated it himself into his native tongue. Prior to the second World War, at precisely the moment when Harold Laski and the intellectual leaders of the British Labor Party were appealing to it as a sacred text of political principle, the Japanese Emperor Hirohito, deeming it a potent source of the contagious disease *kikenshiso* (dangerous thoughts), banished it from the public domain.[1]

[1] Albert William Levi, Introduction to *The Six Great Humanistic Essays of John Stuart Mill* (New York: Washington Square Press, 1963), p. xii.

ON THE LIBERTY OF THOUGHT AND DISCUSSION

John Stuart Mill

The time, it is to be hoped, is gone by when any defence would be necessary of the "liberty of the press" as one of the securities against corrupt or tyrannical government. No argument, we may suppose, can now be needed, against permitting a legislature or an executive, not identified in interest with the people, to prescribe opinions to them, and determine what doctrines or what arguments they shall be allowed to hear. This aspect of the question, besides, has been so often and so triumphantly enforced by preceding writers, that it needs not be specially insisted on in this place. Though the law of England, on the subject of the press, is as servile to this day as it was in the time of the Tudors, there is little danger of its being actually put in force against political discussion, except during some temporary panic, when fear of insurrection drives ministers and judges from their propriety;[1] and, speaking generally, it is not, in constitutional countries, to be apprehended that the government, whether completely responsible to the people or not, will often attempt to control the expression of opinion, except when in doing so it makes itself the organ of the general intolerance of the public. Let us suppose, therefore, that the government is entirely at one with the people, and never thinks of exerting any power of coercion unless in agreement with what it conceives to be their voice. But I deny the right of the people to exercise such coercion, either by themselves or by their government. The power itself is illegitimate. The best govern-

John S. Mill, *Essay on Liberty*, Chapter 2. From *Harvard Classics*, Vol. 25 (1909), pp. 218–259. This material is reprinted with the kind permission of Crowell Collier and Macmillan, Inc.

Passages not essential to Mill's argument have been deleted to save space. The deletions are indicated by a row of spaced periods. Footnotes appear at the end of the selection.

ment has no more title to it than the worst. It is as noxious, or more noxious, when exerted in accordance with public opinion, than when in opposition to it. If all mankind minus one, were of one opinion, and only one person were of the contrary opinion, mankind would be no more justified in silencing that one person, than he, if he had the power, would be justified in silencing mankind. Were an opinion a personal possession of no value except to the owner; if to be obstructed in the enjoyment of it were simply a private injury, it would make some difference whether the injury was inflicted only on a few persons or on many. But the peculiar evil of silencing the expression of an opinion is, that it is robbing the human race; posterity as well as the existing generation; those who dissent from the opinion, still more than those who hold it. If the opinion is right, they are deprived of the opportunity of exchanging error for truth: if wrong, they lose, what is almost as great a benefit, the clearer perception and livelier impression of truth, produced by its collision with error.

It is necessary to consider separately these two hypotheses, each of which has a distinct branch of the argument corresponding to it. We can never be sure that the opinion we are endeavoring to stifle is a false opinion; and if we were sure, stifling it would be an evil still.

First: the opinion which it is attempted to suppress by authority may possibly be true. Those who desire to suppress it, of course deny its truth; but they are not infallible. They have no authority to decide the question for all mankind, and exclude every other person from the means of judging. To refuse a hearing to an opinion, because they are sure that it is false, is to assume that *their* certainty is the same thing as *absolute* certainty. All silencing of discussion is an assumption of infallibility. Its condemnation may be allowed to rest on this common argument, not the worse for being common.

Unfortunately for the good sense of mankind, the fact of their fallibility is far from carrying the weight in their practical judgment, which is always allowed to it in theory; for while every one well knows himself to be fallible, few think it necessary to take any precautions against their own fallibility, or admit the supposition that any opinion of which they feel very certain, may be one of the examples of the error to which they acknowledge themselves to be liable. Absolute princes, or others who are accustomed to unlimited deference, usually feel this complete confidence in their own opinions on nearly all subjects. People more happily situated, who sometimes hear their opinions disrupted, and are not wholly unused to be set right when they are wrong, place the same unbounded reliance only on such of their opinions as are shared by all who surround them, or to whom they habitually defer: for in proportion to a man's want of confidence in his own solitary judgment, does he usually repose, with implicit trust, on the infallibility of "the world" in general. And the world, to each individual, means the part of it with which he comes in contact; his party, his sect, his church, his class of society: the man may be called, by comparison, almost liberal and large-minded to whom it means anything so comprehensive as his own country or his own age. Nor is his faith in this collective authority at all shaken by his being aware that other ages, countries, sects, churches, classes, and parties have thought, and even now think, the exact reverse. He develops upon his own world the responsibility of being in the right against the dissentient worlds of other people; and it never troubles him that mere accident has decided which of these numerous worlds is the object of his reliance, and that the same causes which make him a Churchman in London, would have made him a Buddhist or a Confucian in Pekin. Yet it is as evident in itself as any amount of argument can make it, that ages are no more infallible than individuals; every age having held many opinions which subsequent ages have deemed not only false but absurd; and it is as certain that many opinions, now general, will be rejected by future ages, as it is that many, once general, are rejected by the present.

The objection likely to be made to this argument, would probably take some such form as the following. There is no greater assumption of infallibility in forbidding the propagation of error, than in any other thing which is done by public authority on its own judgment and responsibility. Judgment is given to men that they may use it. Because it may be used erroneously, are men to be told that they ought not to use it at all? To prohibit what they think pernicious, is not claiming exemption from error, but fulfilling the duty incumbent on them, although fallible, of acting on their conscientious conviction. If we were never to act on our opinions, because those opinions may be wrong, we should leave all our interests uncared for, and all our duties unperformed. An objection which applies to all conduct can be no valid objection to any conduct in particular.

It is the duty of governments, and of individuals, to form the truest opinions they can; to form them carefully, and never impose them upon others unless they are quite sure of being right. But when they are sure (such reasoners may say), it is not conscientiousness but cowardice to shrink from acting on their opinions, and allow doctrines which they honestly think dangerous to the welfare of mankind, either in this life or in another, to be scattered abroad without restraint, because other people, in less enlightened times, have persecuted opinions now believed to be true. Let us take care, it may be said, not to make the same mistake: but governments and nations have made mistakes in other things, which are not denied to be fit subjects for the exercise of authority: they have laid on bad taxes, made unjust wars. Ought we therefore to lay on no taxes, and, under whatever provocation, make no wars? Men, and governments, must act to the best of their ability. There is no such thing as absolute certainty, but there is assurance sufficient for the purposes of human life. We may, and must, assume our opinion to be true for the guidance of our own conduct: and it is assuming no more when we forbid bad men to pervert society by the propagation of opinions which we regard as false and pernicious.

I answer, that it is assuming very much more. There is the greatest difference between presuming an opinion to be true, because, with every opportunity for contesting it, it has not been refuted, and assuming its truth for the purpose of not permitting its refutation. Complete liberty of contradicting and disproving our opinion, is the very condition which justifies us in assuming its truth for purposes of action; and on no other terms can a being with human faculties have any rational assurance of being right.

When we consider either the history of opinion, or the ordinary conduct of human life, to what is it to be ascribed that the one and the other are no worse than they are? Not certainly to the inherent force of the human understanding; for, on any matter not self-evident, there are ninety-nine persons totally incapable of judging of it, for one who is capable; and the capacity of the hundredth person is only comparative; for the majority of the eminent men of every past generation held many opinions now known to be erroneous, and did or approved numerous things which no one will now justify. Why is it, then, that there is on the whole a preponderance among mankind of rational opinions and rational conduct? If there really is this preponderance — which there must be, unless human affairs are, and have always been, in an almost desperate state — it is owing to a quality of the human mind, the source of everything respectable in man, either as an intellectual or as a moral being, namely, that his errors are corrigible. He is capable of rectifying his mistakes by discussion and experience. Not by experience alone. There must be discussion, to show how experience is to be interpreted. Wrong opinions and practices gradually yield to fact and argument: but facts and arguments, to produce any effect on the mind, must be brought before it. Very few are able to tell their own story, without comments to bring out their meaning. The whole strength and value, then, of human judgment, depending on the one property, that it can be set right when it is wrong, reliance can be placed on it only when the means of setting it right are kept constantly at hand. In the case of any person whose judgment is really deserving of confidence, how has it become so? Because he has kept his mind open to criticism of his opinions and conduct. Because it has been his practice to listen to all that could be said against him; to profit by as much of it as was just, and expound to himself, and upon occasion to others, the fallacy of what was fallacious. Because he has felt, that the only way in which a human being can make some approach to knowing the whole of a subject, is by hearing what can be said about it by persons of every variety of opinion, and studying all modes in which it can be looked at by every character of mind. No wise man ever acquired his wisdom in any mode but this; nor is it in the nature of human intellect to become wise in any other manner. The steady habit of correcting and completing his own opinion by collating it with those of others, so far from causing doubt and hesitation in carrying it into practice, is the only stable foundation for a just reliance on it: for, being cognizant of all that can, at least obviously, be said against him, and having taken up his position against all gainsayers knowing that he has sought for objections and difficulties, instead of avoiding them, and has shut out no light which can be thrown upon the subject from any quarter — he has a right to think his judgment better than that of any person, or any multitude, who have not gone through a similar process.

It is not too much to require that what the wisest of mankind, those who are best entitled to trust their own judgment, find necessary to warrant their relying on it, should be submitted to by that miscellaneous collection of a few wise and many foolish individuals, called the public. The most intolerant of churches, the Roman Catholic Church, even at the canonization of a saint, admits, and listens patiently to, a "devil's advocate." The holiest of men, it appears, cannot be admitted to posthumous honors, until all that the devil could say against him is known and weighed. If even the Newtonian philosophy were not permitted to be questioned, mankind could not feel as complete assurance of its truth as they now do. The beliefs which we have most warrant for, have no safeguard to rest on, but a standing invitation to the whole world to prove them unfounded. If the challenge is not accepted, or is accepted and the attempt fails, we are far enough from certainty still; but we have done the best that the existing state of human reason admits of; we have neglected nothing that could give the truth a chance of reaching us: if the lists are kept open, we may hope that if there be a better truth, it will be found when the human mind is capable of receiving it; and in the meantime we may rely on having attained such approach to truth, as is possible in our own day. This is the amount of certainty attainable by a fallible being, and this the sole way of attaining it.

Strange it is, that men should admit the validity of the arguments for free discussion, but object to their being "pushed to an extreme"; not seeing that unless the reasons are good for an extreme case, they are not good for any case. Strange that they should imagine that they are not assuming infallibility when they acknowledge that there should be free discussion on all subjects which can possibly be *doubtful*, but think that some particular principle or doctrine should be forbidden to be questioned because it is *so certain*, that is, because *they are certain* that it is certain. To call any proposition certain, while there is any one who would deny its certainty if permitted, but who is not permitted, is to assume that we ourselves, and those who agree with us, are the judges of certainty, and judge without hearing the other side.

In the present age — which has been described as "destitute of faith, but terrified at scepticism" — in which people feel sure, not so much that their opinions are true, as that they should not know what to do without them — the claims of an opinion to be protected from public attack are rested not so much on its truth, as on its importance to society. There are, it is alleged, certain beliefs, so useful, not to say indispensable to well-being, that it is as much the duty of government to uphold those beliefs, as to protect any other of the interests of society. In a case of such necessity, and so directly in the line of their duty, something less than infallibility may, it is maintained, warrant, and even bind, governments, to act on their own opinion, confirmed by the general opinion of mankind. It is also often argued, and still oftener thought, that none but bad men would desire to weaken these salutary beliefs; and there can be nothing wrong, it is thought, in restraining bad men, and prohibiting what only such men would wish to practise. This mode of thinking makes the justification of restraints on discussion not a question of the truth of doctrines, but of their usefulness; and flatters itself by that means to escape the responsibility of claiming to be an infallible judge of opinions. But those who thus satisfy themselves, do not perceive that the assumption of infallibility is merely shifted from one point to another. The usefulness of an opinion is itself matter of opinion: as disputable, as open to discussion and requiring discussion as much, as the opinion itself. There is the same need of an infallible judge of opinions to decide an opinion to be noxious, as to decide it to be false, unless the opinion condemned has full opportunity of defending itself. And it will not do to say that the heretic may be allowed to maintain the utility or harmlessness of his opinion, though forbidden to maintain its truth. The truth of an opinion is part of its utility. If we would know whether or not it is desirable that a proposition should be believed, is it possible to exclude the consideration of whether or not it is true? In the opinion, not of bad men, but of the best men, no belief which is contrary to truth can be really useful: and can you prevent such men from urging that plea, when they are charged with culpability for denying some doctrine which they are told is useful, but which they believe to be false? Those who are on the side of received opinions, never fail to take all possible advantage of this plea; you do not find *them* handling the question of utility as if it could be completely abstracted from that of truth: on the contrary, it is, above all, because their doctrine is "the truth," that the knowledge or the belief of it is held to be so indispensable. There can be no fair discussion of the question of usefulness, when an argument so vital may be employed on one side, but not on the other. And in point of fact, when law or public feeling do not permit the truth of an opinion to be disputed, they are just as little tolerant of a denial of its usefulness. The utmost they allow is an extenuation of its absolute necessity or of the positive guilt of rejecting it.

In order more fully to illustrate the mischief of denying a hearing to opinions because we, in our own judgment, have condemned them, it will be desirable to fix down the discussion to a concrete case; and I choose, by preference, the cases which are least favourable to me — in which the argument against freedom of opinion, both on the score of truth and on that of utility, is considered the strongest. Let the opinions impugned be the belief in a God and in a future state, or any of the commonly received doctrines of morality. To fight the battle on such ground, gives a great advantage to an unfair antagonist; since he will be sure to say (and many who have no desire to be unfair will say it internally), Are these the doctrines which you do not deem sufficiently certain to be taken under the protection of law? Is the belief in a God one of the opinions, to feel sure of which, you hold to be assuming infallibility? But I must be permitted to observe, that it is not the feeling sure of a doctrine (be it what it may) which I call an assumption of infallibility. It is the undertaking to decide that question *for others*, without allowing them to hear what can be said on the contrary side. And I denounce and reprobate this pretension not the less, if put forth on the side of my most solemn convictions. However positive any one's persuasion may be, not only of the falsity, but of the pernicious consequences — not only of the pernicious consequences, but (to adopt expressions which I altogether condemn) the immorality and impiety of an opinion; yet if, in pursuance of that private judgment, though backed by the public judgment of his country or his contemporaries, he prevents the opinion from being heard in its defence, he assumes infallibility. And so far from the assumption being less objectionable or less dangerous because the opinion is called immoral or impious, this is the case of all others in which it is most fatal. These are exactly the occasions on which the men of one generation commit those dreadful mistakes which excite the astonishment and horror of posterity. It is among such that we find the instances memorable in history, when the arm of the law has been employed to root out the best men and the noblest doctrines; with deplorable success as to the men, though some of the doctrines have survived to be (as if in mockery) invoked, in defence of similar conduct towards those who dissent from *them*, or from their received interpretation.

·   ·   ·   ·   ·

A theory which maintains that truth may justifiably be persecuted because persecution cannot possibly do it any harm, cannot be charged with being intentionally hostile to the reception of new truths; but we cannot commend the generosity of its dealing with the persons to whom mankind are indebted for them. To discover to the world something which deeply concerns it, and of which it was previously ignorant; to prove to it that it had been mistaken on some vital point of temporal or spiritual interest, is as important a service as a human being can render to his fellow-creatures, and in certain cases, as in those of the early Christians and of the Reformers, those who think with Dr. Johnson believe it to have been the most precious gift which could be bestowed on mankind. That the authors of such splendid benefits should be requited by martyrdom; that their reward should be to be dealt with as the vilest of criminals, is not, upon this theory, a deplorable error and misfortune, for which humanity should mourn in sackcloth and ashes, but the normal and justifiable state of things. The propounder of a new truth, according to this doctrine, should stand, as stood, in the legislation of the Locrians, the proposer of a new law, with a halter round his neck, to be instantly tightened if the public assembly did not, on hearing his reasons, then and there adopt his proposition. People who defend this mode of treating bene-factors, can not be supposed to set much value on the benefit; and I believe this view of the subject is mostly confined to the sort of persons who think that new truths may have been desirable once, but that we have had enough of them now.

But, indeed, the dictum that truth always triumphs over persecu-tion, is one of those pleasant falsehoods which men repeat after one another till they pass into commonplaces, but which all experience refutes. History teems with instances of truth put down by persecu-tion. If not suppressed forever, it may be thrown back for centuries. To speak only of religious opinions: the Reformation broke out at least twenty times before Luther, and was put down. Arnold of Brescia was put down. Fra Dolcino was put down. Savonarola was put down. The Albigeois were put down. The Vaudois were put down. The Lollards were put down. The Hussites were put down. Even after the era of Luther, wherever persecution was persisted in, it was successful. In Spain, Italy, Flanders, the Austrian empire, Protestantism was rooted out; and, most likely, would have been so in England, had Queen Mary lived, or Queen Elizabeth died. Per-secution has always succeeded, save where the heretics were too strong a party to be effectually persecuted. No reasonable person can doubt that Christianity might have been extirpated in the Roman empire. It spread, and became predominant, because the persecutions were only occasional, lasting but a short time, and separated by long intervals of almost undisturbed propagandism. It is a piece of idle sentimentality that truth, merely as truth, has any inherent power denied to error, of prevailing against the dungeon and the stake. Men are not more zealous for truth than they often are for error, and a sufficient application of legal or even of social penalties will generally succeed in stopping the propagation of either. The real advantage which truth has, consists in this, that when an opinion is true, it may be extinguished once, twice, or many times, but in the course of ages there will generally be found persons to rediscover it, until some one of its reappearances falls on a time when from favourable circumstances it escapes persecution until it has made such head as to withstand all subsequent attempts to suppress it.

It will be said, that we do not now put to death the introducers of new opinions: we are not like our fathers who slew the prophets, we even build sepulchres to them. It is true we no longer put heretics to death; and the amount of penal infliction which modern feeling would probably tolerate, even against the most obnoxious opinions, is not sufficient to extirpate them. But let us not flatter ourselves that we are yet free from the stain even of legal persecution. Penalties for opinion, or at least, for its expression, still exist by law; and their enforcement is not, even in these times, so unexampled as to make it at all incredible that they may some day be revived in full force. In the year 1857, at the summer assizes of the county of Cornwall, an unfortunate man,[2] said to be of unexceptionable conduct in all relations of life, was sentenced to twenty-one months imprisonment, for uttering, and writing on a gate, some offensive words concerning Christianity. Within a month of the same time, at the Old Bailey, two persons, on two separate occasions,[3] were rejected as jurymen, and one of them grossly insulted by the judge and one of the counsel, because they honestly declared that they had no theological belief; and a third, a foreigner,[4] for the same reason, was denied justice against a thief. This refusal of redress took place in virtue of the legal doctrine, that no person can be allowed to give evidence in a court of justice, who does not profess belief in a God (any god is sufficient) and in a future state; which is equivalent to declaring such persons to be outlaws, excluded from the protection of the tribunals; who may not only be robbed or assaulted with impunity, if no one but themselves, or persons of similar opinions, be present, but any one else may be robbed or assaulted with impunity, if the proof of the fact depends on their evidence. The assumption on which this is grounded, is that the oath is worthless, of a person who does not believe in a future state; a proposition which betokens much ignorance of history in those who assent to it (since it is historically true that a large proportion of infidels in all ages have been persons of distinguished integrity and honor); and would be maintained by no one who had the smallest conception how many of the persons in greatest repute with the world, both for virtues and for attainments, are well known, at least to their intimates, to be unbelievers. The rule, besides, is suicidal, and cuts away its own foundation. Under pretence that atheists must be liars, it admits the testimony of all atheists who are willing to lie, and rejects only those who brave the obloquy of publicly confessing a detested creed rather than affirm a falsehood. A rule thus self-convicted of absurdity so far as regards its professed purpose, can be kept in force only as a badge of hatred, a relic of persecution; a persecution, too, having the peculiarity that the qualification for undergoing it is the being clearly proved not to deserve it. The rule, and the theory it implies, are hardly less insulting to believers than to infidels. For if he who does not believe in a future state necessarily lies, it follows that they who do believe are only prevented from lying, if prevented they are, by the fear of hell. We will not do the authors and abettors of the rule the injury of supposing, that the conception which they have formed a Christian virtue is drawn from their own consciousness.

These, indeed, are but rags and remnants of persecution, and may be thought to be not so much an indication of the wish to persecute, as an example of that very frequent infirmity of English minds, which makes them take a preposterous pleasure in the assertion of a bad principle, when they are no longer bad enough to desire to carry it really into practice. But unhappily there is no security in the state of the public mind, that the suspension of worse forms of legal persecution, which has lasted for about the space of a generation, will continue. In this age the quiet surface of routine is as often ruffled by attempts to resuscitate past evils, as to introduce new benefits. What is boasted of at the present time as the revival of religion, is always, in narrow and uncultivated minds, at least as much the revival of bigotry; and where there is the strongest permanent leaven of intolerance in the feelings of a people, which at all times abides in the middle classes of this country, it needs but little to provoke them into actively persecuting those whom they have never ceased to think proper objects of persecution.[5] For it is this — it is the opinions men entertain, and the feelings they cherish, respecting those who disown the beliefs they deem important, which makes this country not a place of mental freedom. For a long time past, the chief mischief of the legal penalties is that they strengthen the social stigma. It is that stigma which is really effective, and so effective is it, that the profession of opinions which are under the ban of society is much less common in England, than is, in many other countries, the avowal of those which incur risk of judicial punishment. In respect to all persons but those whose pecuniary circumstances make them independent of the good will of other people, opinion, on this subject, is as efficacious as law; men might as well be imprisoned, as excluded from the means of earning their bread. Those whose bread is already secured, and who desire no favors from men in power, or from bodies of men, or from the public, have nothing to fear from the open avowal of any opinions, but to be ill-thought of and ill-spoken of, and this it ought not to require a very heroic mould to enable them to bear. There is no room for any appeal *ad misericordiam* in behalf of such persons. But though we do not now inflict so much evil on those who think differently from us, as it was formerly our custom to do, it may be that we do ourselves as much evil as ever by our treatment of them. Socrates was put to death, but the Socratic philosophy rose like the sun in heaven, and spread its illumination over the whole intellectual firmament. Christians were cast to the lions, but the Christian Church grew up a stately and spreading tree, overtopping the older and less vigorous growths, and stifling them by its shade. Our merely social intolerance, kills no one, roots out no opinions, but induces men to disguise them, or to abstain from any active effort for their diffusion. With us, heretical opinions do not perceptibly gain or even lose ground in each decade or generation; they never blaze out far and wide, but continue to smoulder in the narrow circles of thinking and studious persons among whom they originate, without ever lighting up the general affairs of mankind with either a true or a deceptive light. And thus is kept up a state of things very satisfactory to some minds, because, without the unpleasant process of fining or imprisoning anybody, it maintains all prevailing opinions outwardly undisturbed, while it does not absolutely interdict the exercise of reason by dissentients afflicted with the malady of thought. A convenient plan for having peace in the intellectual world, and keeping all things going on therein very much as they do already. But the price paid for this sort of intellectual pacification, is the sacrifice of the entire moral courage of the human mind. A state of things in which a large portion of the most active and inquiring intellects find it advisable to keep the genuine principles and grounds of their convictions within their own breasts, and attempt, in what they address to the public, to fit as much as they can of their own conclusions to premises which they have internally renounced, cannot send forth the open, fearless characters, and logical, consistent intellects who once adorned the thinking world. The sort of men who can be looked for under it, are either mere conformers to commonplace, or time-servers for truth whose arguments on all great subjects are meant for their hearers, and are not those which have convinced themselves. Those who avoid this alternative, do so by narrowing their thoughts and interests to things which can be spoken of without venturing within the region of principles, that is, to small practical matters, which would come right of themselves, if but the minds of mankind were strengthened and enlarged, and which will never be effectually right until then; while that which would strengthen and enlarge men's minds, free and daring speculation on the highest subjects, is abandoned.

Those in whose eyes this reticence on the part of heretics is no evil, should consider in the first place, that in consequence of it there is never any fair and thorough discussion of heretical opinions; and that such of them as could not stand such a discussion, though they may be prevented from spreading, do not disappear. But it is not the minds of heretics that are deteriorated most, by the ban placed on all inquiry which does not end in the orthodox conclusions. The greatest harm done is to those who are not heretics, and whose whole mental development is cramped, and their reason cowed, by the fear of heresy. Who can compute what the world loses in the multitude of promising intellects combined with timid characters, who dare not follow out any bold, vigorous, independent train of thought, lest it should land them in something which would admit of being considered irreligious or immoral? Among them we may occasionally see some man of deep conscientiousness, and subtle and refined understanding, who spends a life of sophisticating with an intellect which he cannot silence, and exhausts the resources of ingenuity in attempting to reconcile the promptings of his conscience and reason with orthodoxy, which yet he does not, perhaps, to the end succeed in doing. No one can be a great thinker who does not recognize, that as a thinker it is his first duty to follow his intellect to whatever conclusions it may lead. Truth gains more even by the errors of one who, with due study and preparation, thinks for himself, than by the true opinions of those who only hold them because they do not suffer themselves to think. Not that it is solely, or chiefly, to form great thinkers, that freedom of thinking is required. On the contrary, it is as much, and even more indispensable, to enable average human beings to attain the mental stature which they are capable of. There have been, and may again be, great individual thinkers, in a general atmosphere of mental slavery. But there never has been, nor ever will be, in that atmosphere, an intellectually active people. Where any people has made a temporary approach to such a character, it has been because the dread of heterodox speculation was for a time suspended. Where there is a tacit convention that principles are not to be disputed; where the discussion of the greatest questions which can occupy humanity is considered to be closed, we cannot hope to find that generally high scale of mental activity which has made some periods of history so remarkable. Never when controversy avoided the subjects which are large and important enough to kindle enthusiasm, was the mind of a people stirred up from its foundations, and the impulse given which raised even persons of the most ordinary intellect to something of the dignity of thinking beings. Of such we have had an example in the condition of Europe during the times immediately following the Reformation; another, though limited to the Continent and to a more cultivated class, in the speculative movement of the latter half of the eighteenth century; and a third, of still briefer duration, in the intellectual fermentation of Germany during the Goethian and Fichtean period. These periods differed widely in the particular opinions which they developed; but were alike in this, that during all three the yoke of authority was broken. In each, an old mental despotism had been thrown off, and no new one had yet taken place. The impulse given at these three periods has made Europe what it now is. Every single improvement which has taken place either in the human mind or in institutions, may be traced distinctly to one or other of them. Appearances have for some time indicated that all three impulses are well-nigh spent; and we can expect no fresh start, until we again assert our mental freedom.

Let us now pass to the division of the argument, and dismissing the supposition that any of the received opinions may be false, let us assume them to be true, and examine into the worth of the manner in which they are likely to be held, when their truth is not freely and openly canvassed. However unwillingly a person who has a strong opinion may admit the possibility that his opinion may be false, he ought to be moved by the consideration that however true it may be, if it is not fully, frequently, and fearlessly discussed, it will be held as a dead dogma, not a living truth.

There is a class of persons (happily not quite so numerous as formerly) who think it enough if a person assents undoubtingly to what they think true, though he has no knowledge whatever of the grounds of the opinion, and could not make a tenable defence of it against the most superficial objections. Such persons, if they can once get their creed taught from authority, naturally think that no good, and some harm, comes of its being allowed to be questioned. Where their influence prevails, they make it nearly impossible for the received opinion to be rejected wisely and considerately, though it may still be rejected rashly and ignorantly; for to shut out discussion entirely is seldom possible, and when it once gets in, beliefs not grounded on conviction are apt to give way before the slightest semblance of an argument. Waiving, however, this possibility — assuming that the true opinion abides in the mind, but abides as a prejudice, a belief independent of, and proof against, argument — this is not the way in which truth ought to be held by a rational being. This is not knowing the truth. Truth, thus held, is but one superstition the more, accidentally clinging to the words which enunciate a truth.

· · · · ·

The greatest orator, save one, of antiquity, has left it on record that he always studied his adversary's case with as great, if not with still greater, intensity than even his own. What Cicero practised as the means of forensic success, requires to be imitated by all who study any subject in order to arrive at the truth. He who knows only his own side of the case, knows little of that. His reasons may be good, and no one may have been able to refute them. But if he is equally unable to refute the reasons on the opposite side; if he does not so much as know what they are, he has no ground for preferring either opinion. The rational position for him would be suspension of judgment, and unless he contents himself with that, he is either led by authority, or adopts, like the generality of the world, the side to which he feels most inclination. Nor is it enough that he should hear the arguments of adversaries from his own teachers, presented as they state them, and accompanied by what they offer as refutations. This is not the way to do justice to the arguments, or bring them into real contact with his own mind. He must be able to hear them from persons who actually believe them; who defend them in earnest, and do their very utmost for them. He must know them in their most plausible and persuasive form; he must feel the whole force of the difficulty which the true view of the subject has to encounter and dispose of, else he will never really possess himself of the portion of truth which meets and removes that difficulty. Ninety-nine in a hundred of what are called educated men are in this condition, even of those who can argue fluently for their opinions. Their conclusion may be true, but it might be false for anything they know: they have never thrown themselves into the mental position of those who think differently from them, and considered what such persons may have to say; and consequently they do not, in any proper sense of the word, know the doctrine which they themselves profess. They do not know those parts of it which explain and justify the remainder; the considerations which show that a fact which seemingly conflicts with another is reconcilable with it, or that, of two apparently strong reasons, one and not the other ought to be preferred. All that part of the truth which turns the scale, and decides the judgment of a completely informed mind, they are strangers to; nor is it ever really known, but to those who have attended equally and impartially to both sides, and endeavored to see the reasons of both in the strongest light. So essential is this discipline to a real understanding of moral and human subjects, that if opponents of all important truths do not exist, it is indispensable to imagine them and supply them with the strongest arguments which the most skilful devil's advocate can conjure up.

To abate the force of these considerations, an enemy of free discussion may be supposed to say, that there is no necessity for mankind in general to know and understand all that can be said against or for their opinions by philosophers and theologians. That it is not needful for common men to be able to expose all the misstatements or fallacies of an ingenious opponent. That it is enough if there is always somebody capable of answering them, so that nothing likely to mislead uninstructed persons remains unrefuted. That simple minds, having been taught the obvious grounds of the truths inculcated on them, may trust to authority for the rest, and being aware that they have neither knowledge nor talent to resolve every difficulty which can be raised, may repose in the assurance that all those which have been raised have been or can be answered, by those who are specially trained to the task.

Conceding to this view of the subject the utmost that can be claimed for it by those most easily satisfied with the amount of the understanding of truth which ought to accompany the belief of it; even so, the argument for free discussion is no way weakened. For even this doctrine acknowledges that mankind ought to have a rational assurance that all objections have been satisfactorily answered; and how are they to be answered if that which requires to be answered is not spoken? or how can the answer be known to be satisfactory, if the objectors have no opportunity of showing that it is unsatisfactory? If not the public, at least the philosophers and theologians who are to resolve the difficulties, must make themselves familiar with those difficulties in their most puzzling form; and this cannot be accomplished unless they are freely stated, and placed in the most advantageous light which they admit of. The Catholic Church has its own way of dealing with this embarrassing problem. It makes a broad separation between those who can be permitted to receive its doctrines on conviction, and those who must accept them on trust. Neither, indeed, are allowed any choice as to what they will accept; but the clergy, such at least as can be fully confided in, may admissibly and meritoriously make themselves acquainted with the arguments of opponents, in order to answer them, and may, therefore, read heretical books; the laity, not unless by special permission, hard to be obtained. This discipline recognizes a knowledge of the enemy's case as beneficial to the teachers, but finds means, consistent with this, of denying it to the rest of the world: thus giving to the *élite* more mental culture, though not more mental freedom, than it allows to the mass. By this device it succeeds in obtaining the kind of mental superiority which its purposes require; for though culture without freedom never made a large and liberal mind, it can make a clever *nisi prius* advocate of a cause. But in countries professing Protestantism, this resource is denied; since Protestants hold, at least in theory, that the responsibility for the choice of a religion must be borne by each for himself, and cannot be thrown off upon teachers. Besides, in the present state of the world, it is practically impossible that writings which are read by the instructed can be kept from the uninstructed. If the teachers of mankind are to be cognizant of all that they ought to know, everything must be free to be written and published without restraint.

If, however, the mischievous operation of the absence of free discussion, when the received opinions are true, were confined to leaving men ignorant of the grounds of those opinions, it might be thought that this, if an intellectual, is no moral evil, and does not affect the worth of the opinions, regarded in their influence on the character. The fact, however, is, that not only the grounds of the opinion are forgotten in the absence of discussion, but too often the meaning of the opinion itself. The words which convey it, cease to suggest ideas, or suggest only a small portion of those they were originally employed to communicate. Instead of a vivid conception and a living belief, there remain only a few phrases retained by rote; or, if any part, the shell and husk only of the meaning is retained, the finer essence being lost. The great chapter in human history which this fact occupies and fills, cannot be too earnestly studied and meditated on.

It is illustrated in the experience of almost all ethical doctrines and religious creeds. They are all full of meaning and vitality to those who originate them, and to the direct disciples of the originators. Their meaning continues to be felt in undiminished strength, and is perhaps brought out into even fuller consciousness, so long as the struggle lasts to give the doctrine or creed an ascendency over other creeds. At last it either prevails, and becomes the general opinion, or its progress stops; it keeps possession of the ground it has gained, but ceases to spread further. When either of these results has become apparent, controversy on the subject flags, and gradually dies away. The doctrine has taken its place, if not as a received opinion, as one of the admitted sects or divisions of opinion: those who hold it have generally inherited, not adopted it; and conversion from one of these doctrines to another, being now an exceptional fact, occupies little place in the thoughts of their professors. Instead of being, as at first, constantly on the alert either to defend themselves against the world, or to bring the world over to them, they have subsided into acquiescence, and neither listen, when they can help it, to arguments against their creed, nor trouble dissentients (if there be such) with arguments in its favor. From this time may usually be dated the decline in the living power of the doctrine. We often hear the teachers of all creeds lamenting the difficulty of keeping up in the minds of believers a lively apprehension of the truth which they nominally recognize, so that it may penetrate the feelings, and acquire a real mastery over the conduct. No such difficulty is complained of while the creed is still fighting for its existence: even the weaker combatants then know and feel what they are fighting for, and the difference between it and other doctrines; and in that period of every creed's existence, not a few persons may be found, who have realized its fundamental principles in all the forms of thought, have weighed and considered them in all their important bearings, and have experienced the full effect on the character, which belief in that creed ought to produce in a mind thoroughly imbued with it. But when it has come to be an hereditary creed, and to be received passively, not actively — when the mind is no longer compelled, in the same degree as at first, to exercise its vital powers on the questions which its belief presents to it, there is a progressive tendency to forget all of the belief except the formularies, or to give it a dull and torpid assent, as if accepting it on trust dispensed with the necessity of realizing it in consciousness, or testing it by personal experience; until it almost ceases to connect itself at all with the inner life of the human being. Then are seen the cases, so frequent in this age of the world as almost to form the majority, in which the creed remains as it were outside the mind, encrusting and petrifying it against all other influences addressed to the higher parts of our nature; manifesting its power by not suffering any fresh and living conviction to get in, but itself doing nothing for the mind or heart, except standing sentinel over them to keep them vacant.

To what an extent doctrines intrinsically fitted to make the deepest impression upon the mind may remain in it as dead beliefs, without being ever realized in the imagination, the feelings, or the understanding, is exemplified by the manner in which the majority of believers hold the doctrines of Christianity. By Christianity I here mean what is accounted such by all churches and sects — the maxims and precepts contained in the New Testament. These are considered sacred, and accepted as laws, by all professing Christians. Yet it is scarcely too much to say that no one Christian in a thousand guides or tests his individual conduct by reference to those laws. The standard to which he does refer it, is the custom of his nation, his class, or his religious profession. He has thus, on the one hand, a collection of ethical maxims, which he believes to have been vouchsafed to him by infallible wisdom as rules for his government; and on the other, a set of every-day judgments and practices, which go a certain length with some of those maxims, not so great a length with others, stand in direct opposition to some, and are, on the whole, a compromise between the Christian creed and the interests and suggestions of worldly life. To the first of these standards he gives his homage; to the other his real allegiance. All Christians believe that the blessed are the poor and humble, and those who are ill-used by the world; that it is easier for a camel to pass through the eye of a needle than for a rich man to enter the kingdom of heaven; that they should judge not, lest they be judged; that they should swear not at all; that they should love their neighbor as themselves; that if one take their cloak, they should give him their coat also; that they should take no thought for the morrow; that if they would be perfect, they should sell all that they have and give it to the poor. They are not insincere when they say that they believe these things. They do believe them, as people believe what they have always heard lauded and never discussed. But in the sense of that living belief which regulates conduct, they believe these doctrines just up to the point to which it is usual to act upon them. The doctrines in their integrity are serviceable to pelt adversaries with; and it is understood that they are to be put forward (when possible) as the reasons for whatever people do that they think laudable. But any one who reminded them that the maxims require an infinity of things which they never even think of doing would gain nothing but to be classed among those very unpopular characters who affect to be better than other people. The doctrines have no hold on ordinary believers —are not a power in their minds. They have an habitual respect for the sound of them, but no feeling which spreads from the words to the things signified, and forces the mind to take *them* in, and make them conform to the formula. Whenever conduct is concerned, they look round for Mr. A and B to direct them how far to go in obeying Christ.

. . . . .

It still remains to speak of one of the principal causes which make diversity of opinion advantageous, and will continue to do so until mankind shall have entered a stage of intellectual advancement which at present seems at an incalculable distance. We have hitherto considered only two possibilities: that the received opinion may be false, and some other opinion, consequently, true; or that, the received opinion being true, a conflict with the opposite error is essential to a clear apprehension and deep feeling of its truth. But there is a commoner case than either of these; when the conflicting doctrines, instead of being one true and the other false, share the truth between them; and the nonconforming opinion is needed to supply the remainder of the truth, of which the received doctrine embodies only a part. Popular opinions, on subjects not palpable to sense, are often true, but seldom or never the whole truth. They are a part of the truth; sometimes a greater, sometimes a smaller part, but exaggerated, distorted, and disjoined from the truths by which they ought to be accompanied and limited. Heretical opinions, on the other hand, are generally some of these suppressed and neglected truths, bursting the bonds which kept them down, and either seeking reconciliation with the truth contained in the common opinion, or fronting it as enemies, and setting themselves up, with similar exclusiveness, as the whole truth. The latter case is hitherto the most frequent, as, in the human mind, one-sidedness has always been the rule, and many-sidedness the exception. Hence, even in revolutions of opinion, one part of the truth usually sets while another rises. Even progress, which ought to superadd, for the most part only substitutes one partial and incomplete truth for another; improvement consisting chiefly in this, that the new fragment of truth is more wanted, more adapted to the needs of the time, than that which it displaces. Such being the partial character of prevailing opinions, even when resting on a true foundation; every opinion which embodies somewhat of the portion of truth which the common opinion omits, ought to be considered precious, with whatever amount of error and confusion that truth may be blended. No sober judge of human affairs will feel bound to be indignant because those who force on our notice truths which we should otherwise have overlooked, overlook some of those which we see. Rather, he will think that so long as popular truth is one-sided, it is more desirable than otherwise that unpopular truth should have one-sided asserters too; such being usually the most energetic, and the most likely to compel reluctant attention to the fragment of wisdom which they proclaim as if it were the whole.

.   .   .   .   .

It may be objected, "But *some* received principles, especially on the highest and most vital subjects, are more than half-truths. The Christian morality, for instance, is the whole truth on that subject and if any one teaches a morality which varies from it, he is wholly in error." As this is of all cases the most important in practice, none can be fitter to test the general maxim. But before pronouncing what Christian morality is or is not, it would be desirable to decide what is meant by Christian morality. If it means the morality of the New Testament, I wonder that any one who derives his knowledge of this from the book itself, can suppose that it was announced, or intended, as a complete doctrine of morals. The Gospel always refers to a preëxisting morality, and confines its precepts to the particulars in which that morality was to be corrected, or superseded by a wider and higher; expressing itself, moreover, in terms most general, often impossible to be interpreted literally, and possessing rather the impressiveness of poetry or eloquence than the precision of legislation. To extract from it a body of ethical doctrine, has never been possible without eking it out from the Old Testament, that is, from a system elaborate indeed, but in many respects barbarous, and intended only for a barbarous people. Saint Paul, a declared enemy of this Judaical mode of interpreting the doctrine and filling up the scheme of his Master, equally assumes a preëxisting morality, namely, that of the Greeks and Romans; and his advice to Christians is in a great measure a system of accommodation to that; even to the extent of giving an apparent sanction to slavery. What is called Christian, but should rather be termed theological, morality, was not the work of Christ or the Apostles, but is of much later origin, having been gradually built up by the Catholic Church of the first five centuries, and though not implicitly adopted by moderns and Protestants, has been much less modified by them than might have been expected. For the most part, indeed, they have contented themselves with cutting off the additions which had been made to it in the Middle Ages, each sect supplying the place by fresh additions, adapted to its own character and tendencies. That mankind owe a great debt to this morality, and to its early teachers, I should be the last person to deny; but I do not scruple to say of it, that it is, in many important points, incomplete and one-sided, and that unless ideas and feelings, not sanctioned by it, had contributed to the formation of European life and character, human affairs would have been in a worse condition than they now are. Christian morality (so called) has all the characters of a reaction; it is, in great part, a protest against Paganism. Its ideal is negative rather than positive; passive rather than active; Innocence rather than Nobleness; Abstinence from Evil, rather than energetic Pursuit of Good: in its precepts (as has been well said) "thou shalt not" predominates unduly over "thou shalt." In its horror of sensuality, it made an idol of asceticism, which has been gradually compromised away into one of legality. It holds out the hope of heaven and the threat of hell, as the appointed and appropriate motives to a virtuous life: in this falling far below the best of the ancients, and doing what lies in it to give to human morality an essentially selfish character, by disconnecting each man's feelings of duty from the interests of his fellow-creatures, except so far as a self-interested inducement is offered to him for consulting them. It is essentially a doctrine of passive obedience; it inculcates submission to all authorities found established; who indeed are not to be actively obeyed when they command what religion forbids, but who are not to be resisted, far less rebelled against, for any amount of wrong to ourselves. And while, in the morality of the best Pagan nations, duty to the State holds even a disproportionate place, infringing on the just liberty of the individual; in purely Christian ethics that grand department of duty is scarcely noticed or acknowledged. It is in the Koran, not the New Testament, that we read the maxim — "A ruler who appoints any man to an office, when there is in his dominions another man better qualified for it, sins against God and against the State." What little recognition the idea of obligation to the public obtains in modern morality, is derived from Greek and Roman sources, not from Christian; as, even in the morality of private life, whatever exists of magnanimity, high-mindedness, personal dignity, even the sense of honor, is derived from the purely human, not the religious part of our education, and never could have grown out of a standard of ethics in which the only worth, professedly recognized, is that of obedience.

·   ·   ·   ·   ·

I do not pretend that the most unlimited use of the freedom of enunciating all possible opinions would put an end to the evils of religious or philosophical sectarianism. Every truth which men of narrow capacity are in earnest about is sure to be asserted, inculcated, and in many ways ever acted on, as if no other truth existed in the world, or at all events none that could limit or qualify the first. I acknowledge that the tendency of all opinions to become sectarian is not cured by the freest discussion, but is often heightened and exacerbated thereby; the truth which ought to have been, but was not, seen, being rejected all the more violently because proclaimed by persons regarded as opponents. But it is not on the impassioned partisan, it is on the calmer and more disinterested bystander, that this collision of opinions works its salutary effect. Not the violent conflict between parts of the truth, but the quiet suppression of half of it, is the formidable evil: there is always hope when people are forced to listen to both sides; it is when they attend only to one that errors harden into prejudices, and truth itself ceases to have the effect of truth, by being exaggerated into falsehood. And since there are few mental attributes more rare than that judicial faculty which can sit in intelligent judgment between two sides of a question, of which only one is represented by an advocate before it, truth has no chance but in proportion as every side of it, every opinion which embodies any fraction of the truth, not only finds advocates, but is so advocated as to be listened to.

We have now recognized the necessity to the mental well-being of mankind (on which all their other well-being depends) of freedom of opinion, and freedom of the expression of opinion, on four distinct grounds; which we will now briefly recapitulate.

First, if any opinion is compelled to silence, that opinion may, for aught we can certainly know, be true. To deny this is to assume our own infallibility.

Secondly, though the silenced opinion be an error, it may, and very commonly does, contain a portion of truth; and since the general or prevailing opinion on any object is rarely or never the whole truth, it is only by the collision of adverse opinions that the remainder of the truth has any chance of being supplied.

Thirdly, even if the received opinion be not only true, but the whole truth; unless it is suffered to be, and actually is, vigorously and earnestly contested, it will, by most of those who receive it, be held in the manner of a prejudice, with little comprehension or feeling of its rational grounds. And not only this, but, fourthly, the meaning of the doctrine itself will be in danger of being lost, or enfeebled, and deprived of its vital effect on the character and conduct: the dogma becoming a mere formal profession, inefficacious for good, but cumbering the ground, and preventing the growth of any real and heartfelt conviction, from reason or personal experience.

Before quitting the subject of freedom of opinion, it is fit to take notice of those who say, that the free expression of all opinions should be permitted, on condition that the manner be temperate, and do not pass the bounds of fair discussion. Much might be said on the impossibility of fixing where these supposed bounds are to be placed; for if the test be offence to those whose opinion is attacked, I think experience testifies that this offence is given whenever the attack is telling and powerful, and that every opponent who pushes them hard, and whom they find it difficult to answer, appears to them, if he shows any strong feeling on the subject, an intemperate opponent. But this, though an important consideration in a practical point of view, merges in a more fundamental objection. Undoubtedly the manner of asserting an opinion, even though it be a true one, may be very objectionable, and may justly incur severe censure. But the principal offences of the kind are such as it is mostly impossible, unless by accidental self-betrayal, to bring home to conviction. The gravest of them is, to argue sophistically, to suppress facts or arguments, to misstate the elements of the case, or misrepresent the opposite opinion. But all this, even to the most aggravated degree, is so continually done in perfect good faith, by persons who are not considered, and in many other respects may not deserve to be considered, ignorant or incompetent, that it is rarely possible on adequate grounds conscientiously to stamp the misrepresentation as morally culpable; and still less could law presume to interfere with this kind of controversial misconduct. With regard to what is commonly meant by intemperate discussion, namely, invective, sarcasm, personality, and the like, the denunciation of these weapons would deserve more sympathy if it were ever proposed to interdict them equally to both sides; but it is only desired to restrain the employment of them against the prevailing opinion: against the unprevailing they may not only be used without general disapproval, but will be likely to obtain for him who uses them the praise of honest zeal and righteous indignation. Yet whatever mischief arises from their use, is greatest when they are employed against the comparatively defenceless; and whatever unfair advantage can be derived by any opinion from this mode of asserting it, accrues almost exclusively to received opinions. The worst offence of this kind which can be committed by a polemic, is to stigmatize those who hold the contrary opinion as bad and immoral men. To calumny of this sort, those who hold any unpopular opinion are peculiarly exposed, because they are in general few and uninfluential, and nobody but themselves feels much interest in seeing justice done them; but this weapon is, from the nature of the case, denied to those who attack a prevailing opinion: they can neither use it with safety to themselves, nor if they could, would it do anything but recoil on their own cause. In general, opinions contrary to those commonly received can only obtain a hearing by studied moderation of language, and the most cautious avoidance of unnecessary offence, from which they hardly ever deviate even in a slight degree without losing ground: while unmeasured vituperation employed on the side of the prevailing opinion, really does deter people from professing contrary opinions, and from listening to those who profess them. For the interest, therefore, of truth and justice, it is far more important to restrain this employment of vituperative language than the other; and, for example, if it were necessary to choose, there would be much more need to discourage offensive attacks on infidelity, than on religion. It is, however, obvious that law and authority have no business with restraining either, while opinion ought, in every instance, to determine its verdict by the circumstances of the individual case; condemning every one, on whichever side of the argument he places himself, in whose mode of advocacy either want of candor, or malignity, bigotry or intolerance of feeling manifest themselves, but not inferring these vices from the side which a person takes, though it be the contrary side of the question to our own; and giving merited honor to every one, whatever opinion he may hold, who has calmness to see and honesty to state what his opponents and their opinions really are, exaggerating nothing to their discredit, keeping nothing back which tells, or can be supposed to tell, in their favor. This is the real morality of public discussion; and if often violated, I am happy to think that there are many controversialists who to a great extent observe it, and a still greater number who conscientiously strive towards it.

Footnotes

[1] These words had scarcely been written, when, as if to give them an emphatic contradiction, occurred the Government Press Prosecutions of 1858. That ill-judged interference with the liberty of public discussion has not, however, induced me to alter a single word in the text, nor has it at all weakened my conviction that, moments of panic excepted, the era of pains and penalties for political discussion has, in our own country, passed away. For, in the first place, the prosecutions were not persisted in; and in the second, they were never, properly speaking, political prosecutions. The offence charged was not that of criticizing institutions, or the acts of persons of rulers, but of circulating what was deemed an immoral doctrine, the lawfulness of Tyrannicide.

If the arguments of the present chapter are of any validity, there ought to exist the fullest liberty of professing and discussing, as a matter of ethical conviction, any doctrine, however immoral it may be considered. It would, therefore, be irrelevant and out of place to examine here, whether the doctrine of Tyrannicide deserves that title. I shall content myself with saying, that the subject has been at all times one of the open questions of morals; that the act of a private citizen in striking down a criminal, who, by raising himself above the law, has placed himself beyond the reach of legal punishment or control, has been accounted by whole nations, and by some of the best and wisest of men, not a crime, but an act of exalted virtue; and that, right or wrong, it is not of the nature of assassination, but of civil war. As such, I hold that the instigation to it, in a specific case, may be a proper subject of punishment, but only if an overt act has followed, and at least a probable connection can be established between the act and the instigation. Even then, it is not a foreign government, but the very government assailed, which alone, in the exercise of self-defence, can legitimately punish attacks directed against its own existence.

[2] Thomas Pooley, Bodim Assizes, July 31, 1857. In December following, he received a free pardon from the Crown.

[3] George Jacob Holyoake, August 17, 1857; Edward Truelove, July, 1857.

[4] Baron de Gleichen, Marlborough Street Police Court, August 4, 1857.

[5] Ample warning may be drawn from the large infusion of the passions of a persecutor, which mingled with the general display of the worst parts of our national character on the occasion of the Sepoy insurrection. The ravings of fanatics or charlatans from the pulpit may be unworthy of notice; but the heads of the Evangelical party have announced as their principle, for the government of Hindoos and Mahomedans, that no schools

be supported by public money in which the Bible is not taught, and by necessary consequence that no public employment be given to any but real or pretended Christians. An Under-Secretary of State, in a speech delivered to his constituents on the 12th of November, 1857, is reported to have said: "Toleration of their faith" (the faith of a hundred millions of British subjects), "the superstition which they called religion, by the British Government, had had the effect of retarding the ascendancy of the British name, and preventing the salutary growth of Christianity. . . . Toleration was the great corner-stone of the religious liberties of this country; but do not let them abuse that precious word toleration. As he understood it, it meant the complete liberty to all, freedom of worship, *among Christians, who worshipped upon the same foundation.* It meant toleration of all sects and denominations of *Christians who believed in the one mediation."* I desire to call attention to the fact, that a man who has been deemed fit to fill a high office in the government of this country, under a liberal Ministry, maintains the doctrine that all who do not believe in the divinity of Christ are beyond the pale of toleration. Who, after this imbecile display, can indulge the illusion that religious persecution has passed away, never to return?

John Trenchard *and*
Thomas Gordon: "Cato"

In attempting to justify the need to break away from England and establish their own principles of government, the American colonists had to turn to Old World writers for ideas and inspiration on such matters as government structure, civil liberties, and state-church relations. The writings of Milton, Montesquieu, Pope, Addison, and Locke had great influence on James Otis, Benjamin Franklin, Thomas Paine, John Dickinson, Peter Zenger, and others instrumental in pleading the colonists' cause.

Among the English writers who greatly influenced the colonists were John Trenchard and Thomas Gordon, who collaborated in writing political tracts under the pseudonym of "Cato." *Cato's Letters* were first published in 1720, and between 1733 and 1755 they went through six editions in England; in America, according to Clinton Rossiter, they were "the most popular, quotable, esteemed source of political ideas in the colonial period."[1] Leonard Levy, in his *Freedom of Speech and Press in Early American History: Legacy of Suppression*, points to *Cato's Letters* as the most widely known source of libertarian thought in England and America during the eighteenth century.[2] In 1735, when "Peter Zenger's lawyer sought theoretic grounds for attacking the traditional concept of seditious libel he turned for authority to Trenchard and Gordon's *Cato's Letters*."[3] Benjamin Franklin recommended that college students be taught the

---

[1] Clinton Rossiter, *Seedtime of the Republic* (New York: Harcourt, Brace & World, 1953), p. 141.

[2] Leonard W. Levy, *Freedom of Speech and Press in Early American History: Legacy of Suppression* (New York: Harper & Row, 1963), p. 133.

[3] Bernard Bailyn and J. N. Garrett (eds.), *Pamphlets of the American Revolution* (Cambridge, Mass.: Harvard University Press, 1965), I, 36.

English language by studying, among other things, *Cato's Letters*.[4] Their influence on Franklin was so great that instead of composing his own letter to *The New England Courant* in July, 1722, he sent for publication a lengthy portion of number fifteen of *Cato's Letters*, "Of Freedom of Speech: That the same is inseparable from Publick Liberty," saying that he preferred it to anything he had written.[5]

The letter reprinted here is an example of the free-speech pamphleteering which had great logical and emotional impact on the colonists. The eighteenth-century spelling and punctuation in the original tract have been modernized.

[4] Benjamin Franklin, *Proposals Relating to the Education of Youth in Pensilvania* (Philadelphia: Press of the University of Pennsylvania, 1931), pp. 13–14.

[5] Benjamin Franklin, *The Writings of Benjamin Franklin* (New York: Haskell, 1907), II, 25.

CATO'S LETTERS

Saturday, February 4, 1720. No. 15
Of Freedom of Speech: That the same is inseparable from Publick Liberty

Without freedom of thought, there can be no such thing as wisdom; and no such thing as public liberty, without freedom of speech: which is the right of every man, as far as by it he does not hurt and control the right of another; and this is the only check which it ought to suffer, the only bounds which it ought to know.

This sacred privilege is so essential to free government that the security of property and the freedom of speech always go together; and in those wretched countries where a man cannot call his tongue his own, he can scarce call anything else his own. Whoever would overthrow the liberty of the nation must begin by subduing the freedom of speech, a thing terrible to public traitors.

This secret was so well known to the court of King Charles I that his wicked Ministry procured a proclamation to forbid the people to talk of Parliaments, which those traitors had laid aside. To assert the undoubted right of the subject and defend his Majesty's legal prerogative was called disaffection and punished as sedition. Nay, people were forbidden to talk of religion in their families, for the Priests had combined with the Ministers to cook up tyranny and suppress truth and the law. While the late King James, when Duke of York, went avowedly to Mass, men were fined, imprisoned, and undone for saying that he was a Papist; and, that King Charles II might live more securely a Papist, there was an Act of Parliament made declaring it treason to say that he was one.

That men ought to speak well of their governors is true, while their governors deserve to be well spoken of; but to do public mischief without hearing of it is only the prerogative and felicity of tyranny; a free people will be showing that they are so by their freedom of speech.

The administration of government is nothing else but the attendance of the trustees of the people upon the interest and affairs of the people; and as it is the part and business of the people, for whose sake alone all public matters are or ought to be transacted, to see whether they be well or ill transacted, so it is the interest and ought to be the ambition of all honest magistrates to have their deeds openly examined and publicly scanned; only the wicked governors of men dread what is said of them; *Audivit Tiberius probra queis lacerabitur, atque perculsus est* [Tiberius heard criticisms by which he was assailed, and he was stricken. (*Lacerabitur* actually means *will be assailed,* but this must be a mistake for the past tense *lacerabatur*)]. The public censure was true, else he had not felt it bitter.

Freedom of speech is ever the symptom as well as the effect of good government. In old Rome, all was left to the judgment and pleasure of the people who examined the public proceedings with such discretion and censured those who administered them with such equity and mildness that in the space of three hundred years not five public ministers suffered unjustly. Indeed, whenever the commons proceeded to violence, the great ones had been the aggressors.

Guilt only dreads liberty of speech which drags it out of its lurking holes and exposes its deformity and horror to daylight. Horatius, Valerius, Cincinnatus, and other virtuous and undesigning magistrates of the Roman Commonwealth had nothing to fear from liberty of speech. Their virtuous administration, the more it was examined the more it brightened and gained by enquiry. When Valerius, in particular, was accused upon some slight grounds of affecting the Diadem, he who was the first Minister of Rome did not accuse the people for examining his conduct but approved his innocence in a speech to them; he gave such satisfaction to them and gained such popularity to himself that they gave him a new name, *inde cognomen factum Publicolae est*, to denote that he was their favorite and their friend. *Latae deinde leges. Ante omnes de provocatione* ADVERSUS MAGISTRATUS AD POPULUM, Livii lib. ii. cap. 8. [Hence was derived Publicola's cognomen. . . . Then laws were passed, especially one concerning appeal to the people against magistrates.]

But things afterwards took another turn; Rome, with the loss of its liberty lost also its freedom of speech; then men's words began to be feared and watched; then first began the poisonous race of informers, banished indeed under the righteous administration of Titus, Nerva,

Trajan, Aurelius, but encouraged and enriched under the vile ministry of Sejanus, Tigellinus, Pallas, and Cleander; *Querilibet, quod in secreta nostra non inquirant principes, nisi quos odimus,* says Pliny to Trajan [I should like to complain that the only emperors who inquire into our secret affairs are the ones whom we hate].

The best princes have ever encouraged and promoted freedom of speech; they know that upright measures would defend themselves and that all upright men would defend them. Tacitus, speaking of the reign of some of the princes above-mentioned, says with ecstasy, *Rara temporum felicitate, ubi sentire quae velis, & quae sentias dicere liceat:* A blessed time, when you might think what you would, and speak what you thought!

The same was the opinion and practice of the wise and virtuous Timoleon, deliverer of the great city of Syracuse from slavery. He being accused by Demoenetus, a popular orator, in a full assembly of the people, of several misdemeanors committed by him while he was General, gave no other answer than that he was highly obliged to the Gods for granting him a request that he had often made to them, namely, that he might live to see the Syracusians enjoy that liberty of speech which they now seemed to be masters of.

And that great Commander M. Marcellus, who won more battles than any Roman Captain of his age, being accused by the Syracusians, while he was now a fourth-time Consul of having done them indignities and hostile wrongs contrary to the League, rose from his seat in the Senate as soon as the charge against him was opened, and passing (as a private man) into the place where the accused were wont to make their defence, gave free liberty to the Syracusians to impeach him; which when they had done, he and they went out of the Court together to attend the issues of the cause; nor did he express the least ill will or resentment towards these his accusers, but being acquitted, received their city into his protection. Had he been guilty, he would neither have shown such temper nor courage.

I doubt not but old Spencer and his son, who were the chief ministers and betrayers of Edward II, would have been very glad to have stopped the mouths of all the honest men in England. They dreaded to be called traitors because they were traitors. And I dare say Queen Elizabeth's Walsingham, who deserved no reproaches, feared none. Misrepresentation of public measures is easily overthrown by representing public measures truly; when they are honest, they ought to be publicly known that they may be publicly commended; but if they be knavish or pernicious, they ought to be publicly exposed in order to be publicly detested.

To assert that King James was a Papist and a tyrant was only as far hurtful to him as it was true of him; and if the Earl of Strafford had not deserved to be impeached, he need not have feared a Bill of Attainder. If our directors and their confederates be not such knaves as the world thinks them, let them prove to all the world that the world thinks wrong, and that they are guilty of none of those villainies which all the world lays to their charge. Others, too, who would be thought to have no part of their guilt, must, before they are thought innocent, show that they did all that was in their power to prevent that guilt and to check their proceedings.

Freedom of speech is the great bulwark of liberty; they prosper and die together; and it is the terror of traitors and oppressors and a barrier against them. It produces excellent writers and encourages men of fine genius. Tacitus tells us that the Roman Commonwealth bred great and numerous authors who wrote with equal boldness and eloquence; but when it was enslaved, those great wits were no more. *Postquam bellatum apud Actium; atque omnem potestatem ad unum conferri pacis intersuit, magna illa ingenia cessere* [After the battle of Actium, when it became expedient for the sake of peace to confer power upon one man, those mighty talents ceased]. Tyranny had usurped the place of equality, which is the soul of liberty, and destroyed public courage. The minds of men, terrified by unjust power, degenerated into all the vileness and methods of servitude; abject sycophancy and blind submission grew the only means of preferments and indeed of safety; men durst not open their mouths but to flatter.

Pliny the Younger observes that this dread of tyranny had such effect that the Senate, the great Roman Senate, became at last stupid and dumb: *Mutam ac sedentariam assentiendi necessitatem* [The silent and passive necessity of conformity]. Hence, says he, our spirit and genius are stupefied, broken, and sunk forever. And in one of his epistles, speaking of the works of his uncle, he makes an apology for eight of them, as not written with the same vigor which was to be found in the rest; for that these eight were written in the reign of Nero, when the spirit of writing was cramped by fear; *Dubii sermonis octo scripsit sub* Nerone — *cum omne studiorum genus paulo liberius & erectius periculosum servitus fecisset* [He wrote eight (books) in the time of Nero about ambiguous speech, when slavery had made dangerous every variety of study that was a little too free and independent].

All ministers, therefore, who were oppressors or intended to be oppressors, have been loud in their complaints against freedom of speech and the license of the press, and always restrained, or endeavored to restrain, both. In consequence of this, they have browbeaten writers, punished them violently and against law, and burnt their works, by all which they showed how much truth alarmed them and how much they were at enmity with truth.

There is a famous instance of this in Tacitus; he tells us, that Cremutius Cordus, having in his annals praised Brutus and Cassius, gave offense to Sejanus, first Minister, and to some inferior sycophants in the court of Tiberius, who, conscious of their own characters, took the praise bestowed on every worthy Roman to be so many reproaches pointed at themselves; they therefore complain of the book to the Senate which, being now only the machine of tyranny, condemned it to be burnt. But this did not prevent its spreading. *Libros cremandos censuere Patres; sed manserunt occultati & editi* [The Fathers (Senators) voted to burn the books; but they survived, circulated in secret]; being censured, it was the more sought after. From hence, says Tacitus, we may wonder at the stupidity of those statesmen who hope to extinguish, by the terror of their power, the memory of their actions; for quite otherwise, the punishment of good writers gains credit to their writings; *Nam contra, punitis ingeniis, gliscit auctoritas* [To the contrary, authority waxed strong by means of penalties]. Nor did ever any government who practiced impolitic severity get anything by it but infamy to themselves and renown to those who suffered under it. This also is an observation of Tacitus: *Neque aliud reges, qui ea saevitiae usi sunt, nisi dedecus sibi, atque gloriam illis peperere* [And the kings who displayed such ferocity accomplished nothing but disgrace for themselves and glory for their victims].

Freedom of speech, therefore, being of such infinite importance to the preservation of liberty, everyone who loves liberty ought to encourage freedom of speech. Hence it is that I, living in a country of liberty and under the best Prince upon earth, shall take this very favorable opportunity of serving mankind by warning them of the hideous mischiefs that they will suffer if ever corrupt and wicked men shall hereafter get possession of any state, and the power of betraying their master; and, in order to do this, I will show them by what steps they will probably proceed to accomplish their traitorous ends. This may be the subject of my next.

Valerius Maximus tells us that Lentulus Marcellinus, the Roman Consul, having complained in a popular assembly of the overgrown power of Pompey, the people answered him with a shout of approbation, upon which the Consul told them, "Shout on Gentlemen, shout on, and use those bold signs of liberty while you may, for I do not know how long they will be allowed of you."

God be thanked, we Englishmen have neither lost our liberties nor are in danger of losing them. Let us always cherish this matchless blessing, almost peculiar to ourselves, that our posterity may, many ages hence, ascribe their freedom to our zeal. The defense of liberty is a noble, a heavenly office which can only be performed where liberty is. For, as the same Valerius Maximus observes, *Quid ergo Libertas sine* Catone? *Non magis quam* Cato *sine Libertate.* [What then is liberty without Cato? Nothing more than Cato without liberty.]

The Alien and Sedition Acts of 1798

Several periods in American history stand out as periods of suppression of free expression. One was from 1798 to 1800 with the passage of the Alien and Sedition Acts. Under the Sedition Act, Jeffersonian Republicans were tried and convicted for their criticisms and attacks against the Federalists and the administration of John Adams. Several scholars have indicated that the circumstances did not warrant the passage of these acts. Professor Thomas I. Emerson has written: "There was a consistent tendency to overestimate the need for restriction upon freedom of expression. No one now questions that the Alien and Sedition Acts were not required to preserve internal order to protect the country against any external danger."[1] Supreme Court Justice Holmes, in his dissenting opinion in *Abrams* v. *United States* arguing against the "bad tendency" test, wrote: "I had conceived that the United States through many years had shown its repentance for the Sedition Act of 1798, by repaying fines that it imposed." Civil libertarian Zechariah Chafee, Jr., observed in his *Free Speech in the United States* that in the prosecutions under the Sedition Act "words were once more made punishable for their judicially supposed bad tendency."[2] The lesson to be learned from these prosecutions under the Sedition Act, says Professor Chafee, is "that the most essential element of free speech is the rejection of bad tendency as the test of a criminal utterance [and it] was never more clearly recognized than in Jefferson's preamble to the Virginia

[1] Thomas I. Emerson, "Toward a General Theory of the First Amendment" *Yale Law Review*, 72 (April 1963), p. 891.

[2] Zechariah Chafee, Jr., *Free Speech in the United States* (Cambridge, Mass.: Harvard University Press, 1941), p. 27.

Act for establishing Religious Freedom."[3] Chafee quotes from Jefferson:

> To suffer the civil Magistrate to intrude his powers into the field of opinion, and to restrain the profession or propagation of principles on supposition of their ill tendency, is a dangerous fallacy, which at once destroys all religious liberty, because he being of course judge of that tendency, will make his opinions the rule of judgment, and approve or condemn the sentiments of others only as they shall square with or differ from his own.[4]

The Alien Acts, although not as directly related to the question of free speech as the Sedition Act, are included here to reflect the climate of the times and the attempts of the Federalists to suppress dissent. The text for the acts comes from Volume One of *United States Statutes at Large*.

Professor James Smith's chapter "The Sedition Law, Free Speech, and the American Political Process" from his book *Freedom's Fetters* is reprinted for background on the Sedition Act, its "bad tendency" test implications, its application against the Jeffersonian Republicans, and its more far-reaching effects.

[3] *Ibid.*, p. 28.
[4] *Ibid.*, p. 29.

AN ACT CONCERNING ALIENS

SECTION 1. *Be it enacted by the Senate and House of Representatives of the United States of America in Congress assembled,* That it shall be lawful for the President of the United States at any time during the continuance of this act, to *order* all such *aliens* as he shall judge dangerous to the peace and safety of the United States, or shall have reasonable grounds to suspect are concerned in any treasonable or secret machinations against the government thereof, to depart out of the territory of the United States, within such time as shall be expressed in such order, which order shall be served on such alien by delivering him a copy thereof, or leaving the same at his usual abode, and returned to the office of the Secretary of State, by the marshal or other person to whom the same shall be directed. And in case any alien, so ordered to depart, shall be found at large within the United States after the time limited in such order for his departure, and not having obtained a *license* from the President to reside therein, or having obtained such *license* shall not have conformed thereto, every such alien shall, on conviction thereof, be imprisoned for a term not exceeding three years, and shall never after be admitted to become a citizen of the United States. *Provided always, and be it further enacted,* that if any alien so ordered to depart shall prove to the satisfaction of the President, by evidence to be taken before such person or persons as the President shall direct, who are for that purpose hereby authorized to administer oaths, that no injury or danger to the United States will arise from suffering such alien to reside therein, the President may grant a *license* to such alien to remain within the United States for such time as he shall judge proper, and at such place as he may designate. And the President may also require of such alien to enter into a bond to the United States, in such penal sum as he may direct, with one or more sufficient sureties to the satisfaction of the person authorized by the President to take the same, conditioned for the good behavior of such alien during his residence in the United States, and not violating his license, which license the President may revoke, whenever he shall think proper.

SEC. 2. *And be it further enacted,* That it shall be lawful for the President of the United States, whenever he may deem it necessary for the public safety, to order to be removed out of the territory thereof, any alien who may or shall be in prison in pursuance of this act; and to cause to be arrested and sent out of the United States such of those aliens as shall have been ordered to depart therefrom and shall not have obtained a license as aforesaid, in all cases where, in the opinion of the President, the public safety requires a speedy removal. And if any alien so removed or sent out of the United States by the President shall voluntarily return thereto, unless by permission of the President of the United States, such alien on conviction thereof, shall be imprisoned so long as, in the opinion of the President, the public safety may require.

SEC. 3. *And be it further enacted,* That every master or commander of any ship or vessel which shall come into any port of the United States after the first day of July next, shall immediately on his arrival make report in writing to the collector or other chief officer of the customs of such port, of all aliens, if any, on board his vessel, specifying their names, age, the place of nativity, the country from which they shall have come, the nation to which they belong and owe allegiance, their occupation and a description of their persons, as far as he shall be informed thereof, and on failure, every such master and commander shall forfeit and pay three hundred dollars, for the payment whereof on default of such master or commander, such vessel shall also be holden, and may by such collector or other officer of the customs be detained. And it shall be the duty of such collector or other officer of the customs, forthwith to transmit to the office of the department of state true copies of all such returns.

SEC. 4. *And be it further enacted,* That the circuit and district courts of the United States, shall respectively have cognizance of all crimes and offences against this act. And all marshals and other officers of the United States are required to execute all precepts and orders of the President of the United States issued in pursuance or by virtue of this act.

SEC. 5. *And be it further enacted,* That it shall be lawful for any alien who may be ordered to be removed from the United States, by virtue of this act, to take with him such part of his goods, chattels, or other property, as he may find convenient; and all property left in the

United States by any alien, who may be removed, as aforesaid, shall be, and remain subject to his order and disposal, in the same manner as if this act had not been passed.

SEC. 6. *And be if further enacted,* That this act shall continue and be in force for and during the term of two years from the passing thereof.

APPROVED, June 25, 1798.

AN ACT RESPECTING ALIEN ENEMIES

SECTION 1. *Be it enacted by the Senate and House of Representatives of the United States of America in Congress assembled,* That whenever there shall be a declared war between the United States and any foreign nation or government, or any invasion or predatory incursion shall be perpetrated, attempted, or threatened against the territory of the United States, by any foreign nation or government, and the President of the United States shall make public proclamation of the event, all natives, citizens, denizens, or subjects of the hostile nation or government, being males of the age of fourteen years and upwards, who shall be within the United States, and not actually naturalized, shall be liable to be apprehended, restrained, secured and removed, as alien enemies. And the President of the United States shall be, and he is hereby authorized, in any event, as aforesaid, by his proclamation thereof, or other public act, to direct the conduct to be observed, on the part of the United States, towards the aliens who shall become liable, as aforesaid; the manner and degree of the restraint to which they shall be subject, and in what cases, and upon what security their residence shall be permitted, and to provide for the removal of those, who, not being permitted to reside within the United States, shall refuse or neglect to depart therefrom; and to establish any other regulations which shall be found necessary in the premises and for the public safety: Provided, that aliens resident within the United States, who shall become liable as enemies, in the manner aforesaid, and who shall not be chargeable with actual hostility, or other crime against the public safety, shall be allowed, for the recovery, disposal, and removal of their goods and effects, and for their departure, the full time which is, or shall be stipulated by any treaty, where any shall have been between the United States, and the hostile nation or government, of which they shall be natives, citizens, denizens or subjects: and where no such treaty shall have existed, the President of the United States may ascertain and declare such reasonable time as may be consistent with the public safety, and according to the dictates of humanity and national hospitality.

46

Sec. 2. *And be it further enacted,* That after any proclamation shall be made as aforesaid, it shall be the duty of the several courts of the United States, and of each state, having criminal jurisdiction, and of the several judges and justices of the courts of the United States, and they shall be, and are hereby respectively, authorized upon complaint, against any alien or alien enemies, as aforesaid, who shall be resident and at large within such jurisdiction or district, to the danger of the public peace or safety, and contrary to the tenor or intent of such proclamation, or other regulations which the President of the United States shall and may establish in the premises, to cause such alien or aliens to be duly apprehended and convened before such court, judge or justice; and after a full examination and hearing on such complaint, and sufficient cause therefor appearing, shall and may order such alien or aliens to be removed out of the territory of the United States, or to give sureties of their good behaviour, or to be otherwise restrained, conformably to the proclamation or regulations which shall and may be established as aforesaid, and may imprison, or otherwise secure such alien or aliens, until the order which shall and may be made, as aforesaid, shall be performed.

Sec. 3. *And be it further enacted,* That it shall be the duty of the marshal of the district in which any alien enemy shall be apprehended, who by the President of the United States, or by order of any court, judge or justice, as aforesaid, shall be required to depart, and to be removed, as aforesaid, to provide therefor, and to execute such order, by himself or his deputy, or other discreet person or persons to be employed by him, by causing a removal of such alien out of the territory of the United States; and for such removal the marshal shall have the warrant of the President of the United States, or of the court, judge or justice ordering the same, as the case may be.

Approved, July 6, 1798.

THE SEDITION ACT OF JULY 14, 1798

An Act in addition to the act entitled
"An act for the punishment of
certain crimes against the United States."

SECTION 1. *Be it enacted by the Senate and House of Representatives of the United States of America, in Congress assembled,* That if any persons shall unlawfully combine or conspire together, with intent to oppose any measure or measures of the government of the United States, which are or shall be directed by proper authority, or to impede the operation of any law of the United States, or to intimidate or prevent any person holding a place or office in or under the government of the United States, from undertaking, performing or executing his trust or duty; and if any person or persons, with intent as aforesaid, shall counsel, advise or attempt to procure any insurrection, riot, unlawful assembly, or combination, whether such conspiracy, threatening, counsel, advice, or attempt shall have the proposed effect or not, he or they shall be deemed guilty of a high misdemeanor, and on conviction, before any court of the United States having jurisdiction thereof, shall be punished by a fine not exceeding five thousand dollars, and by imprisonment during a term not less than six months nor exceeding five years; and further, at the discretion of the court may be holden to find sureties for his good behaviour in such sum, and for such time, as the said court may direct.

SEC. 2. *And be it further enacted,* That if any person shall write, print, utter or publish, or shall cause or procure to be written, printed, uttered or published, or shall knowingly and willingly assist or aid in writing, printing, uttering or publishing any false, scandalous and malicious writing or writings against the government of the United States, or either house of the Congress of the United States, or the President of the United States, with intent to defame the said government, or either house of the said Congress, or the said President, or to bring them, or either of them, into contempt or disrepute; or to excite

48

against them, or either or any of them, the hatred of the good people of the United States, or to stir up sedition within the United States, or to excite any unlawful combinations therein, for opposing or resisting any law of the United States, or any act of the President of the United States, done in pursuance of any such law, or of the powers in him vested by the constitution of the United States, or to resist, oppose, or defeat any such law or act, or to aid, encourage or abet any hostile designs of any foreign nation against the United States, their people or government, then such person, being thereof convicted before any court of the United States having jurisdiction thereof, shall be punished by a fine not exceeding two thousand dollars, and by imprisonment not exceeding two years.

SEC. 3. *And be it further enacted and declared,* That if any person shall be prosecuted under this act, for the writing or publishing any libel aforesaid, it shall be lawful for the defendant, upon the trial of the cause, to give in evidence in his defence, the truth of the matter contained in the publication charged as a libel. And the jury who shall try the cause, shall have a right to determine the law and the fact, under the direction of the court, as in other cases.

SEC. 4. *And be it further enacted,* That this act shall continue and be in force until the third day of March, one thousand eight hundred and one, and no longer: *Provided,* that the expiration of the act shall not prevent or defeat a prosecution and punishment of any offence against the law, during the time it shall be in force.

APPROVED, July 14, 1798.

THE SEDITION LAW, FREE SPEECH, AND THE AMERICAN POLITICAL PROCESS

James Smith

> The influence of discussion has presided at the creation of intellectual freedom.
>
> WALTER BAGEHOT

Popular government rests on the right of the public to choose between opposing views. Since an informed public opinion is vital to republican government, freedom of expression is necessary for the formation of that opinion. If people cannot communicate their thoughts to one another without running the risk of prosecution, no other liberty can be secure, because freedom of speech and of the press are essential to any meaning of liberty.

The years between 1798 and 1801 afford the first instance under the Constitution in which American political leaders faced the problem of defining the role of public criticism in a representative government. During this period of changing political ideas, the basic pattern of the American political process emerged, and the essential features of the American civil liberties tradition were formulated. The failure of repressive measures to silence criticism of elected officials reemphasized the new and revolutionary political principle which had been the basis of the War of Independence: the idea that government rests upon the consent of the governed.

The view which the law takes of the offense of publishing and uttering seditious words depends upon the attitude it holds concerning

Reprinted from J. M. Smith: *Freedom's Fetters: The Alien and Sedition Laws and American Civil Liberties.* Copyright © 1956 by Cornell University. Used by permission of Cornell University Press.

Footnotes appear at the end of the selection.

the relation of the rulers to the people. Are the people the superiors of the rulers, or are the rulers the superiors of the people? The first view holds that sovereignty resides with the people and not with the government. The so-called rulers are the elected agents and servants of the people, who may discuss questions relating not only to government policy but also to punishment or dismissal of dishonest, inadequate, or unpopular agents. If anyone disagrees with the faultfinding, he may advocate the cause of the agents. The most that can happen is the replacement of the agent with another more to the people's liking.[1]

The criminal law of seditious libel which emerged in England during the seventeenth and eighteenth centuries developed at a time when the accepted view made the rulers the superiors of the people.[2] By virtue of their exalted positions, the rulers were considered the wise and good guides of the country. Authority, therefore, had to be approached with proper decorum. Mistakes might be pointed out in respectful petitions, but whether the rulers were mistaken or not, no censure could be leveled against them. The people could not make adverse comments in conversation, in clandestine pamphlets or, later, in newspapers. The only lawful method of presenting grievances was through their lawful representatives in the legislature, who might be petitioned in an orderly and dignified manner.[3]

This view made words punishable, because to find fault with the government tended to undermine the respect of the people for it and to reduce its dignity and authority. The "bad-tendency" test, moreover, presumed that criticism tended to overthrow the state. There was no need to prove any intention on the part of the defendant to produce disaffection or to excite an insurrection; it was enough if he intended to publish the blame. The law of seditious libel was thus the product of the view that the government was master.[4]

It was to this English common law concept that the Federalists turned for their model. Even so, they attempted to adapt the authoritarian practice to the basic realities of popular government by working out a compromise between the rights of the authorities and the rights of the people. An aristocratic party which deplored political democracy, they based their defense of the right of authorities to freedom from public criticism, paradoxically enough, on the fact that the American government rested on the consent of the governed. They contended that the election of officials by the people demonstrated the confidence which the people had in those officers. Once those officials had been elevated by the people to the highest offices in the land, they became the "constituted authorities" who ran things until the next election. Thus, the Federalists exalted the officeholder above the mass of the citizens. It was a greater offense to criticize one of the rulers than it was to criticize one of the people themselves, because the rulers partook of the majesty of the whole people.

The Federalist theory of government, moreover, held that the right of political participation was not the province of all men but the prerogative of a chosen few. As Jay put it, "those who own the country are the most fit persons to participate in the government of it." The Sedition Law was consistent with the Federalist concept of an elite ruling class. Thinking that the stability of American society depended on "the few, the rich, and the well born," they opposed any criticism which might threaten their positions as rulers by undermining public confidence in their administration. Because they had been in power since the adoption of the Constitution, they looked upon themselves as the peculiar guardians of the nation's welfare. By identifying their administration with the government, and the government with the Constitution, the Federalists concluded that criticism of their administration was an attempt to subvert the Constitution and to overthrow the government.

The Republicans agreed that the government of the United States rested on the people, but they widened the concept of "public confidence" to coincide with "public opinion." Elected officials could lose the confidence of the people as well as gain it. To continue to merit public confidence, their measures had to meet public approval. Public opinion was not a cyclical phenomenon which appeared every two years to be registered at the polls. It was in continuous process of formulation and could be conveyed constitutionally in speeches or in the press. The people did not vote themselves out of further political participation by the act of voting in elected officials. They were free to examine the conduct of the authorities; they could denounce it as well as praise it. They did not have to wait until election time to withdraw their confidence from an agent whom they decided was unworthy of it.

The Republicans based their arguments against the Sedition Law on the ground that it destroyed "the responsibility of public servants and public measures to the people." Madison specifically condemned the law, because it exposed the United States, "which acquired the honour of taking the lead among nations towards perfecting political principles," to the disgrace of retreating "towards the exploded doctrine that the administrators of the Government are the masters and not the servants of the people."[5]

Although the Federalists asserted that the Sedition Law was declaratory of the English common law, they also announced that it mitigated the rigors of the law as expounded by Blackstone. It made the intent of the speaker, as well as the tendency of his words, an essential element in the crime of seditious libel. Moreover, it allowed truth as a justification and made the jury the judge of the criminality of the utterances. Of what value to the accused were these three procedural safeguards?

The interpretation which the courts put on the truth provision made it worse than useless as an aid to the defendant. Under the rulings handed down by the judges of the Supreme Court on circuit, this supposed safeguard actually reversed the normal criminal law presumption of innocence. Instead of the government's having to prove that the words of the accused were false, scandalous, and malicious, the defendant had to prove that they were true. As Judge Samuel Chase put it, the accused had to prove all of his statements "to the marrow. If he asserts three things and proves but two," the jurist said, "he fails in his defense, for he must prove the whole of his assertions to be true." This is a clear illustration of the doctrine of presumptive guilt; in practice, the courts presumed the defendant guilty until he proved himself innocent.

Moreover, the accused was required not only to prove the truth of every word in every statement but, in one instance, to prove an entire count in an indictment by the same witness. Even though the statement contained more than one point, the defendant could not introduce different witnesses to prove different points. According to Judge Chase, this practice would have been "irregular and subversive of every principle of law."[6]

The court also refused to distinguish between a false statement of facts and erroneous opinions. Indeed, the expression of any opinion on future events could be condemned as false under the interpretation given section three of the law. Although the prosecutor could no more prove the falsity of a prediction than the defendant could prove its truth, the statement was considered false because the defendant had failed to carry the burden of proof.

What was the effect of the clause requiring that bad intent should be proved? In every case, the government prosecutors and the judges presumed the bad intent of the speaker from the bad tendency of the words. Moreover, it was the tendency of the words to find fault with elected officials which was penalized and not the intent to cause violence. Although the Vermont and New York indictments used the words "with force and arms," these were merely legal epithets thrown into the indictment. There was no effort to prove that Congressman Lyon, editor Haswell, Assemblyman Peck, or Mrs. Greenleaf intended to use force and violence or even that the tendency of their criticism was to bring about ruptures of the public peace. Lyon's prosecution was based on the "force and arms" concept, even though he was running for re-election himself. By presuming the bad intent of the speaker from the bad tendency of the words, the courts narrowed the legal test of criminality to the pre-Revolutionary common law test; persons were punished if the tendency of their words was to undermine public confidence in the elected officials and thus to render it less likely that they might be re-elected.[7]

Finally, the function of the trial jury was reduced almost to that of a rubber stamp. It is evident from the replies of grand juries to charges from federal judges, and from the verdicts of the trial juries, that both were Federalist-dominated, if not made up exclusively of Federalists. The rigor with which the trial judges restricted challenges of jurors by defense attorneys virtually prevented any examination for political bias and led to extensive criticism of the courts. Congressman Matthew Lyon, the first victim of the law, claimed that all of his trial jurors were chosen from towns which were hostile to him. The Callender case, however, is the only one in which it can be proved positively that the trial jury was Federalist to a man. Whether the juries were deliberately packed or not, they were usually chosen by the federal marshal, who was a Federalist and who became the keeper of the prisoner upon conviction. In no event can the juries be called impartial. Indeed, Beveridge observes that "the juries were nothing more than machines that registered the will, opinion, or even inclination of the national judges and the United States district attorneys. In short, in these prosecutions, trial by jury in any real sense was not to be had."[8]

Under the Sedition Law, the jury was to decide on the criminality of the utterance; one of its vital functions was to decide on the intent of the speaker. The proper duty of the court in sedition cases was to aid the jury in reaching a decision, by instructing it on what the law was in one set of circumstances or in another. The judges were given no power to pass on the facts of publication or intent.[9] In practice, however, they determined the intent of the defendant.

In the trial of Thomas Cooper, Judge Chase ruled that the defendant's effort to prove the truth of his publication demonstrated his bad intent. The defendant's attempt to utilize the legal defense allowed by the Sedition Law, the judge declared, "showed that he intended to dare and defy the Government, and to provoke them, and his subsequent conduct satisfies my mind that such was his disposition. For he justifies the publication, and declares it to be formed in truth. It is proved to be his publication."

Thus the judge ruled, and directed the jury to find, that Cooper had published the words and that he had done so with wicked intent. "It is the boldest attempt I have known to poison the minds of the people," he told the jury. It was poison not because it incited the people to force and violence but because it criticized President John Adams in an election year, tending to defeat his campaign against Thomas Jefferson. In short, the instructions of the judges made verdicts of guilty virtually inevitable.[10]

To summarize, then, the clause on truth was nullified by the courts; the right of the jury to decide the criminality of the writing was usurped by the presiding judges; and the test of intent was reduced to the seventeenth-century common law test of bad tendency. Without these procedural safeguards, the Sedition Law was almost a duplicate of the English common law of seditious libel. Since intent was presumed from tendency, the test of criminality became the same: the tendency of the words to bring rulers into disrepute.

The evidence is conclusive that the Sedition Law, as enforced, reduced the limits of speech and press in the United States to those set by the English common law in the days, before the American Revolution. This was the standard advocated by the Federalists who enacted the law, and it was the standard applied by the Federalist judges who interpreted the law.

The basic question, then, is this: is the pre-Revolutionary rule the guide to the liberties protected by the First Amendment? Is the bad-tendency test compatible with free and open discussion of public affairs by the people? Formulated in an age of authority, the common law doctrine of seditious utterances was antirepublican to the core. When Blackstone wrote his *Commentaries* in 1769, he was trying to describe the law as it then existed. Although prior censorship had expired seventy-five years before he wrote, the British government continued to institute numerous sedition prosecutions.[11] Blackstone discussed the importance of a free press in a free state, but he insisted that liberty of the press meant only that no restraints could be laid upon writings prior to their publication.[12]

In stressing the sovereignty of the legislature, Blackstone emphasized the supremacy of the government over the subject. Whatever liberties the people possessed were conferred by the government. They had no "inalienable right" to liberty of the press; that had been created automatically when Parliament failed to extend the Licensing Act of 1695. So long as the writings were not censored before being printed, the press was free. Blackstone's definition, however, legalized suppression any time after the moment of publication; the most vital or the most harmless discussion of public policy could be punished if it was obnoxious to the authorities. Common law asserted the right of the state to punish those who wrote true statements about public magistrates if they tended to expose them to public hatred, contempt, and ridicule. Such statements were punishable because "the direct tendency of these libels is the breach of the public peace, by stirring up the objects of them to revenge, and perhaps to bloodshed." In criminal proceedings, truth was no defense. It was the provocation to action, and not the falsity of the statement, which was punished. The tendency to disturb the public peace was the measure of criminality. Moreover, the common law presumed that the tendency of all libel was bad. It placed the judges of the King's Bench in a position to condemn any writings which had a tendency to excite and move the people to change the existing order of things.[13] Sir James Fitzjames Stephen has observed that the practical enforcement of the law of seditious libel in England "was wholly inconsistent with any serious public discussion of political affairs." As long as it was recognized as the law of the land, any political discussion existed only by sufferance of the government.[14]

This was the model to which the Federalists turned in 1798. Not only did they define the First Amendment by the pre-Revolutionary English common law, but they also urged the necessity of imitating the repressive alien and sedition legislation which Great Britain had passed to combat the social and political forces unleashed by the

French Revolution. Although England enforced these measures as wartime precautions, the Federalists insisted on the need for a similar policy whether war came or not. Indeed, the Sedition Law was to expire not at the end of the diplomatic impasse with France but with the end of President Adams' term of office. By following the British precedents, the Federalists subscribed to the authoritarian view that the government is the master, not the servant, of the people.

The American Revolution culminated in the formulation and establishment in the United States of a form of government which rested on the will of the governed. Growing out of the natural-rights philosophy of the seventeenth and eighteenth centuries, this revolutionary theory of government was founded on the principle that governments are instituted to secure, among other things, the liberties of the individual. A written Constitution established a limited government, which was barred from invading these "inalienable rights."

The meaning of the First Amendment did not crystallize in 1791, when the Bill of Rights was added to the Constitution. Not until the years from 1798 to 1801, when the Sedition Act was debated and enforced, did the limits of liberty of speech and of the press become an issue which focused attention squarely on its definition as a part of the American experiment in self-government.[15] The first thing to be kept in mind in determining the meaning of the First Amendment is that it was added by the people as a further bulwark guarding civil liberties in the United States from governmental interference.[16] Moreover, the rights protected by the proviso were those prevailing not in England but in the United States.[17]

One of the political catalysts of the American Revolution was the effort of the British to subdue the popular press in colonial America. This attempt was twofold. Under the Stamp Act of 1765, a prohibitive tax was placed on the paper used by the presses. Had this law been executed, it would have forced the inexpensive press out of circulation, thus suppressing colonial discussion of politics in the popular papers. A second method used to crush colonial opposition to ministerial policies was an accelerated use of the law of seditious libel.[18] Indeed, when George III issued his proclamation of rebellion against the American colonies, he gave as its official title "A Proclamation, By the King, for Suppressing Rebellion and Sedition."[19]

There are several important pronouncements prior to the debates of 1798 which indicate that liberty of the press in the post-Revolutionary United States meant more than the English common law rule.

Many of the colonial publications on political affairs were considered seditious and even treasonable under the common law and its loose administration by the king's judges.[20] That one of the objects of the American Revolution was to abolish the common law restriction on liberty of the press, especially on political discussion, is illustrated by one of the addresses framed by the First Continental Congress in 1774. In a letter addressed to the inhabitants of Quebec, Congress enumerated five rights basic to a free government. One of these was liberty of the press. "Besides the advancement of truth, science, morality, and arts in general," its importance consisted "in its diffusion of liberal sentiments on the administration of Government, its ready communication of thought between subjects, and the consequential promotion of union among them, whereby oppressive officers are shamed or intimidated into more honourable and just modes of conducting affairs."[21]

This statement of liberty of the press specifically denies the right of the government to censure remarks because of their tendency to bring magistrates into public shame and contempt. Indeed, it asserts the opposite right of criticizing administrative officials chosen by the "free and full consent" of the governed.

The Declaration of Independence, of course, was the classic repudiation of the idea that the government was the master of the people. The Virginia Act for Establishing Religious Freedom, written by the author of the Declaration, is another Revolutionary document which sets forth a philosophical justification of the right of a person to intellectual freedom.[22] The Preamble includes a declaration for individual liberty not only in religion but also in civil affairs:

> To suffer the civil magistrate to intrude his powers into the field of opinion and to restrain the profession or propagation of principles on supposition of their ill tendency, is a dangerous falacy [sic], which at once destroys all religious liberty, because he being of course judge of that tendency, will make his opinions the rule of judgment, and approve or condemn the sentiment of others only as they shall square with or differ from his own; that it is time enough for the rightful purposes of government for its officers to interfere when principles break out into overt acts against peace and good order; and finally, that truth is great and will prevail if left to herself; that she is the proper and sufficient antagonist to error, and has nothing to fear from the conflict unless by human interposition disarmed of her natural

weapons, free argument and debate; errors ceasing to be dangerous when it is permitted freely to contradict them.[23]

The basic doctrine of this bill, which Jefferson always ranked next to the Declaration of Independence, was its rejection of the bad-tendency test in the field of opinion. In a line which was deleted when the bill passed, Jefferson stated "that the opinions of men are not the object of civil government, nor under its jurisdiction." Even without this line, however, the Virginia Act for Establishing Religious Freedom announced the right of an individual to choose his beliefs, religious or political, free from compulsion.

The fact that the rights of free speech and of a free press are linked with the rights of conscience, assembly, and petition in the First Amendment throws much light on the meaning of the guarantees added to the Constitution at the insistence of the American people. Whereas the First Amendment secures the separation of church and state, England had a state-supported church. Moreover, the right of assembly was severely restricted in England at the time the Bill of Rights was ratified in the United States.[24] The First Amendment certainly did not follow the English example in the field of religion and assembly. As Madison emphasized in the congressional debates over the rights incorporated in the First Amendment, "The freedom of the press and rights of conscience, those choicest privileges of the people, are unguarded in the British Constitution." Although any invasion of them by the government always was resisted in Parliament by able advocates, he observed that the Magna Charta did not contain any provision for the security of rights "respecting which the people of America are most alarmed."[25] The First Amendment can no more be considered an endorsement of the English common law definition of the press than it can be interpreted as an adoption of English practices in the field of religion and assembly.

Indeed, Madison based his explanation of the First Amendment in 1799 on the essential difference "between the nature of the British Government and the nature of the American Governments." In England, Parliament was omnipotent; in the United States, "the People, not the Government, possess the absolute sovereignty." In the United States, the legislatures are not omnipotent, nor are the magistrates infallible. "The nature of governments elective, limited, and responsible in all their branches," Madison continued, "may well be supposed

to require a greater freedom of animadversion than might be tolerated" by one that is composed of an hereditary king and upper
house, neither elected by, nor responsible to, the people, and an
omnipotent lower house.[26]

There is other contemporary evidence which indicates that freedom
of speech and of the press in the United States was viewed as a liberal
protection guaranteeing free discussion of public matters. In his essay
on the press, Benjamin Franklin asserted that "if by the *Liberty of the
Press* were understood merely the Liberty of discussing the Propriety
of Public Measures and political opinions, let us have as much of it as
you please."[27]

One of the strongest statements on the American meaning of the
liberty of the press was contained in the reply of the Federalist envoys
to France in answer to Talleyrand's protest against remarks in the
American press critical of the Directory. "The genius of the Constitution," wrote Pinckney, Marshall, and Gerry in a passage which
their fellow Federalists ignored, "and the opinion of the people of the
United States, cannot be overruled by those who administer the Government. Among those principles deemed sacred in America," they
continued, "among those sacred rights considered as forming the bulwark of their liberty which the Government contemplates with awful
reverence and would approach only with the most cautious circum-
spection, there is no one of which the importance is more deeply
impressed on the public mind than the liberty of the press."[28]

All these statements went much farther than the Blackstonian
theory which held that liberty of the press prevented only government censorship. Although they all agreed that the absence of censorship was an important part of that freedom, they also asserted the
right of the people to participate in free and full discussion of public
affairs. They were declarations based on American experience, not
on British precedents. They rejected the authoritarian view that the
rulers are the superiors of the people.

In his *History of the Criminal Law of England*, Stephen asserted
that to those who believe that the people are the masters of the
government, "and who carry it out to all its consequences, there can
be no such offence as sedition. There may indeed be breaches of the
peace which may destroy or threaten life, limb, or property, and there
may be incitements to such offences, but," he maintained, "no imagin-
able censure of the government, short of censure which has an

immediate tendency to produce such a breach of the peace, ought to be regarded as criminal." Although Stephen considered this statement too extreme for England in view of her historical development, this is the view expounded by the American people in the Declaration of Independence, fought for in the American Revolution, and established in the state and federal constitutions. In short, the English common law crime of sedition and the American principle of popular government cannot coexist.[29]

In every case in which the law was enforced, a political crime was punished for the same reason that all political crimes have ever been punished — for expressions of discontent with the authorities. As Professor Henry Schofield has pointed out, the sedition cases clearly demonstrated "the great danger . . . that men will be fined and imprisoned, under the guise of being punished for their bad motives, or bad intent and ends, simply because the powers that be do not agree with their opinions, and spokesmen of minorities may be terrorized and silenced when they are most needed by the community and most useful to it, and when they stand most in need of the protection of the law against a hostile, arrogant majority."[30]

Calling the Sedition Law the greatest and most fatal error of the Federalist party, Charles Francis Adams, the grandson and biographer of John Adams, noted that republican government cannot function without free discussion. "It cannot be denied," he wrote, "that the attempt to punish individuals for mere expressions of opinion of public measures and public men, to subject them perhaps to fine and imprisonment, and certainly to heavy and burdensome charges in their defense, for exercising a latitude of speech however extreme, in the heat and excitement attending the political conflicts of a free country, verged too closely upon an abridgment of the liberty of speech and of the press to be quite reconcilable to the theory of free institutions."[31]

The Alien and Sedition Laws played a prominent role in shaping the American tradition of civil liberties. Based on the concept that the government was master, these laws provoked a public response which clearly demonstrated that the people occupied that position. The severity of the Sedition Law failed to prevent the "overthrow" of the Adams administration by the Jeffersonian "disorganizers." Indeed, the law furnished a ready text which the Democratic-Republicans used to incite the American people to legal "insurgency" at the polls; the election resulted in the repudiation of the party which tried to protect itself behind the Sedition Law. It elevated to power a party whose leaders stressed the concept that freedom of opinion is an essential part of an all-encompassing freedom of the mind; for Jefferson and Madison the First Freedom occupied a high, preferred position as the only effectual guardian of every other right. To them, as to the United States Supreme Court later, the defeat of the Federalists illustrated the common understanding that the First Amendment abolished the English common law crime of seditious libel, of which the Sedition Law was merely declaratory.[32]

The adherence of the people to the Republicans marked the beginning of a new political era. As John Adams himself pointed out, the election resulted in the "revolution of 1801":[33] the Age of Federalism was at an end. Public opinion had never been without its influence on the conduct of government but it had been grudgingly acknowledged by the Federalists. It now became the basis of American democratic development. As early as 1794, Madison had stated concisely what has since become the traditional American view: "If we advert to the nature of Republican Government, we shall find that the censorial power is in the people over the Government, and not in the Government over the people."[34]

The sharp and lasting defeat administered to the Federalists at the beginning of the nineteenth century made a deep impression on the party leaders of that century. Not until the entry of the United States into World War I did Congress again impose restrictions on utterances and publications and thus encroach on the civil liberties tradition founded on the resentment against the laws of 1798.[35] The Sedition Act of 1918, however, was a wartime measure which was repealed in 1921. The first peacetime sedition statute was not passed until 1940, when Congress enacted the Alien Registration Act, commonly called the Smith Act.

With these two exceptions, the United States has preferred to abide by the principles enunciated by Jefferson in his first inaugural address. Referring to the election of 1800 as a "contest of opinion" which had been decided by "the voice of the nation," the new president reasserted the right of the people "to think freely and to speak and to write what they think." Although he stoutly defended the right of the majority to rule, he cautioned that its will "to be rightful must be reasonable. The minority," he declared, "possess their equal rights, which equal law must protect, and to violate would be oppression."

In a passage which condemned the Sedition Law without naming it, he restated the fundamental principle of the American experiment in popular government:

> If there be any among us who would wish to dissolve this Union or to change its republican form, let them stand undisturbed as monuments of the safety with which error of opinion may be tolerated where reason is left free to combat it. I know, indeed, that some honest men fear that a republican government can not be strong, that this Government is not strong enough; but would the honest patriot, in the full tide of successful experiment, abandon a government which has so far kept us free and firm on the theoretic and visionary fear that this Government, the world's best hope, may by possibility want energy to preserve itself? I trust not. I believe this, on the contrary, the strongest Government on earth. I believe it the only one where every man, at the call of the law, would fly to the standard of the law, and would meet invasions of the public order as his own personal concern. Sometimes it is said that man can not be trusted with the government of himself. Can he, then, be trusted with the government of others? Or have we found angels in the forms of kings to govern him? Let history answer this question.[36]

The American experiment in self-government, which was conceived in liberty, was dedicated to the proposition that public discussion is a political duty; that men may disagree on public issues; that the opportunity to speak their minds on supposed grievances affords the best means of deciding on proper remedies; that in the marketplace, or on the battleground, of opinions, the people will be able to distinguish truth from error; and that the sounder principles and measures will prevail. Without free speech and a free press, representative government is not truly representative. Without them, popular government cannot function.

Footnotes

[1] Sir James Fitzjames Stephen, *A History of the Criminal Law of England* (London, 1883), II, 299–300.
Portions of this chapter were published in *The William and Mary Quarterly*, 3d ser., 9 (1952), 497–511.

[2] Williams S. Holdsworth, *A History of English Law* (London, 1903–1938), VIII, 378.

[3] *Ibid.*, 337–338. Also see George Chase, ed., *Blackstone's Commentaries,* 3d ed. (New York, 1894), bk. IV, ch. vii, 915–918; Zechariah Chafee, *Free Speech in the United States* (Cambridge, Mass., 1941), 3–35; Henry Schofield, "Freedom of the Press in the United States," *Essays on Constitutional Law and Equity* (Boston, 1921), II, 510.

[4] Holdsworth, *History of English Law*, VIII, 341. This commentator defines seditious libel as "the intentional publication of a writing which reflected on the government." This is the substance of Coke's case, *De Libellis famosis* (1606), which Stephen calls "the nearest approach to a definition of the crime with which I am acquainted."

[5] Address of the General Assembly to the People of the Commonwealth of Virginia, Jan. 23, 1799, *Madison's Writings* (Hunt ed.), VI, 338.

[6] For Chief Justice John Marshall's disagreements, see *Chase Trial*, 70.

[7] For an outstanding analysis of "intent" and "tendency," see Chafee, *Free Speech in the United States*, 23–25.

[8] Beveridge, *Marshall*, III, 42. He also asserts that "in many States the United States Marshals selected what persons they pleased as members of the grand juries and trial juries. These officers of the National courts were, without exception, Federalists; in many cases Federalist politicians. When making up juries they selected only persons of the same manner of thinking as that of the marshals and judges themselves."

Also see Anderson, "Alien and Sedition Laws," Amer. Hist. Assoc., *Annual Report for 1912*, 125–126; Warren, *The Supreme Court in United States History*, rev. ed. (Boston, 1937), I, 164–168, and the Papers of George Bancroft Relating to the Administration of John Adams (N.Y. Pub. Lib.).

[9] Carroll, "Freedom of Speech and of the Press in the Federalist Period: The Sedition Act," *Michigan Law Review*, 18 (1920), 644n.

[10] The two leading legal writers on the Sedition Law have observed that the summing up of the judges to the juries "left nothing for honest jurors to do but return verdicts of guilty." See *ibid.*, 641, and Henry Schofield, "Freedom of the Press," *Essays on Constitutional Law*, II, 534.

[11] Wilkes's famous case had been before the English public for six years when Blackstone's work appeared. In the next year, the ministers of George III began the even more important prosecutions of the printers of Junius' letters. Sir Thomas Erskine May, *The Constitutional History of England, since the Accession of George the Third, 1760–1860, with a Supplementary Chapter, 1861–1871* (New York, 1889), II, 113–114.

[12] *Blackstone's Commentaries*, bk. IV, ch. vii, 915–918.

[13] For Blackstone's reference to the role of the expiration of the Licensing Act in the establishment of liberty of the press, see *Commentaries*, 915–918.

For a discussion of why Parliament failed to extend the act, see Thomas Babington Macaulay, *The History of England From the Accession of James II* (New York, 1856), IV, 488–490.

[14] Stephen, *History of the Criminal Law*, II, 348. Not until 1843 did England admit truth as a defense in criminal libel suits, and then it was allowed only in rebuttal. See Lord Campbell's Act, 6 and 7 Victoria, C. 96, s.6.

[15] Chafee, *Free Speech in the United States*, 29.

[16] Schofield, "Freedom of the Press," *Essays on Constitutional Law*, II, 569, says that the constitutional declarations of liberty of speech and of the press are the original work of the American people in the sphere of law and government.

In Number 84 of *The Federalist*, Hamilton argued that the Constitution conferred no power by which restrictions might be imposed on the press.

[17] Albert J. Beveridge, "The Effect of the French Revolution on England and America," *Chicago Legal News*, 53 (1920), 103.

[18] Clyde Augustus Duniway, *The Development of Freedom of the Press in Massachusetts* (New York, 1906), 124–136; Arthur M. Schlesinger, "The Colonial Newspapers and the Stamp Act," *New England Quarterly*, 8 (1935), 63–83. Also see Edmund S. and Helen M. Morgan, *The Stamp Act Crisis: Prologue to Revolution* (Chapel Hill, 1953), 187, and Chafee, *Free Speech in the United States*, 21. For the increased use of the law of seditious libel in England during the pre-Revolutionary period, see May, *Constitutional History of England*, II, 110, 114.

[19] Peter Force, *American Archives* (Washington, 1840), 4th ser., III, 240–241. The proclamation was issued Aug. 23, 1775.

[20] Bradley Chapin, "The American Revolution as Lese Majesty," *Pennsylvania Magazine of History and Biography*, 79 (July, 1955), 310–330. Also see Chapin, "The Law of Treason during the American Revolution, 1765–1783" (doctoral dissertation, Cornell University, 1951).

[21] "Letter Addressed to the Inhabitants of the Province of Quebec," Oct. 26, 1774, W. C. Ford, ed., *Journal of the Continental Congress* (Washington, 1904), I, 108.

[22] Although the bill did not become law until 1785, it was written in 1777 and was printed as early as 1779. For a facsimile of the 1779 text, see Julian P. Boyd and others, eds., *The Papers of Thomas Jefferson* (Princeton, 1950), II, 304.

[23] *Jefferson Papers* (Boyd ed.), II, 546.

[24] Philip A. Brown, *The French Revolution in English History* (London, 1918).

[25] *Annals*, IC. 434. For a thorough discussion of *The Birth of the Bill of Rights, 1776–1791*, see the excellent study by Robert Allen Rutland.

[26] Report on the Virginia Resolutions, 1799–1800 session, Virginia State Assembly, *Madison's Writings* (Hunt ed.), VI, 387–388.

[27] "The Court of the Press," Sept. 12, 1789, *Franklin's Writings* (Smyth ed.), X, 38. For an analysis of this essay and Harper's interpretation, see Chapter VIII.

[28] "Envoys to the French Minister of Exterior Affairs," *Annals*, 5C, 3449.

[29] Stephen, *History of Criminal Law of England*, II, 300; Schofield, "Freedom of the Press," *Essays on Constitutional Law*, II, 535. 520–521. For a lucid discussion of *Freedom of the Press*, see the recent book by William L. Chenery (New York, 1955).

[30] Schofield, *Essays*, II, 540.

[31] Adams, *Life and Works of John Adams*, I, 560–561.

[32] In *U.S.* v. *Hudson and Goodwin*, 7 Cranch 32 (1812), the Supreme Court rejected the argument that the United States possessed common law jurisdiction over the crime of seditious libel and ruled that crimes against the United States must be established by statutes. The court specifically stated that "although this question is brought up now for the first time to be decided by this Court, we consider it as having been long since settled in *public opinion*. In no other case for many years has this jurisdiction been asserted; and the general acquiescence of legal men shews the prevalence of opinion in favor of the negative of the proposition." The italics are mine.

The reaction against the federal statute of 1798 also had its effect on state prosecutions for seditious libel, rendering them less and less frequent until they ceased altogether. Edward S. Corwin, "Freedom of Speech and Press under the First Amendment: A Résumé," *Yale Law Journal*, 30 (1920), 48, reprinted in American Association of Law Schools, *Select Essays in Constitutional Law*, II, 1063.

[33] *Adams' Works*, X, 162.

[34] *Annals*, 3C, 2S (Nov. 27, 1794), 934.

[35] Robert E. Cushman, "Alien and Sedition Laws," *Encyclopedia of Social Sciences* (New York, 1930), I, 635. Also see Chafee, *Free Speech in the United States, passim*.

[36] Richardson, *Messages*, I, 322.

Freedom of Speech and the Abolitionists

During the first half of the nineteenth century, Americans of different religious persuasions and social reformers of various kinds were subject to harassment, violence, and persecution for propagating and practicing their beliefs. Mormons suffered atrocities and in some states were subjected to a reign of terror; Catholic convents were burned or wrecked; Abolitionists were harassed and their meetings disrupted, and some were tarred and feathered, run out of town, or killed.

The following selection deals with the suppression and attempted suppression in the South and the North of Americans disseminating antislavery doctrines, especially during the two decades preceding the Civil War.

Professor Nye is the author of several books, including *The Cultural Life of the New Nation, 1776–1830, William Lloyd Garrison and the Humanitarian Reformers*, and coauthor of the two-volume work *A History of the United States*. He received the Pulitzer Prize for biography in 1945 for his book *George Bancroft: Brahmin Rebel*.

THE DAY OF THE MOB

Russel B. Nye

Before 1830, though sensitive to antislavery talk, the South nevertheless allowed a limited amount of free discussion. Yet at the same time signs of displeasure indicated a growing public uneasiness about the slavery question. One "Hieronymous" in 1825 complained of newspaper comments on slavery; a meeting in Smithfield, Virginia, was broken up by local magistrates in 1827; and the Manumission Society of North Carolina in 1826 deplored the increasing tendency in the South to stifle criticism of its domestic institutions. The most rigid control of antislavery discussion before 1830 existed in South Carolina, but after that date fears of Garrisonian abolition and slave revolt spread suspicion of antislavery opinion throughout the South in general.

It was imperative, after the beginnings of the aggressive phase of abolition, for the dominant slaveholding group to prevent the dissemination of antislavery doctrines. The South could be self-critical; a decade of reports from Southern commercial conventions reprinted in *DeBow's Review* shows that slaveholders themselves recognized that slavery had its faults, yet it is significant that none of the resolutions passed by these conventions ever had really practical results. To retain political and economic control of the South, the slaveholders believed that no deep-seated criticism of slavery could safely be tolerated. This group, with its chief institution at stake, could not allow frank discussion of it, and, for obvious reasons, hoped to identify its private interests with the public welfare of the South at large.

In the deep South the suppression of antislavery criticism after 1830 was relatively simple, for there, as one historian phrased it, "existed the most perfect agreement known in Anglo-Saxon history." In the upper South, where cotton and Negroes were less of an issue, repression was more difficult, and though independent thinkers were discouraged, recalcitrants continued to appear in the border states until the Civil War. But throughout the South it was possible by the passage of state and local legislation to control and minimize, and, if need be, to prohibit entirely antislavery opinion and discussion among Southerners, and to prevent the spread of such doctrines in the region by Northerners.

With the exception of Kentucky, every Southern state eventually passed laws controlling and limiting speech, press, and discussion. The decision of an Alabama court in 1837, for example, made any person "who shall proclaim to our slaves the doctrine of universal emancipation . . . a subject for criminal justice." The Virginia Code of 1849 punished by imprisonment up to a year, and a fine up to $500, any person who "by speaking or writing maintains that owners have no right of property in slaves," while Louisiana's penalty for conversation "having a tendency to promote discontent among free colored people, or insubordination among slaves" ranged from twenty-one years at hard labor to death. The passage of such laws was justified as a means of preventing slave revolts, presumably stirred up by abolitionists. Not all Southerners agreed that these measures were necessary. The Richmond *Whig* thought the Virginia law of 1836 "far worse than lynching or lynch law," while the Louisville *Gazette*, applauding Kentucky's refusal to pass restrictive legislation, thought the preservation of free speech more important than the suppression of antislavery opinion. Such objections were unusual, however, and the laws remained on the statute books, reaffirmed and strengthened in subsequent years.

Though these statutes served to hamper free expression of antislavery opinion in the South, they did not fully suppress it. Most of the laws dealt out punishment for "incendiary" talk, or "opinions tending to incite insurrection," — terms vaguely defined and charges difficult to establish — a fact recognized by Southern courts, whose verdicts were usually lenient. Legal processes were often slow, loopholes could be found, and there were strong feelings in the South that better ways of controlling antislavery opinions ought to be found. To remedy these defects and to provide swifter and more effective punishment, the South turned to the citizen-mob, long known on the frontier as "lynch law." Though isolated cases of mob action occurred before 1833, the development of the mob as a means of suppressing abolitionism reached its climax during the period 1833–1840, receding in the North after 1845 and continuing with undiminished force in the South until the Civil War.

There were in the South two threats to the security of slavery: the Southerner who entertained unsound opinions, and the Northerner (whether abolition agent or casual traveller) who might spread anti-slavery doctrine. To silence the one and eject the other, if legal means were too slow or not justified by the case, the citizen-mob, in the opinion of the proslavery element, was by far the most effective instrument. By appealing to the popular dread of racial amalgamation and Negro equality, and most of all by raising the specter of slave revolt, mobs were not difficult to organize in the South. Governor Hammond of South Carolina advised his legislature that abolitionism could be "silenced in but one way — Terror — Death," and a group of citizens who cooperated to suppress abolitionism, he believed, was "no more a mob than a rally of shepherds to chase a wolf out of their pastures." As Southern proslavery opinion became more unified, the mob came to be known, in most Southern states, as a "vigilance committee," or "committee of safety," and to be granted quasi-legal status in many Southern communities.

.   .   .   .   .

Though its activities were obviously violations of Federal and state laws guaranteeing free speech and expression, the vigilance committee was, in Southern opinion, a necessary community organization. Free speech, as it was defined in the slave states, did not allow criticism of slavery — a perfectly logical attitude from the proslavery point of view. If it was right to have slavery, it was right to have its defenses; if speech against slavery was wrong, there was no other alternative than to suppress it, by law or without law.

Definitions of free speech in the South provide some interesting insight into the proslavery mind. The Frankfort, Kentucky, *Commonwealth* believed no one was entitled to speak on the subject of slavery "unless he speak in terms acceptable to those who alone have any responsibilities and powers in regard to the question." The Norfolk, Virginia, *Herald* said that "free speech" meant only "implicit obedience to our laws. . . . The thing is very simple, and cannot be possibly misunderstood, we should think . . ." Richard Yeadon of the Charleston *Courier* defined it as "freedom to discuss slavery with the whites, but not with Negroes"; a Southerner, he pointed out with some logic, might not be allowed to preach "agrarianism and sedition" to the Irish laborers of New York. A "Lady of Georgia" could not understand the objections to the whole issue — "We have made up our minds about it, and because our decision does not suit abolitionists, they clamor that we wish to restrain the discussion." *The Western Presbyterian Herald* gave the definition most generally accepted in the South: "Freedom of speech is to be distinguished from licentiousness. No man has a moral right to use the power of speech in defiance of reason and revelation." Based on such grounds, the vigilance committee claimed that it possessed moral, if not legal, reasons for existence, and from a Southern viewpoint what it did was not a violation of freedom of speech.

The extent of Southern vigilance committee activity during the years 1835 to 1860 is almost impossible to determine. Judging from the newspaper accounts carefully kept by the abolitionist newspapers, and making allowances for cases which received no notice in the press, Garrison's figure of three hundred "lynchings," as they were usually termed, seems not too high. Though the years after 1850 were those of greatest violence, the beginning of vigilance committee activity dated roughly from 1835. In that year the Charleston post office was raided and abolitionist literature burned by such a committee, and four Ohioans, suspected of slave-tampering, were whipped at Kanawha Salines, Virginia, by a "committee of safety." In May of 1836 a committee of fifty, incensed at Dr. Nelson's Palmyra College in Missouri, cleared the county of suspected abolitionists. In June the Reverend Aaron Kitchell of New Jersey, an itinerant preacher, was tarred and feathered by a committee of twelve in Hillsborough, Georgia. In January of 1837 John Hopper (son of the Quaker abolitionist Isaac Hopper) barely escaped a dangerous mob in Savannah, Georgia, after a local committee found a colonizationist pamphlet in his baggage. Later in the year a British sea-captain was beaten by a mob in Jacksonville, Florida, for antislavery views.

The experience of George Rye of Woodstock, Virginia, was perhaps typical of how some committees operated. Rye expressed himself against slavery so well in talking with friends in 1836 that one of them asked him to write out his arguments for private perusal. The next year, after Rye had defended a local minister for preaching a sermon on colonization, his false friend showed Rye's paper to the local committee of vigilance, who summarized and published it in a local newspaper as an example of "incendiary talk." On the basis of these opinions, which the committee itself had published, Rye was tried, convicted, and fined for attempting to foment slave insurrections.

.   .   .   .   .

The greatest activity on the part of Southern vigilance committees came in the 'fifties. By that time the organization of Southern opinion had reached its final stage, the technique of the citizen-mob had been perfected, and increased tension in South-North relations had excited Southern feelings to the breaking point. A wave of slave revolt scares during the 'fifties caused suspicion to fall on Southerner and travelling Northerner alike, and the merest indication of antislavery sentiment was likely to attract the attention of a local committee. The system spread during the decade until some states, such as South Carolina, were networks of interlocking committees, and at least one serious case of organized mob action occurred every year after 1850.

In January, 1850, Elijah Harris, an itinerant schoolteacher from Dunbarton, New Hampshire, was arrested on a writ issued by the justice of the peace of Clinton, Barnwell District, South Carolina. He was arraigned not before the court, but before the local committee of safety, which convicted him of carrying in his trunk an antislavery sermon by a New Hampshire minister. The committee shaved his head, tarred and feathered him, and gave him twelve hours to leave town. During the same month a Scotsman, Robert Edmond, a native of Charleston, South Carolina, was tarred and feathered on suspicion of teaching Negroes to read, and later in the year Jackson Evans of Ebenezer, South Carolina, received similar treatment for "expressing abolition opinions." In October, 1850, the Georgetown, South Carolina, committee, suspecting a Maine sea-captain and his first officer of abolitionism, whipped them and put them on their ship with twenty-four hours to leave the harbor. Captain Elisha Betts of Eufaula, Alabama, an aged veteran of the Indian wars, was discovered by the local committee to be a subscriber to *The National Era*. Though Betts protested that neither his ideas nor those of the *Era* were incendiary, he was exiled from the community and advised to leave the state.

Northern travelling agents and merchants had an especially difficult time in the South after 1850. Dr. L. B. Coles of Boston, a book salesman and lecturer on physiology, was jailed in Columbia, South Carolina, in January, 1851, under an old local law forbidding the sale of books printed outside the state. No lawyer would take his case, but after his baggage had been searched and his letters examined by the local committee, he was fined and released. At Cheraw, South Carolina, John Malone, a New York window-shade salesman, was heard to say that he did not believe "a poor white man stood as good a chance in a slave state as in a free one." For this statement, judged to be incendiary, he was arraigned with his employer, James Colwell, before the local vigilance committee and convicted. A delegation of five men took the two culprits to Wilmington, North Carolina, where a guard took them to Norfolk, Virginia. Norfolk authorities jailed them for two days and put them on a New York steamer. At Troy, Alabama, a one-legged clockmender from New York State was ducked and ridden out of town on a rail as "a thoroughly dangerous man" for "speaking freely about free soil" in July of 1851. The Reverend Edward Matthews, an agent of the American Free Mission Society and a friend of Cassius Clay's, was arrested near Richmond, Kentucky; his clothes were ripped off, he was thrown eleven times into a pond, and driven out of town by the local committee.

Native Southerners fared little better. Nathan Bird Watson of Warrenton, Georgia, was convicted by the local committee of safety of "promulgating abolition opinions, and visiting Negro houses . . . , as we suppose, for the purpose of inciting our free and slave population to insurrection and insubordination." The committee blacked his face, put him on the next train for Atlanta, and notified the committees of surrounding communities of his offense. The Reverend McBride and the Reverend Crooks of the Wesleyan Methodist Church were driven from their circuits in Guilford County, North Carolina, during 1851, by a committee (which included a minister, a member of the state legislature, and several Methodist elders) for expressing antislavery opinions.

The case which most graphically illustrated the power that committees of vigilance came to possess in the South was that of John Cornutt, a slaveholder of Grayson County, Virginia. When a local Wesleyan minister was accused of inciting slaves to revolt because he preached a sermon against slavery to his white congregation, Cornutt, a man of some community standing, protested the charge as absurd. As a result, he was tarred and feathered and lashed by the local committee of safety. However, Cornutt recognized some of his assailants and swore out warrants for their arrest. The committee met and passed resolutions warning all lawyers against taking the case on pain of additional tar and feathers, and warned the judge and court that the case was not to be tried. But the court did meet, only to be broken up by a mob led by the committee. Immediately afterward a mass meeting voted to form a new vigilance committee of two hundred members, to be divided into sub-committees. Further, it voted that the names of all presumed antislavery men in the county and of those holding suspicious opinions were to be reported to the central committee; that no clerks of county or circuit courts were to be permitted to issue writs against citizens for acts committed while expelling or punishing abolitionists; that no sheriff was to be permitted to serve such writs; that all candidates for county office must subscribe to these doctrines; and that all election officials must pledge to cast out the votes of known abolitionists in all elections. Cornutt and the judge who convened the court, it was added, must give the committee "positive assurance" of their soundness on the slavery question or leave the county immediately. Neighboring Wythe County endorsed the resolutions and promised to follow suit.

.   .   .   .   .

It was evident to the people of the Northern states that vigilance committee justice in the South threatened the whole American tradition of civil liberties. The abolitionists pointed out that where slavery existed, the rights of man were always subverted; depriving the Southern white man of his right to free speech was simply the first step toward depriving the Northern citizen of his. "What liberty," asked William Goodell, after making an analysis of Southern laws governing discussion of slavery, "is there for *white* people in the South? They share deeply in the bondage of the blacks." And after reprinting a letter from a Southern subscriber, recounting a brush with a vigilance committee, James G. Birney remarked, "Such is the liberty of the white man where slavery reigns." The widespread opposition in the South to the circulation of Helper's *The Impending Crisis,* a book addressed not to Negroes but to Southern whites, impressed the North with the truth of the abolitionist claim. When Owen Lovejoy, during a particularly bitter passage-at-arms over Helper's book in the House, asked if he could repeat his remarks in Richmond, Martin of Virginia replied with deadly seriousness, "We would hang you higher than Haman."

The full implication of these things was not lost on Northerners. William Thomas, though he refused "to utter one syllable in favor of the peculiar sentiments of the abolitionists," expressed the fear that the acts of Southern committees of vigilance foreshadowed a determined attempt to destroy American rights; after the civil rights of the white citizen were erased, would there not be substituted for them the laws of the mob and those who controlled it? The Columbus *Ohio Observer* thought that "When it once becomes general to substitute mobs for law, our liberties are gone, and we are a ruined nation," and the Boston *Observer* editorialized, "Let it once be established that a mob may, under any pretense, usurp the functions of the courts of justice, and Liberty will have fallen upon her own sword." Warning the South against the consequences of tolerating vigilance committees, another Northerner remarked:

> The man, then, who presumes to intimate that because a particular community may be opposed awhile to certain opinions, that that community have a right, therefore, by mob law, or any other law . . . to forcibly suppress the discussion and constitutional promulgation of those opinions . . . is encouraging the prevalence of a doctrine fraught with imminent danger to the constitution itself.

There can be little doubt that such committees exercised a more powerful control over the life of the white man than any other agency in the South. That this control was increasing rather than diminishing is illustrated by the organizational pattern of one of the last committees to be formed, that of Bibb County, Alabama. All citizens, according to its constitution, became members of the General Committee upon signature in the "book." Any twenty such signers constituted a quorum, empowered to "denounce any man as a bad man, and unworthy to reside amongst honest men . . . , to be expelled from the neighborhood." The chairman of the General Committee selected a "secret committee" of five to fifteen members, whose identities were to remain secret, and who, "in appropriate disguises," were assigned to carry out the expulsion orders of a meeting of any twenty members. Beginning with the formation of the first citizens' groups in the early eighteen-thirties, the development of the vigilance committee system tended inevitably in this direction. Had it not been for the intervention of war, there is ample reason to believe that such enormous grants of power to these committees would have become general practice throughout the South.

The concurrent development of a move to suppress free speech on the slavery question in the North, though less violent and a shorter duration, did much to convince a large segment of previously neutral or hostile opinion that, in sanctioning mob action against the abolitionist groups, the North was seriously endangering its own liberties. In seizing upon the issue of free speech versus mob law, antislavery men turned the controversy to their advantage. In defending a fundamental right of democracy they saw that they might also convince Northerners that the institution of slavery was in itself a danger to democratic principles. The period of mob violence in the free states ranged from 1833 to 1845; after the latter date cases of mob action were relatively infrequent, though by no means non-existent. The reasons which lay behind the formation of Southern vigilance committees were obvious — fear of slave revolt, racial equality, and racial amalgamation — but in the North the most powerful of these clearly did not apply.

Yet it is undeniably true that for nearly fifteen years the citizenry and officialdom of several Northern states either condoned or actively assisted in suppressing an unpopular minority. What, then, led citizens of free states to promote and sanction antiabolitionist mobs? Although the constitutions of all the states, slave and free, contained guarantees of free speech, press, and assembly, apparently a sizeable number of communities were willing to resort to extra-legal means to suppress abolition opinion. As an Ohioan wrote in 1836:

> When a body of men with such feeling and principles begins to distract the nation with their mad schemes, it is high time for a community to notice them. I am no advocate of Lynch law, but I must say that if Lynch law is to be practised, I know of no fitter subjects for its operation than such fanatics.

Northern mobs, like Southern ones, were organized and led by prominent, respected members of the community. The abolitionists, in fact, coined a term to describe them — "respectable mobs." Oliver Johnson, Phillips, Garrison, Birney, and Goodell, all of whom made a study of mobs, agreed, in Goodell's words, that they were

> . . . either countenanced, instigated, or palliated by that description of citizens who complacently consider themselves and are commonly denominated the *higher classes of society* — the men of wealth, of

office, of literature, of elegant leisure, including politicians, and that portion of the clergy who naturally associate with that class just described, or are dependent on them.

Garrison's analysis of Northern mobs is probably the most authoritative. They were, he believed, supported by several groups: first, by those who believed abolitionism a threat to peace and order, men who simply disliked agitation; second, by those who, for business reasons, believed abolitionism a threat to Southern trade connections; third, by those who believed abolitionists to be infidels, anti-Biblical, religiously unorthodox; fourth, by those who feared racial equality and amalgamation; and fifth, by those who believed the slavery controversy, if unchecked, might break up the Union. *The National Anti Slavery Standard* agreed on the whole with Garrison's analysis, believing that mob leadership was ordinarily drawn from the ranks of "first, the aristocracy of wealth," who saw in the movement a threat to economic interest; second, those who ". . . are unwilling that the negroes should be turned loose to remain among us, in the full enjoyment of equal rights, in civil and religious society," and third, from the hoodlum element, "drunken and deceived mobocrats whose arguments consist of vulgar blackguardism, brickbats, and rotten eggs."

The resolutions of the mass meetings called to protest abolition activity bear out these explanations. Before breaking up an abolition gathering at nearby Putnam, a mob in Zanesville, Ohio, placarded the town with exhortations to "rid ourselves of the disgrace of amalgamation." Another mob in Martinsville, Ohio, attacked an abolition meeting for the reason that abolitionists were "for equalizing with the Black and trying to reduce all the White laboring men to the same condition." A meeting in Utica, New York, in 1836, labelled the coming abolitionist convention in that city as dangerous to peace, to the constitution, to the stability of the Union, and an insult to New York's Southern friends. The Clermont County, Ohio, Anti Slavery Society was accused by a public protest meeting of "designing to divide the Union . . . , to excite slaves to insurrection and murder, attempting a union of Church and State," and of "scheming . . . to gain honor and distinction."

Politics, too, played a part in arousing antiabolitionist sentiment. James Birney thought it "remarkable that no mob had ever attacked the abolitionists except after special training by politicians who had something to hope from the favor of the South. . . . It is the editors of a venal press, to-be expectants of office, congressmen, judges, postmasters, etc., that we are to look for the cause of these frequent and shameful outrages." But according to contemporary accounts, the chief motives for attacks on abolitionists in the North apparently were economic, social, religious, and political, in approximately that order of importance.

The method of organizing Northern antiabolitionist mobs resembled the pattern established in the South, though Northern groups were much less united and much less permanent. It began with a mass meeting of citizens, addressed by prominent members of the community, which passed resolutions condemning abolitionist activity in general or the acts of a particular abolitionist or society. A group of executive officers was elected by the meeting, with a subcommittee to warn the offenders, and in some cases to take action against them. The committee usually dissolved after doing its work, leaving no permanent organization.

Northern mobs usually were little more than an annoyance to the abolitionists. William Birney thought them "as a general thing, not dangerous either to life or limb, or beyond the power of the police to control," and Weed, an Ohio lecturer, wrote, "These mobocrats are all great cowards and seldom do anything but make swelling threats . . . I have been in a great many mobs but have never apprehended a great deal of danger." In breaking up abolition meetings, the mobs rarely resorted to physical violence, but instead were usually no more than rude and rowdy. Throwing eggs, ink, or paint; shaving the tails of horses or driving them off; placing red pepper or asafoetida in the meetinghouse stove; drowning out the speaker with drums, horns, or shouts; blockading the building in which the meeting was to be held or in a few cases setting it on fire — these were common methods of dispersing abolitionist meetings.

Abolitionist newspapers were ordinarily handled more drastically — throwing away type, pounding the press with hammers, dumping it in a river or pond, or burning the building. More dangerous was an occasional stoning or clubbing. Mount Eaton, Ohio, reported a man killed in 1846 by a brick, and Fred Douglass' hand was crippled by an Indiana mob. Most annoying to abolition agents was the damage done to clothes, which, on an agent's meager salary, constituted a large item of expense. Some agents wore "storm suits" of old clothes when a mob threatened.

Abolitionist agents, during their training period, were taught how to conduct themselves in the presence of a mob. They were warned at the beginning of the trials they faced, and what their choice entailed. "Let every abolitionist," Theodore Weld told prospective antislavery agents, "debate the matter once and for all, and settle it with himself whether he is an abolitionist from *impulse* or *principle* — whether he can lie upon the rack — and clasp the faggot and tread with steady step the scaffold. . . ." They were told not to be discouraged, that mob action was really an indication that abolitionism was gaining in a community. "Every abolition lecture they break up is a ruinous victory to the cause of slavery," reminded *The Anti Slavery Record*. Don't provoke mobs, it continued, but do everything to avoid them. Proceed as if a mob could not occur, and act surprised if one does. If a mob breaks into a meeting, keep on as long as possible, hoping that the intruders will eventually tire. Do not resist violence — "Be persecuted if you must" — and after the mob has retired, find out and publish the names of its instigators and leaders. Although a good many in the North believed that the abolitionists deliberately drew attacks in order to gain sympathy, evidence to support the accusation is difficult to establish.

.   .   .   .   .

New York City experienced perhaps the worst disorders. Close and profitable connections with the slave states, and a fairly large and influential group of resident Southerners, combined to make the city an antiabolitionist stronghold. New York merchants regarded abolitionism as a threat to Southern trade relations; the fact that the names of the Tappans were linked to New York, which was also the headquarters of the American Anti Slavery Society, was highly embarrassing. It was not uncommon for business firms to insert notices in the newspapers assuring Southern customers that they held no sympathy with the abolitionists, and frequent resolutions of censure against them were passed at directors' meetings.

The organization of the New York City Anti Slavery Society on October 2, 1833, provided the occasion for the city's first conspicuous disturbance. On that date Leavit, Green, Rankin, Goodell, Elizur

Wright, and Lewis and Arthur Tappan intended to call a meeting at Clinton Hall to launch the city's first abolition society, but before the meeting the city was placarded by signs, signed "Many Southerners," which urged all citizens unsympathetic to abolition to break it up. Discretion led the abolitionists to change their meeting place to Chatham Street Chapel. A large crowd gathered at Clinton Hall on the appointed evening, however, and held an antiabolitionist meeting, addressed by General Robert Bogardus, F. A. Tallmadge of New York, and other prominent citizens. Resolutions affirmed that "our duty to our country, and to our Southern brethren in particular, renders it improper and inexpedient to agitate a question pregnant with peril and difficulty to the common weal," and at the conclusion of the meeting a portion of the crowd moved on Chatham Street Chapel. The abolitionists, however, had finished a few minutes before the arrival of the Clinton Hall group, who satisfied themselves by conducting a mock meeting burlesquing them.

On July 8, 1834, a meeting of the American Anti Slavery Society at Chatham Street Chapel was invaded and broken up. Since the meeting was attended by free Negroes, the race question seems to have been at least partially responsible. According to the New York *Daily Advertiser*, the Sacred Music Society had hired the chapel for the same evening, and, upon arriving, found an abolitionist meeting in progress. Demands for the use of the hall, it was claimed, led to an attack by the Negroes upon members of the music society, joined by others from both camps. Lewis Tappan was stoned on the way home, but escaped injury. On the evening of the 9th, crowds began to gather about the chapel again, on the strength of a rumored abolitionist meeting. When no abolitionists appeared, the crowd broke into the chapel and held another antiabolitionist meeting. In an ugly mood, it next invaded the Bowery Theater and broke up a production of *Metamora* because of a rumor that the British stage manager had made anti-American remarks. The group next moved on to Lewis Tappan's home to sack it and burn the furniture in the street. Later, after the churches of Drs. Ludlow and Cox (believed to be abolitionists) had been damaged by the mob, barricades began to appear in the streets.

The next day the riot burst out with augmented violence. The Tappans' store was attacked, but police drove off the rioters, who then invaded the Negro section and wrecked three Negro churches, a Negro school, and about twenty Negro homes. As violence grew, Mayor C.

W. Lawrence, after two proclamations, deputized several citizens and called out the militia. The riots gradually subsided. Although the members of the American Anti Slavery Society issued a flat denial of responsibility, Mayor Lawrence specifically declared them to be the cause of the disturbance, while several newspapers condoned the riots on the ground that abolitionists could neither merit nor enjoy any legal protection against mobs. The three-day riots evidently had the desired effect, for the extremist Richmond *Enquirer* thought them ". . . highly gratifying to the people of the South, as a strong, and indeed conclusive manifestation that the public sentiment of the north will itself suffice to put down that fanatical spirit of false philanthropy and real incendiarism."

The riots of 1834 were the worst suffered by the city. Meetings of New Yorkers in 1835 and 1836 reaffirmed their determination "to frustrate and defeat the mischievous schemes of designing demagogues and deluded fanatics," but nothing happened until 1850, when the sixteenth anniversary meeting of the American Anti Slavery Society at the Broadway Tabernacle was annoyed by a group led by Isaiah Rynders, a Tammany politician, and forced to disperse. Both the New York *Globe* and *The Herald* urged the mobs on, *The Herald* saying, "The merchants, men of business, and men of property in this city should frown down the meeting of these madmen, if they would save themselves." Newspapers in general, however, decried the mobs and pointed out the danger to free speech.

. . . . . .

From the earliest phase of the controversy over slavery, the abolitionists were conscious of the close relationship between their cause and that of free discussion. Judge Jay in 1835 appealed to "every genuine republican to resist with energy and decision so palpable an outrage" as suppression of abolitionist liberty of speech, since it was a heritage common to all Americans. Birney believed that the right to discuss slavery eventually involved the perpetuation of all free institutions, warning that "the salvation of the country now depends upon *our* living down and working down, these mobs." The Vermont Anti Slavery Society resolved that to allow any self-appointed group to suppress free discussion was "to acquiesce in the subversion of the fundamental principles of all freedom." Abolition societies, in their announcements, resolutions, and constitutions, carefully quoted all of the constitutional guarantees of free speech and stressed the importance of keeping them inviolate. Freedom of expression, it was maintained, was a basic minority right, not just for abolitionists, but for all Americans. "If it is surrendered," said Lewis Gunn, "we ourselves are slaves . . .; it lies at the foundation of all our other rights."

The abolitionist cause therefore from the first stood upon firm moral ground by identifying itself with a fundamental democratic privilege. If free speech were slavery's greatest foe, in attacking slavery, the abolitionists were, in effect, preserving that fundamental right. Why was it, the abolitionists asked, that prison reform, prohibition of alcoholic beverages, women's rights, or any other reform could be preached without opposition, but that antislavery agitation was immediately to be put down? Mobs and gag-laws betrayed the essential weakness of the very cause they were meant to strengthen. If abolitionists were wicked men, and their cause wrong, why did not the proslavery faction allow them to condemn themselves out of their own mouths?

The abolitionists pointed out that if free discussion were right, and that if slavery could not be maintained in the face of it, slavery must therefore be wrong. If slavery could not survive criticism, and if the right to discuss and criticize it freely were threatened by slavery's existence, the American people would have to choose between the two. "The contest," said Francis Jackson, "is therefore between liberty and slavery. If slavery cannot exist with free discussion — so neither can liberty breathe without it. Losing this, we too, shall not be freemen indeed, but little, if at all, superior to the millions we now seek to emancipate."

The effect upon Northern opinion of the period of mob law was, as the abolitionists anticipated, largely sympathetic to their cause. The fact that suppression of free speech affected every man who held a stake in the American tradition assisted them greatly in enlisting support from non-abolitionists and neutrals. In putting down the abolitionists, it was argued, the North was establishing a precedent that could be invoked against any minority whose opinions did not meet the public favor. As Professor Follen of Harvard pointed out, "A mob excited against abolition now may excite another mob far more dangerous to others than it is to us. It is impossible to prescribe limits to lawless acts of popular violence." Many in the North recognized the validity of the argument. The Vermont *Watchman and State Gazette*, while admitting its disagreement with abolitionism, at the same time disapproved of "all measures to put down discussion by force," and a meeting in Lowell, Massachusetts, called to stir up opposition to abolition, ended by affirming the right of all abolitionists to be heard, and to resist "the imperious demands of Southern tyranny." The Detroit Presbytery in 1836 went on record as favoring free speech for abolitionists as "a privilege no human government has a right to take away," and the Reverend Albert Barnes told the alumni of Hamilton College that "the most appalling danger that threatens our country is the threatened restriction of the right of free discussion."

The death of Lovejoy, coupled with the attacks upon Garrison, Birney, and Pennsylvania Hall, and the increasing frequency of incidents involving abolitionist speakers and presses in the free states, shocked a great segment of opinion in the North into agreement with the abolitionist contention that a basic constitutional right was at stake in the controversy over slavery. Prominent men such as Webster, Channing, and Alexander Everett lent their weight to the abolitionist side; and newspaper opinion, always sensitive of threats to free discussion, expressed the fear that mob action might become dangerously out of hand. The Adrian, Michigan, *Expositor*, which was not an abolitionist newspaper, summarized the Northern reaction by saying:

> We tell you, gentlemen, when you encourage such proceedings you are handling edged tools — you know not how soon such weapons may turn against yourselves. . . . We repeat, the liberty of speech and of the press must be respected, or you are violators of the very principles of that compact you profess so ardently to love.

The end of the period of violence in the North came with the shift of public opinion after 1840. Though the abolitionists' right to free speech was never again seriously threatened in the North, they continued to warn the nation that until slavery was dead, free speech was never out of danger. With all their faults of intolerance, intensity, fanaticism, and narrow single-mindedness, the abolitionists nevertheless laid claim to a principle without which the nation could not exist, and the attempt to suppress them in the North by denying them expression was bound to fail. There was too much at stake for the free states to risk willingly the traditional right of the citizen to express his opinion. To thousands of Northerners, the abolitionist contention that their cause and that of civil liberty were joined seemed believable and logical.

The abolitionists from the start held every moral advantage. They were the martyrs, the oppressed and persecuted, the defenders of free speech and free criticism. When the abolitionists emerged as guardians of white liberties, as well as crusaders for those of blacks, their cause gained immeasurably in moral strength. The influence of the era of mob violence, and the threat to free discussion occasioned by it, was a significant factor in cementing support in the North for the antislavery movement.

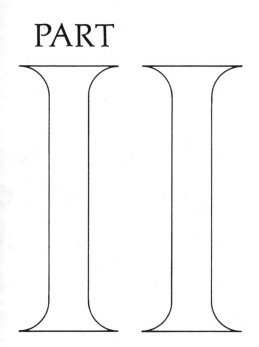

Landmark
Court Decisions

Freedom of Speech and World War I

On April 6, 1917, Congress declared war against Germany. On June 15, 1917, the Espionage Act was passed, and although most of it related to actual espionage and protection of military secrets, part was directed against conspiracy and some types of expression. Charges were brought against hundreds of individuals as a result of the Espionage Act, but none of the cases reached the United States Supreme Court until World War I was over. The Court's first decision on these cases came in 1919, in *Schenck* v. *United States*. Charles Schenck was charged with violation of the 1917 Espionage Act, and the Court, in a unanimous decision, found against him. In this decision, Justice Oliver Wendell Holmes, Jr., first applied his "clear and present danger" test.

On May 16, 1918, the Espionage Act was amended to include what is sometimes referred to as the Sedition Act. The 1918 amendment was eventually repealed in 1921, but the 1917 act remained in effect. The 1918 amendment dealt more than the original Espionage Act with advocacy, teaching, printing, speaking, inciting — more with "speech." The defendants in the *Abrams* case were indicted under the 1918 amendment, and in a seven to two decision the Court upheld the conviction. Justices Holmes and Brandeis dissented, and much of the dissent is devoted to an elaboration of the "clear and present danger" test presented by Holmes earlier the same year in the *Schenck* decision.

All four selections, the 1917 Espionage Act and the *Schenck* decision, the 1918 amendment and the *Abrams* decision, are included here in their entirety.

ESPIONAGE ACT OF JUNE 15, 1917

CHAP. 30. — An Act to punish acts of interference with the foreign relations, the neutrality, and the foreign commerce of the United States, to punish espionage, and better to enforce the criminal laws of the United States, and for other purposes.

Be it enacted by the Senate and House of Representatives of the United States of America in Congress assembled:

Title I

Espionage

SECTION 1. That (a) whoever, for the purpose of obtaining information respecting the national defense with intent or reason to believe that the information to be obtained is to be used to the injury of the United States, or to the advantage of any foreign nation, goes upon, enters, flies over, or otherwise obtains information concerning any vessel, aircraft, work of defense, navy yard, naval station, submarine base, coaling station, fort, battery, torpedo station, dockyard, canal, railroad, arsenal, camp, factory, mine, telegraph, telephone, wireless, or signal station, building, office, or other place connected with the national defense, owned or constructed, or in progress of construction by the United States or under the control of the United States, or of any of its officers or agents, or within the exclusive jurisdiction of the United States, or any place in which any vessel, aircraft, arms, munitions, or other materials or instruments for use in time of war are being made, prepared, repaired, or stored, under any contract or agreement with the United States, or with any person on behalf of the United States, or otherwise on behalf of the United States, or any prohibited place within the meaning of section six of this title; or (b) whoever for the purpose aforesaid, and with like intent or reason to believe, copies, takes, makes, or obtains, or attempts, or induces or aids another to copy, take, make, or obtain, any sketch, photograph, photographic negative, blue print, plan, map, model, instrument, appliance, document, writing, or note of anything connected with the national defense; or (c) whoever, for the purpose aforesaid, receives or obtains or agrees or attempts or induces or aids another to receive or obtain from any person, or from any source whatever, any document, writing, code book, signal book, sketch, photograph, photographic negative, blue print, plan, map, model, instrument, appliance, or note, of anything connected with the national defense, knowing or having reason to believe, at the time he receives or obtains, or agrees or attempts or induces or aids another to receive or obtain it, that it has been or will be obtained, taken, made or disposed of by any person contrary to the provisions of this title; or (d) whoever, lawfully or unlawfully having possession of, access to, control over, or being intrusted with any document, writing, code book, signal book, sketch, photograph, photographic negative, blue print, plan, map, model, instrument, appliance, or note relating to the national defense, willfully communicates or transmits or attempts to communicate or transmit the same to any person not entitled to receive it, or willfully retains the same and fails to deliver it on demand to the officer or employee of the United States entitled to receive it; or (e) whoever, being intrusted with or having lawful possession or control of any document, writing, code book, signal book, sketch, photograph, photographic negative, blue print, plan, map, model, note, or information, relating to the national defense, through gross negligence permits the same to be removed from its proper place of custody or delivered to anyone in violation of his trust, or to be lost, stolen, abstracted, or destroyed, shall be punished by a fine of not more than $10,000, or by imprisonment for not more than two years, or both.

SEC. 2. (a) Whoever, with intent or reason to believe that it is to be used to the injury of the United States or to the advantage of a foreign nation, communicates, delivers, or transmits, or attempts to, or aids or induces another to, communicate, deliver, or transmit, to any foreign government, or to any faction or party or military or naval force within a foreign country, whether recognized or unrecognized by the United States, or to any representative, officer, agent, employee, subject, or citizen thereof, either directly or indirectly, any document, writing, code book, signal book, sketch, photograph, photographic negative, blue print, plan, map, model, note, instrument, appliance, or information relating to the national defense, shall be punished by imprisonment for not more than twenty years: *Provided,* That whoever shall violate the provisions of subsection (a) of this section in time of war shall be punished by death or imprisonment for not more than thirty years; and (b) whoever, in time of war, with intent that the same shall be communicated to the enemy, shall collect, record, publish, or communicate, or attempt to elicit any information with respect to the movement, numbers, description, condition, or disposition of any of the armed forces, ships, aircraft, or war materials of the United States, or with respect to the plans or conduct, or supposed plans or conduct of any naval or military operations, or with respect to any works or measures undertaken for or connected with, or intended for the fortification or defense of any place, or any other information relating to the public defense, which might be useful to the enemy, shall be punished by death or by imprisonment for not more than thirty years.

SEC. 3. Whoever, when the United States is at war, shall willfully make or convey false reports or false statements with intent to interfere with the operation or success of the military or naval forces of the United States or to promote the success of its enemies and whoever, when the United States is at war, shall willfully cause or attempt to cause insubordination, disloyalty, mutiny, or refusal of duty, in the military or naval forces of the United States, or shall willfully obstruct the recruiting or enlistment service of the United States, to the injury of the service or of the United States, shall be punished by a fine of not more than $10,000 or imprisonment for not more than twenty years, or both.

SEC. 4. If two or more persons conspire to violate the provisions of sections two or three of this title, and one or more of such persons does any act to effect the object of the conspiracy, each of the parties to such conspiracy shall be punished as in said sections provided in the case of the doing of the act the accomplishment of which is the object of such conspiracy. Except as above provided conspiracies to commit offenses under this title shall be punished as provided by section thirty-seven of the Act to codify, revise, and amend the penal laws of the United States approved March fourth, nineteen hundred and nine.

SEC. 5. Whoever harbors or conceals any person who he knows, or has reasonable grounds to believe or suspect, has committed, or is about to commit, an offense under this title shall be punished by a fine of not more than $10,000 or by imprisonment for not more than two years, or both.

SEC. 6. The President in time of war or in case of national emergency may by proclamation designate any place other than those set forth in subsection (a) of section one hereof in which anything for the use of the Army or Navy is being prepared or constructed or stored as a prohibited place for the purposes of this title: *Provided*, That he shall determine that information with respect thereto would be prejudicial to the national defense.

SEC. 7. Nothing contained in this title shall be deemed to limit the jurisdiction of the general courts-martial, military commissions, or naval courts-martial under sections thirteen hundred and forty-two, thirteen hundred and forty-three, and sixteen hundred and twenty-four of the Revised Statutes as amended.

SEC. 8. The provisions of this title shall extend to all Territories, possessions, and places subject to the jurisdiction of the United States whether or not contiguous thereto, and offenses under this title when committed upon the high seas or elsewhere within the admiralty and maritime jurisdiction of the United States and outside the territorial limits thereof shall be punishable hereunder.

SEC. 9. The Act entitled "An Act to prevent the disclosure of national defense secrets," approved March third, nineteen hundred and eleven, is hereby repealed.

AMENDMENT OF MAY 16, 1918 TO SECTION 3 OF THE ESPIONAGE ACT

CHAP. 75. — An Act to amend section three, title one, of the Act entitled "An Act to punish acts of interference with the foreign relations, the neutrality, and the foreign commerce of the United States, to punish espionage, and better to enforce the criminal laws of the United States, and for other purposes," approved June fifteenth, nineteen hundred and seventeen, and for other purposes.

Be it enacted by the Senate and House of Representatives of the United States of America in Congress assembled, That section three of title one of the Act entitled "An Act to punish acts of interference with the foreign relations, the neutrality, and the foreign commerce of the United States, to punish espionage, and better to enforce the criminal laws of the United States, and for other purposes," approved June fifteenth, nineteen hundred and seventeen, be, and the same is hereby, amended so as to read as follows:

SEC. 3. Whoever, when the United States is at war, shall willfully make or convey false reports or false statements with intent to interfere with the operation or success of the military or naval forces of the United States, or to promote the success of its enemies, or shall willfully make or convey false reports or false statements, or say or do anything except by way of bona fide and not disloyal advice to an investor or investors, with intent to obstruct the sale by the United States of bonds or other securities of the United States or the making of loans by or to the United States, and whoever, when the United States is at war, shall willfully cause or attempt to cause, or incite or attempt to incite, insubordination, disloyalty, mutiny, or refusal of duty, in the military or naval forces of the United States, or shall willfully obstruct or attempt to obstruct the recruiting or enlistment service of the United States, and whoever, when the United States is at war, shall willfully utter, print, write, or publish any disloyal, profane, scurrilous, or abusive language about the form of government of the United States, or the Constitution of the United States, or the military or naval forces of the United States, or the flag of the United

States, or the uniform of the Army or Navy of the United States, or any language intended to bring the form of government of the United States, or the Constitution of the United States, or the military or naval forces of the United States, or the flag of the United States, or the uniform of the Army or Navy of the United States into contempt, scorn, contumely, or disrepute, or shall willfully utter, print, write, or publish any language intended to incite, provoke, or encourage resistance to the United States, or to promote the cause of its enemies, or shall willfully display the flag of any foreign enemy, or shall willfully by utterance, writing, printing, publication, or language spoken, urge, incite, or advocate any curtailment of production in this country of any thing or things, product or products, necessary or essential to the prosecution of the war in which the United States may be engaged, with intent by such curtailment to cripple or hinder the United States in the prosecution of the war, and whoever shall willfully advocate, teach, defend, or suggest the doing of any of the acts or things in this section enumerated, and whoever shall by word or act support or favor the cause of any country with which the United States is at war or by word or act oppose the cause of the United States therein, shall be punished by a fine of not more than $10,000 or imprisonment for not more than twenty years, or both: *Provided*, That any employee or official of the United States Government who commits any disloyal act or utters any unpatriotic or disloyal language, or who, in an abusive and violent manner criticizes the Army or Navy or the flag of the United States shall be at once dismissed from the service. Any such employee shall be dismissed by the head of the department in which the employee may be engaged, and any such official shall be dismissed by the authority having power to appoint a successor to the dismissed official."

Sec. 2. That section one of Title XII and all other provisions of the Act entitled "An Act to punish acts of interference with the foreign relations, the neutrality, and the foreign commerce of the United States, to punish espionage, and better to enforce the criminal laws of the United States, and for other purposes," approved June fifteenth, nineteen hundred and seventeen, which apply to section three of Title I thereof shall apply with equal force and effect to said section three as amended.

Title XII of the said Act of June fifteenth, nineteen hundred and seventeen, be, and the same is hereby, amended by adding thereto the following section:

"Sec. 4. When the United States is at war, the Postmaster General may, upon evidence satisfactory to him that any person or concern is using the mails in violation of any of the provisions of this Act, instruct the postmaster at any post office at which mail is received addressed to such person or concern to return to the postmaster at the office at which they were originally mailed all letters or other matter so addressed, with the words 'Mail to this address undeliverable under Espionage Act' plainly written or stamped upon the outside thereof, and all such letters or other matters so returned to such postmasters shall be by them returned to the senders thereof under such regulations as the Postmaster General may prescribe."

Approved, May 16, 1918.

SCHENCK v. UNITED STATES

249 U.S 47 (1919)

MR. JUSTICE HOLMES delivered the opinion of the court.

This is an indictment in three counts. The first charges a conspiracy to violate the Espionage Act of June 15, 1917, c. 30, § 3, 40 Stat. 217, 219, by causing and attempting to cause insubordination, &c., in the military and naval forces of the United States, and to obstruct the recruiting and enlistment service of the United States, when the United States was at war with the German Empire, to wit, that the defendants wilfully conspired to have printed and circulated to men who had been called and accepted for military service under the Act of May 18, 1917, a document set forth and alleged to be calculated to cause such insubordination and obstruction. The count alleges overt acts in pursuance of the conspiracy, ending in the distribution of the document set forth. The second count alleges a conspiracy to commit an offence against the United States, to wit, to use the mails for the transmission of matter declared to be non-mailable by Title XII, § 2 of the Act of June 15, 1917, to wit, the above mentioned document, with an averment of the same overt acts. The third count charges an unlawful use of the mails for the transmission of the same matter and otherwise as above. The defendants were found guilty on all the counts. They set up the First Amendment to the Constitution forbidding Congress to make any law abridging the freedom of speech, or of the press, and bringing the case here on that ground have argued some other points also of which we must dispose.

It is argued that the evidence, if admissible, was not sufficient to prove that the defendant Schenck was concerned in sending the documents. According to the testimony Schenck said he was general secretary of the Socialist party and had charge of the Socialist headquarters from which the documents were sent. He identified a book found there as the minutes of the Executive Committee of the party. The book showed a resolution of August 13, 1917, that 15,000 leaflets should be printed on the other side of one of them in use, to be mailed to men who had passed exemption boards, and for distribution.

95

Schenck personally attended to the printing. On August 20 the general secretary's report said "Obtained new leaflets from printer and started work addressing envelopes" &c.; and there was a resolve that Comrade Schenck be allowed $125 for sending leaflets through the mail. He said that he had about fifteen or sixteen thousand printed. There were files of the circular in question in the inner office which he said were printed on the other side of the one-sided circular and were there for distribution. Other copies were proved to have been sent through the mails to drafted men. Without going into confirmatory details that were proved, no reasonable man could doubt that the defendant Schenck was largely instrumental in sending the circulars about. As to the defendant Baer there was evidence that she was a member of the Executive Board and that the minutes of its transactions were hers. The argument as to the sufficiency of the evidence that the defendants conspired to send the documents only impairs the seriousness of the real defence.

It is objected that the documentary evidence was not admissible because obtained upon a search warrant, valid so far as appears. The contrary is established. *Adams* v. *New York,* 192 U.S. 585; *Weeks* v. *United States,* 232 U.S. 383, 395, 396. The search warrant did not issue against the defendant but against the Socialist headquarters at 1326 Arch Street and it would seem that the documents technically were not even in the defendants' possession. See *Johnson* v. *United States,* 228 U.S. 457. Notwithstanding some protest in argument the notion that evidence even directly proceeding from the defendant in a criminal proceeding is excluded in all cases by the Fifth Amendment is plainly unsound. *Holt* v. *United States,* 218 U.S. 245, 252, 253.

The document in question upon its first printed side recited the first section of the Thirteenth Amendment, said that the idea embodied in it was violated by the Conscription Act and that a conscript is little better than a convict. In impassioned language it intimated that conscription was despotism in its worst form and a monstrous wrong against humanity in the interest of Wall Street's chosen few. It said "Do not submit to intimidation," but in form at least confined itself to peaceful measures such as a petition for the repeal of the act. The other and later printed side of the sheet was headed "Assert Your Rights." It stated reasons for alleging that any one violated the Constitution when he refused to recognize "your right to assert your opposition to the draft," and went on "If you do not assert and support your rights, you are helping to deny or disparage rights which it is the solemn duty of all citizens and residents of the United States to retain." It described the arguments on the other side as coming from cunning politicians and a mercenary capitalist press, and even silent consent to the conscription law as helping to support an infamous conspiracy. It denied the power to send our citizens away to foreign shores to shoot up the people of other lands, and added that words could not express the condemnation such cold-blooded ruthlessness deserves, &c., &c., winding up "You must do your share to maintain, support and uphold the rights of the people of this country." Of course the document would not have been sent unless it had been intended to have some effect, and we do not see what effect it could be expected to have upon persons subject to the draft except to influence them to obstruct the carrying of it out. The defendants do not deny that the jury might find against them on this point.

But it is said, suppose that that was the tendency of this circular, it is protected by the First Amendment to the Constitution. Two of the strongest expressions are said to be quoted respectively from well-known public men. It well may be that the prohibition of laws abridging the freedom of speech is not confined to previous restraints, although to prevent them may have been the main purpose, as intimated in *Patterson* v. *Colorado*, 205 U.S. 454, 462. We admit that in many places and in ordinary times the defendants in saying all that was said in the circular would have been within their constitutional rights. But the character of every act depends upon the circumstances in which it is done. *Aikens* v. *Wisconsin*, 195 U.S. 194, 205, 206. The most stringent protection of free speech would not protect a man in falsely shouting fire in a theatre and causing a panic. It does not even protect a man from an injunction against uttering words that may have all the effect of force. *Gompers* v. *Bucks Stove & Range Co.*, 221 U.S. 418, 439. The question in every case is whether the words used are used in such circumstances and are of such a nature as to create a clear and present danger that they will bring about the substantive evils that Congress has a right to prevent. It is a question of proximity and degree. When a nation is at war many things that might be said in time of peace are such a hindrance to its effort that their utterance will not be endured so long as men fight and that no Court could regard them as protected by any constitutional right. It seems to be admitted that if an actual obstruction of the recruiting service were proved, liability for words that produced that effect might be enforced. The statute of 1917 in § 4 punishes conspiracies to obstruct as well as actual obstruction. If the act (speaking, or circulating a paper), its tendency and the intent with which it is done are the same, we perceive no ground for saying that success alone warrants making the act a crime. *Goldman* v. *United States,* 245 U.S. 474, 477. Indeed that case might be said to dispose of the present contention if the precedent covers all *media concludendi.* But as the right to free speech was not referred to specially, we have thought fit to add a few words.

It was not argued that a conspiracy to obstruct the draft was not within the words of the Act of 1917. The words are "obstruct the recruiting or enlistment service," and it might be suggested that they refer only to making it hard to get volunteers. Recruiting heretofore usually having been accomplished by getting volunteers the word is apt to call up that method only in our minds. But recruiting is gaining fresh supplies for the forces, as well by draft as otherwise. It is put as an alternative to enlistment or voluntary enrollment in this act. The fact that the Act of 1917 was enlarged by the amending Act of May 16, 1918, c. 75, 40 Stat. 553, of course, does not affect the present indictment and would not, even if the former act had been repealed. Rev. Stats., § 13.

Judgments affirmed.

ABRAMS v. UNITED STATES

250 U.S. 616 (1919)

MR. JUSTICE CLARKE delivered the opinion of the court.

On a single indictment, containing four counts, the five plaintiffs in error, hereinafter designated the defendants, were convicted of conspiring to violate provisions of the Espionage Act of Congress (§ 3, Title I, of Act approved June 15, 1917, as amended May 16, 1918, 40 Stat. 553).

Each of the first three counts charged the defendants with conspiring, when the United States was at war with the Imperial Government of Germany, to unlawfully utter, print, write and publish: In the first count, "disloyal, scurrilous and abusive language about the form of Government of the United States;" in the second count, language "intended to bring the form of Government of the United States into contempt, scorn, contumely and disrepute;" and in the third count, language "intended to incite, provoke and encourage resistance to the United States in said war." The charge in the fourth count was that the defendants conspired "when the United States was at war with the Imperial German Government, . . . unlawfully and wilfully, by utterance, writing, printing and publication, to urge, incite and advocate curtailment of production of things and products, to wit, ordnance and ammunition, necessary and essential to the prosecution of the war." The offenses were charged in the language of the act of Congress.

It was charged in each count of the indictment that it was a part of the conspiracy that the defendants would attempt to accomplish their unlawful purpose by printing, writing and distributing in the City of New York many copies of a leaflet or circular, printed in the English language, and of another printed in the Yiddish language, copies of which, properly identified, were attached to the indictment.

All of the five defendants were born in Russia. They were intelligent, had considerable schooling, and at the time they were arrested they had lived in the United States terms varying from five to ten years, but none of them had applied for naturalization. Four of them testified as witnesses in their own behalf and of these, three frankly avowed that they were "rebels," "revolutionists," "anarchists," that they did not believe in government in any form, and they declared that they had no interest whatever in the Government of the United States. The fourth defendant testified that he was a "socialist" and believed in "a proper kind of government, not capitalistic," but in his classification the Government of the United States was "capitalistic."

It was admitted on the trial that the defendants had united to print and distribute the described circulars and that five thousand of them had been printed and distributed about the 22d day of August, 1918. The group had a meeting place in New York City, in rooms rented by defendant Abrams, under an assumed name, and there the subject of printing the circulars was discussed about two weeks before the defendants were arrested. The defendant Abrams, although not a printer, on July 27, 1918, purchased the printing outfit with which the circulars were printed and installed it in a basement room where the work was done at night. The circulars were distributed some by throwing them from a window of a building where one of the defendants was employed and others secretly, in New York City.

The defendants pleaded "not guilty," and the case of the Government consisted in showing the facts we have stated, and in introducing in evidence copies of the two printed circulars attached to the indictment, a sheet entitled "Revolutionists Unite for Action," written by the defendant Lipman, and found on him when he was arrested, and another paper, found at the headquarters of the group, and for which Abrams assumed responsibility.

Thus the conspiracy and the doing of the overt acts charged were largely admitted and were fully established.

On the record thus described it is argued, somewhat faintly, that the acts charged against the defendants were not unlawful because within the protection of that freedom of speech and of the press which is guaranteed by the First Amendment to the Constitution of the United States, and that the entire Espionage Act is unconstitutional because in conflict with that Amendment.

This contention is sufficiently discussed and is definitely negatived in *Schenck* v. *United States* and *Baer* v. *United States*, 249 U.S. 47; and in *Frohwerk* v. *United States*, 249 U.S. 204.

The claim chiefly elaborated upon by the defendants in the oral argument and in their brief is that there is no substantial evidence in the record to support the judgment upon the verdict of guilty and that the motion of the defendants for an instructed verdict in their favor was erroneously denied. A question of law is thus presented, which calls for an examination of the record, not for the purpose of weighing conflicting testimony, but only to determine whether there was some evidence, competent and substantial, before the jury, fairly tending to sustain the verdict. *Troxell v. Delaware, Lackawanna & Western R. R. Co.*, 227 U.S. 434, 442; *Lancaster v. Collins*, 115 U.S. 222, 225; *Chicago & Northwestern Ry. Co. v. Ohle*, 117 U.S. 123, 129. We shall not need to consider the sufficiency, under the rule just stated, of the evidence introduced as to all of the counts of the indictment, for, since the sentence imposed did not exceed that which might lawfully have been imposed under any single count, the judgment upon the verdict of the jury must be affirmed if the evidence is sufficient to sustain any one of the counts. *Evans v. United States*, 153 U.S. 608; *Claassen v. United States*, 142 U.S. 140; *Debs v. United States*, 249 U.S. 211, 216.

The first of the two articles attached to the indictment is conspicuously headed, "The Hypocrisy of the United States and her Allies." After denouncing President Wilson as a hypocrite and a coward because troops were sent into Russia, it proceeds to assail our Government in general, saying: "His [the President's] shameful, cowardly silence about the intervention in Russia reveals the hypocrisy of the plutocratic gang in Washington and vicinity."

It continues: "He [the President] is too much of a coward to come out openly and say: 'We capitalistic nations cannot afford to have a proletarian republic in Russia.' " Among the capitalistic nations Abrams testified the United States was included.

Growing more inflammatory as it proceeds, the circular culminates in:

> The Russian Revolution cries: Workers of the World! Awake! Rise! Put down your enemy and mine!
>
> Yes! friends, there is only one enemy of the workers of the world and that is CAPITALISM.

This is clearly an appeal to the "workers" of this country to arise and put down by force the Government of the United States which they characterize as their "hypocritical," "cowardly" and "capitalistic" enemy. It concludes: "Awake! Awake, you Workers of the World! Revolutionists."

The second of the articles was printed in the Yiddish language and in the translation is headed, "Workers — Wake up." After referring to "his Majesty, Mr. Wilson, and the rest of the gang; dogs of all colors!", it continues: "Workers, Russian emigrants, you who had the least belief in the honesty of *our* Government," which defendants admitted referred to the United States Government, "must now throw away all confidence, must spit in the face the false, hypocritic, military propaganda which has fooled you so relentlessly, calling forth your sympathy, your help, to the prosecution of the war."

The purpose of this obviously was to persuade the persons to whom it was addressed to turn a deaf ear to patriotic appeals in behalf of the Government of the United States, and to cease to render it assistance in the prosecution of the war.

It goes on:

> With the money which you have loaned, or are going to loan them, they will make bullets not only for the Germans, but also for the Workers Soviets of Russia. *Workers in the ammunition factories, you are producing bullets, bayonets, cannon, to murder not only the Germans, but also your dearest, best, who are in Russia and are fighting for freedom.*

It will not do to say, as is now argued, that the only intent of these defendants was to prevent injury to the Russian cause. Men must be held to have intended, and to be accountable for, the effects which their acts were likely to produce. Even if their primary purpose and intent was to aid the cause of the Russian Revolution, the plan of action which they adopted necessarily involved, before it could be realized, defeat of the war program of the United States, for the obvious effect of this appeal, if it should become effective, as they hoped it might, would be to persuade persons of character such as those whom they regarded themselves as addressing, not to aid government loans and not to work in ammunition factories, where their work would produce "bullets, bayonets, cannon" and other munitions of war, the use of which would cause the "murder" of Germans and Russians.

Again, the spirit becomes more bitter as it proceeds to declare that —

> America and her Allies have betrayed (the Workers). Their robberish aims are clear to all men. The destruction of the Russian Revolution, that is the politics of the march to Russia.

Workers, our reply to the barbaric intervention has to be a general strike! An open challenge only will let the Government know that not only the Russian Worker fights for freedom, but also *here in America lives the spirit of Revolution.*

This is not an attempt to bring about a change of administration by candid discussion, for no matter what may have incited the outbreak on the part of the defendant anarchists, the manifest purpose of such a publication was to create an attempt to defeat the war plans of the Government of the United States, by bringing upon the country the paralysis of a general strike, thereby arresting the production of all munitions and other things essential to the conduct of the war.

This purpose is emphasized in the next paragraph, which reads:

Do not let the Government scare you with their wild punishment in prisons, hanging and shooting. We must not and will not betray the splendid fighters of Russia. *Workers, up to fight.*

After more of the same kind, the circular concludes: "Woe unto those who will be in the way of progress. Let solidarity live!" It is signed, "The Rebels."

That the interpretation we have put upon these articles, circulated in the greatest port of our land, from which great numbers of soldiers were at the time taking ship daily, and in which great quantities of war supplies of every kind were at the time being manufactured for transportation overseas, is not only the fair interpretation of them, but that it is the meaning which their authors consciously intended should be conveyed by them to others is further shown by the additional writings found in the meeting place of the defendant group and on the person of one of them. One of these circulars is headed: "Revolutionists! Unite for Action!"

After denouncing the President as "Our Kaiser" and the hypocrisy of the United States and her Allies, this article concludes:

Socialists, Anarchists, Industrial Workers of the World, Socialists, Labor party men and other revolutionary organizations *Unite for action* and let us save the Workers' Republic of Russia!
Know you lovers of freedom that in order to save the Russian revolution, we must keep the armies of the allied countries busy at home.

Thus was again avowed the purpose to throw the country into a state of revolution if possible and to thereby frustrate the military program of the Government.

The remaining article, after denouncing the President for what is characterized as hostility to the Russian revolution, continues:

> We, the toilers of America, who believe in real liberty, shall *pledge ourselves*, in case the United States will participate in that bloody conspiracy against Russia, *to create so great a disturbance that the autocrats of America shall be compelled to keep their armies at home, and not be able to spare any for Russia.*

It concludes with this definite threat of armed rebellion:

> If they will use arms against the Russian people to enforce their standard of order, *so will we use arms,* and they shall never see the ruin of the Russian Revolution.

These excerpts sufficiently show, that while the immediate occasion for this particular outbreak of lawlessness, on the part of the defendant alien anarchists, may have been resentment caused by our Government sending troops into Russia as a strategic operation against the Germans on the eastern battle front, yet the plain purpose of their propaganda was to excite, as the supreme crisis of the war, disaffection, sedition, riots, and, as they hoped, revolution, in this country for the purpose of embarrassing and if possible defeating the military plans of the Government in Europe. A technical distinction may perhaps be taken between disloyal and abusive language applied to the *form* of our Government or language intended to bring the *form* of our Government into contempt and disrepute, and language of like character and intended to produce like results directed against the President and Congress, the agencies through which that form of government must function in time of war. But it is not necessary to a decision of this case to consider whether such distinction is vital or merely formal, for the language of these circulars was obviously intended to provoke and to encourage resistance to the United States in the war, as the third count runs, and, the defendants, in terms, plainly urged and advocated a resort to a general strike of workers in ammunition factories for the purpose of curtailing the production of ordnance and munitions necessary and essential to the prosecution of the war as is charged in the fourth count. Thus it is clear not only that some evidence but that much persuasive evidence was before the jury tending to prove that the defendants were guilty as charged in both the third and fourth counts of the indictment and under the long established rule of law hereinbefore stated the judgment of the District Court must be

Affirmed.

MR. JUSTICE HOLMES dissenting.

This indictment is founded wholly upon the publication of two leaflets which I shall describe in a moment. The first count charges a conspiracy pending the war with Germany to publish abusive language about the form of government of the United States, laying the preparation and publishing of the first leaflet as overt acts. The second count charges a conspiracy pending the war to publish language intended to bring the form of government into contempt, laying the preparation and publishing of the two leaflets as overt acts. The third count alleges a conspiracy to encourage resistance to the United States in the same war and to attempt to effectuate the purpose by publishing the same leaflets. The fourth count lays a conspiracy to incite curtailment of production of things necessary to the prosecution of the war and to attempt to accomplish it by publishing the second leaflet to which I have referred.

The first of these leaflets says that the President's cowardly silence about the intervention in Russia reveals the hypocrisy of the plutocratic gang in Washington. It intimates that "German militarism combined with allied capitalism to crush the Russian revolution" — goes on that the tyrants of the world fight each other until they see a common enemy — working class enlightenment, when they combine to crush it; and that now militarism and capitalism combined, though not openly, to crush the Russian revolution. It says that there is only one enemy of the workers of the world and that is capitalism; that it is a crime for workers of America, &c., to fight the workers' republic of Russia, and ends "Awake! Awake, you Workers of the World! Revolutionists." A note adds "It is absurd to call us pro-German. We hate and despise German militarism more than do you hypocritical tyrants. We have more reasons for denouncing German militarism than has the coward of the White House."

The other leaflet, headed "Workers — Wake Up," with abusive language says that America together with the Allies will march for Russia to help the Czecho-Slovaks in their struggle against the Bolsheviki, and that this time the hypocrites shall not fool the Russian emigrants, and friends of Russia in America. It tells the Russian emigrants that they now must spit in the face of the false military propaganda by which their sympathy and help to the prosecution of the war have been called forth and says that with the money they have lent or are going to lend "they will make bullets not only for the Germans but also for the Workers Soviets of Russia," and further, "Workers in the ammunition factories, you are producing bullets, bayonets, cannon, to murder not only the Germans, but also your dearest, best, who are in Russia and are fighting for freedom." It then appeals to the same Russian emigrants at some length not to consent to the "inquisitionary expedition to Russia," and says that the destruction of the Russian revolution is "the politics of the march to Russia." The leaflet winds up by saying "Workers, our reply to this barbaric intervention has to be a general strike!," and after a few words on the spirit of revolution, exhortations not to be afraid, and some usual tall talk ends "Woe unto those who will be in the way of progress. Let solidarity live! The Rebels."

No argument seems to me necessary to show that these pronunciamentos in no way attack the form of government of the United States, or that they do not support either of the first two counts. What little I have to say about the third count may be postponed until I have considered the fourth. With regard to that it seems too plain to be denied that the suggestion to workers in the ammunition factories that they are producing bullets to murder their dearest, and the further advocacy of a general strike, both in the second leaflet, do urge curtailment of production of things necessary to the prosecution of the war within the meaning of the Act of May 16, 1918, c. 75, 40 Stat. 553, amending § 3 of the earlier Act of 1917. But to make the conduct criminal that statute requires that it should be "with intent by such curtailment to cripple or hinder the United States in the prosecution of the war." It seems to me that no such intent is proved.

I am aware, of course, that the word *intent* as vaguely used in ordinary legal discussion means no more than knowledge at the time of the act that the consequences said to be intended will ensue. Even less than that will satisfy the general principle of civil and criminal liability. A man may have to pay damages, may be sent to prison, at common law might be hanged, if at the time of his act he knew facts from which common experience showed that the consequences would follow, whether he individually could foresee them or not. But, when words are used exactly, a deed is not done with intent to produce a consequence unless that consequence is the aim of the deed. It may be obvious, and obvious to the actor, that the consequence will follow, and he may be liable for it even if he regrets it, but he does not do the act with intent to produce it unless the aim to produce it is the proximate motive of the specific act, although there may be some deeper motive behind.

It seems to me that this statute must be taken to use its words in a strict and accurate sense. They would be absurd in any other. A patriot might think that we were wasting money on aeroplanes, or making more cannon of a certain kind than we needed, and might advocate curtailment with success, yet even if it turned out that the curtailment hindered and was thought by other minds to have been obviously likely to hinder the United States in the prosecution of the war, no one would hold such conduct a crime. I admit that my illustration does not answer all that might be said but it is enough to show what I think and to let me pass to a more important aspect of the case. I refer to the First Amendment to the Constitution that Congress shall make no law abridging the freedom of speech.

I never have seen any reason to doubt that the questions of law that alone were before this Court in the cases of *Schenck, Frohwerk* and *Debs*, 249 U.S. 47, 204, 211, were rightly decided. I do not doubt for a moment that by the same reasoning that would justify punishing persuasion to murder, the United States constitutionally may punish speech that produces or is intended to produce a clear and imminent danger that it will bring about forthwith certain substantive evils that the United States constitutionally may seek to prevent. The power undoubtedly is greater in time of war than in time of peace because war opens dangers that do not exist at other times.

But as against dangers peculiar to war, as against others, the principle of the right to free speech is always the same. It is only the present danger of immediate evil or an intent to bring it about that warrants Congress in setting a limit to the expression of opinion where private rights are not concerned. Congress certainly cannot forbid all effort to change the mind of the country. Now nobody can suppose that the surreptitious publishing of a silly leaflet by an unknown man, without more, would present any immediate danger that its opinions would hinder the success of the government arms or have any appreciable tendency to do so. Publishing those opinions for the very purpose of obstructing however, might indicate a greater danger and at any rate would have the quality of an attempt. So I assume that the second leaflet if published for the purposes alleged in the fourth count might be punishable. But it seems pretty clear to me that nothing less than that would bring these papers within the scope of this law. An actual intent in the sense that I have explained is necessary to constitute an attempt, where a further act of the same individual is required to complete the substantive crime, for reasons given in *Swift & Co. v. United States*, 196 U.S. 375, 396. It is necessary where the success of the attempt depends upon others because if that intent is not present the actor's aim may be accomplished without bringing about the evils sought to be checked. An intent to prevent interference with the revolution in Russia might have been satisfied without any hindrance to carrying on the war in which we were engaged.

I do not see how anyone can find the intent required by the statute in any of the defendants' words. The second leaflet is the only one that affords even a foundation for the charge, and there, without invoking the hatred of German militarism expressed in the former one, it is evident from the beginning to the end that the only object of the paper is to help Russia and stop American intervention there against the popular government — not to impede the United States in the war that it was carrying on. To say that two phrases taken literally might import a suggestion of conduct that would have interference with the war as an indirect and probably undesired effect seems to me by no means enough to show an attempt to produce that effect.

I return for a moment to the third count. That charges an intent to provoke resistance to the United States in its war with Germany. Taking the clause in the statute that deals with that in connection with the other elaborate provisions of the act, I think that resistance to the United States means some forcible act of opposition to some proceeding of the United States in pursuance of the war. I think the intent must be the specific intent that I have described and for the reasons that I have given I think that no such intent was proved or existed in fact. I also think that there is no hint at resistance to the United States as I construe the phrase.

In this case sentences of twenty years imprisonment have been imposed for the publishing of two leaflets that I believe the defendants had as much right to publish as the Government has to publish the Constitution of the United States now vainly invoked by them. Even if I am technically wrong and enough can be squeezed from these poor and puny anonymities to turn the color of legal litmus paper; I will add, even if what I think the necessary intent were shown; the most nominal punishment seems to me all that possibly could be inflicted, unless the defendants are to be made to suffer not for what the indictment alleges but for the creed that they avow — a creed that I believe to be the creed of ignorance and immaturity when honestly held, as I see no reason to doubt that it was held here, but which, although made the subject of examination at the trial, no one has a right even to consider in dealing with the charges before the Court.

Persecution for the expression of opinions seems to me perfectly logical. If you have no doubt of your premises or your power and want a certain result with all your heart you naturally express your wishes in law and sweep away all opposition. To allow opposition by speech seems to indicate that you think the speech impotent, as when a man says that he has squared the circle, or that you do not care whole-heartedly for the result, or that you doubt either your power or your premises. But when men have realized that time has upset many fighting faiths, they may come to believe even more than they believe the very foundations of their own conduct that the ultimate good desired is better reached by free trade in ideas — that the best test of truth is the power of the thought to get itself accepted in the competition of the market, and that truth is the only ground upon which their wishes safely can be carried out. That at any rate is the theory of our Constitution. It is an experiment, as all life is an experiment. Every year if not every day we have to wager our salvation upon some prophecy based upon imperfect knowledge. While that experiment is part of our system I think that we should be eternally vigilant against attempts to check the expression of opinions that we loathe and believe to be fraught with death, unless they so imminently threaten immediate interference with the lawful and pressing purposes of the law that an immediate check is required to save the country. I wholly disagree with the argument of the Government that the First Amendment left the common law as to seditious libel in force. History seems to me against the notion. I had conceived that the United States through many years had shown its repentance for the Sedition Act of 1798, by repaying fines that it imposed. Only the emergency that makes it immediately dangerous to leave the correction of evil counsels to time warrants making any exception to the sweeping command, "Congress shall make no law . . . abridging the freedom of speech." Of course I am speaking only of expressions of opinion and exhortations, which were all that were uttered here, but I regret that I cannot put into more impressive words my belief that in their conviction upon this indictment the defendants were deprived of their rights under the Constitution of the United States.

Mr. Justice Brandeis concurs with the foregoing opinion.

State Antisedition Laws in the 1920's

In the *Schenck* and *Abrams* cases the United States Supreme Court dealt with federal statutes; in the following two decisions, *Gitlow v. New York* and *Whitney v. California*, it dealt with state criminal anarchy and criminal syndicalism acts. In the *Gitlow* case, decided in 1925, the Court found against Gitlow, with Holmes and Brandeis dissenting. Holmes, writing the dissenting opinion, stood by his "clear and present danger" test. Justice Sanford, writing for the majority, based the majority decision almost entirely on the "bad tendency" test. As Zechariah Chafee, Jr., has observed, "the words 'tend' and 'tending' are as frequent in his opinion as in an English charge during the prosecution of a reformer in the French Revolutionary Wars."[1]

Although Gitlow's conviction was upheld, the majority's decision implies an acceptance of the principle that "freedom of speech and of the press — which are protected by the First Amendment from abridgment by Congress — are among the fundamental personal rights and 'liberties' protected by the due process clause of the Fourteenth Amendment from impairment by the States." The *Gitlow* decision established the doctrine that the First Amendment was in effect incorporated into the Fourteenth Amendment and hence applicable to the various states of the nation; freedom of speech, declared the Court, may be protected against state laws by the Fourteenth Amendment. The brief Holmes-Brandeis dissent was based on the "clear and present danger" test, but as in previous cases, that test did not help much in protecting free expression.

---

[1] Zechariah Chafee, Jr., *Free Speech in the United States* (Cambridge, Mass.: Harvard University Press, 1941), p. 323.

In 1927, the Court upheld the conviction of Miss Anita Whitney for her violation of California's Criminal Syndicalism Act. Brandeis filed a concurring opinion, in which Holmes joined. In the next to last paragraph, Brandeis explains why he had to concur to uphold the conviction. But this concurring opinion is one of the classic statements attacking suppression, defending free speech, and explaining the function of free expression in the American society. Governor C. C. Young of California, who pardoned Miss Whitney soon after the Court's decision, relied heavily on the Brandeis opinion in explaining his reasons for the pardon.

The *Gitlow* decision appears here in its entirety. The entire *Whitney* decision is not included here since it is only in the concurring opinion of Brandeis and Holmes that an extended discussion of freedom of speech appears.

GITLOW v. NEW YORK*

268 U.S. 652 (1925)

MR. JUSTICE SANFORD delivered the opinion of the Court.

Benjamin Gitlow was indicted in the Supreme Court of New York, with three others, for the statutory crime of criminal anarchy. New York Penal Laws, §§ 160, 161. He was separately tried, convicted, and sentenced to imprisonment. The judgment was affirmed by the Appellate Division and by the Court of Appeals. 195 App. Div. 773; 234 N.Y. 132 and 539. The case is here on writ of error to the Supreme Court, to which the record was remitted. 260 U.S. 703.

The contention here is that the statute, by its terms and as applied in this case, is repugnant to the due process clause of the Fourteenth Amendment. Its material provisions are:

§ 160. *Criminal anarchy defined.* Criminal anarchy is the doctrine that organized government should be overthrown by force or violence, or by assassination of the executive head or of any of the executive officials of government, or by any unlawful means. The advocacy of such doctrine either by word of mouth or writing is a felony.

§ 161. *Advocacy of criminal anarchy.* Any person who:

1. By word of mouth or writing advocates, advises or teaches the duty, necessity or propriety of overthrowing or overturning organized government by force or violence, or by assassination of the executive head or of any of the executive officials of government, or by any unlawful means; or,

2. Prints, publishes, edits, issues or knowingly circulates, sells, distributes or publicly displays any book, paper, document, or written or printed matter in any form, containing or advocating, advising or teaching the doctrine that organized government should be overthrown by force, violence or any unlawful means . . . , is guilty of a felony and punishable

by imprisonment or fine, or both.

---

* Footnotes and case citations have been deleted.

The indictment was in two counts. The first charged that the defendant had advocated, advised and taught the duty, necessity and propriety of overthrowing and overturning organized government by force, violence and unlawful means, by certain writings therein set forth entitled "The Left Wing Manifesto"; the second that he had printed, published and knowingly circulated and distributed a certain paper called "The Revolutionary Age," containing the writings set forth in the first count advocating, advising and teaching the doctrine that organized government should be overthrown by force, violence and unlawful means.

The following facts were established on the trial by undisputed evidence and admissions: The defendant is a member of the Left Wing Section of the Socialist Party, a dissenting branch or faction of that party formed in opposition to its dominant policy of "moderate Socialism." Membership in both is open to aliens as well as citizens. The Left Wing Section was organized nationally at a conference in New York City in June, 1919, attended by ninety delegates from twenty different States. The conference elected a National Council, of which the defendant was a member, and left to it the adoption of a "Manifesto." This was published in The Revolutionary Age, the official organ of the Left Wing. The defendant was on the board of managers of the paper and was its business manager. He arranged for the printing of the paper and took to the printer the manuscript of the first issue which contained the Left Wing Manifesto, and also a Communist Program and a Program of the Left Wing that had been adopted by the conference. Sixteen thousand copies were printed, which were delivered at the premises in New York City used as the office of the Revolutionary Age and the headquarters of the Left Wing, and occupied by the defendant and other officials. These copies were paid for by the defendant, as business manager of the paper. Employees at this office wrapped and mailed out copies of the paper under the defendant's direction; and copies were sold from this office. It was admitted that the defendant signed a card subscribing to the Manifesto and Program of the Left Wing, which all applicants were required to sign before being admitted to membership; that he went to different parts of the State to speak to branches of the Socialist Party about the principles of the Left Wing and advocated their adoption; and that he was responsible for the Manifesto as it appeared, that "he knew of the publication, in a general way and he knew of its publication afterwards, and is responsible for its circulation."

There was no evidence of any effect resulting from the publication and circulation of the Manifesto.

No witnesses were offered in behalf of the defendant.

Extracts from the Manifesto are set forth in the margin. Coupled with a review of the rise of Socialism, it condemned the dominant "moderate Socialism" for its recognition of the necessity of the democratic parliamentary state; repudiated its policy of introducing Socialism by legislative measures; and advocated, in plain and unequivocal language, the necessity of accomplishing the "Communist Revolution" by a militant and "revolutionary Socialism," based on "the class struggle" and mobilizing the "power of the proletariat in action," through mass industrial revolts developing into mass political strikes and "revolutionary mass action," for the purpose of conquering and destroying the parliamentary state and establishing in its place, through a "revolutionary dictatorship of the proletariat," the system of Communist Socialism. The then recent strikes in Seattle and Winnipeg were cited as instances of a development already verging on revolutionary action and suggestive of proletarian dictatorship, in which the strike-workers were "trying to usurp the functions of municipal government"; and revolutionary Socialism, it was urged, must use these mass industrial revolts to broaden the strike, make it general and militant, and develop it into mass political strikes and revolutionary mass action for the annihilation of the parliamentary state.

At the outset of the trial the defendant's counsel objected to the introduction of any evidence under the indictment on the grounds that, as a matter of law, the Manifesto "is not in contravention of the statute," and that "the statute is in contravention of" the due process clause of the Fourteenth Amendment. This objection was denied. They also moved, at the close of the evidence, to dismiss the indictment and direct an acquittal "on the grounds stated in the first objection to evidence," and again on the grounds that "the indictment does not charge an offense" and the evidence "does not show an offense." These motions were also denied.

The court, among other things, charged the jury, in substance, that they must determine what was the intent, purpose and fair meaning of the Manifesto; that its words must be taken in their ordinary meaning, as they would be understood by people whom it might reach; that a mere statement or analysis of social and economic facts and historical incidents, in the nature of an essay, accompanied by prophecy as to the future course of events, but with no teaching, advice or advocacy of action, would not constitute the advocacy, advice or teaching of a doctrine for the overthrow of government within the meaning of the statute; that a mere statement that unlawful acts might accomplish such a purpose would be insufficient, unless there was a teaching, advising and advocacy of employing such unlawful acts for the purpose of overthrowing government; and that if the jury had a reasonable doubt that the Manifesto did teach, advocate or advise the duty, necessity or propriety of using unlawful means for the overthrowing of organized government, the defendant was entitled to an acquittal.

The defendant's counsel submitted two requests to charge which embodied in substance the statement that to constitute criminal anarchy within the meaning of the statute it was necessary that the language used or published should advocate, teach or advise the duty, necessity or propriety of doing "some definite or immediate act or acts" of force, violence or unlawfulness directed toward the overthrowing of organized government. These were denied further than had been charged. Two other requests to charge embodied in substance the statement that to constitute guilt the language used or published must be "reasonably and ordinarily calculated to incite certain persons" to acts of force, violence or unlawfulness, with the object of overthrowing organized government. These were also denied.

The Appellate Division, after setting forth extracts from the Manifesto and referring to the Left Wing and Communist Programs published in the same issue of the Revolutionary Age, said:

> It is perfectly plain that the plan and purpose advocated . . . contemplate the overthrow and destruction of the governments of the United States and of all the States, not by the free action of the majority of the people through the ballot box in electing representatives to authorize a change of government by amending or changing the Constitution, . . . but by immediately organizing the industrial proletariat into militant Socialist unions and at the earliest opportunity through mass strike and force and violence, if necessary, compelling the government to cease to function, and then through a proletarian

dictatorship, taking charge of and appropriating all property and administering it and governing through such dictatorship until such time as the proletariat is permitted to administer and govern it. . . . The articles in question are not a discussion of ideas and theories.

They advocate a doctrine deliberately determined upon and planned for militantly disseminating a propaganda advocating that it is the duty and necessity of the proletariat engaged in industrial pursuits to organize to such an extent that, by massed strike, the wheels of government may ultimately be stopped and the government overthrown . . .

The Court of Appeals held that the Manifesto "advocated the overthrow of this government by violence, or by unlawful means." In one of the opinions representing the views of a majority of the court, it was said:

It will be seen . . . that this defendant through the manifesto . . . advocated the destruction of the state and the establishment of the dictatorship of the proletariat. . . . To advocate . . . the commission of this conspiracy or action by mass strike whereby government is crippled, the administration of justice paralyzed, and the health, morals and welfare of a community endangered, and this for the purpose of bringing about a revolution in the state, is to advocate the overthrow of organized government by unlawful means.

In the other it was said:

As we read this manifesto . . . we feel entirely clear that the jury were justified in rejecting the view that it was a mere academic and harmless discussion of the advantages of communism and advanced socialism [and] in regarding it as a justification and advocacy of action by one class which would destroy the rights of all other classes and overthrow the state itself by use of revolutionary mass strikes. It is true that there is no advocacy in specific terms of the use of . . . force or violence. There was no need to be. Some things are so commonly incident to others that they do not need to be mentioned when the underlying purpose is described.

And both the Appellate Division and the Court of Appeals held the statute constitutional.

The specification of the errors relied on relates solely to the specific rulings of the trial court in the matters herein before set out. The correctness of the verdict is not questioned, as the case was submitted to the jury. The sole contention here is, essentially, that as there was no evidence of any concrete result flowing from the publication of the Manifesto or of circumstances showing the likelihood of such result, the statute as construed and applied by the trial court penalizes the mere utterance, as such, of "doctrine" having no quality of incitement, without regard either to the circumstances of its utterance or to the likelihood of unlawful sequences; and that, as the exercise of the right of free expression with relation to government is only punishable "in circumstances involving likelihood of substantive evil," the statute contravenes the due process clause of the Fourteenth Amendment. The argument in support of this contention rests primarily upon the following propositions: 1st, That the "liberty" protected by the Fourteenth Amendment includes the liberty of speech and of the press; and 2nd, That while liberty of expression "is not absolute," it may be restrained "only in circumstances where its exercise bears a causal relation with some substantive evil, consummated, attempted or likely," and as the statute "takes no account of circumstances," it unduly restrains this liberty and is therefore unconstitutional.

The precise question presented, and the only question which we can consider under this writ of error, then is, whether the statute, as construed and applied in this case by the state courts, deprived the defendant of his liberty of expression in violation of the due process clause of the Fourteenth Amendment.

The statute does not penalize the utterance or publication of abstract "doctrine" or academic discussion having no quality of incitement to any concrete action. It is not aimed against mere historical or philosophical essays. It does not restrain the advocacy of changes in the form of government by constitutional and lawful means. What it prohibits is language advocating, advising or teaching the overthrow of organized government by unlawful means. These words imply urging to action. Advocacy is defined in the Century Dictionary as: "1. The act of pleading for, supporting, or recommending; active espousal." It is not the abstract "doctrine" of overthrowing organized government by unlawful means which is denounced by the statute, but the advocacy of action for the accomplishment of that purpose. It was so construed and applied by the trial judge, who specifically charged the jury that:

> A mere grouping of historical events and a prophetic deduction
> from them would neither constitute advocacy, advice or teaching of a

doctrine for the overthrow of government by force, violence or un-lawful means. [And] if it were a mere essay on the subject, as sug-gested by counsel, based upon deductions from alleged historical events, with no teaching, advice or advocacy of action, it would not constitute a violation of the statute. . . .

The Manifesto, plainly, is neither the statement of abstract doctrine nor, as suggested by counsel, mere prediction that industrial disturb-ances and revolutionary mass strikes will result spontaneously in an inevitable process of evolution in the economic system. It advocates and urges in fervent language mass action which shall progressively foment industrial disturbances and through political mass strikes and revolutionary mass action overthrow and destroy organized parlia-mentary government. It concludes with a call to action in these words: "The proletariat revolution and the Communist reconstruction of society — *the struggle for these* — is now indispensable. . . . The Communist International calls the proletariat of the world to the final struggle!" This is not the expression of philosophical abstraction, the mere prediction of future events; it is the language of direct incite-ment.

The means advocated for bringing about the destruction of or-ganized parliamentary government, namely, mass industrial revolts usurping the functions of municipal government, political mass strikes directed against the parliamentary state, and revolutionary mass action for its final destruction, necessarily imply the use of force and vio-lence, and in their essential nature are inherently unlawful in a con-stitutional government of law and order. That the jury were war-ranted in finding that the Manifesto advocated not merely the abstract doctrine of overthrowing organized government by force, violence and unlawful means, but action to that end, is clear.

For present purposes we may and do assume that freedom of speech and of the press — which are protected by the First Amendment from abridgment by Congress — are among the fundamental personal rights and "liberties" protected by the due process clause of the Four-teenth Amendment from impairment by the States. We do not regard the incidental statement in *Prudential Ins. Co. v. Cheek*, 259 U.S. 530, 543, that the Fourteenth Amendment imposes no restrictions on the States concerning freedom of speech, as determinative of this ques-tion.

It is a fundamental principle, long established, that the freedom of speech and of the press which is secured by the Constitution, does not confer an absolute right to speak or publish, without responsibility, whatever one may choose, or an unrestricted and unbridled license that gives immunity for every possible use of language and prevents the punishment of those who abuse this freedom. 2 Story on the Constitution, 5th ed., § 1580, p. 634; *Robertson v. Baldwin*, 165 U.S. 275, 281; *Patterson v. Colorado*, 205 U.S. 454, 462; *Fox v. Washington*, 236 U.S. 273, 276; *Schenck v. United States*, 249 U.S. 47, 52; *Frohwerk v. United States*, 249 U.S. 204, 206; *Debs v. United States*, 249 U.S. 211, 213; *Schaefer v. United States*, 251 U.S. 466, 474; *Gilbert v. Minnesota*, 254 U.S. 325, 332; *Warren v. United States*, (C.C.A.) 183 Fed. 718, 721. Reasonably limited, it was said by Story in the passage cited, this freedom is an inestimable privilege in a free government; without such limitation, it might become the scourge of the republic.

That a State in the exercise of its police power may punish those who abuse this freedom by utterances inimical to the public welfare, tending to corrupt public morals, incite to crime, or disturb the public peace, is not open to question. *Robertson v. Baldwin, supra*, p. 281; *Patterson v. Colorado, supra*, p. 462; *Fox v. Washington, supra*, p. 277; *Gilbert v. Minnesota, supra*, p. 339; *People v. Most*, 171 N.Y. 423, 431; *State v. Holm*, 139 Minn. 267, 275; *State v. Hennessy*, 114 Wash. 351, 359; *State v. Boyd*, 86 N. J. L. 75, 79; *State v. McKee*, 73 Conn. 18, 27. Thus it was held by this Court in the Fox Case, that a State may punish publications advocating and encouraging a breach of its criminal laws; and, in the *Gilbert Case*, that a State may punish utterances teaching or advocating that its citizens should not assist the United States in prosecuting or carrying on war with its public enemies.

And, for yet more imperative reasons, a State may punish utterances endangering the foundations of organized government and threatening its overthrow by unlawful means. These imperil its own existence as a constitutional State. Freedom of speech and press, said Story, *supra*, does not protect disturbances to the public peace or the attempt to subvert the government. It does not protect publications or teachings which tend to subvert or imperil the government or to impede or hinder it in the performance of its governmental duties. *State v. Holm, supra*, p. 275. It does not protect publications prompting the overthrow of government by force; the punishment of those who publish articles which tend to destroy organized society being essential to the security of freedom and the stability of the State. *People v. Most, supra,* pp. 431, 432. And a State may penalize utterances which openly advocate the overthrow of the representative and constitutional form of government of the United States and the several States, by violence or other unlawful means. *People v. Lloyd,* 304 Ill. 23, 34. See also, *State v. Tachin,* 92 N. J. L. 269, 274; and *People v. Steelik,* 187 Cal. 361, 375. In short this freedom does not deprive a State of the primary and essential right of self-preservation; which, so long as human governments endure, they cannot be denied. *Turner v. Williams,* 194 U.S. 279, 294. In *Toledo Newspaper Co. v. United States,* 247 U.S. 402, 419, it was said:

> The safeguarding and fructification of free and constitutional institutions is the very basis and mainstay upon which the freedom of the press rests, and that freedom, therefore, does not and cannot be held to include the right virtually to destroy such institutions.

By enacting the present statute the State has determined, through its legislative body, that utterances advocating the overthrow of organized government by force, violence and unlawful means, are so inimical to the general welfare and involve such danger of substantive evil that they may be penalized in the exercise of its police power. That determination must be given great weight. Every presumption is to be indulged in favor of the validity of the statute. *Mugler v. Kansas,* 123 U.S. 623, 661. And the case is to be considered "in the light of the principle that the State is primarily the judge of regulations required in the interest of public safety and welfare"; and that its police "statutes may only be declared unconstitutional where they are arbitrary or unreasonable attempts to exercise authority vested in the State in the public interest." *Great Northern Ry. v. Clara City,* 246 U.S. 434, 439. That utterances inciting to the overthrow of organized government by unlawful means, present a sufficient danger of substantive evil to bring their punishment within the range of legislative discretion, is clear. Such utterances, by their very nature, involve danger to the public peace and to the security of the State. They threaten breaches of the peace and ultimate revolution. And the immediate danger is none the less real and substantial, because the effect of a given utterance cannot be accurately foreseen. The State cannot reasonably be required to measure the danger from every such utterance in the nice balance of a jeweler's scale. A single revolutionary spark may kindle a fire that, smouldering for a time, may burst into a sweeping and destructive conflagration. It cannot be said that the State is acting arbitrarily or unreasonably when in the exercise of its judgment as to the measures necessary to protect the public peace and safety, it seeks to extinguish the spark without waiting until it has enkindled the flame or blazed into the conflagration. It cannot reasonably be required to defer the adoption of measures for its own peace and safety until the revolutionary utterances lead to actual disturbances of the public peace or imminent and immediate danger of its own destruction; but it may, in the exercise of its judgment, suppress the threatened danger in its incipiency. In *People* v. *Lloyd,* *supra,* p. 35, it was aptly said:

> Manifestly, the legislature has authority to forbid the advocacy of a doctrine designed and intended to overthrow the government without waiting until there is a present and imminent danger of the success of the plan advocated. If the State were compelled to wait until the apprehended danger became certain, then its right to protect itself would come into being simultaneously with the overthrow of the government, when there would be neither prosecuting officers nor courts for the enforcement of the law.

We cannot hold that the present statute is an arbitrary or unreasonable exercise of the police power of the State unwarrantably infringing the freedom of speech or press; and we must and do sustain its constitutionality.

This being so it may be applied to every utterance — not too trivial to be beneath the notice of the law — which is of such a character and used with such intent and purpose as to bring it within the prohibition of the statute. This principle is illustrated in *Fox* v. *Washington,* *supra,* p. 277; *Abrams* v. *United States,* 250 U.S. 616, 624; *Schaefer* v. *United States, supra,* pp. 479, 480; *Pierce* v. *United States,* 252 U.S. 239, 250, 251; and *Gilbert* v. *Minnesota, supra,* p. 333. In other words, when the legislative body has determined generally, in the constitutional exercise of its discretion, that utterances of a certain kind involve such danger of substantive evil that they may be punished, the question whether any specific utterance coming within the prohibited class is likely, in and of itself, to bring about the substantive evil, is not open to consideration. It is sufficient that the statute itself be constitutional and that the use of the language comes within its prohibition.

It is clear that the question in such cases is entirely different from that involved in those cases where the statute merely prohibits certain acts involving the danger of substantive evil, without any reference to language itself, and it is sought to apply its provisions to language used by the defendant for the purpose of bringing about the prohibited results. There, if it be contended that the statute cannot be applied to the language used by the defendant because of its protection by the freedom of speech or press, it must necessarily be found, as an original question, without any previous determination by the legislative body, whether the specific language used involved such likelihood of bringing about the substantive evil as to deprive it of the constitutional protection. In such cases it has been held that the general provisions of the statute may be constitutionally applied to the specific utterance of the defendant if its natural tendency and probable effect was to bring about the substantive evil which the legislative body might prevent. *Schenck* v. *United States, supra,* p. 51; *Debs* v. *United States, supra,* pp. 215, 216. And the general statement in the *Schenck Case,* p. 52, that the "question in every case is whether the words are used in such circumstances and are of such a nature as to create a clear and present danger that they will bring about the substantive evils," — upon which great reliance is placed in the defendant's argument — was manifestly intended, as shown by the context, to apply only in cases of this class, and has no application to those like the present, where the legislative body itself has previously determined the danger of substantive evil arising from utterances of a specified character.

The defendant's brief does not separately discuss any of the rulings of the trial court. It is only necessary to say that, applying the general rules already stated, we find that none of them involved any invasion of the constitutional rights of the defendant. It was not necessary, within the meaning of the statute, that the defendant should have advocated "some definite or immediate act or acts" of force, violence or unlawfulness. It was sufficient if such acts were advocated in general terms; and it was not essential that their immediate execution should have been advocated. Nor was it necessary that the language should have been "reasonably and ordinarily calculated to incite certain persons" to acts of force, violence or unlawfulness. The advocacy need not be addressed to specific persons. Thus, the publication and circulation of a newspaper article may be an encouragement or endeavor to persuade to murder, although not addressed to any person in particular. *Queen v. Most,* L.R., 7 Q.B.D. 244.

We need not enter upon a consideration of the English common law rule of seditious libel or the Federal Sedition Act of 1798, to which reference is made in the defendant's brief. These are so unlike the present statute, that we think the decisions under them cast no helpful light upon the questions here.

And finding, for the reasons stated, that the statute is not in itself unconstitutional, and that it has not been applied in the present case in derogation of any constitutional right, the judgment of the Court of Appeals is

Affirmed.

Mr. Justice Holmes, dissenting.

Mr. Justice Brandeis and I are of opinion that this judgment should be reversed. The general principle of free speech, it seems to me, must be taken to be included in the Fourteenth Amendment, in view of the scope that has been given to the word "liberty" as there used, although perhaps it may be accepted with a somewhat larger latitude of interpretation than is allowed to Congress by the sweeping language that governs or ought to govern the laws of the United States. If I am right, then I think that the criterion sanctioned by the full Court in *Schenck v. United States,* 249 U.S. 47, 52, applies. "The question in every case is whether the words used are used in such circumstances and are of such a nature as to create a clear and present danger that they will bring about the substantive evils that [the State] has a right to prevent." It is true that in my opinion this criterion was departed from in *Abrams v. United States,* 250 U.S. 616, but the convictions that I expressed in that case are too deep for it to be possible for me as yet to believe that it and *Schaefer v. United States,* 251 U.S. 466, have settled the law. If what I think the correct test is applied, it is manifest that there was no present danger of an attempt to overthrow the Government by force on the part of the admittedly small minority who shared the defendant's views. It is said that this manifesto was more than a theory, that it was an incitement. Every idea is an incitement. It offers itself for belief and if believed it is acted on unless some other belief outweighs it or some failure of energy stifles the movement at its birth. The only difference between the expression of an opinion and an incitement in the narrower sense is the speaker's enthusiasm for the result. Eloquence may set fire to reason. But whatever may be thought of the redundant discourse before us it had no chance of starting a present conflagration. If in the long run the beliefs expressed in proletarian dictatorship are destined to be accepted by the dominant forces of the community, the only meaning of free speech is that they should be given their chance and have their way.

If the publication of this document had been laid as an attempt to induce an uprising against government at once and not at some indefinite time in the future it would have presented a different question. The object would have been one with which the law might deal, subject to the doubt whether there was any danger that the publication could produce any result, or in other words, whether it was not futile and too remote from possible consequences. But the indictment alleges the publication and nothing more.

WHITNEY v. CALIFORNIA

274 U.S. 357 (1927)*

. . . . .

MR. JUSTICE BRANDEIS, concurring.

Miss Whitney was convicted of the felony of assisting in organizing, in the year 1919, the Communist Labor Party of California, of being a member of it, and of assembling with it. These acts are held to constitute a crime, because the party was formed to teach criminal syndicalism. The statute which made these acts a crime restricted the right of free speech and of assembly theretofore existing. The claim is that the statute, as applied, denied to Miss Whitney the liberty guaranteed by the Fourteenth Amendment.

The felony which the statute created is a crime very unlike the old felony of conspiracy or the old misdemeanor of unlawful assembly. The mere act of assisting in forming a society for teaching syndicalism, of becoming a member of it, or of assembling with others for that purpose is given the dynamic quality of crime. There is guilt although the society may not contemplate immediate promulgation of the doctrine. Thus the accused is to be punished, not for contempt, incitement or conspiracy, but for a step in preparation, which, if it threatens the public order at all, does so only remotely. The novelty in the prohibition introduced is that the statute aims, not at the practice of criminal syndicalism, nor even directly at the preaching of it, but at association with those who propose to preach it.

Despite arguments to the contrary which had seemed to me persuasive, it is settled that the due process clause of the Fourteenth Amendment applies to matters of substantive law as well as to matters of procedure. Thus all fundamental rights comprised within the term *liberty* are protected by the Federal Constitution from invasion by the States. The right of free speech, the right to teach and the right of assembly are, of course, fundamental rights. See *Meyer v. Nebraska,* 262 U.S. 390; *Pierce v. Society of Sisters,* 268 U.S. 510; *Gitlow v. New York,* 268 U.S. 652, 666; *Farrington v. Tokushige,* 273 U.S. 284.

* Footnotes and case citations have been deleted.

These may not be denied or abridged. But, although the rights of free speech and assembly are fundamental, they are not in their nature absolute. Their exercise is subject to restriction, if the particular restriction proposed is required in order to protect the State from destruction or from serious injury, political, economic or moral. That the necessity which is essential to a valid restriction does not exist unless speech would produce, or is intended to produce, a clear and imminent danger of some substantive evil which the State constitutionally may seek to prevent has been settled. See *Schenck* v. *United States*, 249 U.S. 47, 52.

It is said to be the function of the legislature to determine whether at a particular time and under the particular circumstances the formation of, or assembly with, a society organized to advocate criminal syndicalism constitutes a clear and present danger of substantive evil; and that by enacting the law here in question the legislature of California determined that question in the affirmative. Compare *Gitlow* v. *New York*, 268 U.S. 652, 668–671. The legislature must obviously decide, in the first instance, whether a danger exists which calls for a particular protective measure. But where a statute is valid only in case certain conditions exist, the enactment of the statute cannot alone establish the facts which are essential to its validity. Prohibitory legislation has repeatedly been held invalid, because unnecessary, where the denial of liberty involved was that of engaging in a particular business. The power of the courts to strike down an offending law is no less when the interests involved are not property rights, but the fundamental personal rights of free speech and assembly.

This Court has not yet fixed the standard by which to determine when a danger shall be deemed clear; how remote the danger may be and yet be deemed present; and what degree of evil shall be deemed sufficiently substantial to justify resort to abridgement of free speech and assembly as the means of protection. To reach sound conclusions on these matters, we must bear in mind why a State is, ordinarily, denied the power to prohibit dissemination of social, economic and political doctrine which a vast majority of its citizens believes to be false and fraught with evil consequence.

Those who won our independence believed that the final end of the State was to make men free to develop their faculties; and that in its government the deliberative forces should prevail over the arbitrary. They valued liberty both as an end and as a means. They believed liberty to be the secret of happiness and courage to be the secret of liberty. They believed that freedom to think as you will and to speak as you think are means indispensable to the discovery and spread of political truth; that without free speech and assembly discussion would be futile; that with them, discussion affords ordinarily adequate protection against the dissemination of noxious doctrine; that the greatest menace to freedom is an inert people; that public discussion is a political duty; and that this should be a fundamental principle of the American Government. They recognized the risks to which all human institutions are subject. But they knew that order cannot be secured merely through fear of punishment for its infraction; that it is hazardous to discourage thought, hope and imagination; that fear breeds repression; that repression breeds hate; that hate menaces stable government; that the path of safety lies in the opportunity to discuss freely supposed grievances and proposed remedies; and that the fitting remedy for evil counsels is good ones. Believing in the power of reason as applied through public discussion, they eschewed silence coerced by law — the argument of force in its worst form. Recognizing the occasional tyrannies of governing majorities, they amended the Constitution so that free speech and assembly should be guaranteed.

Fear of serious injury cannot alone justify suppression of free speech and assembly. Men feared witches and burnt women. It is the function of speech to free men from the bondage of irrational fears. To justify suppression of free speech there must be reasonable ground to fear that serious evil will result if free speech is practiced. There must be reasonable ground to believe that the danger apprehended is imminent. There must be reasonable ground to believe that the evil to be prevented is a serious one. Every denunciation of existing law tends in some measure to increase the probability that there will be violation of it. Condonation of a breach enhances the probability. Expressions of approval add to the probability. Propagation of the criminal state of mind by teaching syndicalism increases it. Advocacy of law-breaking heightens it still further. But even advocacy of violation, however reprehensible morally, is not a justification for denying free speech where the advocacy falls short of incitement and there is nothing to indicate that the advocacy would be immediately acted on. The wide difference between advocacy and incitement, between preparation and attempt, between assembling and conspiracy, must be borne in mind. In order to support a finding of clear and present danger it must be shown either that immediate serious violence was to be expected or was advocated, or that the past conduct furnished reason to believe that such advocacy was then contemplated.

Those who won our independence by revolution were not cowards. They did not fear political change. They did not exalt order at the cost of liberty. To courageous, self-reliant men, with confidence in the power of free and fearless reasoning applied through the processes of popular government, no danger flowing from speech can be deemed clear and present, unless the incidence of the evil apprehended is so imminent that it may befall before there is opportunity for full discussion. If there be time to expose through discussion the falsehood and fallacies, to avert the evil by the processes of education, the remedy to be applied is more speech, not enforced silence. Only an emergency can justify repression. Such must be the rule if authority is to be reconciled with freedom. Such, in my opinion, is the command of the Constitution. It is therefore always open to Americans to challenge a law abridging free speech and assembly by showing that there was no emergency justifying it.

Moreover even imminent danger cannot justify resort to prohibition of these functions essential to effective democracy unless the evil apprehended is relatively serious. Prohibition of free speech and assembly is a measure so stringent that it would be inappropriate as the means for averting a relatively trivial harm to society. A police measure may be unconstitutional merely because the remedy, although effective as means of protection, is unduly harsh or oppressive. Thus, a State might, in the exercise of its police power, make any trespass upon the land of another a crime, regardless of the results or of the intent or purpose of the trespasser. It might, also, punish an attempt, a conspiracy, or an incitement to commit the trespass. But it is hardly conceivable that this Court would hold constitutional a statute which punished as a felony the mere voluntary assembly with a society formed to teach that pedestrians had the moral right to cross unenclosed, unposted, waste lands and to advocate their doing so, even if there was imminent danger that advocacy would lead to a trespass. The fact that speech is likely to result in some violence or in destruction of property is not enough to justify its suppression. There must be the probability of serious injury to the State. Among free men, the deterrents ordinarily to be applied to prevent crime are education and punishment for violations of the law, not abridgment of the rights of free speech and assembly.

The California Syndicalism Act recites in § 4:

> Inasmuch as this act concerns and is necessary to the immediate preservation of the public peace and safety, for the reason that at the present time large numbers of persons are going from place to place in this state advocating, teaching and practicing criminal syndicalism, this act shall take effect upon approval by the Governor.

This legislative declaration satisfies the requirement of the constitution of the State concerning emergency legislation. *In re McDermott*, 180 Cal. 783. But it does not preclude enquiry into the question whether, at the time and under the circumstances, the conditions existed which are essential to validity under the Federal Constitution. As a statute, even if not void on its face, may be challenged because invalid as applied, *Dahnke-Walker Milling Co. v. Bondurant*, 257 U.S. 282, the result of such an enquiry may depend upon the specific facts of the particular case. Whenever the fundamental rights of free speech and assembly are alleged to have been invaded, it must remain open to a defendant to present the issue whether there actually did exist at the time a clear danger; whether the danger, if any, was imminent; and whether the evil apprehended was one so substantial as to justify the stringent restriction interposed by the legislature. The legislative declaration, like the fact that the statute was passed and was sustained by the highest court of the State, creates merely a rebuttable presumption that these conditions have been satisfied.

Whether in 1919, when Miss Whitney did the things complained of, there was in California such clear and present danger of serious evil, might have been made the important issue in the case. She might have required that the issue be determined either by the court or the jury. She claimed below that the statute as applied to her violated the Federal Constitution; but she did not claim that it was void because there was no clear and present danger of serious evil, nor did she request that the existence of these conditions of a valid measure thus restricting the rights of free speech and assembly be passed upon by the court or a jury. On the other hand, there was evidence on which the court or jury might have found that such danger existed. I am unable to assent to the suggestion in the opinion of the Court that assembling with a political party, formed to advocate the desirability of a proletarian revolution by mass action at some date necessarily far in the future, is not a right within the protection of the Fourteenth Amendment. In the present case, however, there was other testimony which tended to establish the existence of a conspiracy, on the part of members of the International Workers of the World, to commit present serious crimes; and likewise to show that such a conspiracy would be furthered by the activity of the society of which Miss Whitney was a member. Under these circumstances the judgment of the state court cannot be disturbed.

Our power of review in this case is limited not only to the question whether a right guaranteed by the Federal Constitution was denied, *Murdock* v. *City of Memphis*, 20 Wall. 590; *Haire* v. *Rice*, 204 U.S. 291, 301; but to the particular claims duly made below, and denied. *Seaboard Air Line Ry.* v. *Duvall*, 225 U.S. 477, 485–488. We lack here the power occasionally exercised on review of judgments of lower federal courts to correct in criminal cases vital errors, although the objection was not taken in the trial court. *Wiborg* v. *United States*, 163 U.S. 632, 658–660; *Clyatt* v. *United States*, 197 U.S. 207, 221–222. This is a writ of error to a state court. Because we may not enquire into the errors now alleged, I concur in affirming the judgment of the state court.

Mr. Justice Holmes joins in this opinion.

Freedom of Speech: Inflammatory Utterances and Public Order

The following three cases which reached the Supreme Court of the United States deal with maintaining public order and with various kinds of abusive and inflammatory utterances.

In *Chaplinsky v. New Hampshire* (1942), the Court unanimously affirmed a New Hampshire conviction for disorderly conduct based on utterances calling a policeman "a God damned racketeer" and "a damned fascist." Out of the decision came the "fighting words" doctrine: to warrant conviction for vile language uttered in a public place, the abusive words have to be spoken individually to the addressee in a face-to-face situation. In upholding the state statute, the Court cited a New Hampshire state court decision:

> The statute, as construed, does no more than prohibit the face-to-face words plainly likely to cause a breach of the peace by the addressee, words whose speaking constitutes a breach of the peace by the speaker — including 'classical fighting words,' words in current use less 'classical' but equally likely to cause violence, and other disorderly words, including profanity, obscenity, and threats.

In 1949, the Supreme Court reversed the Chicago conviction of Arthur Terminiello, a Catholic priest then under suspension by his bishop for causing a breach of the peace. Like Chaplinsky, Terminiello uttered abusive and inflammatory language, referring to the antagonistic crowd outside the auditorium in which he was speaking as "scum" and attacking the "Communistic Zionistic Jews," causing his audience to shout their approval with "Yes, send the Jews back to

Russia;" and "Kill the Jews." In a five to four decision, the Court found the trial court's charge to the jury, which had interpreted "breach of the peace" to include speech that "stirs the public to anger, invites dispute, brings about a condition of unrest, or creates a disturbance," to be an unconstitutional restriction on free speech.

The *Chaplinsky* decision appears here in its entirety. The *Terminiello* decision includes the majority opinion and Justice Jackson's dissent.

The case of Irving Feiner, a Syracuse University student, appears here in a different form. Instead of the Supreme Court's decision in *Feiner v. New York* (1951), a chapter from *Freedoms, Courts, Politics: Studies in Civil Liberties,* by Lucius Barker and Twiley Barker, Jr., is reprinted so that the student can follow a freedom of speech case from beginning to end — from the arrest, through the various lower courts, and finally to the United States Supreme Court. The chapter does an excellent job of presenting the events leading up to Feiner's arrest, the arguments presented in the lower courts, and the Supreme Court's majority and minority opinions.

CHAPLINSKY *v.* NEW HAMPSHIRE*

315 U.S. 568 (1942)

MR. JUSTICE MURPHY delivered the opinion of the Court.

Appellant, a member of the sect known as Jehovah's Witnesses, was convicted in the municipal court of Rochester, New Hampshire, for violation of Chapter 378, § 2, of the Public Laws of New Hampshire:

> No person shall address any offensive, derisive or annoying word to any other person who is lawfully in any street or other public place, nor call him by any offensive or derisive name, nor make any noise or exclamation in his presence and hearing with intent to deride, offend or annoy him, or to prevent him from pursuing his lawful business or occupation.

The complaint charged that appellant,

> . . . with force and arms, in a certain public place in said city of Rochester, to wit, on the public sidewalk on the easterly side of Wakefield Street, near unto the entrance of the City Hall, did unlawfully repeat, the words following, addressed to the complainant, that is to say, "You are a God damned racketeer" and "a damned Fascist and the whole government of Rochester are Fascists or agents of Fascists," the same being offensive, derisive and annoying words and names.

Upon appeal there was a trial *de novo* of appellant before a jury in the Superior Court. He was found guilty and the judgment of conviction was affirmed by the Supreme Court of the State. 91 N.H. 310, 18 A. 2d 754.

By motions and exceptions, appellant raised the questions that the statute was invalid under the Fourteenth Amendment of the Constitution of the United States, in that it placed an unreasonable restraint on freedom of speech, freedom of the press, and freedom of worship, and because it was vague and indefinite. These contentions were overruled and the case comes here on appeal.

There is no substantial dispute over the facts. Chaplinsky was dis-

---

* Footnotes and case citations have been deleted.

tributing the literature of his sect on the streets of Rochester on a busy Saturday afternoon. Members of the local citizenry complained to the City Marshal, Bowering, that Chaplinsky was denouncing all religion as a "racket." Bowering told them that Chaplinsky was lawfully engaged, and then warned Chaplinsky that the crowd was getting restless. Some time later, a disturbance occurred and the traffic officer on duty at the busy intersection started with Chaplinsky for the police station, but did not inform him that he was under arrest or that he was going to be arrested. On the way, they encountered Marshal Bowering, who had been advised that a riot was under way and was therefore hurrying to the scene. Bowering repeated his earlier warning to Chaplinsky, who then addressed to Bowering the words set forth in the complaint.

Chaplinsky's version of the affair was slightly different. He testified that, when he met Bowering, he asked him to arrest the ones responsible for the disturbance. In reply, Bowering cursed him and told him to come along. Appellant admitted that he said the words charged in the complaint, with the exception of the name of the Deity.

Over the appellant's objection the trial court excluded, as immaterial, testimony relating to appellant's mission "to preach the true facts of the Bible," his treatment at the hands of the crowd, and the alleged neglect of duty on the part of the police. This action was approved by the court below, which held that neither provocation nor the truth of the utterance would constitute a defense to the charge.

It is now clear that

> Freedom of speech and freedom of the press, which are protected by the First Amendment from infringement by Congress, are among the fundamental personal rights and liberties which are protected by the Fourteenth Amendment from invasion by state action. *Lovell v. Griffin*, 303 U.S. 444, 450.

Freedom of worship is similarly sheltered. *Cantwell v. Connecticut*, 310 U.S. 296, 303.

Appellant assails the statute as a violation of all three freedoms, speech, press and worship, but only an attack on the basis of free speech is warranted. The spoken, not the written, word is involved. And we cannot conceive that cursing a public officer is the exercise of religion in any sense of the term. But even if the activities of the appellant which preceded the incident could be viewed as religious in character, and therefore entitled to the protection of the Fourteenth

Amendment, they would not cloak him with immunity from the legal consequences for concomitant acts committed in violation of a valid criminal statute. We turn, therefore, to an examination of the statute itself.

Allowing the broadest scope to the language and purpose of the Fourteenth Amendment, it is well understood that the right of free speech is not absolute at all times and under all circumstances. There are certain well-defined and narrowly limited classes of speech, the prevention and punishment of which have never been thought to raise any Constitutional problem. These include the lewd and obscene, the profane, the libelous, and the insulting or "fighting" words — those which by their very utterance inflict injury or tend to incite an immediate breach of the peace. It has been well observed that such utterances are no essential part of any exposition of ideas, and are of such slight social value as a step to truth that any benefit that may be derived from them is clearly outweighed by the social interest in order and morality.

> Resort to epithets or personal abuse is not in any proper sense communication of information or opinion safe-guarded by the Constitution, and its punishment as a criminal act would raise no question under that instrument. *Cantwell* v. *Connecticut*, 310 U.S. 296, 309–310.

The state statute here challenged comes to us authoritatively construed by the highest court of New Hampshire. It has two provisions — the first relates to words or names addressed to another in a public place; the second refers to noises and exclamations. The court said: "The two provisions are distinct. One may stand separately from the other. Assuming, without holding, that the second were unconstitutional, the first could stand if constitutional." We accept that construction of severability and limit our consideration to the first provision of the statute.

On the authority of its earlier decisions, the state court declared that the statute's purpose was to preserve the public peace, no words being "forbidden except such as have a direct tendency to cause acts of violence by the persons to whom, individually, the remark is addressed." It was further said:

> The word "offensive" is not to be defined in terms of what a particular addressee thinks. . . . The test is what men of common intelligence would understand would be words likely to cause an average addressee

to fight. . . . The English language has a number of words and expressions which by general consent are "fighting words" when said without a disarming smile. . . . Such words, as ordinary men know, are likely to cause a fight. So are threatening, profane or obscene revilings. Derisive and annoying words can be taken as coming within the purview of the statute as heretofore interpreted only when they have this characteristic of plainly tending to excite the addressee to a breach of the peace. The statute, as construed, does no more than prohibit the face-to-face words plainly likely to cause a breach of the peace by the addressee, words whose speaking constitutes a breach of the peace by the speaker — including "classical fighting words," words in current use less "classical" but equally likely to cause violence, and other disorderly words, including profanity, obscenity and threats.

We are unable to say that the limited scope of the statute as thus construed contravenes the Constitutional right of free expression. It is a statute narrowly drawn and limited to define and punish specific conduct lying within the domain of state power, the use in a public place of words likely to cause a breach of the peace. Cf. *Cantwell* v. *Connecticut*, 310 U.S. 296, 311; *Thornhill* v. *Alabama*, 310 U.S. 88, 105. This conclusion necessarily disposes of appellant's contention that the statute is so vague and indefinite as to render a conviction thereunder a violation of due process. A statute punishing verbal acts, carefully drawn so as not unduly to impair liberty of expression, is not too vague for a criminal law. Cf. *Fox* v. *Washington*, 236 U.S. 273, 277.

Nor can we say that the application of the statute to the facts disclosed by the record substantially or unreasonably impinges upon the privilege of free speech. Argument is unnecessary to demonstrate that the appellations "damned racketeer" and "damned Fascist" are epithets likely to provoke the average person to retaliation, and thereby cause a breach of the peace.

The refusal of the state court to admit evidence of provocation and evidence bearing on the truth of falsity of the utterances, is open to no Constitutional objection. Whether the facts sought to be proved by such evidence constitute a defense to the charge, or may be shown in mitigation, are questions for the state court to determine. Our function is fulfilled by a determination that the challenged statute, on its face and as applied, does not contravene the Fourteenth Amendment.

Affirmed.

TERMINIELLO v. CHICAGO

337 U.S. 1 (1949)

Mr. Justice Douglas delivered the opinion of the Court.

Petitioner after jury trial was found guilty of disorderly conduct in violation of a city ordinance of Chicago[1] and fined. The case grew out of an address he delivered in an auditorium in Chicago under the auspices of the Christian Veterans of America. The meeting commanded considerable public attention. The auditorium was filled to capacity with over eight hundred persons present. Others were turned away. Outside of the auditorium a crowd of about one thousand persons gathered to protest against the meeting. A cordon of policemen was assigned to the meeting to maintain order; but they were not able to prevent several disturbances. The crowd outside was angry and turbulent.

Petitioner in his speech condemned the conduct of the crowd outside and vigorously, if not viciously, criticized various political and racial groups whose activities he denounced as inimical to the nation's welfare.

The trial court charged that "breach of the peace" consists of any "misbehavior which violates the public peace and decorum"; and that the "misbehavior may constitute a breach of the peace if it stirs the public to anger, invites dispute, brings about a condition of unrest, or creates a disturbance, or if it molests the inhabitants in the enjoyment of peace and quiet by arousing alarm." Petitioner did not take exception to that instruction. But he maintained at all times that the ordinance as applied to his conduct violated his right of free speech under the Federal Constitution. The judgment of conviction was affirmed by the Illinois Appellate Court (332 Ill. App. 17, 74 N.E. 2d 45)

---

[1] "All persons who shall make, aid, countenance, or assist in making any improper noise, riot, disturbance, breach of the peace, or diversion tending to a breach of the peace, within the limits of the city . . . shall be deemed guilty of disorderly conduct, and upon conviction thereof, shall be severally fined not less than one dollar nor more than two hundred dollars for each offense." Municipal Code of Chicago, 1939, § 193–1.

and by the Illinois Supreme Court. 396 Ill. 41, 71 N.E. 2d 2; 400 Ill. 23, 79 N.E. 2d 39. The case is here on a petition for certiorari which we granted because of the importance of the question presented.

The argument here has been focused on the issue of whether the content of petitioner's speech was composed of derisive, fighting words, which carried it outside the scope of the constitutional guarantees. See *Chaplinsky* v. *New Hampshire*, 315 U.S. 568; *Cantwell* v. *Connecticut*, 310 U.S. 296, 310. We do not reach that question, for there is a preliminary question that is dispositive of the case.

As we have noted, the statutory words "breach of the peace" were defined in instructions to the jury to include speech which "stirs the public to anger, invites dispute, brings about a condition of unrest, or creates a disturbance. . . ." That construction of the ordinance is a ruling on a question of state law that is as binding on us as though the precise words had been written into the ordinance. See *Hebert* v. *Louisiana*, 272 U.S. 312, 317; *Winters* v. *New York*, 333 U.S. 507, 514.

The vitality of civil and political institutions in our society depends on free discussion. As Chief Justice Hughes wrote in *De Jonge* v. *Oregon*, 299 U.S. 353, 365, it is only through free debate and free exchange of ideas that government remains responsive to the will of the people and peaceful change is effected. The right to speak freely and to promote diversity of ideas and programs is therefore one of the chief distinctions that sets us apart from totalitarian regimes.

Accordingly a function of free speech under our system of government is to invite dispute. It may indeed best serve its high purpose when it induces a condition of unrest, creates dissatisfaction with conditions as they are, or even stirs people to anger. Speech is often provocative and challenging. It may strike at prejudices and preconceptions and have profound unsettling effects as it presses for acceptance of an idea. That is why freedom of speech, though not absolute, *Chaplinsky* v. *New Hampshire, supra,* pp. 571–572, is nevertheless protected against censorship or punishment, unless shown likely to produce a clear and present danger of a serious substantive evil that rises far above public inconvenience, annoyance, or unrest. See *Bridges* v. *California*, 314 U.S. 252, 262; *Craig* v. *Harney*, 331 U.S. 367, 373. There is no room under our Constitution for a more restrictive view. For the alternative would lead to standardization of ideas either by legislatures, courts, or dominant political or community groups.

The ordinance as construed by the trial court seriously invaded this province. It permitted conviction of petitioner if his speech stirred people to anger, invited public dispute, or brought about a condition of unrest. A conviction resting on any of those grounds may not stand. The fact that petitioner took no exception to the instruction is immaterial. No exception to the instructions was taken in *Stromberg* v. *California*, 283 U.S. 359. But a judgment of conviction based on a general verdict under a state statute was set aside in that case, because one part of the statute was unconstitutional. The statute had been challenged as unconstitutional and the instruction was framed in its language. The Court held that the attack on the statute as a whole was equally an attack on each of its individual parts. Since the verdict was a general one and did not specify the ground upon which it rested, it could not be sustained. For one part of the statute was unconstitutional and it could not be determined that the defendant was not convicted under that part.

The principle of that case controls this one. As we have said, the gloss which Illinois placed on the ordinance gives it a meaning and application which are conclusive on us. We need not consider whether as construed it is defective in its entirety. As construed and applied it at least contains parts that are unconstitutional. The verdict was a general one; and we do not know on this record but what it may rest on the invalid clauses.

The statute as construed in the charge to the jury was passed on by the Illinois courts and sustained by them over the objection that as so read it violated the Fourteenth Amendment. The fact that the parties did not dispute its construction makes the adjudication no less ripe for our review, as the *Stromberg* decision indicates. We can only take the statute as the state courts read it. From our point of view it is immaterial whether the state law question as to its meaning was controverted or accepted. The pinch of the statute is in its application. It is that question which the petitioner has brought here. To say therefore that the question on this phase of the case is whether the trial judge gave a wrong charge is wholly to misconceive the issue.

But it is said that throughout the appellate proceedings the Illinois courts assumed that the only conduct punishable and punished under the ordinance was conduct constituting "fighting words." That emphasizes, however, the importance of the rule of the *Stromberg* case.

Petitioner was not convicted under a statute so narrowly construed. For all anyone knows he was convicted under the parts of the ordinance (as construed) which, for example, make it an offense merely to invite dispute or to bring about a condition of unrest. We cannot avoid that issue by saying that all Illinois did was to measure petitioner's conduct, not the ordinance, against the Constitution. Petitioner raised both points — that his speech was protected by the Constitution; that the inclusion of his speech within the ordinance was a violation of the Constitution. We would, therefore, strain at technicalities to conclude that the constitutionality of the ordinance as construed and applied to petitioner was not before the Illinois courts. The record makes clear that petitioner at all times challenged the constitutionality of the ordinance as construed and applied to him.

Reversed.

MR. JUSTICE JACKSON, dissenting.

The Court reverses this conviction by reiterating generalized approbations of freedom of speech with which, in the abstract, no one will disagree. Doubts as to their applicability are lulled by avoidance of more than passing reference to the circumstances of Terminiello's speech and judging it as if he had spoken to persons as dispassionate as empty benches, or like a modern Demosthenes practicing his Philippics on a lonely seashore.

. But the local court that tried Terminiello was not indulging in theory. It was dealing with a riot and with a speech that provoked a hostile mob and incited a friendly one, and threatened violence between the two. When the trial judge instructed the jury that it might find Terminiello guilty of inducing a breach of the peace if his behavior stirred the public to anger, invited dispute, brought about unrest, created a disturbance or molested peace and quiet by arousing alarm, he was not speaking of these as harmless or abstract conditions. He was addressing his words to the concrete behavior and specific consequences disclosed by the evidence. He was saying to the jury, in effect, that if this particular speech added fuel to the situation already so inflamed as to threaten to get beyond police control, it could be punished as inducing a breach of peace. When the light of the evidence not recited by the Court is thrown upon the Court's opinion, it discloses that underneath a little issue of Terminiello and his hundred-dollar fine lurk some of the most far-reaching constitutional questions that can confront a people who value both liberty and order. This Court seems to regard these as enemies of each other and to be of the view that we must forego order to achieve liberty. So it fixes its eyes on a conception of freedom of speech so rigid as to tolerate no concession to society's need for public order.

An old proverb warns us to take heed lest we "walk into a well from looking at the stars." To show why I think the Court is in some danger of doing just that, I must bring these deliberations down to earth by a long recital of facts.

Terminiello, advertised as a Catholic Priest, but revealed at the trial to be under suspension by his Bishop, was brought to Chicago from Birmingham, Alabama, to address a gathering that assembled in response to a call signed by Gerald L. K. Smith, which, among other things, said:

> The same people who hate Father Coughlin hate Father Terminiello. They have persecuted him, hounded him, threatened him, but he has remained unaffected by their anti-Christian campaign against him. You will hear all sorts of reports concerning Father Terminiello. But remember that he is a Priest in good standing and a fearless lover of Christ and America.

The jury may have considered that this call attempted to capitalize the hatreds this man had stirred and foreshadowed, if it did not intend to invite the kind of demonstration that followed.

Terminiello's own testimony shows the conditions under which he spoke. So far as material it follows:

> We got there [the meeting place] approximately fifteen or twenty minutes past eight. The car stopped at the front entrance. There was a crowd of three or four hundred congregated there shouting and cursing and picketing. . . .
>
> When we got there the pickets were not marching; they were body to body and covered the sidewalk completely, some on the steps so that we had to form a flying wedge to get through. Police escorted us to the building, and I noticed four or five others there.
>
> They called us "God damned Fascists, Nazis, ought to hang the so and so's." When I entered the building I heard the howls of the people outside. . . . There were four or five plainclothes officers standing at the entrance to the stage and three or four at the entrance to the back door.

The officers threatened that if they broke the door again they would arrest them and every time they opened the door a little to look out something was thrown at the officers, including ice-picks and rocks.

A number of times the door was broken, was partly broken through. There were doors open this way and they partly opened and the officers looked out two or three times and each time ice-picks, stones and bottles were thrown at the police at the door. I took my place on the stage, before this I was about ten or fifteen minutes in the body of the hall.

I saw a number of windows broken by stones or missiles. I saw the back door being forced open, pushed open.

The front door was broken partly open after the doors were closed. There were about seven people seated on the stage. Smith opened the meeting with prayer, the Pledge of Allegiance to the Flag and singing of "America." There were other speakers who spoke before me and before I spoke I heard things happening in the hall and coming from the outside.

I saw rocks being thrown through windows and that continued throughout at least the first half of the meeting, probably longer, and again attempts were made to force the front door, rather the front door was forced partly. The howling continued on the outside, cursing could be heard audibly in the hall at times. Police were rushing in and out of the front door protecting the front door, and there was a general commotion, all kinds of noises and violence—all from the outside.

Between the time the first speaker spoke and I spoke, stones and bricks were thrown in all the time. I started to speak about 35 or 40 minutes after the meeting started, a little later than nine o'clock. . . .

The court below, in addition to this recital, heard other evidence, that the crowd reached an estimated number of 1,500. Picket lines obstructed and interfered with access to the building. The crowd constituted "a surging, howling mob hurling epithets" at those who would enter and "tried to tear their clothes off." One young woman's coat was torn off and she had to be assisted into the meeting by policemen. Those inside the hall could hear the loud noises and hear those on the outside yell, "Fascists," "Hitlers" and curse words like "damn Fascists." Bricks were thrown through the windowpanes before and during the speaking. About 28 windows were broken. The street was black with people on both sides for at least a block either way; bottles, stink bombs and brickbats were thrown. Police were unable to control the mob, which kept breaking the windows at the meeting hall, drowning out the speaker's voice at times and breaking in through the back door of the auditorium. About 17 of the group outside were arrested by the police.

Knowing of this environment, Terminiello made a long speech, from the stenographic record of which I omit relatively innocuous passages and add emphasis to what seems especially provocative:

> *Father Terminiello:* Now, I am going to whisper my greetings to you, Fellow Christians. I will interpret it. I said, "Fellow *Christians,*" and I suppose there are *some of the scum got in by mistake,* so I want to tell a story about *the scum:*
>
> . . . And nothing I could say tonight could begin to express the contempt I have for the *slimy scum* that got in by mistake.
>
> . . . The subject I want to talk to you tonight about is the attempt *that is going on right outside this hall tonight,* the attempt that is going on to *destroy America by revolution.* . . .
>
> My friends, it is no longer true that it can't happen here. It is hap-pening here, and it only depends upon you, good people, who are here tonight, depends upon all of us together, as Mr. Smith said. The tide is changing, and if you and I turn and run from that tide, we will all be drowned in this tidal wave of Communism which is going over the world. . . . I am not going to talk to you about the menace of Communism, which is already accomplished, in Russia, where from eight to fifteen million people were murdered in cold blood by their own countrymen, and millions more through Eastern Europe at the close of the war are being murdered by these murderous Russians, hurt, being raped and sent into slavery. *That is what they want for you, that howling mob outside.*
>
> I know I was told one time that my winter quarters were ready for me in Siberia. I was told that. Now, I am talking about the fifty-seven varieties that we have in America, and we have fifty-seven varieties of pinks and reds and pastel shades in this country; and all of it can be traced back to the twelve years we spent under the New Deal, be-cause that was the build-up for what is going on in the world today.

> . . . . .

> Now, Russia promised us we would *ga* [sic] back to the official newspaper of Russia. Primarily, it was back about 1929. They quoted the words of George E. Dimitroff, who at that time was the Executive Secretary of the Communist International. I only quote you this one passage. I could quote thousands of paragraphs for you. Let me quote you: "The worldwide nature of our program is not mere talk,

but an all embracing *blood-soaked reality."* *That is what they want for us, a blood-soaked reality but it was promised to us by the crystal gazers in Washington;* and you know what I mean by the "crystal gazers," I presume.

First of all, we had Queen Eleanor. Mr. Smith said, "Queen Eleanor is now one of the world's communists. She is one who said this— imagine, coming from the spouse of the former President of the United States for twelve long years—this is what she said: "The war is but a step in the revolution. The war is but one step in the revolution, and we know who started the war.' "

Then we have Henry Adolph Wallace, the sixty-million job magician. You know we only need fifty-four million jobs in America and everybody would be working. He wants sixty million jobs, because some of the bureaucrats want two jobs apiece. Here he is, what he says about revolution: "We are in for a profound revolution. Those of us who realize the inevitableness of the revolution, and are anxious that it be *gradual and bloodless* instead of *somewhat bloody. Of course, if necessary, we will have it more bloody."*

And then Chief Justice Stone had this to say: "A way has been found for the effective suppression of speeches and press and religion, despite constitutional guarantee," — from the Chief Justice, from the Chief Justice of the United States.

Now, my friends, they are planning another ruse; and if it ever happens to this cou-try [sic], God help America. They are going to try to put into Mr. Edgar Hoover's position a man by the name of *George Swarzwald.* I think even those who were uneducated on so-called sedition charges, that the majority of the individuals in this department, that Christ-like men and women who realize today what is going on in this country, men who are in this audience today, who want *to know the names of those people, before they are outside, they want to know the names if any. Did you hear any tonight that you recognize? Most of them probably are imported. They are imported from Russia, certainly. If you know the names, please send them to me immediately.* . . .

. . . Didn't you ever read the Morgenthau plan for the starvation of little babies and pregnant women in Germany? Whatever could a child that is born have to do with Hitler or anyone else at the beginning of the war? Why should every child in Germany today not live to be more than two or three months of age? Because Morgenthau wants it that way, and so did F.D.R. . . . *You will know who is behind it when I tell you the story* of a doctor in Akron, Ohio. He boasted to a friend of mine within the last few days, while he was in the service of this country as a doctor, he and others of his kind made it a practice — now, this was not only one man — made it a practice to amputate the limbs of every German they came in contact with whenever they could get away with it; so, that they could never carry a gun. Imagine men of that caliber, sworn to serve this beautiful country of ours, *why should we tolerate them?*

My friends, this moment someone reminded me of the plan to sterilize them. The nurses, they tell me are going to inject diseases in them, syphilis and other diseases in *every one that came there all of one race, all non-Christians.* . . .

Now, we are going to get the threats of the people of Argentine, the people of Spain. We have now declared, according to our officials, to have declared Franco to have taken the place of Hitler. *Franco was the savior of what was left of Europe.*

Now, let me say, I am going to talk about — I almost said, about the Jews. Of course, I would not want to say that. However, I am going to talk about some Jews. I hope that — I am a Christian minister. We must take a Christian attitude. I don't want you to go from this hall with hatred in your heart for any person, for no person. . . .

Now, this danger which we face — let us call them Zionist Jews if you will, let's call them atheistic, communistic Jewish or Zionist Jews, then let us not fear to condemn them. You remember the Apostles when they went into the upper room after the death of the Master, they went in there, after locking the doors; they closed the windows. [At this time there was a very loud noise as if something was being thrown into the building.]

Don't be disturbed. That happened, by the way, while Mr. Gerald Smith was saying "Our Father who art in heaven". [Just then a rock went through the window.] *Do you wonder they were persecuted in other countries in the world?* . . .

You know I have always made a study of the psychology, sociology of mob reaction. It is exemplified out there. Remember there has to be a leader to that mob. He is not out there. He is probably across the street, looking out the window. There must be certain things, money, other things, in order to have a successful mob action; there must be rhythm. There must be some to beat a cadence. Those mobs are chanting; that is the caveman's chant. They were trained to do it. They were trained this afternoon. They are being led; *there will be violence.*

That is why I say to you, men, don't you do it. Walk out of here dignified. The police will protect you. Put the women on the inside, where there will be no hurt to them. Just walk; don't stop and argue. . . . They want to picket our meetings. They don't want us to picket their meetings. It is the same kind of tolerance, if we said there was a bedbug in bed, "We don't care for you," or if we looked under the bed and found a snake and said, "I am going to be tolerant and leave the snake there." We will not be tolerant of that mob out there. We are not going to be tolerant any longer.

We are strong enough. We are not going to be tolerant of their smears any longer. We are going to *stand up and dare them to smear us.* . . .

So, my friends, since we spent much time tonight trying to quiet the howling mob, I am going to bring my thoughts to a conclusion, and the conclusion is this. We must all be like the Apostles before the coming of the Holy Ghost. We must not lock ourselves in an upper room for fear of the Jews. I speak of the Communistic Zionistic Jew, and those are not American Jews. We don't want them here; we want them to go back where they came from.

·   ·   ·   ·   ·

Mr. Smith: I would like to ask that Miss Purcell would please go back to the front of the building and contact the police officer in charge of the detail. We are going to adjourn this meeting if and when Miss Purcell comes back and reports to me that the one in charge of the detail believes it is safe for us to go out on the street. I am sure it is. Sit still. We are not going to have anybody move. If there are any chiselers that want to go, we are going to take up an offering for Father Terminiello. [There was further discussion to stimulate this offering which was not reported.]

Such was the speech. Evidence showed that it stirred the audience not only to cheer and applaud but to expressions of immediate anger, unrest and alarm. One called the speaker a "God damned liar" and was taken out by the police. Another said that "Jews, niggers and Catholics would have to be gotten rid of." One response was, "Yes, the Jews are all killers, murderers. If we don't kill them first, they will kill us." The anti-Jewish stories elicited exclamations of "Oh!" and "Isn't that terrible!" and shouts of "Yes, send the Jews back to Russia," "Kill the Jews," "Dirty kikes," and much more of ugly tenor. This is the specific and concrete kind of anger, unrest and alarm, coupled with that of the mob outside, that the trial court charged the jury might find to be a breach of peace induced by Terminiello. It is difficult to believe that this Court is speaking of the same occasion, but it is the only one involved in this litigation.

Terminiello, of course, disclaims being a fascist. Doubtless many of the indoor audience were not consciously such. His speech, however, followed, with fidelity that is more than coincidental, the pattern of European fascist leaders.

The street mob, on the other hand, included some who deny being communists, but Terminiello testified and offered to prove that the demonstration was communist-organized and communist-led. He offered literature of left-wing organizations calling members to meet and "mobilize" for instruction as pickets and exhorting followers: "All out to fight Fascist Smith."

As this case declares a nation-wide rule that disables local and state authorities from punishing conduct which produces conflicts of this kind, it is unrealistic not to take account of the nature, methods and objectives of the forces involved. This was not an isolated, spontaneous and unintended collision of political, racial or ideological adversaries. It was a local manifestation of a world-wide and standing conflict between two organized groups of revolutionary fanatics, each of which has imported to this country the strong-arm technique developed in the struggle by which their kind has devastated Europe. Increasingly, American cities have to cope with it. One faction organizes a mass meeting, the other organizes pickets to harass it; each organizes squads to counteract the other's pickets; parade is met with counterparade. Each of these mass demonstrations has the potentiality, and more than a few the purpose, of disorder and violence. This technique appeals not to reason but to fears and mob spirit; each is a show of force designed to bully adversaries and to overawe the indifferent. We need not resort to speculation as to the purposes for which these tactics are calculated nor as to their consequences. Recent European history demonstrates both.

Hitler summed up the strategy of the mass demonstration as used by both fascism and communism:

> We should not work in secret conventicles, but in mighty mass demonstrations, and it is not by dagger and poison or pistol that the road can be cleared for the movement but *by the conquest of the streets*. We must teach the Marxists that the future *master of the streets* is National Socialism, just as it will some day be the master of

the state. [Emphasis supplied.] 1 *Nazi Conspiracy and Aggression* (GPO, 1946) 204, 2 *id.* 140, Docs. 2760–PS, 404–PS, from *Mein Kampf.*

First laughed at as an extravagant figure of speech, the battle for the streets became a tragic reality when an organized *Sturmabteilung* began to give practical effect to its slogan that "possession of the streets is the key to power in the state." *Ibid.,* also Doc. 2168–PS. The present obstacle to mastery of the streets by either radical or reactionary mob movements is not the opposing minority. It is the authority of local governments which represent the free choice of democratic and law-abiding elements of all shades of opinion, but who, whatever their differences, submit them to free elections which register the results of their free discussion. The fascist and communist groups, on the contrary, resort to these terror tactics to confuse, bully and discredit those freely chosen governments. Violent and noisy shows of strength discourage participation of moderates in discussions so fraught with violence, and real discussion dries up and disappears. And people lose faith in the democratic process when they see public authority flouted and impotent and begin to think the time has come when they must choose sides in a false and terrible dilemma such as was posed as being at hand by the call for the Terminiello meeting: "Christian Nationalism or World Communism — Which?"

This drive by totalitarian groups to undermine the prestige and effectiveness of local democratic governments is advanced whenever either of them can win from this Court a ruling which paralyzes the power of these officials. This is such a case. The group of which Terminiello is a part claims that his behavior, because it involved a speech, is above the reach of local authorities. If the mild action those authorities have taken is forbidden, it is plain that hereafter there is nothing effective left that they can do. If they can do nothing as to him, they are equally powerless as to rival totalitarian groups. Terminiello's victory today certainly fulfills the most extravagant hopes of both right and left totalitarian groups, who want nothing so much as to paralyze and discredit the only democratic authority that can curb them in their battle for the streets.

I am unable to see that the local authorities have transgressed the Federal Constitution. Illinois imposed no prior censorship or suppression upon Terminiello. On the contrary, its sufferance and protection was all that enabled him to speak. It does not appear that the motive in punishing him is to silence the ideology he expressed as offensive to the State's policy or as untrue, or has any purpose of controlling his thought or its peaceful communication to others. There is no claim that the proceedings against Terminiello are designed to discriminate against him or the faction he represents or the ideas that he bespeaks. There is no indication that the charge against him is a mere pretext to give the semblance of legality to a covert effort to silence him or to prevent his followers or the public from hearing any truth that is in him.

A trial court and jury has found only that in the context of violence and disorder in which it was made, this speech was a provocation to immediate breach of the peace and therefore cannot claim constitutional immunity from punishment. Under the Constitution as it has been understood and applied, at least until most recently, the State was within its powers in taking this action.

Rioting is a substantive evil, which I take it no one will deny that the State and the City have the right and the duty to prevent and punish. Where an offense is induced by speech, the Court has laid down and often reiterated a test of the power of the authorities to deal with the speaking as also an offense.

> The question in every case is whether the words *used are used in such circumstances* and are of *such a nature* as to create a *clear and present danger* that they will bring about the substantive evils that Congress [or the State or City] has a right to prevent. [Emphasis supplied.] Mr. Justice Holmes in *Schenck* v. *United States*, 249 U.S. 47, 52.

No one ventures to contend that the State on the basis of this test, for whatever it may be worth, was not justified in punishing Terminiello. In this case the evidence proves beyond dispute that danger of rioting and violence in response to the speech was clear, present and immediate. If this Court has not silently abandoned this long-standing test and substituted for the purposes of this case an unexpressed but more stringent test, the action of the State would have to be sustained.

Only recently this Court held that a state could punish as a breach of the peace use of epithets such as "damned racketeer" and "damned fascist," addressed to only one person, an official, because likely to provoke the average person to retaliation. But these are mild in comparison to the epithets "slimy scum," "snakes," "bedbugs," and the like, which Terminiello hurled at an already inflamed mob of his adversaries. Mr Justice Murphy, writing for a unanimous Court in *Chaplinsky* v. *New Hampshire*, 315 U.S. 568, 571–572, said:

> There are certain well-defined and narrowly limited classes of speech, the prevention and punishment of which have never been thought to raise any Constitutional problem. These include the lewd and obscene, the profane, the libelous, and the insulting or 'fighting' words — those which by their very utterance inflict injury or tend to incite an immediate breach of the peace. It has been well observed that such utterances are no essential part of any exposition of ideas, and are of such slight social value as a step to truth that any benefit that may be derived from them is clearly outweighed by the social interest in order and morality. "Resort to epithets or personal abuse is not in any proper sense communication of information or opinion as safeguarded by the Constitution, and its punishment as a criminal act would raise no question under that instrument." *Cantwell* v. *Connecticut*, 310 U.S. 296, 309–310.

In the latter case Mr. Justice Roberts for a unanimous Court also said:

> The offense known as breach of the peace embraces a great variety of conduct destroying or menacing public order and tranquility. It includes not only violent acts but acts and words likely to produce violence in others. No one would have the hardihood to suggest that the principle of freedom of speech sanctions incitement to riot or that religious liberty connotes the privilege to exhort others to physical attack upon those belonging to another sect. When clear and present danger of riot, disorder, interference with traffic upon the public streets, or other immediate threat to public safety, peace, or other, appears, the power of the State to prevent or punish is obvious. 310 U.S. 296, 308.

How this present decision, denying state power to punish civilly one who precipitated a public riot involving hundreds of fanatic fighters in a most violent melee, can be squared with those unanimous statements of law, is incomprehensible to me. And the Court recently cited these two statements as indicating that "The essential rights of the First Amendment in some instances are subject to the elemental need for order without which the guarantees of civil rights to others would be a mockery." *United Public Workers* v. *Mitchell,* 330 U.S. 75, 95.

However, these wholesome principles are abandoned today and in their place is substituted a dogma of absolute freedom for irresponsible and provocative utterance which almost completely sterilizes the power of local authorities to keep the peace as against this kind of tactics.

Before giving the First and Fourteenth Amendments to the Constitution this effect, we should recall that our application of the First Amendment to Illinois rests entirely on authority which this Court has voted to itself. The relevant parts of the First Amendment, with emphasis supplied, reads: "*Congress* shall make *no* law . . . abridging the freedom of speech." This restrains no authority except Congress. Read as literally as some would do, it restrains Congress in terms so absolute that no legislation would be valid if it touched free speech, no matter how obscene, treasonable, defamatory, inciting or provoking. If it seems strange that no express qualifications were inserted in the Amendment, the answer may be that limitations were thought to be implicit in the definition of "freedom of speech" as then understood. Or it may have been thought unnecessary to delegate to *Congress* any power over abuses of free speech. The Federal Government was then a new and experimental authority, remote from the people, and it was supposed to deal with a limited class of national problems. Inasmuch as any breaches of peace from abuse of free speech traditionally were punishable by state governments, it was needless to reserve that power in a provision drafted to exclude only Congress from such a field of law-making.

The Fourteenth Amendment forbade states to deny the citizen "due process of law." But its terms gave no notice to the people that its adoption would strip their local governments of power to deal with such problems of local peace and order as we have here. Nor was it hinted by this Court for over half a century that the Amendment might have any such effect. In 1922, with concurrence of the most liberty-alert Justices of all times — Holmes and Brandeis — this Court declared flatly that the Constitution does not limit the power of the State over free speech. *Prudential Insurance Co.* v. *Cheek,* 259 U.S. 530, 543. In later years the Court shifted its dogma and decreed that the Constitution does this very thing and that state power is bound by the same limitation as Congress. *Gitlow* v. *New York*, 268 U.S. 652. I have no quarrel with this history. See *Board of Education* v. *Barnette*, 319 U.S. 624. I recite the method by which the right to limit the State has been derived only from this Court's own assumption of the power, with never a submission of legislation or amendment into which the people could write any qualification to prevent abuse of this liberty, as bearing upon the restraint I consider as becoming in exercise of self-given and unappealable power.

It is significant that provisions adopted by the people with awareness that they applied to their own states have universally contained qualifying terms. The Constitution of Illinois is representative of the provisions put in nearly all state constitutions and reads (Art. II, § 4): "Every person may freely speak, write and publish on all subjects *being responsible for the abuse of that liberty.*" (Emphasis added.) That is what I think is meant by the cryptic phrase "freedom of speech," as used in the Federal Compact, and that is the rule I think we should apply to the states.

This absence from the Constitution of any expressed power to deal with abuse of freedom of speech has enabled the Court to soar aloof from any consideration of the abuses which create problems for the states and to indulge in denials of local authority, some of which seem to me improvident in the light of functions which local governments must be relied on to perform for our free society. Quite apart from any other merits or defects, recent decisions have almost completely immunized this battle for the streets from any form of control.

Streets and parks maintained by the public cannot legally be denied to groups "for communication of ideas." *Hague* v. *C. I. O.*, 307 U.S. 496; *Jamison* v. *Texas*, 318 U.S. 413. Cities may not protect their streets from activities which the law has always regarded subject to control, as nuisances. *Lovell* v. *Griffin*, 303 U.S. 444; *Schneider* v. *State*, 308 U.S. 147. Cities may not protect the streets or even homes of their inhabitants from the aggressions of organized bands operating in large numbers. *Douglas* v. *Jeannette*, 319 U.S. 157. As in this case, the facts are set forth fully only in the dissent, p. 166. See also *Martin* v. *Struthers*, 319 U.S. 141. Neither a private party nor a public authority can invoke otherwise valid state laws against trespass to exclude from their property groups bent on disseminating propaganda. *Marsh* v. *Alabama*, 326 U.S. 501; *Tucker* v. *Texas*, 326 U.S. 517. Picketing is largely immunized from control on the ground that it is free speech, Thornhill v. Alabama, 310 U.S. 88, and police may not regulate sound trucks and loud-speakers, Saia v. New York, 334 U.S. 558, though the Court finds them an evil that may be prohibited altogether. Kovacs v. Cooper, 336 U.S. 77. And one-third of the Court has gone further and declared that a position "that the state may prevent any conduct which induces people to violate the law, or any advocacy of unlawful activity, cannot be squared with the First Amendment . . ." and it is only we who can decide when the limit is passed. Musser v. Utah, 333 U.S. 95, 102. Whatever the merits of any one of these decisions in isolation, and there were sound reasons for some of them, it cannot be denied that their cumulative effect has been a sharp handicap on municipal control of the streets and a dramatic encouragement of those who would use them in a battle of ideologies.

I do not think we should carry this handicap further, as we do today, but should adhere to the principles heretofore announced to safeguard our liberties against abuse as well as against invasion. It should not be necessary to recall these elementary principles, but it has been a long time since some of them were even mentioned in this Court's writing on the subject and results indicate they may have been overlooked.

I begin with the oft-forgotten principle which this case demonstrates, that freedom of speech exists only under law and not independently of it. What would Terminiello's theoretical freedom of speech have amounted to had he not been given active aid by the officers of the law? He could reach the hall only with their help, could talk only because they restrained the mob, and could make his getaway only under their protection. We would do well to recall the words of Chief Justice Hughes in Cox v. New Hampshire, 312 U.S, 569, 574: "Civil liberties, as guaranteed by the Constitution, imply the existence of an organized society maintaining public order without which liberty itself would be lost in the excesses of unrestrained abuses. . . ."

This case demonstrates also that this Court's service to free speech is essentially negative and can consist only of reviewing actions by local magistrates. But if free speech is to be a practical reality, affirmative and immediate protection is required; and it can come only from nonjudicial sources. It depends on local police, maintained by law-abiding taxpayers, and who, regardless of their own feelings, risk themselves to maintain supremacy of law. Terminiello's theoretical right to speak free from interference would have no reality if Chicago should withdraw its officers to some other section of the city, or if the men assigned to the task should look the other way when the crowd threatens Terminiello. Can society be expected to keep these men at Terminiello's service if it has nothing to say of his behavior which may force them into dangerous action?

No one will disagree that the fundamental, permanent and overriding policy of police and courts should be to permit and encourage utmost freedom of utterance. It is the legal right of any American citizen to advocate peaceful adoption of fascism or communism, socialism or capitalism. He may go far in expressing sentiments whether pro-Semitic or anti-Semitic, pro-Negro or anti-Negro, pro-Catholic or anti-Catholic. He is legally free to argue for some anti-American system of government to supersede by constitutional methods the one we have. It is our philosophy that the course of government should be controlled by a consensus of the governed. This process of reaching intelligent popular decisions requires free discussion. Hence we should tolerate no law or custom of censorship or suppression.

But we must bear in mind also that no serious outbreak of mob violence, race rioting, lynching or public disorder is likely to get going without help of some speech-making to some mass of people. A street may be filled with men and women and the crowd still not be a mob. Unity of purpose, passion and hatred, which merges the many minds of a crowd into the mindlessness of a mob, almost invariably is supplied by speeches. It is naive, or worse, to teach that oratory with this object or effect is a service to liberty. No mob has ever protected any liberty, even its own, but if not put down it always winds up in an orgy of lawlessness which respects no liberties.

In considering abuse of freedom by provocative utterances it is necessary to observe that the law is more tolerant of discussion than are most individuals or communities. Law is so indifferent to subjects of talk that I think of none that it should close to discussion. Religious, social and political topics that in other times or countries have not been open to lawful debate may be freely discussed here.

Because a subject is legally arguable, however, does not mean that public sentiment will be patient of its advocacy at all times and in all manners. So it happens that, while peaceful advocacy of communism or fascism is tolerated by the law, both of these doctrines arouse passionate reactions. A great number of people do not agree that introduction to America of communism or fascism is even debatable. Hence many speeches, such as that of Terminiello, may be legally permissible but may nevertheless in some surroundings be a menace to peace and order. When conditions show the speaker that this is the case, as it did here, there certainly comes a point beyond which he cannot indulge in provocations to violence without being answerable to society.

Determination of such an issue involves a heavy responsibility. Courts must beware lest they become mere organs of popular intolerance. Not every show of opposition can justify treating a speech as a breach of peace. Neither speakers nor courts are obliged always and in all circumstances to yield to prevailing opinion and feeling. As a people grow in capacity for civilization and liberty their tolerance will grow, and they will endure, if not welcome, discussion even on topics as to which they are committed. They regard convictions as tentative and know that time and events will make their own terms with theories, by whomever and by whatever majorities they are held, and many will be proved wrong. But on our way to this idealistic state of tolerance the police have to deal with men as they are. The crowd mind is never tolerant of any idea which does not conform to its herd opinion. It does not want a tolerant effort at meeting of minds. It does not know the futility of trying to mob an idea. Released from the sense of personal responsibility that would restrain even the worst individuals in it if alone and brave with the courage of numbers, both radical and reactionary mobs endanger liberty as well as order. The authorities must control them and they are entitled to place some checks upon those whose behavior or speech calls such mobs into being. When the right of society to freedom from probable violence should prevail over the right of an individual to defy opposing opinion, presents a problem that always tests wisdom and often calls for immediate and vigorous action to preserve public order and safety.

I do not think that the Constitution of the United States denies to the states and the municipalities power to solve that problem in the light of local conditions, at least so long as danger to public order is not invoked in bad faith, as a cover for censorship or suppression. The preamble declares domestic tranquility as well as liberty to be an object in founding a Federal Government and I do not think the Forefathers were naive in believing both can be fostered by the law.

Certain practical reasons reinforce the legal view that cities and states should be sustained in the power to keep their streets from becoming the battleground for these hostile ideologies to the destruction and detriment of public order. There is no other power that can do it. Theirs are the only police that are on the spot. The Federal Government has no police force. The Federal Bureau of Investigation is, and should remain, not a police but an investigative service. To date the only federal agency for preserving and restoring order when local authority fails has been the Army. And when the military steps in, the court takes a less liberal view of the rights of the individual and sustains most arbitrary exercises of military power. See *Korematsu v. United States,* 323 U.S. 214. Every failure of local authority to deal with riot problems results in a demand for the establishment of a federal police or intervention by federal authority. In my opinion, locally established and controlled police can never develop into the menace to general civil liberties that is inherent in a federal police.

The ways in which mob violence may be worked up are subtle and various. Rarely will a speaker directly urge a crowd to lay hands on a victim or class of victims. An effective and safer way is to incite mob action while pretending to deplore it, after the classic example of Antony, and this was not lost on Terminiello. And whether one may be the cause of mob violence by his own personification or advocacy of ideas which a crowd already fears and hates, is not solved merely by going through a transcript of the speech to pick out "fighting words." The most insulting words can be neutralized if the speaker will smile when he says them, but a belligerent personality and an aggressive manner may kindle a fight without use of words that in cold type shock us. True judgment will be aided by observation of the individual defendant, as was possible for this jury and trial court but impossible for us.

There are many appeals these days to liberty, often by those who are working for an opportunity to taunt democracy with its stupidity in furnishing them the weapons to destroy it as did Goebbels when he said:

> When democracy granted democratic methods for us in the times of opposition, this [Nazi seizure of power] was bound to happen in a democratic system. However, we National Socialists never asserted that we represented a democratic point of view, but we have declared openly that we used democratic methods only in order to gain the power and that, after assuming the power, we would deny to our

adversaries without any consideration the means which were granted to use in the times of [our] opposition. 1 *Nazi Conspiracy and Aggression* (GPO, 1946) 202, Doc. 2412–PS.

Invocation of constitutional liberties as part of the strategy for overthrowing them presents a dilemma to a free people which may not be soluble by constitutional logic alone.

But I would not be understood as suggesting that the United States can or should meet this dilemma by suppression of free, open and public speaking on the part of any group or ideology. Suppression has never been a successful permanent policy; any surface serenity that it creates is a false security, while conspiratorial forces go underground. My confidence in American institutions and in the sound sense of the American people is such that if with a stroke of the pen I could silence every fascist and communist speaker, I would not do it. For I agree with Woodrow Wilson, who said:

> I have always been among those who believed that the greatest freedom of speech was the greatest safety, because if a man is a fool, the best thing to do is to encourage him to advertise the fact by speaking. It cannot be so easily discovered if you allow him to remain silent and look wise, but if you let him speak, the secret is out and the world knows that he is a fool. So it is by the exposure of folly that it is defeated; not by the seclusion of folly, and in this free air of free speech men get into that sort of communication with one another which constitutes the basis of all common achievement. Address at the Institute of France, Paris, May 10, 1919. 2 *Selected Literary and Political Papers and Addresses of Woodrow Wilson* (1926) 333.

But if we maintain a general policy of free speaking, we must recognize that its inevitable consequence will be sporadic local outbreaks of violence, for it is the nature of men to be intolerant of attacks upon institutions, personalities and ideas for which they really care. In the long run, maintenance of free speech will be more endangered if the population can have no protection from the abuses which lead to violence. No liberty is made more secure by holding that its abuses are inseparable from its enjoyment. We must not forget that it is the free democratic communities that ask us to trust them to maintain peace with liberty and that the factions engaged in this battle are not interested permanently in either. What would it matter to Terminiello if the police batter up some communists or, on the other hand, if the communists batter up some policemen? Either result makes grist for his mill; either would help promote hysteria and the demand for strong-arm methods in dealing with his adversaries. And what, on the other hand, have the communist agitators to lose from a battle with the police?

This Court has gone far toward accepting the doctrine that civil liberty means the removal of all restraints from these crowds and that all local attempts to maintain order are impairments of the liberty of the citizen. The choice is not between order and liberty. It is between liberty with order and anarchy without either. There is danger that, if the Court does not temper its doctrinaire logic with a little practical wisdom, it will convert the constitutional Bill of Rights into a suicide pact.

I would affirm the conviction.

MR. JUSTICE BURTON joins in this opinion.

The Case of an Unpopular Student:

FEINER v. NEW YORK

340 U.S. 315 (1951)

Another Student in Trouble?

"Mayor Costello is a champagne-sipping bum; he does not speak for the Negro people."

"The 15th Ward is run by corrupt politicians, and there are horse rooms operating there."

"President Truman is a drunken bum."

"Mayor O'Dwyer [of New York City] is a bum."

"The American Legion is a Nazi Gestapo."

"The Negroes don't have equal rights; they should rise up in arms and fight for their rights."

These words were alleged to have created a serious disturbance at Harrison and South McBride Streets in the city of Syracuse. They were the words of Irving Feiner, a Syracuse University student. He was protesting the revocation of a speaker's permit, which his organization, the Young Progressives of America, had obtained. What happened was that John Rogge, a former U.S. Assistant Attorney General and a prominent member of the American Progressive party, was invited jointly by the Syracuse University Chapter of the Young Progressives and the local branch of the American Labor party to speak at the Madison public school auditorium of Syracuse. Rogge's speech, among other things, was billed as a protest against the recent conviction for murder of six Negro boys in New Jersey, which Rogge and many others thought unfair. Rogge himself was considered a

Lucius J. Barker and Twiley W. Barker, Jr., *Freedoms, Courts, Politics: Studies in Civil Liberties*, copyright © 1965. Reprinted by permission of Prentice-Hall, Inc., Englewood Cliffs, N.J.

"left-winger," and upon reviewing the situation, Mayor Frank Costello ordered the revocation of Rogge's permit to use the school auditorium.

Consequently, the meeting was shifted to the Syracuse Hotel, and on March 8, 1949, about 6:30 p.m., Feiner began addressing an open air meeting at the corner of Harrison and McBride. In his talk, Feiner denounced those responsible for revoking the permit while simultaneously publicizing the Syracuse Hotel as the new site for Rogge's speech. Feiner spoke from a large box placed on the sidewalk and used loudspeakers fixed on his car. A crowd gathered to hear him. So did Patrolman Roy Cook and Sergeant Dennis Flynn of the Syracuse police department, the latter being dispatched to the scene when notified that there was a "disturbance."

Feiner, in the course of his speech, allegedly referred to the Syracuse city administration as "stinking," to Mayor Costello as a "champagne-sipping bum," to President Harry S. Truman as a "drunken bum," and to the American Legion as "Nazi Gestapo agents."

After Feiner had been speaking for some twenty minutes, the policemen observed that "there was angry muttering throughout the crowd." The officers thought that the crowd, which they estimated at seventy-five, was "hampering the use of the sidewalk," and as a result, pedestrians were being "forced into the road." Generally, the officers said the crowd was restless, pushing, shoving, and muttering angrily. Sergeant Flynn related that "when Feiner said that 'the Negro people do not have equal rights and should rise and fight,' one man came up to him [Flynn] and said 'if you don't get that son of a bitch off of there, I will go over and get him off myself.'" At this point Flynn asked Feiner to get down and stop speaking, but Feiner refused. He was asked to stop a second time. However, Feiner continued speaking, telling the people to go to the Syracuse Hotel to hear John Rogge. Finally, Flynn told Feiner he was under arrest, but as Feiner was leaving his self-made speaker's rostrum, he yelled to the crowd that the "law had arrived and would take over."

When Feiner asked Flynn the grounds for his arrest, the officer said: "for unlawful assembly." Upon reflection, however, the officer changed the charge to "disorderly conduct." Feiner was subsequently charged with violating Sec. 722 (2) of the New York Penal Code, which reads:

Any person who with intent to provoke a breach of the peace or whereby a breach of the peace may be occasioned, commits any of the following acts shall be deemed to have committed the offense of disorderly conduct:

1. Uses offensive, disorderly, threatening, abusive, or insulting language, conduct or behavior;

2. Acts in such a manner as to annoy, disturb, interfere with, obstruct, or be offensive to others;

3. Congregates with others on a public street and refuses to move on when ordered by police;

4. By his actions causes a crowd to collect except when lawfully addressing such a crowd.

From the Streets to the Court

The controversy moved from the streets to court of special sessions of Syracuse, where Judge William H. Bamerick heard the case. On arraignment Feiner pleaded not guilty, and bail was fixed at $1,000. Feiner's trial took place in early May, 1949. The prosecution was led by Daniel Kelly, assistant district attorney, while the defense counsel was Sidney Greenberg. The initial motion by Feiner's attorney was for dismissal. It was denied.

As the trial progressed, it became apparent that the prosecution and defense conceived the case quite differently. The prosecution thought that the case should rest primarily upon the nature of the speech and its immediate impact, while the defense thought that a full development of the circumstances and background was necessary to put the case in proper perspective. This difference in approach was important, since by not fully developing background factors, the case would more clearly focus on "breach of the peace"; on the other hand, to develop these factors would tend to focus more directly on the free speech issue. Defense Counsel Greenberg was particularly concerned here, since he thought that it was the utterance of the unpopular views and the organization to which Feiner belonged that led to his arrest rather than any "clear and present danger" or a great disturbance. But Judge Bamerick sided with the more narrow development of the case:

The point is simply what the defendant was doing or what he was saying at the time and place in question — that is, the place where he was using his loudspeaker apparatus, that is all there is to it — the fact that the meeting place had been changed or another meeting scheduled, or that someone else came from Washington or California or some other place to speak at this meeting, that, it seems to me, is a little beside the point. The point is, what was the defendant doing and saying at that particular time.

There was conflicting testimony on every facet of the case. Witnesses for the prosecution and defense differed on the following points:

1. The Size of the Crowd

According to the two police officers, who were the only witnesses for the prosecution, the crowd numbered about seventy-five to eighty. Though individual listeners were coming and going, both officers maintained that the number remained around that mark. The defense, on the other hand, produced witnesses who testified that the number was about twenty-five to thirty. For example, one housewife, whose home was located across the street from the meeting place, estimated the number at "about twenty-five or twenty-six." Of course whether the crowd numbered seventy-five to eighty or twenty-five to thirty was important, since the prosecution charged that the large crowd caused pedestrian and vehicular traffic to be adversely affected. In the end, the trial judge accepted the testimony of the policemen; hence the record showed the crowd at about seventy-five.

2. The Nature of the Language Used by Feiner

The police testified that the defendant used derogatory terms in attacking public authorities and made inflammatory remarks to the effect that Negroes do not have equal rights and should "rise up in arms and fight for [them]." But defense witnesses disagreed. They testified that Feiner's speech was not of the inflammatory nature described by the police.

The manner in which the trial judge framed the question for determination made the nature of the language used crucial to the outcome of the disorderly conduct charge. In phrasing the question, Judge Bamerick said:

The question here is, what was said and what was done? And it doesn't make any difference whether whatever was said was said with a loudspeaker or not. There are acts and conduct an individual can engage in when you don't even have to have a crowd gathered around which would justify a charge of disorderly conduct. The question is, what did this defendant say and do that particular time and the Court must determine whether those facts, concerning what the defendant did or said, are sufficient to support the charge.

Defense Counsel Greenberg took sharp exception to the manner in which the judge framed the question. "Even assuming that the plaintiff made the statements with which he is charged," countered Greenberg, "no crime has been committed." He continued:

From time immemorial there has been a steady barrage of name calling from one side to the other. History is filled with it. If everyone who was called a name in public life brought the name called to law, as between the common citizen and the public figure, I venture to say that the jails of this country would be pretty substantially full. . . . Lincoln was called a copperhead; and the names they called Franklin Roosevelt, I could talk a whole day on that — they said he was crazy and that he was a Communist. President Truman called someone an S.O.B.

3. The Attitude of the Defendant Toward the Police and Vice Versa

Policemen Flynn and Cook testified that the defendant refused to obey orders, while defense witnesses maintained that he was quick enough in complying with the police orders. Counsel for prosecution and defense commented extensively on this aspect of the case. Much of the discussion centered on whether the defendant gave proper deference tò police orders.

Sergeant Flynn testified that it took about two minutes for the defendant to get off the stand after having been requested to do so by the officer. Concerning this testimony, Defense Counsel Greenberg said that he did not think it "unreasonable . . . to spend two minutes to question the police officer's request and to determine whether the decision of the police or the instruction of the police were reasonable. I think that in order to be obeyed," continued Greenberg, "the instructions of the police must be reasonable, and I certainly don't think it's unreasonable to spend two minutes to decide whether they are or not." Greenberg thought that because a policeman felt that there was "going to be a disturbance" should not by any means be controlling. Prosecutor Kelly, however, disagreed. He thought that the officers were "very lenient." "Two minutes is a lot of time when anything is coming to a climax," said Kelly. "If you take your watch and hold it in your hand," said Kelly, "why all hell could break out in two minutes, and I submit to your honor, has a police officer got to stand by and be at the mercy [or] whim of someone who is disobeying the law to say just when he will wind up?" Concluded Kelly:

> He [Feiner] was requested first to stop, and he disregarded the officer — the officer had just passed through a group of people, and three of those . . . people had said to him, "How long do we have to put up with this?" The officer had a perfect right to do as he did — and even after the second request the defendant still goes on speaking in his flippant manner, disregarding any authority, and wisecracking about the law, still talking to the people and doing something to egg this crowd on to accomplish some purpose which is best known in the mind of this man himself.

4. The Reaction of the Crowd to the Speech

There was also disagreement on the reaction of the crowd to Feiner's speech. The policemen testified that there were "angry mutterings," "discussions of the speech pro and con," as well as the threat of at least one man to assault the speaker. Defense witnesses disagreed. In their opinion, the audience was not of the nature described by the police, and did not show any "strong feelings." Prosecution and defense counsel, as did the witnesses, varied greatly in their description of the crowd reaction. Prosecutor Kelly summarized the situation as follows:

> It appears that these officers were very lenient. They did not go down there with the idea in mind of making an arrest. They watched the situation and mingled with the crowd, and they were able to estimate the temper of that crowd. They heard this dissertation and the comments made by various people and this was climaxed finally by one of the people telling the officer if he did not get the defendant down off the box he would get the son of a bitch off himself. That is followed . . . by the defendant, urging the people to get up in arms

or with arms and fight, and it doesn't make any difference whether he said in arms or with arms because it aroused them to a point where the officer knew that a riot or a disorder was imminent. That is all that was necessary to bring this case within the particular section with which this man is charged with violating.

. . . The effect of his words was to bring a crisis, an outbreak and disorder more imminent every minute, and apparently counsel feels that the defendant should receive some consideration because he finally did get down off the box after being requested three times to do so.

But Defense Counsel Greenberg disagreed. "The most that the [prosecution] has shown by its witnesses, the two police officers, was that there was some muttering in the crowd. And I fail to see," continued Greenberg, "how you can determine either the volume or the extent of it that would be necessary to lead to a breach of the peace or which would tend toward a breach of the peace." Greenberg explained:

I think it's . . . significant that the People have been unable to produce anyone other than the two police officers as witnesses. They claim there were seventy-five people there, and this speech must have been heard over a wide area, yet the People have been unable to bring into Court any witnesses but the police officers.

He concluded that if the prosecution wanted to prove that the crowd was being disturbed they could have "brought in the man they claim approached the police officer and told him to do something about it or he would. And if that man was talking in that frame of mind," said Greenberg, "it seems to me that he was the one that should have been arrested."

Throughout the trial there were frequent clashes between Judge Bamerick and Greenberg. At one point, for example, Prosecutor Kelly remarked that "considering all the circumstances . . . and the class of people to whom the defendant was appealing, the officers were perfectly right in making the arrest. . . ." Immediately Greenberg objected to the manner in which Kelly referred to the Negro people in the Fifteenth Ward as "that class of people." But Judge Bamerick came to Kelly's defense, saying that he did not believe "Kelly intended . . . to cast reflection on the colored people. That is something that should not occur," said the judge, "and I am sure Mr. Kelly agrees with me." Kelly replied, "Absolutely," whereupon the judge put the matter to rest by saying, "So let's not talk any more about that."

There was also controversy concerning the use of character witnesses by the defense. The character witnesses were mainly Syracuse University instructors who knew Feiner. However, because of frequent objections by the prosecution which were sustained by the Court, their testimony was largely stricken. In fact, Judge Bamerick ruled that character witnesses could testify only to "a knowledge of the witness for truth and veracity." But Greenberg was not satisfied with this ruling and at the end of the day's trial (May 5), he researched the law and precedents on the subject, and found that character witnesses were competent to testify to the general good character of the defendant and also to his reputation for peace and quiet.

Armed with this authority, Greenberg arrived the next day and challenged the Court's ruling. He began by citing a number of precedents to support his position, after which the following dialogue took place:

THE COURT: I am familiar with those cases. I was very liberal in my rulings, and I permitted your witnesses to spread out and cover any subject that you wanted to talk about.

GREENBERG: I don't think you understand my remarks. The point is that these witnesses were confined to testifying to the reputation of the witness for truth and veracity.

THE COURT: The questions could have been asked in regard to the other subjects you mentioned.

GREENBERG: I did, and they were denied. I asked whether the witnesses were familiar with the reputation of the defendant on the campus.

THE COURT: No, I'm not going into that any more. I will adhere to the ruling I made yesterday. I permitted your questions covering the campus and even the classroom. I even permitted the witnesses to testify when they knew nothing of the reputation of the defendant in the community.

GREENBERG: Yes, but your honor, under your ruling the questions were confined to truth and veracity.

THE COURT: Have you got any witnesses now?

At this point Greenberg called Marguerite Fisher, an associate professor of political science at Syracuse, to testify as to Feiner's reputation, which she said was good. But Prosecutor Kelly immediately raised objections to the nature of the questions Greenberg asked Professor Fisher. And as he had done so many times previously, Judge Bamerick sustained Kelly's objections and overruled Greenberg's line of questioning.

Such was the nature of the trial. There was little doubt as to the outcome.

A Final Plea and a Judge Has His Say

In his summation, Defense Counsel Greenberg asked the judge to dismiss the charges for lack of evidence. He reasoned that there was a sharp distinction between what is in bad taste and what is disorderly conduct. But once again, Greenberg's motion for dismissal was denied, and the Court gave its verdict. In so doing, Judge Bamerick lectured Feiner, saying:

> Mr. Feiner, . . . you have had a fair trial; you have been ably defended by good counsel, that is a right that is afforded everyone in this country regardless of his position or his race or situation in life. That is a priceless heritage; that is something that is foreign to some of these ideologies in some places in this world, and that some folks in this country seem to like and seem to endorse. Now, awhile ago, a very estimable citizen in this town, . . . delivered a talk here in town at a certain place and I would like to summarize briefly what that outstanding citizen of this town had to say. He spoke on the freedom of speech: something that is prized very highly; something that is talked about very generally nowadays. That, too, is one of the priceless heritages we have in this country, and which we would like to preserve. It is something our forefathers fought and bled for, and they set up this system of equal rights for everyone, including you and including me; and on that subject this man that I have spoken to you about had this to say:
>
>> The importance of Freedom of Speech for which our founding fathers fought and died is a very important right. Freedom of speech is a right which must not be abused in Public any more than in private. . . . When these liberties are abused they endanger our national security. Then this Freedom must be controlled.
>
> Continuing, he said something about Communism — the mention of which has been avoided here so I will omit that. He maintains that people "who advocate change by violence, and who divide a nation

to conquer and pit man against man, and class against class and race against race and color against color and religion against religion, should be denied the right to freedom of speech."
I think that is a good, sound, sensible philosophy. I think our citizens should be permitted to exercise those liberties [he] spoke about. . . . Subject, however, to some regard for the rights of others; subject to other people's convenience; subject to other people's wishes. . . .
I don't think even though you were within your strict legal right, in addressing the American Legion the way you did, I don't think that is an attribute of good citizenship. I have just as much respect for you as for anyone else, but I haven't much respect for the philosophy you endorse. Guilty.

The judge then sentenced Feiner to thirty days in the Onondaga County jail. However, the sentence was stayed and bail was continued at $1,000 pending appeal. Soon thereafter Feiner was expelled from Syracuse in accordance with University policy affecting students found guilty in county courts.

Several aspects of Feiner's trial stand out. First, the Court accepted wholly the testimony of the officers, even though a number of defense witnesses gave conflicting testimony. Second, the judge's lecture prior to rendering his verdict gave the impression that Feiner was convicted largely because of his political views, and the Court record gave the impression that the trial was not *Feiner v. the State*, but *Feiner*, i.e., *Greenberg*, v. *Kelly* (the State) and *Bamerick* (the judge).

Up the Judicial Ladder: Appeals, Appeals, Appeals

The decision of the trial judge was immediately appealed to the Onondaga County court. In the appeal Feiner charged that the state had not proved beyond a reasonable doubt that the defendant committed the acts charged. To buttress this point, the appellant vigorously criticized Judge Bamerick for his total acceptance of the "police version" of what happened, disregarding conflicting testimony altogether. Secondly, Feiner argued that his conviction was an abridgement of the free speech and assembly guarantees of the First and Fourteenth Amendments, as well as Article I, Section 8 of the New York State Constitution. The appeal also alleged that the sentence was excessive.

On August 8, 1949, County Court Judge Leo Breed upheld the decision of the trial court. Rejecting each of the three points raised by the appellant, Judge Breed said that the trial court is in a better position to assess the biases, interests, and motives of the witnesses. Moreover, the decision of the trial court to accept a certain version among conflicting stories should not be disturbed, since not only is it a time-honored principle, but it is also sanctioned by practical wisdom. Second, the Court said that freedom of speech is not absolute and one need not apply the clear and present danger test to convict. In addition, Judge Breed found that Feiner's sentence was not excessive, since the maximum punishment could have been six months. "From the evidence in this case," concluded Judge Breed, "I feel that the officer was justified in drawing the conclusion that unless the apellant desisted in his talk that disorder and violence would result. Police officers are guardians of the public order. It is their duty to prevent disorder in the community and as such they may give reasonable directions."

Following the decision of the county court, Feiner appealed to the Court of Appeals of New York, the highest state court. Basically, the appeal rested on the same grounds it had in the county court, with perhaps two exceptions. First, Attorney Greenberg disagreed with an inference of the county court that Feiner intended to incite a breach of the peace. Accordingly, Greenberg questioned the propriety of inserting this element of intent, since there was no evidence in the record to support it. In addition, the appeal cited *Terminiello* v. *Chicago*, decided in 1949, in which the U.S. Supreme Court ruled that the trial court judge in instructing the jury had construed "breach of the peace" too broadly. In that case, the Court held that "breach of the peace" may not be defined so broadly as to include speech which "stirs the public to anger, invites dispute, brings about a condition of unrest, or creates a disturbance. . . ."

However, on March 2, 1950, in a unanimous decision, the Court of Appeals denied these defense contentions and upheld the lower courts. Judge Albert Conway spoke for the Court. On the question of intent, Judge Conway brushed aside the whole problem by saying that the acts of the appellant were punishable even without the element of intent, since it was not essential to a charge of disorderly conduct. With regard to *Terminiello*, the Court of Appeals held that the two cases (*Feiner* and *Terminiello*) were quite different, since, among other things, Terminiello was not charged with disrupting pedestrian and vehicular traffic as the meeting was held in a private hall, not on a street corner. Judge Conway continued:

> The findings contained in the decision of the trial judge sufficiently establish that the defendant . . . was guilty of disorderly conduct — putting aside, for the moment, constitutional objections to the convictions.
>
> It is perhaps laboring the obvious and oft-repeated to state that the constitutional guarantee of freedom of speech is not absolute. . . . The preservation of order and the prevention of disturbance are of prime importance to the state.
>
> . . . There is no indication that the action of the police officer was taken as a subterfuge or excuse for suppression of defendant's views and opinions. The courts below have found, and we are bound by the finding, that the officer was motivated solely by a proper concern for the preservation of order and the protection of the general welfare, in face of an actual interference with traffic and an imminently threatened disturbance of the peace of the community.

On to the Supreme Court

After exhausting all state judicial remedies, Feiner and his attorney looked to the Supreme Court to correct what they considered an injustice. Feiner was destitute. His friends were few. Only the Civil Rights Congress of New York presented an *amicus curiae* brief on his behalf to the Court of Appeals. The executive secretary of the American Labor party, Arthur Schutzer, lodged what appeared to be a weak protest against "the unlawful attempt of [Judge] William Bamerick . . . to halt political activities." Schutzer also asked the state judicial counsel to investigate the matter. Nothing resulted from either move. In addition, several months after Feiner's conviction, John Rogge withdrew his membership from the Progressive party and rejoined the Democratic party. The only noticeable protest against the upholding of Feiner's conviction by the Court of Appeals of New York came from students at Syracuse University. On May 6, 1949, the students staged a massive demonstration in front of police headquarters that the police chief described as a "near riot." Despite this youthful enthusiasm, Feiner remained a convicted man without friends or money.

Nevertheless, Feiner and his counsel were determined to take the case to the Supreme Court, and they did. On May 29, 1950, the High Court granted Feiner a writ of certiorari and permitted him to proceed in forma pauperis, meaning that the costs involved in his behalf would be at public expense. Prosecutor Kelly and Defense Counsel Greenberg continued to be chief counsel in the case. Both parties carried familiar arguments to the Court, but though basically the same, the arguments appeared sharper, more cogent, and dressed in more sophisticated constitutional garb. The basic position of both sides, as presented to the High Court, are excerpted here.

For the State of New York (Prosecutor Kelly)

In view of the language used, the aspersions cast, and the very apparent unrest in the crowd and despite the right of free speech and free assembly which was not questioned by the officers, still the effect on the crowd whether intentional or otherwise on the part of the speaker clearly spelled out a picture where trouble was imminent and disorder could most easily follow. The officers were not precipitate in their action and the whole scene before them presented a situation where action to prevent disorder was thoroughly warranted and justifiable. The picture before us then cannot be duplicated by any record and who can say that as police officers, guardians of the public peace, they should have done less to preserve public order. It was a good piece of excellent police work on the part of two officers who acted very conservatively to avoid a real threatened breach of the peace.

The duty rested on the Judge of the Court of Special Sessions to determine the accurate version among conflicting stories of witnesses for the People and for the defendant and his decision should not be disturbed.

Whether or not there was a breach of the peace or a threatened breach of the peace within the statute was a question of fact for the Magistrate who heard the case to decide. In fact all that is involved here is a question of fact and whether the opinion of the Magistrate is a sound one.

The Magistrate before whom this case was tried is the best judge of the creditability of the testimony brought out. He was in a position to observe their ideas, prejudices, motives, interests, to study the materiality of their testimony, and to form a decision from all the facts before him more accurately than can be placed before an Appellate

Court on a written record. When the testimony of witnesses is conflicting the Magistrate before whom the trial is held is the best judge of the ultimate truth. He has the picture as a whole to a degree that cannot be duplicated by a record. Can what he observed be questioned as to facts on which his decision is based?

There is nothing ambiguous about the statute under which petitioner was convicted and it most certainly is sufficiently explicit to inform those who are subject to it what conduct on their part will render them liable to its penalties.

For the Petitioner Feiner (Defense Counsel Greenberg)

There is no escaping the fact that [Feiner] was exercising his constitutional right to speak on the streets of his community. Not only did he speak, but he spoke about things that mattered; things that would arouse and excite people, things that would cause them to take action to move the evils about which he spoke. During the course of this speech, he undoubtedly irritated some of his hearers and since he spoke against the administration of the City of Syracuse, he undoubtedly annoyed and disturbed the police officers present on the scene.

The question is not the small annoyances and inconveniences, but is . . . "whether the words used are used in such circumstances and are of such a nature as to create a clear and present danger that they will bring about the substantive evils that Congress has a right to prevent. It is a question of proximity and degree."

We cannot deny that [Feiner] was outraged by this [cancellation of a permit to use a public auditorium]. We cannot deny that he attempted to convey this feeling of outrage to his hearers, to parallel the cancelling of the permit with the unequal treatment given to Negroes in many areas. Obviously, his intent was to arouse his audience, to stir them up, to urge upon them a course of action that would prevent a recurrence of the peremptory cancellation of the permit, and help in the fight for equal rights for Negroes. That he was successful in exciting the crowd is a tribute not only to the soundness of his sentiments, but also to his effectiveness as a public speaker. That he annoyed some of his listeners and caused them to display their annoyance by mild vocal eruptions is not surprising. Less surprising is the fact that he annoyed the police officers present.

The petitioner did not appear at this public meeting to discuss the solar system, flowers, or stamp collecting. He spoke on a provocative subject that mattered a great deal to him. He fully hoped that his words would [receive] a warm response. He fully anticipated that some would disagree with him. As Mr. Justice Jackson stated so eloquently in *Board of Education* v. *Barnette*, 319 U.S. 624, 642: ". . . but freedom to differ is not limited to things that do not matter much. That would be a mere shadow of freedom. The test of its substance is the right to differ as to things that touch the heart of the existing order."

The preceding is not intended to be brazen or flippant. It is intended to bring the conduct of the petitioner and his words, and the conduct of the crowd, down into the bedrock of constitutional guarantees encompassing all the acts and words of the petitioner and of the crowd on the night of March 8th.

We concede that there was one threat of violence. Not by the petitioner, but by one man in the audience who approached one of the police officers and said, "If you don't get that son of a bitch off, I will go over and get him off there myself." The duty of the police officer, at that moment, was clear. It was his duty at the very least, to reprimand the protestor and send him on his way, so that violence would be avoided, or if necessary, to arrest him for threatening violence and threatening to take the law into his own hands. Threatening violence is a well-defined crime in the State of New York, covered by the same statute under which petitioner was convicted. Except in self-defense, violence or threats of violence are criminal acts, punishable under the law. . . . One may well question whether, under the law so far laid down in this case, freedom to speak has become the crime, and freedom to threaten violence lawful.

A Divided Court Gives Its Decision

On January 15, 1951, some three months after oral arguments, the Supreme Court handed down its decision by a 6–3 vote. Chief Justice Frederick M. Vinson spoke for the majority. In the first place, the Court dealt with the claim of the denial of First Amendment rights. In this connection, Vinson said that "in the review of state decisions where First Amendment rights are drawn in question, we of course make an examination of the evidence to ascertain independently whether the right has been violated."

But to begin with, and this was crucial, the Court accepted the trial court's determination of the factual situation. Vinson said that the trial judge's decision "indicated generally that he believed the state's witnesses, and his summation of the testimony was used by two New York courts on review in stating the facts." "Our appraisal of the facts," reasoned Vinson, "is, therefore, based upon the uncontroverted facts and, where controversy exists, upon that testimony which the trial judge did reasonably conclude to be true."

The Court said that freedom of speech does not sanction incitement to riot, nor does it imply that the community has no right to place reasonable regulations on its exercise for the maintenance of peace and order on its streets. "We are well aware," said the Chief Justice, "that the ordinary murmurings and objections of a hostile audience cannot be allowed to silence a speaker, and are also mindful of the possible danger of giving overzealous police officials complete discretion to break up otherwise lawful public meetings." But, continued Vinson, "it is one thing to say that the police cannot be used as an instrument for the oppression of unpopular views, and another to say that, when as here the speaker passes the bounds of argument or persuasion and undertakes incitement to riot, they are powerless to prevent a breach of the peace."

The Court also paid great deference to the lower courts by saying that it could not "condemn the considered judgment of three New York courts approving means which the police, faced with a crisis, used in the exercise of their power and duty to preserve peace and order." Accordingly, Vinson concluded that "the findings of the state courts as to the existing situation and the imminence of greater disorder coupled with petitioner's deliberate defiance of the police officers convince us that we should not reverse this conviction in the name of free speech."

In a concurring opinion, Justice Frankfurter highlighted this deference which the Court accorded to the judgments of the state courts. After reviewing the facts in the case Frankfurter said:

> The estimate of a particular local situation thus comes here with the momentum of the weightiest judicial authority of New York.
>
> This Court has often emphasized that in the exercise of our authority over state court decisions the Due Process Clause must not be construed in an abstract and doctrinaire way by disregarding local conditions. In considering the degree of respect to be given findings by the highest court of a State in cases involving the Due Process Clause, the course of decisions by that court should be taken into account. Particularly within the area of due process colloquially called "civil liberties," it is important whether such a course of decision reflects a cavalier attitude toward civil liberties or real regard

for them. Only unfamiliarity with its decisions and the outlook of its judges could generate a notion that the Court of Appeals of New York is inhospitable to claims of civil liberties or is wanting in respect for this Court's decisions in support of them. It is pertinent, therefore, to note that all members of the New York Court accepted the finding that Feiner was stopped not because of listeners or police officers disagreed with his views but because these officers were honestly concerned with preventing a breach of the peace. This unanimity is all the more persuasive since three members of the Court had dissented, only three months earlier, in favor of Kunz, a man whose vituperative utterances must have been highly offensive to them. *Kunz v. New York,* 340 U.S. 290, 1951.

A Little Disorder, Some Unpopular Views, and an Unfair Conviction — Three Dissent

Justices Hugo L. Black, William O. Douglas, and Sherman Minton dissented. Justice Black issued a particularly sharp dissent. He was convinced that Feiner was convicted for his unpopular views, nothing more. He vigorously criticized the Court for not making an independent evaluation of the facts, especially since "the trial judge fully accepted the testimony of the prosecution witnesses on all important points." "Many times in the past," said Black, "this Court has said that despite findings below, we will examine the evidence for ourselves to ascertain whether federally protected rights have been denied; otherwise review here would fail of its purpose in safe-guarding constitutional guarantees. Even a partial abandonment of this rule marks a dark day for civil liberties in our Nation." The Justice continued:

> But still more has been lost today. Even accepting every "finding of fact" below, I think this conviction makes a mockery of the free speech guarantees of the First and Fourteenth Amendments. The end result of the affirmance here is to approve a simply and readily available technique by which cities and states can with impunity subject all speeches, political or otherwise, on streets or elsewhere, to the supervision and censorship of the local police. I will have no part or parcel in this holding which I view as a long step toward totalitarian authority.

In addition, Black rejected the implication of the Court that the police had no obligation to protect Feiner's constitutional right to talk. Certainly the police have power to prevent breaches of the peace, "but if, in the name of preserving order, they ever can interfere with a lawful public speaker, they must make all reasonable efforts to protect him." Nothing was done, he said, to clear a path on the sidewalk; nor was anything done to discourage the person who threatened Feiner, in a situation where "even a word might have sufficed. Their duty was to protect petitioner's right to talk," continued Black, "even to the extent of arresting the man who threatened to interfere. . . . Instead, they shirked that duty and acted only to suppress the right to speak."

Justice Douglas also wrote a dissenting opinion, in which Justice Minton concurred. Douglas, like Black, thought that unpopular views will commonly provoke "mutterings and unrest and heckling from the crowd." "When a speaker mounts a platform," said Douglas, "it is not unusual to find him resorting to exaggeration, to vilification of ideas and men, and to making of false charges. . . . But those extravagances . . . do not justify penalizing the speaker by depriving him of the platform or by punishing him for his conduct." Douglas concluded:

> A speaker may not, of course, incite a riot any more than he may invite a breach of the peace by the use of "fighting words.". . . But this record shows no such extremes. It shows an unsympathetic audience and the threat of one man to haul the speaker from the stage. It is against that kind of threat that speakers need police protection. If they do not receive it and instead the police throw their weight on the side of those who would break up the meetings, the police become the new censors of speech. Police censorship has all the vices of the censorship from city halls which we have repeatedly struck down.

At long last Feiner's case had run the judicial gamut. On February 17, 1951, almost two years after the trial, Feiner began serving his long-delayed prison sentence.

Freedom of Speech and the Civil Rights Movement

The following three cases which reached the United States Supreme Court all dealt with various aspects of the civil rights sit-ins and demonstrations of the early 1960's. The protest activities of the civil rights movement raised questions regarding their relationship to the First Amendment guarantees. Were the protest activities, under certain circumstances, protected by the First Amendment? Several justices argued that protesters have some rights to express their views and grievances through conduct as well as oral and written communication; these justices recognized the rhetorical function of the sit-ins, stand-ins, and demonstrations.

In *Garner* v. *Louisiana* (1961), the Court decided unanimously to reverse the Louisiana convictions of students who had participated in lunch counter sit-ins. Since there were three separate group arrests, separate cases were designated at the state court level: *State* v. *Garner*, *State* v. *Briscoe*, and *State* v. *Hoston*. Because of the similarities in the three cases, the Supreme Court considered all of them under *Garner* v. *Louisiana;* hence the references in Justice Harlan's concurring opinion to *Garner*, No. 26, *Briscoe*, No. 27, and *Hoston*, No. 28. Justice Harlan's lengthy opinion rejected the majority's reasons for reversal. He said that the convictions should be reversed because the statute under which the students were convicted was unconstitutionally vague and because Louisiana had infringed on an area of constitutionally protected expression. The part of Harlan's decision reprinted here deals directly with the sit-ins and their relationship to freedom of speech protection.

In 1963, the Supreme Court reversed a South Carolina court decision which had convicted 187 student civil rights demonstrators of breach of the peace and fined them from ten to one hundred dollars or five to thirty days in jail. After the South Carolina Supreme Court upheld the convictions, the students appealed to the United States Supreme Court, which held that "under the circumstances disclosed by this record, South Carolina infringed the petitioners' constitutionally protected rights of free speech, free assembly, and freedom to petition for redress of their grievances." Justice Clark dissented. The *Edwards* decision is reprinted here in its entirety.

In 1966, the Supreme Court handed down a decision in *Adderley v. Florida*. The majority of the justices voted to affirm the conviction of civil rights demonstrators, but four dissented. Chief Justice Warren and Justices Douglas, Brennan, and Fortas gave the First Amendment rights a preferred position and saw the majority as discarding *Edwards*. Clearly, the majority saw significant differences in *Edwards* and *Adderley*, the minority important similarities. The *Adderley* decision is reprinted here in its entirety.

GARNER *v.* LOUISIANA

368 U.S. 157 (1961)

MR. JUSTICE HARLAN, concurring.

.   .   .   .   .

Were there no more to these cases, I should have to vote to affirm. But in light of principles established by *Cantwell* v. *Connecticut*, 310 U.S. 296, and consistently since recognized, I think the convictions are subject to other constitutional infirmities.

At the outset it is important to focus on the precise factual situation in each of these cases. Common to all three are the circumstances that petitioners were given the invitation extended to the public at large to patronize these establishments: that they were told that they could be served food only at the Negro lunch counters; that their conduct was not unruly or offensive; and that none of them was ever asked by the owners or their agents to leave the establishments. While in *Briscoe*, No. 27, there was some very slight, but in my view constitutionally adequate, evidence that those petitioners were expressly asked "to move" from the "white" lunch counter, and undisputed evidence that they did not do so, in *Garner*, No. 26, and *Hoston*, No. 28, there was no evidence whatever of any express request to the petitioners in those cases that they move from the "white" lunch counters where they were sitting.

Nor do I think that any such request is fairly to be implied from the fact that petitioners were told by the management that they could not be served food at such counters. The premises in both instances housed merchandising establishments, a drugstore in *Garner*, a department store in *Hoston*, which solicited business from all comers to the stores. I think the reasonable inference is that the management did not want to risk losing Negro patronage in the stores by requesting these petitioners to leave the "white" lunch counters, preferring to rely on the hope that the irritations of white customers or the force of custom would drive them away from the counters. This view seems the more probable in circumstances when, as here, the "sitters'" behavior was entirely quiet and courteous, and, for all we know, the counters may have been only sparsely, if to any extent, occupied by white persons.

In short, I believe that in the *Garner* and *Hoston* cases the records should be taken as indicating that the petitioners remained at the "white" lunch counters with the implied consent of the management, even though a similar conclusion may not be warranted in the *Briscoe* case. Under these circumstances, applying principles announced in *Cantwell*, I would hold all these convictions offensive to the Fourteenth Amendment, in that: (1) in *Garner* and *Hoston* petitioners' conduct, occurring with the managements' implied consent, was a form of expression within the range of protections afforded by the Fourteenth Amendment which could in no event be punished by the State under a *general* breach of the peace statute; and (2) in *Briscoe*, while petitioners' "sitting," over the management's objection, cannot be deemed to be within the reach of such protections, their convictions must nonetheless fall because the Louisiana statute, as there applied (and *a fortiori* as applied in the other two cases), was unconstitutionally vague and uncertain.

In the Cantwell case a Jehovah's Witness had been convicted for breach of the peace under a Connecticut statute embracing what was considered to be the common-law concept of that offense.

> The facts which were held to support the conviction . . . were that he stopped two men in the street, asked, and received, permission to play a phonograph record, and played the record "Enemies," which attacked the religion and church of the two men, who were Catholics. Both were incensed by the contents of the record and were tempted to strike Cantwell [the defendant] unless he went away. On being told to be on his way he left their presence. There was no evidence that he was personally offensive or entered into any argument with those he interviewed. 310 U.S., at 302–303.

Accepting the determination of the state courts that although the defendant himself had not been disorderly or provocative, his conduct under Connecticut law nonetheless constituted a breach of the peace because of its tendency to inflame others, this Court reversed. Starting from the premise that the "fundamental concept of liberty embodied in [the Fourteenth] Amendment embraces the liberties guaranteed by the First Amendment," the Court found that the defendant's activities fell within the protection granted to the "free exercise" of religion. Then recognizing the danger to such liberties of "leaving to the executive and judicial branches too wide a discretion" in the application of a statute "sweeping in a great variety of conduct under a general and indefinite characterization," the Court held that the defendant's activities could not constitutionally be reached under a general breach of the peace statute, but only under one specifically and narrowly aimed at such conduct. 310 U.S., at 307–308. The Court stated:

> Although the contents of the [phonograph] record not unnaturally aroused animosity, we think that, in the absence of a statute narrowly drawn to define and punish specific conduct as constituting a clear and present danger to a substantial interest of the State, the petitioner's communication, considered in the light of the constitutional guarantees, raised no such clear and present menace to public peace and order as to render him liable to conviction of the common law offense in question. [Citing to such cases as *Schenck* v. *United States*, 249 U.S. 47.] 310 U.S., at 311.

I think these principles control the *Garner* and *Hoston* cases. There was more to the conduct of those petitioners than a bare desire to remain at the "white" lunch counter and their refusal of a police request to move from the counter. We would surely have to be blind not to recognize that petitioners were sitting at these counters, where they knew they would not be served, in order to demonstrate that their race was being segregated in dining facilities in this part of the country.

Such a demonstration, in the circumstances of these two cases, is as much a part of the "free trade in ideas," *Abrams* v. *United States*, 250 U.S. 616, 630 (Holmes, J., dissenting), as is verbal expression, more commonly thought of as "speech." It, like speech, appeals to good sense and to "the power of reason as applied through public discussion," *Whitney* v. *California*, 274 U.S. 357, 375 (Brandeis, J., concurring), just as much as, if not more than, a public oration delivered from a soapbox at a street corner. This Court has never limited the right to speak, a protected "liberty" under the Fourteenth Amendment, *Gitlow* v. *New York*, 268 U.S. 652, 666, to mere verbal expression. *Stromberg* v. *California*, 283 U.S. 359; *Thornhill* v. *Alabama*, 310 U.S. 88; *West Virginia State Board of Education* v. *Barnette*, 319

U.S. 624, 633–634. See also *N.A.A.C.P.* v. *Alabama*, 357 U.S. 449, 460. If the act of displaying a red flag as a symbol of opposition to organized government is a liberty encompassed within free speech as protected by the Fourteenth Amendment, *Stromberg* v. *California*, *supra*, the act of sitting at a privately owned lunch counter with the consent of the owner, as a demonstration of opposition to enforced segregation, is surely within the same range of protections. This is not to say, of course, that the Fourteenth Amendment reaches to demonstrations conducted on private property over the objection of the owner (as in *Briscoe*), just as it would surely not encompass verbal expression in a private home if the owner has not consented.

No one can deny the interest that a State has in preserving peace and harmony within its borders. Pursuant to this interest, a state legislature may enact a trespass statute, or a disturbance of the peace statute which either lists in detail the acts condemned by legitimate state policy or proscribes breaches of the peace generally, thus relating the offense to the already developed body of common law defining that crime. Or it may, as Louisiana has done, append to a specific enumeration in a breach of the peace statute a "catch-all" clause to provide for unforeseen but obviously disruptive and offensive behavior which cannot be justified, and which is not within the range of constitutional protection.

But when a State seeks to subject to criminal sanctions conduct which, except for a demonstrated paramount state interest, would be within the range of freedom of expression as assured by the Fourteenth Amendment, it cannot do so by means of a general and all-inclusive breach of the peace prohibition. It must bring the activity sought to be proscribed within the ambit of a statute or clause "narrowly drawn to define and punish specific conduct as constituting a clear and present danger to a substantial interest of the State." *Cantwell* v. *Connecticut, supra*, at 311; *Thornhill* v. *Alabama*, 310 U.S. 88, 105. And of course that interest must be a legitimate one. A State may not "suppress free communication of views, religious or other, under the guise of conserving desirable conditions." *Cantwell, supra,* at 308.

These limitations exist not because control of such activity is beyond the power of the State, but because sound constitutional principles demand of the state legislature that it focus on the nature of the otherwise "protected" conduct it is prohibiting, and that it then make a legislative judgment as to whether that conduct presents so clear and present a danger to the welfare of the community that it may legitimately be criminally proscribed.

The Louisiana Legislature made no such judgment before the petitioners in *Garner* and *Hoston* engaged in their "sit-in" activity. In light of the *Cantwell* case, whose reasoning of course cannot be deemed limited to "expression" taking place on the public streets, cf. *Terminiello v. Chicago*, 337 U.S. 1, *Niemotko v. Maryland*, 340 U.S. 268, 281 (concurring opinion), Louisiana could not, in my opinion, constitutionally reach those petitioners' conduct under subsection (7) — the "catch-all clause" — of its then existing disturbance of the peace statute. In so concluding, I intimate no view as to whether Louisiana could by a specifically drawn statute constitutionally proscribe conduct of the kind evinced in these two cases, or upon the constitutionality of the statute which the State has recently passed. I deal here only with these two cases, and the statute that is before us now.

IV

Finally, I believe that the principles of *Cantwell* lead to the conclusion that this general breach of the peace provision must also be deemed unconstitutional for vagueness and uncertainty, *as applied* in the circumstances of all these cases. As to *Garner* and *Hoston* this affords an alternative ground for reversal. As to *Briscoe*, where the evidence falls short of establishing that those petitioners remained at the "white" lunch counter with the express or implied consent of the owner (notes 4, 5, *supra*), I would rest reversal solely on this ground.[13]

While *Cantwell* was not explicitly founded on that premise, it seems to me implicit in the opinion that a statute which leaves the courts in uncertainty as to whether it was intended to reach otherwise constitutionally protected conduct must by the same token be deemed inadequate warning to a defendant that his conduct has been condemned by the State. See *Chaplinsky v. New Hampshire*, 315 U.S. 568, 573–574. Cf. *Winters v. New York*, 333 U.S. 507, 509–510; *Smith v. California*, 361 U.S. 147, 151; *Thompson v. City of Louisville*, 362 U.S. 199, 206. Such warning is, of course, a requirement of the Fourteenth Amendment. *Lanzetta v. New Jersey*, 306 U.S. 451, 453.

This conclusion finds added support in the cases requiring of state legislatures more specificity in statutes impinging on freedom of expression than might suffice for other criminal enactments. See *Winters* v. *New York, supra,* at 509–510; *Smith* v. *California, supra,* at 151; cf. *Herndon* v. *Lowry,* 301 U.S. 242, 261–264. To the extent that this Louisiana statute is explicit on the subject of expression it prohibits only that which is "unnecessarily loud, offensive, or insulting" or activity carried on "in a violent or tumultuous manner by any three or more persons" (note 1, *supra*). No charge was made or proved that petitioners' conduct met any of those criteria. Nor has the statute been elucidated in this respect before, or since, petitioners' conviction, by any decision of the Louisiana courts of which we have been advised. Cf. *Winters* v. *New York, supra,* at 514; *Terminiello* v. *Chicago,* 337 U.S. 1, 4. Lastly, it is worth observing that in *State* v. *Sanford* the Louisiana Supreme Court seriously questioned on the score of vagueness the validity of that earlier breach of the peace statute under the State Constitution, as there applied to conduct within the same range of constitutional protection.

In the absence of any Louisiana statute purporting to express the State's overriding interest in prohibting petitioners' conduct as a clear and present danger to the welfare of the community, peaceful demonstration on public streets, and on private property with the consent of the owner, was constitutionally protected as a form of expression. Louisiana's breach of the peace statute drew no distinct line between presumably constitutionally protected activity and the conduct of the petitioners in *Briscoe,* as a criminal trespass statute might have done. The fact that in *Briscoe,* unlike *Garner* and *Hoston,* the management did not consent to the petitioners' remaining at the "white" lunch counter does not serve to permit the application of this general breach of the peace statute to the conduct shown in that case. For the statute by its terms appears to be as applicable to "incidents fairly within the protection of the guarantee of free speech," *Winters* v. *New York, supra,* at 509, as to that which is not within the range of such protection. Hence such a law gives no warning as to what may fairly be deemed to be within its compass. See Note, 109 U. of Pa. L. Rev. 67, 75–76, 99–104 (1960).

For the foregoing reasons I dissent from the opinion of the Court, but join in the judgment.

EDWARDS v. SOUTH CAROLINA

372 U.S. 229 (1963)*

Mr. Justice Stewart delivered the opinion of the Court.

The petitioners, 187 in number, were convicted in a magistrate's court in Columbia, South Carolina, of the common-law crime of breach of the peace. Their convictions were ultimately affirmed by the South Carolina Supreme Court, 239 S.C. 339, 123 S.E. 2d 247. We granted certiorari, 369 U.S. 870, to consider the claim that these convictions cannot be squared with the Fourteenth Amendment of the United States Constitution.

There was no substantial conflict in the trial evidence. Late in the morning of March 2, 1961, the petitioners, high school and college students of the Negro race, met at the Zion Baptist Church in Columbia. From there, at about noon, they walked in separate groups of about 15 to the South Carolina State House grounds, an area of two city blocks open to the general public. Their purpose was "to submit a protest to the citizens of South Carolina, along with the Legislative Bodies of South Carolina, our feelings and our dissatisfaction with the present condition of discriminatory actions against Negroes, in general, and to let them know that we were dissatisfied and that we would like for the laws which prohibited Negro privileges in this State to be removed."

Already on the State House grounds when the petitioners arrived were 30 or more law enforcement officers, who had advance knowledge that the petitioners were coming. Each group of petitioners entered the grounds through a driveway and parking area known in the record as the "horseshoe." As they entered, they were told by the law enforcement officials that "they had a right, as a citizen, to go through the State House grounds, as any other citizen has, as long as they were peaceful." During the next half hour or 45 minutes, the petitioners, in the same small groups, walked single file or two abreast

* Footnotes and case citations have been deleted.

in an orderly way through the grounds, each group carrying placards bearing such messages as "I am proud to be a Negro" and "Down with segregation." During this time a crowd of some 200 to 300 onlookers had collected in the horseshoe area and on the adjacent sidewalks. There was no evidence to suggest that these onlookers were anything but curious, and no evidence at all of any threatening remarks, hostile gestures, or offensive language on the part of any member of the crowd. The City Manager testified that he recognized some of the onlookers, whom he did not identify, as "possible trouble makers," but his subsequent testimony made clear that nobody among the crowd actually caused or threatened any trouble. There was no obstruction of pedestrian or vehicular traffic within the State House grounds. No vehicle was prevented from entering or leaving the horseshoe area. Although vehicular traffic at a nearby street intersection was slowed down somewhat, an officer was dispatched to keep traffic moving. There were a number of bystanders on the public sidewalks adjacent to the State House grounds, but they all moved on when asked to do so, and there was no impediment of pedestrian traffic. Police protection at the scene was at all times sufficient to meet any foreseeable possibility of disorder.

In the situation and under the circumstances thus described, the police authorities advised the petitioners that they would be arrested if they did not disperse within 15 minutes. Instead of dispersing, the petitioners engaged in what the City Manager described as "boisterous," "loud," and "flamboyant" conduct, which, as his later testimony made clear, consisted of listening to a "religious harangue" by one of their leaders, and loudly singing "The Star Spangled Banner" and other patriotic and religious songs, while stamping their feet and clapping their hands. After 15 minutes had passed, the police arrested the petitioners and marched them off to jail.

Upon this evidence the state trial court convicted the petitioners of breach of the peace, and imposed sentences ranging from a $10 fine or five days in jail, to a $100 fine or 30 days in jail. In affirming the judgments, the Supreme Court of South Carolina said that under the law of that State the offense of breach of the peace "is not susceptible of exact definition," but that the "general definition of the offense" is as follows:

In general terms, a breach of the peace is a violation of public order, a disturbance of the public tranquility, by any act or conduct inciting to violence . . . , it includes any violation of any law enacted to preserve peace and good order. It may consist of an act of violence or an act likely to produce violence. It is not necessary that the peace be actually broken to lay the foundation for a prosecution for this offense. If what is done is unjustifiable and unlawful, tending with sufficient directness to break the peace, no more is required. Nor is actual personal violence an essential element in the offense. . . .

By peace, as used in the law in this connection, is meant the tranquility enjoyed by citizens of a municipality or community where good order reigns among its members, which is the natural right of all persons in political society. 239 S.C., at 343–344, 123 S. E. 2nd, at 249.

The petitioners contend that there was a complete absence of any evidence of the commission of this offense, and that they were thus denied one of the most basic elements of due process of law. *Thompson* v. *Louisville,* 362 U.S. 199; see *Garner* v. *Louisiana,* 368 U.S. 157; *Taylor* v. *Louisiana,* 370 U.S. 154. Whatever the merits of this contention, we need not pass upon it in the present case. The state courts have held that the petitioners' conduct constituted breach of the peace under state law, and we may accept their decision as binding upon us to that extent. But it nevertheless remains our duty in a case such as this to make an independent examination of the whole record. *Blackburn* v. *Alabama,* 361 U.S. 199, 205, n. 5; *Pennekamp* v. *Florida,* 328 U.S. 331, 335; *Fiske* v. *Kansas,* 274 U.S. 380, 385–386. And it is clear to us that in arresting, convicting, and punishing the petitioners under the circumstances disclosed by this record, South Carolina infringed the petitioners' constitutionally protected rights of free speech, free assembly, and freedom to petition for redress of their grievances.

It has long been established that these First Amendment freedoms are protected by the Fourteenth Amendment from invasion by the States. *Gitlow* v. *New York,* 268 U.S. 652; *Whitney* v. *California,* 274 U.S. 357; *Stromberg* v. *California,* 283 U.S. 359; *De Jonge* v. *Oregon,* 299 U.S. 353; *Cantwell* v. *Connecticut,* 310 U.S. 296. The circumstances in this case reflect an exercise of these basic constitutional rights in their most pristine and classic form. The petitioners felt aggrieved by laws of South Carolina which allegedly "prohibited Negro privileges in this State." They peaceably assembled at the site of the State Government and there peaceably expressed their grievances "to the citizens of South Carolina, along with the Legislative Bodies of South Carolina." Not until they were told by police officials that they must disperse on pain of arrest did they do more. Even then, they but sang patriotic and religious songs after one of their leaders had delivered a "religious harangue." There was no violence or threat of violence on their part, or on the part of any member of the crowd watching them. Police protection was "ample."

This, therefore, was a far cry from the situation in *Feiner* v. *New York*, 340 U.S. 315, where two policemen were faced with a crowd which was "pushing, shoving and milling around," *id.*, at 317, where at least one member of the crowd "threatened violence if the police did not act," *id.*, at 317, where "the crowd was pressing closer around petitioner and the officer," *id.*, at 318, and where "the speaker passes the bounds of argument or persuasion and undertakes incitement to riot." *Id.*, at 321. And the record is barren of any evidence of "fighting words." See *Chaplinsky* v. *New Hampshire*, 315 U.S. 568.

We do not review in this case criminal convictions resulting from the evenhanded application of a precise and narrowly drawn regulatory statute evincing a legislative judgment that certain specific conduct be limited or proscribed. If, for example, the petitioners had been convicted upon evidence that they had violated a law regulating traffic, or had disobeyed a law reasonably limiting the periods during which the State House grounds were open to the public, this would be a different case. See *Cantwell* v. *Connecticut*, 310 U.S. 296, 307–308; *Garner* v. *Louisiana*, 368 U.S. 157, 202 (concurring opinion). These petitioners were convicted of an offense so generalized as to be, in the words of the South Carolina Supreme Court, "not susceptible of exact definition." And they were convicted upon evidence which showed no more than that the opinions which they were peaceably expressing were sufficiently opposed to the views of the majority of the community to attract a crowd and necessitate police protection.

The Fourteenth Amendment does not permit a State to make criminal the peaceful expression of unpopular views. "[A] function of free speech under our system of government is to invite dispute. It may indeed best serve its high purpose when it induces a condition of unrest, creates dissatisfaction with conditions as they are, or even stirs people to anger. Speech is often provocative and challenging. It may strike at prejudices and preconceptions and have profound unsettling effects as it presses for acceptance of an idea. That is why freedom of speech . . . is . . . protected against censorship or punishment, unless shown likely to produce a clear and present danger of a serious substantive evil that rises far above public inconvenience, annoyance, or unrest. . . . There is no room under our Constitution for a more restrictive view. For the alternative would lead to standardization of ideas either by legislatures, courts, or dominant political or community groups." *Terminiello* v. *Chicago*, 337 U.S. 1, 4–5. As in the *Terminiello* case, the courts of South Carolina have defined a criminal offense so as to permit conviction of the petitioners if their speech "stirred people to anger, invited public dispute, or brought about a condition of unrest. A conviction resting on any of those grounds may not stand." *Id.*, at 5.

As Chief Justice Hughes wrote in *Stromberg* v. *California*,

> The maintenance of the opportunity for free political discussion to the end that government may be responsive to the will of the people and that changes may be obtained by lawful means, an opportunity essential to the security of the Republic, is a fundamental principle of our constitutional system. A statute which upon its face, and as authoritatively construed, is so vague and indefinite as to permit the punishment of the fair use of this opportunity is repugnant to the guaranty of liberty contained in the Fourteenth Amendment. . . . 283 U.S. 359, 369.

For these reasons we conclude that these criminal convictions cannot stand.

Reversed.

Mr. Justice Clark, dissenting.

The convictions of the petitioners, Negro high school and college students, for breach of the peace under South Carolina law are accepted by the Court "as binding upon us to that extent" but are held violative of "petitioners' constitutionally protected rights of free speech, free assembly, and freedom to petition for redress of their grievances." Petitioners, of course, had a right to peaceable assembly, to espouse their cause and to petition, but in my view the manner in which they exercised those rights was by no means the passive demonstration which this Court relates; rather, as the City Manager of Columbia testified, "a dangerous situation was really building up" which South Carolina's courts expressly found had created "an actual interference with traffic and an imminently threatened disturbance of the peace of the community." Since the Court does not attack the state courts' findings and accepts the convictions as "binding" to the extent that the petitioners' conduct constituted a breach of the peace, it is difficult for me to understand its understatement of the facts and reversal of the convictions.

The priceless character of First Amendment freedoms cannot be gainsaid, but it does not follow that they are absolutes immune from necessary state action reasonably designed for the protection of society. See *Cantwell* v. *Connecticut*, 310 U.S. 296, 304 (1940); *Schneider* v. *State*, 308 U.S. 147, 160 (1939). For that reason it is our duty to consider the context in which the arrests here were made. Certainly the city officials would be constitutionally prohibited from refusing petitioners access to the State House grounds merely because they disagreed with their views. See *Niemotko* v. *Maryland*, 340 U.S. 268 (1951). But here South Carolina's courts have found: "There is no indication whatever in this case that the acts of the police officers were taken as a subterfuge or excuse for the suppression of the appellants' views and opinions." It is undisputed that the city officials specifically granted petitioners permission to assemble, imposing only the requirement that they be "peaceful." Petitioners then gathered on the State House grounds, during a General Assembly session, in a large number of almost 200, marching and carrying placards with slogans such as "Down with segregation" and "You may jail our bodies but not our souls." Some of them were singing.

The activity continued for approximately 45 minutes, during the busy noon-hour period, while a crowd of some 300 persons congregated in front of the State House and around the area directly in front of its entrance, known as the "horseshoe," which was used for vehicular as well as pedestrian ingress and egress. During this time there were no efforts made by the city officials to hinder the petitioners in their rights of free speech and assembly; rather, the police directed their efforts to the traffic problems resulting from petitioners' activities. It was only after the large crowd had gathered, among which the City Manager and Chief of Police recognized potential troublemakers, and which together with the students had become massed on and around the "horseshoe" so closely that vehicular and pedestrian traffic was materially impeded, that any action against the petitioners was taken. Then the City Manager, in what both the state intermediate and Supreme Court found to be the utmost good faith, decided that danger to peace and safety was imminent. Even at this juncture no orders were issued by the City Manager for the police to break up the crowd, now about 500 persons, and no arrests were made. Instead, he approached the recognized leader of the petitioners and requested him to tell the various groups of petitioners to disperse within 15 minutes, failing which they would be arrested. Even though the City Manager might have been honestly mistaken as to the imminence of danger, this was certainly a reasonable request by the city's top executive officer in an effort to avoid a public brawl. But the response of petitioners and their leader was defiance rather than cooperation. The leader immediately moved from group to group among the students, delivering a "harangue" which, according to testimony in the record, "aroused [them] to a fever pitch causing this boisterousness, this singing and stomping."

For the next 15 minutes the petitioners sang "I Shall Not Be Moved" and various religious songs, stamped their feet, clapped their hands, and conducted what the South Carolina Supreme Court found to be a "noisy demonstration in defiance of [the dispersal] orders." 239 S.C. 339, 345, 123 S.E. 2d 247, 250. Ultimately, the petitioners were arrested, as they apparently planned from the beginning, and convicted on evidence the sufficiency of which the Court does not challenge. The question thus seems to me whether a State is constitutionally prohibited from enforcing laws to prevent breach of the peace in a situation where city officials in good faith believe, and the record shows, that disorder and violence are imminent, merely because the activities constituting that breach contain claimed elements of constitutionally protected speech and assembly. To me the answer under our cases is clearly in the negative.

Beginning, as did the South Carolina courts, with the premise that the petitioners were entitled to assemble and voice their dissatisfaction with segregation, the enlargement of constitutional protection for the conduct here is as fallacious as would be the conclusion that free speech necessarily includes the right to broadcast from a sound truck in the public streets. *Kovacs v. Cooper,* 336 U.S. 77 (1949). This Court said in *Thornhill v. Alabama,* 310 U.S. 88, 105 (1940), that "[t]he power and the duty of the State to take adequate steps to preserve the peace and to protect the privacy, the lives, and the property of its residents cannot be doubted." Significantly, in holding that the petitioner's picketing was constitutionally protected in that case the Court took pains to differentiate it from "picketing *en masse* or otherwise conducted which might occasion . . . imminent and aggravated danger . . . ." *Ibid.* Here the petitioners were permitted without hindrance to exercise their rights of free speech and assembly. Their arrests occurred only after a situation arose in which the law-enforcement officials on the scene considered that a dangerous disturbance was imminent. The County Court found that "[t]he evidence is clear that the officers were motivated solely by a proper concern for the preservation of order and the protection of the general welfare in the face of an actual interference with traffic and an imminently threatened disturbance of the peace of the community." In affirming, the South Carolina Supreme Court said the action of the police was "reasonable and motivated solely by a proper concern for the preservation of order and prevention of further interference with traffic upon the public streets and sidewalks." 239 S.C., at 345, 123 S.E. 2d, at 249–250.

In *Cantwell* v. *Connecticut, supra,* at 308, this Court recognized that "[w]hen clear and present danger of riot, disorder, interference with traffic upon the public streets, or other immediate threat to public safety, peace, or order, appears, the power of the State to prevent or punish is obvious." And in *Feiner* v. *New York,* 340 U.S. 315 (1951), we upheld a conviction for breach of the peace in a situation no more dangerous than that found here. There the demonstration was conducted by only one person and the crowd was limited to approximately 80, as compared with the present lineup of some 200 demonstrators and 300 onlookers. There the petitioner was "endeavoring to arouse the Negro people against the whites, urging that they rise up in arms and fight for equal rights." *Id.,* at 317. Only one person — in a city having an entirely different historical background — was exhorting adults. Here 200 youthful Negro demonstrators were being aroused to a "fever pitch" before a crowd of some 300 people who undoubtedly were hostile. Perhaps their speech was not so animated but in this setting their actions, their placards reading "You may jail our bodies but not our souls" and their chanting of "I Shall Not Be Moved," accompanied by stamping feet and clapping hands, created a much greater danger of riot and disorder. It is my belief that anyone conversant with the almost spontaneous combustion in some Southern communities in such a situation will agree that the City Manager's action may well have averted a major catastrophe.

The gravity of the danger here surely needs no further explication. The imminence of that danger has been emphasized at every stage of this proceeding, from the complaints charging that the demonstrations "tended directly to immediate violence" to the State Supreme Court's affirmance on the authority of *Feiner, supra.* This record, then, shows no steps backward from a standard of "clear and present danger." But to say that the police may not intervene until the riot has occurred is like keeping out the doctor until the patient dies. I cannot subscribe to such a doctrine. In the words of my Brother Frankfurter:

> This Court has often emphasized that in the exercise of our authority over state court decisions the Due Process Clause must not be construed in an abstract and doctrinaire way by disregarding local conditions. . . . It is pertinent, therefore, to note that all members of the New York Court accepted the finding that Feiner was stopped not because the listeners or police officers disagreed with his views but because these officers were honestly concerned with preventing a breach of the peace. . . .
>
> As was said in *Hague v. C. I. O., supra,* uncontrolled official suppression of the speaker "cannot be made a substitute for the duty to maintain order." 307 U.S. at 516. Where conduct is within the allowable limits of free speech, the police are peace officers for the speaker as well as for his hearers. But the power effectively to preserve order cannot be displaced by giving a speaker complete immunity. Here, there were two police officers present for 20 minutes. They interfered only when they apprehended imminence of violence. It is not a constitutional principle that, in acting to preserve order, the police must proceed against the crowd, whatever its size and temper, and not against the [demonstrators]. 340 U.S., at 288–289 (concurring opinion in *Feiner v. New York* and other cases decided that day).

I would affirm the convictions.

ADDERLEY v. FLORIDA

385 U.S. 39 (1966)*

MR. JUSTICE BLACK delivered the opinion of the Court.

Petitioners, Harriett Louise Adderley and 31 other persons, were convicted by a jury in a joint trial in the County Judge's Court of Leon County, Florida, on a charge of "trespass with a malicious and mischievous intent" upon the premises of the county jail contrary to § 821.18 of the Florida statutes set out below. Petitioners, apparently all students of the Florida A. & M. University in Tallahassee, had gone from the school to the jail about a mile away, along with many other students, to "demonstrate" at the jail their protests of arrests of other protesting students the day before, and perhaps to protest more generally against state and local policies and practices of racial segregation, including segregation of the jail. The county sheriff, legal custodian of the jail and jail grounds, tried to persuade the students to leave the jail grounds. When this did not work, he notified them that they must leave, that if they did not leave he would arrest them for trespassing, and that if they resisted he would charge them with that as well. Some of the students left but others, including petitioners, remained and they were arrested. On appeal the convictions were affirmed by the Florida Circuit Court and then by the Florida District Court of Appeal, 175 So. 2d 249. That being the highest state court to which they could appeal, petitioners applied to us for certiorari contending that, in view of petitioners' purpose to protest against jail and other segregation policies, their conviction denied them "rights of free speech, assembly, petition, due process of law and equal protection of the laws as guaranteed by the Fourteenth Amendment to the Constitution of the United States." On this "Question Presented" we granted certiorari. 382 U.S. 1023. Petitioners present their argument on this question in four separate points, and for convenience we deal with each of their points in the order in which they present them.

---

* Footnotes and case citations have been deleted.

I

Petitioners have insisted from the beginning of this case that it is controlled by and must be reversed because of our prior cases of *Edwards* v. *South Carolina*, 372 U.S. 229, and *Cox* v. *Louisiana*, 379 U.S. 536, 559. We cannot agree.

The *Edwards* case, like this one, did come up when a number of persons demonstrated on public property against their State's segregation policies. They also sang hymns and danced, as did the demonstrators in this case. But here the analogies to this case end. In *Edwards*, the demonstrators went to the South Carolina State Capitol grounds to protest. In this case they went to the jail. Traditionally, state capitol grounds are open to the public. Jails, built for security purposes, are not. The demonstrators at the South Carolina Capitol went in through a public driveway and as they entered they were told by state officials there that they had a right as citizens to go through the State House grounds as long as they were peaceful. Here the demonstrators entered the jail grounds through a driveway used only for jail purposes and without warning to or permission from the sheriff. More importantly, South Carolina sought to prosecute its State Capitol demonstrators by charging them with the common-law crime of breach of the peace. This Court in *Edwards* took pains to point out at length the indefinite, loose, and broad nature of this charge; indeed, this Court pointed out at p. 237 that the South Carolina Supreme Court had itself declared that the "breach of the peace" charge is "not susceptible of exact definition." South Carolina's power to prosecute, it was emphasized at p. 236, would have been different had the State proceeded under a "precise and narrowly drawn regulatory statute evincing a legislative judgment that certain specific conduct be limited or proscribed" such as, for example, "limiting the periods during which the State House grounds were open to the public. . . ." The South Carolina breach-of-the-peace statute was thus struck down as being so broad and all-embracing as to jeopardize speech, press, assembly and petition, under the constitutional doctrine enunciated in *Cantwell* v. *Connecticut*, 310 U.S. 296, 307–308, and followed in many subsequent cases. And it was on this same ground of vagueness that in *Cox* v. *Louisiana, supra,* at 551–552, the Louisiana breach-of-the-peace law used to prosecute Cox was invalidated.

The Florida trespass statute under which these petitioners were charged cannot be challenged on this ground.   It is aimed at conduct of one limited kind, that is, for one person or persons to trespass upon the property of another with a malicious and mischievous intent. There is no lack of notice in this law, nothing to entrap or fool the unwary.

Petitioners seem to argue that the Florida trespass law is void for vagueness because it requires a trespass to be "with a malicious and mischievous intent. . . ." But these words do not broaden the scope of trespass so as to make it cover a multitude of types of conduct as does the common-law breach-of-the-peace charge. On the contrary, these words narrow the scope of the offense. The trial court charged the jury as to their meaning and petitioners have not argued that this definition, set out below, is not a reasonable and clear definition of the terms. The use of these terms in the statute, instead of contributing to uncertainty and misunderstanding, actually makes its meaning more understandable and clear.

II

Petitioners in this Court invoke the doctrine of abatement announced by this Court in *Hamm v. City of Rock Hill*, 379 U.S. 306. But that holding was that the Civil Rights Act of 1964, 78 Stat. 241, which made it unlawful for places of public accommodation to deny service to any person because of race, effected an abatement of prosecutions of persons for seeking such services that arose prior to the passage of the Act. But this case in no way involves prosecution of petitioners for seeking service in establishments covered by the Act. It involves only an alleged trespass on jail grounds — a trespass which can be prosecuted regardless of the fact that it is the means of protesting segregation of establishments covered by the Act.

III

Petitioners next argue that "petty criminal statutes may not be used to violate minorities' constitutional rights." This of course is true but this abstract proposition gets us nowhere in deciding this case.

IV

Petitioners here contend that "Petitioners' convictions are based on a total lack of relevant evidence." If true, this would be a denial of due process under *Garner v. Louisiana,* 368 U.S. 157, and *Thompson v. City of Louisville,* 362 U.S. 199. Both in the petition for certiorari and in the brief on the merits petitioners state that their summary of the evidence "does not conflict with the facts contained in the Circuit Court's opinion" which was in effect affirmed by the District Court of Appeal. 175 So. 2d 249. That statement is correct and petitioners' summary of facts, as well as that of the Circuit Court, shows an abundance of facts to support the jury's verdict of guilty in this case.

In summary both these statements show testimony ample to prove this: Disturbed and upset by the arrest of their schoolmates the day before, a large number of Florida A. & M. students assembled on the school grounds and decided to march down to the county jail. Some apparently wanted to be put in jail too, along with the students already there. A group of around 200 marched from the school and arrived at the jail singing and clapping. They went directly to the jail-door entrance where they were met by a deputy sheriff, evidently surprised by their arrival. He asked them to move back, claiming they were blocking the entrance to the jail and fearing that they might attempt to enter the jail. They moved back part of the way, where they stood or sat, singing, clapping and dancing, on the jail driveway and on an adjacent grassy area upon the jail premises. This particular jail entrance and driveway were not normally used by the public, but by the sheriff's department for transporting prisoners to and from the courts several blocks away and by commercial concerns for servicing the jail. Even after their partial retreat, the demonstrators continued to block vehicular passage over this driveway up to the entrance of the jail. Someone called the sheriff who was at the moment apparently conferring with one of the state court judges about incidents connected with prior arrests for demonstrations. When the sheriff returned to the jail, he immediately inquired if all was safe inside the jail and was told it was. He then engaged in a conversation with two of the leaders. He told them that they were trespassing upon jail property and that he would give them 10 minutes to leave or he would arrest them. Neither of the leaders did anything to disperse the crowd, and one of them told the sheriff that they wanted to get arrested. A local minister talked with some of the demonstrators and told them not to enter the jail, because they could not arrest themselves, but just to remain where they were. After about 10 minutes, the sheriff, in a voice loud enough to be heard by all, told the demonstrators that he was the legal custodian of the jail and its premises, that they were trespassing on county property in violation of the law, that they should all leave forthwith or he would arrest them, and that if they attempted to resist arrest, he would charge them with that as a separate offense. Some of the group then left. Others, including all petitioners, did not leave. Some of them sat down. In a few minutes, realizing that the remaining demonstrators had no intention of leaving, the sheriff ordered his deputies to surround those remaining on jail premises and placed them, 107 demonstrators, under arrest. The sheriff unequivocally testified that he did not arrest any persons other than those who were on the jail premises. Of the three petitioners testifying, two insisted that they were arrested before they had a chance to leave, had they wanted to, and one testified that she did not intend to leave. The sheriff again explicitly testified that he did not arrest any person who was attempting to leave.

Under the foregoing testimony the jury was authorized to find that the State had proven every essential element of the crime, as it was defined by the state court. That interpretation is, of course, binding on us, leaving only the question of whether conviction of the state offense, thus defined, unconstitutionally deprives petitioners of their rights to freedom of speech, press, assembly or petition. We hold it does not. The sheriff, as jail custodian, had power, as the state courts have here held, to direct that this large crowd of people get off the grounds. There is not a shred of evidence in this record that this power was exercised, or that its exercise was sanctioned by the lower courts, because the sheriff objected to what was being sung or said by the demonstrators or because he disagreed with the objectives of their protest. The record reveals that he objected only to their presence on that part of the jail grounds reserved for jail uses. There is no evidence at all that on any other occasion had similarly large groups of the public been permitted to gather on this portion of the jail grounds for any purpose. Nothing in the Constitution of the United States prevents Florida from even-handed enforcement of its general trespass statute against those refusing to obey the sheriff's order to remove themselves from what amounted to the curtilage of the jailhouse. The State, no less than a private owner of property, has power to preserve the property under its control for the use to which it is lawfully dedicated. For this reason there is no merit to the petitioners' argument that they had a constitutional right to stay on the property, over the jail custodian's objections, because this "area chosen for the peaceful civil rights demonstration was not only 'reasonable' but also particularly appropriate. . . ." Such an argument has as its major unarticulated premise the assumption that people who want to propagandize protests or views have a constitutional right to do so whenever and however and wherever they please. That concept of constitutional law was vigorously and forthrightly rejected in two of the cases petitioners rely on, *Cox* v. *Louisiana, supra,* at 554–555 and 563–564. We reject it again. The United States Constitution does not forbid a State to control the use of its own property for its own lawful nondiscriminatory purpose.

These judgments are   *Affirmed.*

Mr. Justice Douglas, with whom The Chief Justice, Mr. Justice Brennan, and Mr. Justice Fortas concur, dissenting.

The First Amendment, applicable to the States by reason of the Fourteenth (*Edwards* v. *South Carolina,* 372 U.S. 229, 235), provides that "Congress shall make no law . . . abridging . . . the right of the people peaceably to assemble, and to petition the Government for a redress of grievances." These rights, along with religion, speech, and press, are preferred rights of the Constitution, made so by reason of that explicit guarantee and what Edmond Cahn in Confronting Injustice (1966) referred to as "The Firstness of the First Amendment." With all respect, therefore, the Court errs in treating the case as if it were an ordinary trespass case or an ordinary picketing case.

The jailhouse, like an executive mansion, a legislative chamber, a courthouse, or the statehouse itself (*Edwards* v. *South Carolina, supra*) is one of the seats of government, whether it be the Tower of London, the Bastille, or a small county jail. And when it houses political prisoners or those who many think are unjustly held, it is an obvious center for protest. The right to petition for the redress of grievances has an ancient history and is not limited to writing a letter or sending a telegram to a congressman; it is not confined to appearing before the local city council, or writing letters to the President or

Governor or Mayor. See *N. A. A. C. P.* v. *Button,* 371 U.S. 415, 429–431. Conventional methods of petitioning may be, and often have been, shut off to large groups of our citizens. Legislators may turn deaf ears; formal complaints may be routed endlessly through a bureaucratic maze; courts may let the wheels of justice grind very slowly. Those who do not control television and radio, those who cannot afford to advertise in newspapers or circulate elaborate pamphlets may have only a more limited type of access to public officials. Their methods should not be condemned as tactics of obstruction and harassment as long as the assembly and petition are peaceable, as these were.

There is no question that petitioners had as their purpose a protest against the arrest of Florida A. & M. students for trying to integrate public theatres. The sheriff's testimony indicates that he well understood the purpose of the rally. The petitioners who testified unequivocally stated that the group was protesting the arrests, and state and local policies of segregation, including segregation of the jail. This testimony was not contradicted or even questioned. The fact that no one gave a formal speech, that no elaborate handbills were distributed, and that the group was not laden with signs would seem to be immaterial. Such methods are not the *sine qua non* of petitioning for the redress of grievances. The group did sing "freedom" songs. And history shows that a song can be a powerful tool of protest. See *Cox* v. *Louisiana,* 379 U.S. 536, 546–548. There was no violence; no threat of violence; no attempted jail break; no storming of a prison; no plan or plot to do anything but protest. The evidence is uncontradicted that the petitioners' conduct did not upset the jailhouse routine; things went on as they normally would. None of the group entered the jail. Indeed, they moved back from the entrance as they were instructed. There was no shoving, no pushing, no disorder or threat of riot. It is said that some of the group blocked part of the driveway leading to the jail entrance. The chief jailer, to be sure, testified that vehicles would not have been able to use the driveway. Never did the students locate themselves so as to cause interference with persons or vehicles going to or coming from the jail. Indeed, it is undisputed that the sheriff and deputy sheriff, in separate cars, were able to drive up the driveway to the parking places near the entrance and that no one obstructed their path. Further, it is undisputed that the entrance to the jail was not blocked. And whenever the students were requested to move they did so. If there was congestion, the solution was a further request to move to the lawns or parking areas, not complete ejection and arrest. The claim is made that a tradesman waited inside the jail because some of the protestants were sitting around and leaning on his truck. The only evidence supporting such a conclusion is the testimony of a deputy sheriff that the tradesman "came to the door . . . and then did not leave." His remaining is just as consistent with a desire to satisfy his curiosity as it is with a restraint. Finally, the fact that some of the protestants may have felt their cause so just that they were willing to be arrested for making their protest outside the jail seems wholly irrelevant. A petition is nonetheless a petition, though its futility may make martyrdom attractive.

We do violence to the First Amendment when we permit this "petition for redress of grievances" to be turned into a trespass action. It does not help analogize this problem to the problem of picketing. Picketing is a form of protest usually directed against private interests. I do not see how rules governing picketing in general are relevant to this express constitutional right to assemble and to petition for redress of grievances. In the first place the jailhouse grounds were not marked with "NO TRESPASSING!" signs, nor does respondent claim that the public was generally excluded from the grounds. Only the sheriff's fiat transformed lawful conduct into an unlawful trespass. To say that a private owner could have done the same if the rally had taken place on private property is to speak of a different case, as an assembly and a petition for redress of grievances run to government, not to private proprietors.

The Court forgets that prior to this day our decisions have drastically limited the application of state statutes inhibiting the right to go peacefully on public property to exercise First Amendment rights. As Mr. Justice Roberts wrote in *Hague* v. *C. I. O.*, 307 U.S. 496, 515–516:

> Wherever the title of streets and parks may rest, they have immemorially been held in trust for the use of the public and, time out of mind, have been used for purposes of assembly, communicating thoughts between citizens, and discussing public questions. Such use of the streets and public places has, from ancient times, been a part of the privileges, immunities, rights, and liberties of citizens. The privilege of a citizen of the United States to use the streets and parks for communication of views on national questions may be regulated in the interest of all; it is not absolute, but relative, and must be exercised in subordination to the general comfort and convenience, and in con-

sonance with peace and good order; but it must not, in the guise of regulation, be abridged or denied.

Such was the case of *Edwards* v. *South Carolina,* where aggrieved people "peaceably assembled at the site of the State Government" to express their grievances to the citizens of the State as well as to the legislature. *Supra,* at 235. *Edwards* was in the tradition of *Cox* v. *New Hampshire,* 312 U.S. 569, where the public streets were said to be "immemorially associated" with "the right of assembly and the opportunities for the communication of thought and the discussion of public questions." *Id.,* at 574. When we allow Florida to construe her "malicious trespass" statute to bar a person from going on property knowing it is not his own and to apply that prohibition to public property, we discard *Cox* and *Edwards.* Would the case be any different if, as is common, the demonstration took place outside a building which housed both the jail and the legislative body? I think not.

There may be some public places which are so clearly committed to other purposes that their use for the airing of grievances is anomalous. There may be some instances in which assemblies and petitions for redress of grievances are not consistent with other necessary purposes of public property. A noisy meeting may be out of keeping with the serenity of the statehouse or the quiet of the courthouse. No one, for example, would suggest that the Senate gallery is the proper place for a vociferous protest rally. And in other cases it may be necessary to adjust the right to petition for redress of grievances to the other interests inhering in the uses to which the public property is normally put. See *Cox* v. *New Hampshire, supra; Poulos* v. *New Hampshire,* 345 U.S. 395. But this is quite different from saying that all public places are off limits to people with grievances. See *Hague* v. *C. I. O., supra; Cox* v. *New Hampshire, supra; Jamison* v. *Texas,* 318 U.S. 413, 415–416; *Edwards* v. *South Carolina, supra.* And it is farther yet from saying that the "custodian" of the public property in his discretion can decide when public places shall be used for the communication of ideas, especially the constitutional right to assemble and petition for redress of grievances. See *Hague* v. *C. I. O., supra; Schneider* v. *State,* 308 U.S. 147, 163–164; *Cantwell* v. *Connecticut,* 310 U.S. 296; *Largent* v. *Texas,* 318 U.S. 418; *Niemotko* v. *Maryland,* 340 U.S. 268; *Shuttlesworth* v. *City of Birmingham,* 382 U.S. 87. For to place such discretion in any public official, be he the "custodian" of the public property or the local police commissioner (cf. *Kunz* v. *New York,* 340 U.S. 290), is to place those who assert their First Amendment rights at his mercy. It gives him the awesome power to decide whose ideas may be expressed and who shall be denied a place to air their claims and petition their government. Such power is out of step with all our decisions prior to today where we have insisted that before a First Amendment right may be curtailed under the guise of a criminal law, any evil that may be collateral to the exercise of the right, must be isolated and defined in a "narrowly drawn" statute (*Cantwell* v. *Connecticut, supra,* at 307) lest the power to control excesses of conduct be used to suppress the constitutional right itself. See *Stromberg* v. *California,* 283 U.S. 359, 369; *Herndon* v. *Lowry,* 301 U.S. 242, 258–259; *Edwards* v. *South Carolina, supra,* at 238; *N. A. A. C. P.* v. *Button, supra,* at 433.

That tragic consequence happens today when a trespass law is used to bludgeon those who peacefully exercise a First Amendment right to protest to government against one of the most grievous of all modern oppressions which some of our States are inflicting on our citizens.

What we do today disregards the admonition in *De Jonge* v. *Oregon,* 299 U.S. 353, 364–365:

> These [First Amendment] rights may be abused by using speech or press or assembly in order to incite to violence and crime. The people through their legislatures may protect themselves against that abuse. But the legislative intervention can find constitutional justification only by dealing with the abuse. The rights themselves must not be curtailed. The greater the importance of safeguarding the community from incitements to the overthrow of our institutions by force and violence, the more imperative is the need to preserve inviolate the constitutional rights of free speech, free press and free assembly in order to maintain the opportunity for free political discussion, to the end that government may be responsive to the will of the people and that changes, if desired, may be obtained by peaceful means. Therein lies the security of the Republic, the very foundation of constitutional government.

Today a trespass law is used to penalize people for exercising a constitutional right. Tomorrow a disorderly conduct statute, a breach-of-the-peace statute, a vagrancy statute will be put to the same end. It is said that the sheriff did not make the arrests because of the views which petitioners espoused. That excuse is usually given, as we know from the many cases involving arrests of minority groups for breaches of the peace, unlawful assemblies, and parading without a permit. The charge against William Penn, who preached a nonconformist doctrine in a street in London, was that he caused "a great concourse and tumult of people" in contempt of the King and "to the great disturbance of his peace." 6 How. St. Tr. 951, 955. That was in 1670. In modern times, also, such arrests are usually sought to be justified by some legitimate function of government. Yet by allowing these orderly and civilized protests against injustice to be suppressed, we only increase the forces of frustration which the conditions of second-class citizenship are generating amongst us.

Freedom of Speech and Antiwar Protests

The involvement of the United States in the Vietnamese civil war brought with it antiwar protests which raised questions about the forms of dissent protected by the First Amendment. Demonstrations, draft card burnings, flag burnings, parades, petitions, and other persuasive means of communication were used by the protesters. The following decisions deal with questions of great national interest: Can students be reclassified from II-S to I-A for participating in antiwar protests? Is burning one's draft card an act of "symbolic speech" protected by the First Amendment?

Peter Wolff and Richard Shortt v. Selective Service Local Board No. 16, Selective Service Local Board No. 66, and Col. Paul Akst, individually and as Director of the New York City Headquarters Selective Service System is a 1967 United States Court of Appeals decision dealing with the reclassification of two students for their war protest activities. Although reluctant to bring any phase of the operation of the Selective Service under judicial scrutiny, the Court spoke of the preferred position of the First Amendment rights:

> Only the most weighty consideration could induce us to depart from this long-standing policy [of not interfering with the operations of the Selective Service System]. But of all constitutional rights, the freedoms of speech and of assembly are the most perishable, yet the most vital to the preservation of American democracy. Historically, these preferred and paramount rights have continually come under attack from the best intentioned sources.

Speaking directly to the free speech issue, the Court said:

> Here it is not relevant whether or not appellants will ever be inducted. The effect of the reclassification itself is immediately to cur-

tail the exercise of First Amendment rights, for there can be no doubt that the threat of receiving a I-A classification upon voicing dissent from our national policies has an immediate impact on the behavior of appellants and others similarly situated.

It had been held repeatedly that the mere threat of the imposition of unconstitutional sanctions will cause immediate and irreparable injury to the free exercise of rights as fragile and sensitive to suppression as the freedom of speech and assembly and the right to vote.

The United States District Court's decision appears here in its entirety.

In *United States* v. *O'Brien* (1968), the United States Supreme Court vacated the decision of the Court of Appeals for the First Circuit. It reinstated the judgment and sentence of the District Court of Massachusetts, which convicted David O'Brien of violating a part of the Selective Service Act by burning his Selective Service registration certificate in protest against the Selective Service System and United States participation in the war in Vietnam. Chief Justice Warren, speaking for the majority, again and again refers to "governmental interests" and "substantial Government interest," indicating the Court's reliance on the "balancing of interests" test. The following contention seems central to the Court's decision:

> We think it also apparent that the Nation has a vital interest in having a system for raising armies that functions with maximum efficiency and is capable of easily and quickly responding to continually changing circumstances. For these reasons, the Government has a substantial interest in assuring the continuing availability of issued Selective Service certificates.

Except for the footnotes, the Court's decision appears here in its entirety.

Peter Wolff and Richard Shortt v. Selective Service Local Board No. 16, Selective Service Local Board No. 66, and Col. Paul Akst, individually and as Director of the New York City Headquarters Selective Service System, 372 F.2d 817 (1967)*

MEDINA, CIRCUIT JUDGE:

Peter Wolff and Richard Shortt, registrants of Selective Service Boards No. 66 in Queens County and No. 16 in New York County were classified II-S because of their status as full-time students at the University of Michigan. On October 15, 1965 these students and others participated in a demonstration to protest American involvement in Vietnam, at the offices of a Selective Service local board in Ann Arbor, Michigan. At the request of the New York City Director of Selective Service the local boards reclassified the two students I-A. The request was based upon the assertion that by participating in the demonstration the students became "delinquents" by reason of their alleged violation of Section 12(a) of the Universal Military Training and Service Act. Claiming that the local boards acted wholly without jurisdiction and in violation of their First Amendment rights of free speech and assembly and of their Sixth Amendment rights as well, Wolff and Shortt brought this action against the local boards and the Director to bring about a return of their student deferments. On motion, based upon the allegations appearing on the face of the complaint, Judge McLean dismissed the action for lack of "a justiciable controversy" and Wolff and Shortt appeal.

We disagree. The two local boards did act without jurisdiction, the record shows that attempts to secure relief within the Selective Service System would be futile, and the threat to First Amendment rights is of

Peter Wolff and Richard Shortt v. *Selective Service Local Board No. 16, Selective Service Local Board No. 66, and Col. Paul Akst, individually and as Director of the New York City Headquarters Selective Service System.* 372 F. 2d 817 (1967). Reprinted by permission of the West Publishing Company.

* Footnotes and case citations have been deleted.

such immediate and irreparable consequences not simply to these students but to others as to require prompt action by the courts to avoid an erosion of these precious constitutional rights. Under this combination of circumstances an injunction could properly issue. But the question, whether the matter in controversy exceeds the value of $10,000 exclusive of interest and costs, not decided below, remains open and must be passed upon in due course.

I

Section 12 of the Act is a lengthy penal statute covering offenses committed by registrants and by members of local boards. Jurisdiction over these offenses is given to the United States District Courts. With respect to some of these offenses, however, such as the failure of any person knowingly to "fail to neglect or refuse to perform any duty required of him under or in execution of this title," to the extent that the statute affects registrants, the jurisdiction of the District Court is, in effect, concurrent with the administrative jurisdiction of the local boards. Thus a parallel clause of the regulations provides that if a registrant fails to produce certain requested information or to appear for questioning, he may under 32 CFR Section 1642.4(a) be declared a delinquent and classified or reclassified I-A. Also under Section 12 various draftees have been convicted in United States District Courts for failure to appear for induction. See *United States* v. *Mitchell*, 369 F.2d 323 (2 Cir. 1966) and *United States* v. *Hogans*, 369 F.2d 359 (2 Cir. 1966).

[1, 2] The conduct of these New York students, registrants in Local Boards Nos. 16 and 66 in participating in the demonstration in Michigan on October 15, 1965, could, as Judge McLean assumed, be claimed to fall under another provision of Section 12 which makes it a federal criminal offense for any person to "knowingly hinder or interfere or attempt to do so in any way, by force or violence or otherwise, with the administration of this title" and no regulation authorizes a draft board to declare a registrant a delinquent or to reclassify him for such action. As jurisdiction over offenses of this character is exclusively granted to the District Courts, we hold that the Local Boards lacked authority to decide that Wolff and Shortt were "delinquents" by reason of their violation of the terms of this portion of Section 12.

Accordingly, as these two students have never been indicted or tried or convicted of this offense in a District Court, the two Local Boards, appellees, exceeded their jurisdiction by reclassifying the two students I-A.

[3] There is nothing to prevent the prosecution of registrants or others for conduct by them in violation of either federal or state criminal laws, subject to such defenses as may be alleged and established. What we hold in this case is that it is not the function of local boards in the Selective Service System to punish these registrants by reclassifying them I-A because they protested as they did over the Government's involvement in Vietnam.

II

Despite the foregoing, the Government takes the position that the District Court properly concluded that it lacked the power to proceed in this matter and that the dismissal of the complaint may be affirmed on several grounds.

[4–6] Irrespective of the existence of the power to do so, the courts, and particularly this Court, have been extremely reluctant to bring any phase of the operation of the Selective Service System under judicial scrutiny. The very nature of the Service demands that it operate with maximum efficiency, unimpeded by external interference. Only the most weighty consideration could induce us to depart from this long-standing policy. But of all constitutional rights, the freedoms of speech and of assembly are the most perishable, yet the most vital to the preservation of American democracy. Historically, these preferred and paramount rights have continually come under attack from the best intentioned sources. And once the erosion of these rights is permitted to begin, it is exceedingly difficult to halt and the intervening damage may be irreparable. Here it is the free expression of views on issues of critical current national importance that is jeopardized. On such topics perhaps more than any other, it is imperative that the public debate be full and that each segment of our society be permitted freely to express its views. Thus the allegations of the complaint in this case that the draft boards have unlawfully suppressed criticism must take precedence over the policy of nonintervention in the affairs of the Selective Service.

We turn, then, to the arguments of the Government that the District Court lacks the power to pass upon the issues.

A. Subject Matter Jurisdiction

[7, 8]   Appellants have invoked the general federal question of jurisdiction of the District Court under 28 U.S.C. § 1331. As the controversy involves the alleged violation of rights arising out of the Federal Constitution and federal statutes, appellants' view must be correct unless some federal statute other than Section 1331 makes an exception in matters affecting the administration of the Selective Service Act. We are told that 50 U.S.C. App. § 460(b) (3) which provides that "the decisions of such local board shall be final" is such a statute. But it is difficult to understand how the Government can so argue at this date in the light of the express rejection of such a construction of Section 460(b) (3) in *Estep* v. *United States,* 327 U.S. 114, 66 S.Ct. 423, 90 L.Ed. 567 (1946). In that case the Supreme Court noted that the "authority of the local boards" is "circumscribed both by the Act and by the regulations" and is "limited to action 'within their respective jurisdictions.'" Thus the Court concluded that "it is only orders 'within their respective jurisdictions' that are made final." 327 U.S. at 120, 66 S.Ct. at 426. Regarding Section 460 the Court explained:

> The provision making the decisions of the local boards "final" means to us that Congress chose not to give administrative action under this Act the customary scope of judicial review which obtains under other statutes. It means that the courts are not to weigh the evidence to determine whether the classification made by the local boards was justified. The decisions of the local boards made in conformity with the regulations are final even though they may be erroneous. The question of jurisdiction of the local board is reached only if there is no basis in fact for the classification which it gave the registrant. 327 U.S. at 122–123, 66 S.Ct. at 427.

The Government concedes, of course, that the courts have jurisdiction to review classification orders in criminal prosecutions or in an appropriate habeas corpus proceeding but it asserts that the courts lack the "power" to inquire into classifications at an earlier point. All of which seems to us to admit jurisdiction over subject matter and affect merely a quite different point, namely the presence of a justiciable controversy, a subject to which we shall now direct our attention.

B. *Justiciability*

[9–11] The Government further argues that this case is not ripe for adjudication because appellants have failed to exhaust their administrative remedies and because they cannot demonstrate irreparable injury. The courts ordinarily will not adjudicate a matter which may become moot through subsequent action by the executive. Nor will the courts hear a cause when the action complained of has not caused or is not certain to cause injury to the complaining party. In other words, a federal court cannot render an advisory opinion.

[12–15] Thus in the usual run of Selective Service cases, the registrant must wait until he receives an induction order, and has either obeyed it or is prosecuted for refusing to obey it, before the courts may review his classification. This is so because, in nearly all cases, it is service in the armed forces itself, and not the mere classification, that constitutes the alleged injury. Thus, should it develop that for independent reasons such as physical disability the registrant is not actually wanted by the armed forces, he will never have sustained a legally redressible injury. Perhaps it is true that a mere adverse classification will cause a disarray of plans and emotional upset but this is an acceptable price to pay for the efficient functioning of the Selective Service and it has been universally held that such injury is not sufficient to entitle a registrant to preinduction order relief.

But, while the general run of cases do not present a justiciable controversy, it does not follow that no case can. Here it is not relevant whether or not appellants will ever be inducted. The effect of the reclassification itself is immediately to curtail the exercise of First Amendment rights, for there can be no doubt that the threat of receiving a I-A classification upon voicing dissent from our national policies has an immediate impact on the behavior of appellants and others similarly situated.

[16, 17] It has been held repeatedly that the mere threat of the imposition of unconstitutional sanctions will cause immediate and irreparable injury to the free exercise of rights as fragile and sensitive to suppression as the freedoms of speech and assembly and the right to

vote. *Baggett* v. *Bullitt*, 377 U.S. 360, 84 S.Ct. 1316, 12 L.Ed.2d 377 (1964); *NAACP* v. *Button*, 371 U.S. 415, 83 S.Ct. 328, 9 L.Ed.2d 405 (1963); *Smith* v. *People of State of California*, 361 U.S. 147, 80 S.Ct. 215, 4 L.Ed.2d 205 (1959). Since it is the mere threat of unconstitutional sanctions which precipitates the injury, the courts must intervene at once to vindicate the threatened liberties.

Dombrowski v. *Pfister*, 380 U.S. 479, 85 S.Ct. 1116, 14 L.Ed.2d 22 (1965), is very much in point. There a civil rights organization sought an injunction against various state officials against the threatened enforcement of a Subversives Control Law. It was alleged that the prosecution was being conducted without any real expectation of success and was in fact a deliberate harassment of the plaintiff. A three-judge District Court dismissed the complaint on the ground that there had been no showing of irreparable injury to federal rights and that the case was a proper one for abstention. Quite similarly to our case, the Supreme Court allowed that the inconveniences which normally accompany a prosecution were insufficient to invoke federal court intervention and that the rights of the appellants could ultimately be vindicated through the normal procedures. Nevertheless, the Court reversed the District Court and held, first, that irreparable injury had been alleged and, second, that abstention was not appropriate. Regarding the first point, the Court said:

> [T]he allegations in this complaint depict a situation in which defense of the State's criminal prosecution will not assure adequate vindication of constitutional rights. They suggest that a substantial loss or impairment of freedoms of expression will occur if appellants must await the state court's disposition and ultimate review in this Court of any adverse determination. These allegations, if true, clearly show irreparable injury.

[18]   Moreover, the decision of the Supreme Court in *Cameron* v. *Johnson*, 381 U.S. 741, 85 S.Ct. 1751, 14 L.Ed.2d 715 (1965), wherein the District Court had found the statute in question not void on its face, makes it clear that the *Dombrowski* rationale is not to be limited to statutes which are unconstitutional per se. Certainly the justiciability of a given case cannot rest upon a distinction between a statute void on its face and a statute which is being applied in an unconstitutional fashion, for the chilling effect of the illegal Government action is equally great.

Similarly in *United States* v. *Wood*, 295 F.2d 772 (5 Cir. 1961), the federal government secured an injunction under the Civil Rights Act of 1957 against a state criminal prosecution. The Government successfully contended that the mere threat of this prosecution so interfered with the exercise of basic constitutional rights that a legally cognizable injury had resulted.

Here the injury caused by the threatened impairment of appellants' constitutional rights is magnified by the uncertainty as to the standard which the Service has applied. As there is no statute or regulation to guide the local boards, the registrant cannot know whether sit-ins alone will be deemed a basis for reclassification or whether sidewalk demonstrations or even more remote conduct are to be included. See Note, Federal-Question Abstention, 80 Harv.L.Rev. 604, 613 (1967).

[19, 20]   Where basic constitutional rights are imperiled, the courts have not required a series of injured parties to litigate the permissible scope of the statute or administrative interpretation but have nullified the unconstitutional action and required the Government to start in the first instance with a statute or interpretation that will not so overhang free expression that the legitimate exercise of constitutionally protected rights is suppressed. See also *NAACP* v. *Button, supra; United States* v. *Raines*, 362 U.S. 17, 80 S.Ct. 519, 4 L.Ed.2d 524 (1960); *Winters* v. *People of State of New York*, 333 U.S. 507, 68 S.Ct. 665, 92 L.Ed. 840 (1948). In our case intervention is especially appropriate because for reasons independent of the First Amendment the entire course of conduct of the appellee boards is illegal and cannot be saved by any amount of narrowing construction.

C. *Exhaustion of Administrative Remedies*

[21, 22]   Normally it is desirable not only that the administration function with a minimum of judicial interference but also that, when the administration does err, it be free to work out its own problems. But, as noted above, there are competing policies and when as here a serious threat to the exercise of First Amendment rights exists, the policy favoring the preservation of these rights must prevail.

[23]   Furthermore, the narrow facts presented on this appeal show clearly that no purpose would be served by relegating appellants to their administrative remedies.

Appellants were part of a larger group of demonstrators. Some of appellants' companions were similarly reclassified I-A and have completed their appeals within the administration. The national appeal board has concluded unanimously that the reclassifications were valid and, further, the National Director of the Selective Service has stated repeatedly that the reclassifications were proper. There are no facts which have been brought to our attention which would lead to a contrary result in appellants' case and we are most reluctant in a case of this importance to require appellants to proceed along the same futile path that others have trod before.

[24] When there is nothing to be gained from the exhaustion of administrative remedies and the harm from the continued existence of the administrative ruling is great, the courts have not been reluctant to discard this doctrine. See *McCulloch* v. *Sociedad Nacional*, 372 U.S. 10, 83 S.Ct. 671, 9 L.Ed.2d 547 (1963); *Leedom* v. *Kyne*, 358 U.S. 184, 79 S.Ct. 180, 3 L.Ed.2d 210 (1958); *Lichter* v. *United States*, 334 U.S. 742, 68 S.Ct. 1294, 92 L.Ed. 1694 (1948); *Glover* v. *United States*, 286 F.2d 84 (8 Cir. 1961); *Bullard Co.* v. *N. L. R. B.*, 253 F.Supp. 391 (D.D.C.1966).

III

We are well aware that many reported cases contain language, often by way of dictum, as in *Witmer* v. *United States*, 348 U.S. 375, 75 S.Ct. 392, 99 L.Ed. 428 (1955), relied upon below, to the general effect that the review of classification orders is possible only in criminal proceedings or on habeas corpus petitions. But we have discovered no case which contained the allegation that the classification by the board had the immediate effect of depriving the registrant of his First Amendment rights. Nor, in fact, have we discovered any case in which the board exceeded its jurisdiction as clearly as did the appellee boards in this case.

Wholly aside from the First Amendment considerations which we believe compel our intervention at this time, it has in the past been suggested that when a local board acts in flagrant disregard of the applicable regulations and thus in clear excess of its jurisdiction, the courts may intervene at any time to rectify the situation. Thus in *Schwartz* v. *Strauss*, 206 F.2d 767 (2 Cir. 1953), Judge Frank remarked that he had no doubt that a court would have jurisdiction to review a classification where on undisputed facts the board's lack of jurisdiction was manifest. On the merits, however, he found that the board had acted properly as a matter of law. And in *Townsend* v. *Zimmerman*, 237 F.2d 376 (6 Cir. 1956), Judge Stewart, now Justice Stewart, enjoined a threatened induction when it appeared clearly as a matter of law that the board had violated the regulations in issuing its order.

IV

[25]   Because Judge McLean was of the opinion that this suit was not presently justiciable, he had no occasion to determine whether or not appellants could demonstrate the presence of the requisite amount in controversy. It is an unfortunate gap in the statutory jurisdiction of the federal courts that our ability to hear a suit of this nature depends on whether appellants can satisfactorily show injury in the amount of $10,000 but the fact remains and on remand the District Court must determine this question.

Reversed.

UNITED STATES *v.* O'BRIEN

391 U.S. 367 (1968)

MR. CHIEF JUSTICE WARREN delivered the opinion of the Court.

On the morning of March 31, 1966, David Paul O'Brien and three companions burned their Selective Service registration certificates on the steps of the South Boston Courthouse. A sizable crowd, including several agents of the Federal Bureau of Investigation, witnessed the event. Immediately after the burning, members of the crowd began attacking O'Brien and his companions. An FBI agent ushered O'Brien to safety inside the courthouse. After he was advised of his right to counsel and to silence, O'Brien stated to FBI agents that he had burned his registration certificate because of his beliefs, knowing that he was violating federal law. He produced the charred remains of the certificate, which, with his consent, were photographed.

For this act, O'Brien was indicted, tried, convicted, and sentenced in the United States District Court for the District of Massachusetts. He did not contest the fact that he had burned the certificate. He stated in argument to the jury that he burned the certificate publicly to influence others to adopt his antiwar beliefs, as he put it, "so that other people would reevaluate their positions with Selective Service, with the armed forces, and reevaluate their place in the culture of today, to hopefully consider my position."

The indictment upon which he was tried charged that he "willfully and knowingly did mutilate, destroy, and change by burning . . . [his] Registration Certificate (Selective Service System Form No. 2); in violation of Title 50, App., United States Code, Section 462(b)." Section 462(b) is part of the Universal Military Training and Service Act of 1948. Section 462(b)(3), one of six numbered subdivisions of § 462 (b), was amended by Congress in 1965, 79 Stat. 586 (adding the words italicized below), so that at the time O'Brien burned his certificate an offense was committed by any person,

who forges, alters, *knowingly destroys, knowingly mutilates,* or in any manner changes any such certificate . . . [italics supplied].

In the District Court, O'Brien argued that the 1965 Amendment prohibiting the knowing destruction or mutilation of certificates was unconstitutional because it was enacted to abridge free speech, and because it served no legitimate legislative purpose. The District Court rejected these arguments, holding that the statute on its face did not abridge First Amendment rights, that the court was not competent to inquire into the motives of Congress in enacting the 1965 Amendment, and that the Amendment was a reasonable exercise of the power of Congress to raise armies.

On appeal, the Court of Appeals for the First Circuit held the 1965 Amendment unconstitutional as a law abridging freedom of speech. At the time the Amendment was enacted, a regulation of the Selective Service System required registrants to keep their registration certificates in their "personal possession at all times." 32 CFR § 1617.1 (1962). Wilful violations of regulations promulgated pursuant to the Universal Military Training and Service Act were made criminal by statute. 50 U. S. C. App. § 462(b)(6). The Court of Appeals, therefore, was of the opinion that conduct punishable under the 1965 Amendment was already punishable under the nonpossession regulation, and consequently that the Amendment served no valid purpose; further, that in light of the prior regulation, the Amendment must have been "directed at public as distinguished from private destruction." On this basis, the court concluded that the 1965 Amendment ran afoul of the First Amendment by singling out persons engaged in protests for special treatment. The court ruled, however, that O'Brien's conviction should be affirmed under the statutory provision, 50 U. S. C. App. § 462(b)(6), which in its view made violation of the nonpossession regulation a crime, because it regarded such violation to be a lesser included offense of the crime defined by the 1965 Amendment.

The Government petitioned for certiorari, in No. 232, arguing that the Court of Appeals erred in holding the statute unconstitutional, and that its decision conflicted with decisions by the Courts of Appeals for the Second and Eighth Circuits upholding the 1965 Amendment against identical constitutional challenges. O'Brien cross-petitioned for certiorari, in No. 233, arguing that the Court of Appeals erred in sustaining his conviction on the basis of a crime which he was neither charged nor tried. We granted the Government's petition to resolve the conflict in the circuits, and we also granted O'Brien's cross-petition. We hold that the 1965 Amendment is constitutional both as enacted and as applied. We therefore vacate the judgment of the Court of Appeals and reinstate the judgment and sentence of the District Court without reaching the issue raised by O'Brien in No. 233.

I

When a male reaches the age of 18, he is required by the Universal Military Training and Service Act to register with a local draft board. He is assigned a Selective Service number, and within five days he is issued a registration certificate (SSS Form No. 2). Subsequently, and based on a questionnaire completed by the registrant, he is assigned a classification denoting his eligibility for induction, and "[a]s soon as practicable" thereafter he is issued a Notice of Classification (SSS Form No. 110). This initial classification is not necessarily permanent, and if in the interim before induction the registrant's status changes in some relevant way, he may be reclassified. After such a reclassification, the local board "as soon as practicable" issues to the registrant a new Notice of Classification.

Both the registration and classification certificates are small white cards, approximately 2 by 3 inches. The registration certificate specifies the name of the registrant, the date of registration, and the number and address of the local board with which he is registered. Also inscribed upon it are the date and place of the registrant's birth, his residence at registration, his physical description, his signature, and his Selective Service number. The Selective Service number itself indicates his State of registration, his local board, his year of birth, and his chronological position in the local board's classification record.

The classification certificate shows the registrant's name, Selective Service number, signature, and eligibility classification. It specifies whether he was so classified by his local board, an appeal board, or the President. It contains the address of his local board and the date the certificate was mailed.

Both the registration and classification certificates bear notices that the registrant must notify his local board in writing of every change in address, physical condition, and occupational, marital, family, dependency, and military status, and of any other fact which might change his classification. Both also contain a notice that the registrant's Selective Service number should appear on all communications to his local board.

Congress demonstrated its concern that certificates issued by the Selective Service System might be abused well before the 1965 Amendment here challenged. The 1948 Act, 62 Stat. 604, itself prohibited many different abuses involving "any registration certificate, ... or any other certificate issued pursuant to or prescribed by the provisions of this title, or rules or regulations promulgated hereunder. ..." 62 Stat. 622. Under §§ 12(b)(1)–(5) of the 1948 Act, it was unlawful (1) to transfer a certificate to aid a person in making false identification; (2) to possess a certificate not duly issued with the intent of using it for false identification; (3) to forge, alter, "or in any manner" change a certificate or any notation validly inscribed thereon; (4) to photograph or make an imitation of a certificate for the purpose of false identification; and (5) to possess a counterfeited or altered certificate. 62 Stat. 622. In addition, as previously mentioned, regulations of the Selective Service System required registrants to keep both their registration and classification certificates in their personal possession at all times. 32 CFR § 1617.1 (1962) (Registration Certificates); 32 CFR § 1623.5 (1962) (Classification Certificates). And § 12(b)(6) of the Act, 62 Stat. 622, made knowing violation of any provision of the Act or rules and regulations promulgated pursuant thereto a felony.

By the 1965 Amendment, Congress added to § 12(b)(3) of the 1948 Act the provision here at issue, subjecting to criminal liability not only one who "forges, alters, or in any manner changes" but also one who "knowingly destroys, [or] knowingly mutilates" a certificate. We note at the outset that the 1965 Amendment plainly does not abridge free speech on its face, and we do not understand O'Brien to argue otherwise. Amended § 12(b)(3) on its face deals with conduct having no connection with speech. It prohibits the knowing destruction of certificates issued by the Selective Service System, and there is nothing necessarily expressive about such conduct. The Amendment does not distinguish between public or private destruction, and it does not punish only destruction engaged in for the purpose of expressing views. Compare *Stromberg* v. *California*, 283 U.S. 359 (1931). A law prohibiting destruction of Selective Service certificates no more abridges free speech on its face than a motor vehicle law prohibiting the destruction of drivers' licenses, or a tax law prohibiting the destruction of books and records.

O'Brien nonetheless argues that the 1965 Amendment is unconstitutional in its application to him, and is unconstitutional as enacted because what he calls the "purpose" of Congress was "to suppress freedom of speech." We consider these arguments separately.

II

O'Brien first argues that the 1965 Amendment is unconstitutional as applied to him because his act of burning his registration certificate was protected "symbolic speech" within the First Amendment. His argument is that the freedom of expression which the First Amendment guarantees includes all modes of "communication of ideas by conduct," and that his conduct is within this definition because he did it in "demonstration against the war and against the draft."

We cannot accept the view that an apparently limitless variety of conduct can be labeled "speech" whenever the person engaging in the conduct intends thereby to express an idea. However, even on the assumption that the alleged communicative element in O'Brien's conduct is sufficient to bring into play the First Amendment, it does not necessarily follow that the destruction of a registration certificate is constitutionally protected activity. This Court has held that when "speech" and "nonspeech" elements are combined in the same course of conduct, a sufficiently important governmental interest in regulating the nonspeech element can justify incidental limitations on First Amendment freedoms. To characterize the quality of the governmental interest which must appear, the Court has employed a variety of descriptive terms: compelling; substantial; subordinating; paramount; cogent; strong. Whatever imprecision inheres in these terms, we think it clear that a government regulation is sufficiently justified if it is within the constitutional power of the Government; if it furthers an important or substantial governmental interest; if the governmental interest is unrelated to the suppression of free expression; and if the incidental restriction of alleged First Amendment freedom is no greater than is essential to the furtherance of that interest. We find that the 1965 Amendment of § 12(b)(3) of the Universal Military Training and Service Act meets all of these requirements, and consequently that O'Brien can be constitutionally convicted for violating it.

The constitutional power of Congress to raise and support armies and to make all laws necessary and proper to that end is broad and sweeping. *Lichter* v. *United States,* 334 U.S. 742, 755–758 (1948); *Selective Draft Law Cases,* 245 U.S. 366 (1918); see also *Ex parte Quirin,* 317 U.S. 1, 25–26 (1942). The power of Congress to classify and conscript manpower for military service is "beyond question." *Lichter* v. *United States, supra,* at 756; *Selective Draft Law Cases, supra.* Pursuant to this power, Congress may establish a system of registration for individuals liable for training and service, and may require such individuals within reason to cooperate in the registration system. The issuance of certificates indicating the registration and eligibility classification of individuals is a legitimate and substantial administrative aid in the functioning of this system. And legislation to insure the continuing availability of issued certificates serves a legitimate and substantial purpose in the system's administration.

O'Brien's argument to the contrary is necessarily premised upon his unrealistic characterization of Selective Service certificates. He essentially adopts the position that such certificates are so many pieces of paper designed to notify registrants of their registration or classification, to be retained or tossed in the wastebasket according to the convenience or taste of the registrant. Once the registrant has received notification, according to this view, there is no reason for him to retain the certificates. O'Brien notes that most of the information on a registration certificate serves no notification purpose at all; the registrant hardly needs to be told his address and physical characteristics. We agree that the registration certificate contains much information of which the registrant needs no notification. This circumstance, however, leads not to the conclusion that the certificate serves no purpose but that, like the classification certificate, it serves purposes in addition to initial notification. Many of these purposes would be defeated by the certificates' destruction or mutilation. Among these are:

1. The registration certificate serves as proof that the individual described thereon has registered for the draft. The classification certificate shows the eligibility classification of a named but undescribed individual. Voluntarily displaying the two certificates is an easy and painless way for a young man to dispel a question as to whether he

might be delinquent in his Selective Service obligations. Correspondingly, the availability of the certificates for such display relieves the Selective Service System of the administrative burden it would otherwise have in verifying the registration and classification of all suspected delinquents. Further, since both certificates are in the nature of "receipts" attesting that the registrant has done what the law requires, it is in the interest of the just and efficient administration of the system that they be continually available, in the event, for example, of a mix-up in the registrant's file. Additionally, in a time of national crisis, reasonable availability to each registrant of the two small cards assures a rapid and uncomplicated means for determining his fitness for immediate induction, no matter how distant in our mobile society he may be from his local board.

2. The information supplied on the certificates facilitates communication between registrants and local boards, simplifying the system and benefiting all concerned. To begin with, each certificate bears the address of the registrant's local board, an item unlikely to be committed to memory. Further, each card bears the registrant's Selective Service number, and a registrant who has his number readily available so that he can communicate it to his local board when he supplies or requests information can make simpler the board's task in locating his file. Finally, a registrant's inquiry, particularly through a local board other than his own, concerning his eligibility status is frequently answerable simply on the basis of his classification certificate; whereas, if the certificate were not reasonably available and the registrant were uncertain of his classification, the task of answering his questions would be considerably complicated.

3. Both certificates carry continual reminders that the registrant must notify his local board of any change of address, and other specified changes in his status. The smooth functioning of the system requires that local boards be continually aware of the status and whereabouts of registrants, and the destruction of certificates deprives the system of a potentially useful notice device.

4. The regulatory scheme involving Selective Service certificates includes clearly valid prohibitions against the alteration, forgery, or similar deceptive misuse of certificates. The destruction or mutilation of certificates obviously increases the difficulty of detecting and tracing abuses such as these. Further, a mutilated certificate might itself be used for deceptive purposes.

The many functions performed by Selective Service certificates establish beyond doubt that Congress has a legitimate and substantial interest in preventing their wanton and unrestrained destruction and assuring their continuing availability by punishing people who knowingly and wilfully destroy or mutilate them. And we are unpersuaded that the pre-existence of the nonpossession regulations in any way negates this interest.

In the absence of a question as to multiple punishment, it has never been suggested that there is anything improper in Congress' providing alternative statutory avenues of prosecution to assure the effective protection of one and the same interest. Compare the majority and dissenting opinions in *Gore* v. *United States,* 357 U.S. 386 (1958). Here, the preexisting avenue of prosecution was not even statutory. Regulations may be modified or revoked from time to time by administrative discretion. Certainly, the Congress may change or supplement a regulation.

Equally important, a comparison of the regulations with the 1965 Amendment indicates that they protect overlapping but not identical governmental interests, and that they reach somewhat different classes of wrongdoers. The gravamen of the offense defined by the statute is the deliberate rendering of certificates unavailable for the various purposes which they may serve. Whether registrants keep their certificates in their personal possession at all times, as required by the regulations, is of no particular concern under the 1965 Amendment, as long as they do not mutilate or destroy the certificates so as to render them unavailable. Although as we note below we are not concerned here with the nonpossession regulations, it is not inappropriate to observe that the essential elements of nonpossession are not identical with those of mutilation or destruction. Finally, the 1965 Amendment, like § 12(b) which it amended, is concerned with abuses involving *any* issued Selective Service certificates, not only with the registrant's own certificates. The knowing destruction or mutilation of someone else's certificates would therefore violate the statute but not the nonpossession regulations.

We think it apparent that the continuing availability to each registrant of his Selective Service certificates substantially furthers the smooth and proper functioning of the system that Congress has established to raise armies. We think it also apparent that the Nation has a vital interest in having a system for raising armies that functions with maximum efficiency and is capable of easily and quickly responding to continually changing circumstances. For these reasons, the Government has a substantial interest in assuring the continuing availability of issued Selective Service certificates.

It is equally clear that the 1965 Amendment specifically protects this substantial governmental interest. We perceive no alternative means that would more precisely and narrowly assure the continuing availability of issued Selective Service certificates than a law which prohibits their wilful mutilation or destruction. Compare *Sherbert v. Verner*, 374 U.S. 398, 407–408 (1963), and the cases cited therein. The 1965 Amendment prohibits such conduct and does nothing more. In other words, both the governmental interest and the operation of the 1965 Amendment are limited to the noncommunicative aspect of O'Brien's conduct. The governmental interest and the scope of the 1965 Amendment are limited to preventing a harm to the smooth and efficient functioning of the Selective Service System. When O'Brien deliberately rendered unavailable his registration certificate, he wilfully frustrated this governmental interest. For this noncommunicative impact of his conduct, and for nothing else, he was convicted.

The case at bar is therefore unlike one where the alleged governmental interest in regulating conduct arises in some measure because the communication allegedly integral to the conduct is itself thought to be harmful. In *Stromberg v. California*, 283 U.S. 359 (1931), for example, this Court struck down a statutory phrase which punished people who expressed their "opposition to organized government" by displaying "any flag, badge, banner, or device." Since the statute there was aimed at suppressing communication it could not be sustained as a regulation of noncommunicative conduct. See also, *NLRB v. Fruit & Vegetable Packers Union*, 377 U.S. 58, 79 (concurring opinion) (1964).

In conclusion, we find that because of the Government's substantial interest in assuring the continuing availability of issued Selective Service certificates, because amended § 462(b) is an appropriately narrow means of protecting this interest and condemns only the independent noncommunicative impact of conduct within its reach, and because the noncommunicative impact of O'Brien's act of burning his registration certificate frustrated the Government's interest, a sufficient governmental interest has been shown to justify O'Brien's conviction.

III

O'Brien finally argues that the 1965 Amendment is unconstitutional as enacted because what he calls the "purpose" of Congress was "to suppress freedom of speech." We reject this argument because under settled principles the purpose of Congress, as O'Brien uses that term, is not a basis for declaring this legislation unconstitutional.

It is a familiar principle of constitutional law that this Court will not strike down an otherwise constitutional statute on the basis of an alleged illicit legislative motive. As the Court long ago stated:

> The decisions of this court from the beginning lend no support whatever to the assumption that the judiciary may restrain the exercise of lawful power on the assumption that a wrongful purpose or motive has caused the power to be exerted. *McCray v. United States,* 195 U.S. 27, 56 (1904).

This fundamental principle of constitutional adjudication was reaffirmed and the many cases were collected by Mr. Justice Brandeis for the Court in *Arizona v. California,* 283 U.S. 423, 455 (1931).

Inquiries into congressional motives or purposes are a hazardous matter. When the issue is simply the interpretation of legislation, the Court will look to statements by legislators for guidance as to the purpose of the legislature, because the benefit to sound decision making in this circumstance is thought sufficient to risk the possibility of misreading Congress' purpose. It is entirely a different matter when we are asked to void a statute that is, under well-settled criteria, constitutional on its face, on the basis of what fewer than a handful of Congressmen said about it. What motivates one legislator to make a speech about a statute is not necessarily what motivates scores of others to enact it, and the stakes are sufficiently high for us to eschew guesswork. We decline to void essentially on the ground that it is unwise legislation which Congress had the undoubted power to enact and which could be reenacted in its exact form if the same or another legislator made a "wiser" speech about it.

O'Brien's position, and to some extent that of the court below, rests upon a misunderstanding of *Grosjean v. American Press Co.,* 297 U.S. 233 (1936), and *Gomillion v. Lightfoot,* 364 U.S. 339 (1960). These cases stand, not for the proposition that legislative motive is a proper basis for declaring a statute unconstitutional, but that the inevitable effect of a statute on its face may render it unconstitutional. Thus, in *Grosjean* the Court, having concluded that the right of publications to be free from certain kinds of taxes was a freedom of the press protected by the First Amendment, struck down a statute which on its face did nothing other than impose just such a tax. Similarly, in *Gomillion*, the Court sustained a complaint which, if true, established that the "inevitable effect," 364 U.S., at 341, of the redrawing of municipal boundaries was to deprive the petitioners of their right to vote for no reason other than that they were Negro. In these cases, the purpose of the legislation was irrelevant, because the inevitable effect — the "necessary scope and operation," *McCray* v. *United States*, 195 U.S. 27, 59 (1904) — abridged constitutional rights. The statute attacked in the instant case has no such inevitable unconstitutional effect, since the destruction of Selective Service certificates is in no respect inevitably or necessarily expressive. Accordingly, the statute itself is constitutional.

We think it not amiss, in passing, to comment upon O'Brien's legislative-purpose argument. There was little floor debate on this legislation in either House. Only Senator Thurmond commented on. its substantive features in the Senate. 111 Cong. Rec. 19746, 20433. After his brief statement, and without any additional substantive comments, the bill, H.R. 10306, passed the Senate. 111 Cong. Rec. 20434. In the House debate only two Congressmen addressed themselves to the Amendment — Congressmen Rivers and Bray. 111 Cong. Rec. 19871, 19872. The bill was passed after their statements without any further debate by a vote of 393 to 1. It is principally on the basis of the statements by these three Congressmen that O'Brien makes his congressional-"purpose" argument. We note that if we were to examine legislative purpose in the instant case, we would be obliged to consider not only these statements but also the more authoritative reports of the Senate and House Armed Services Committees. The portions of those reports explaining the purpose of the Amendment are reproduced in the Appendix in their entirety. While both reports make clear a concern with the "defiant" destruction of so-called "draft cards" and with "open" encouragement to others to destroy their cards, both reports also indicate that this concern stemmed from an apprehension that unrestrained destruction of cards would disrupt the smooth functioning of the Selective Service System.

IV

Since the 1965 Amendment to § 12 (b)(3) of the Universal Military Training and Service Act is constitutional as enacted and as applied, the Court of Appeals should have affirmed the judgment of conviction entered by the District Court. Accordingly, we vacate the judgment of the Court of Appeals, and reinstate the judgment and sentence of the District Court. This disposition makes unnecessary consideration of O'Brien's claim that the Court of Appeals erred in affirming his conviction on the basis of the nonpossession regulation.

It is so ordered.

MR. JUSTICE MARSHALL took no part in the consideration or decision of these cases.

Appendix to Opinion of the Court

Portions of the Reports of the Committees on Armed Services of the Senate and House Explaining the 1965 Amendment

The "Explanation of the Bill" in the Senate Report is as follows:

Section 12 (b) (3) of the Universal Military Training and Service Act of 1951, as amended, provides, among other things, that a person who forges, alters, or changes a draft registration certificate is subject to a fine of not more than $10,000 or imprisonment of not more than 5 years, or both. There is no explicit prohibition in this section against the knowing destruction or mutilation of such cards.

The committee has taken notice of the defiant destruction and mutilation of draft cards by dissident persons who disapprove of national policy. If allowed to continue unchecked this contumacious conduct represents a potential threat to the exercise of the power to raise and support armies.

For a person to be subject to fine or imprisonment the destruction or mutilation of the draft card must be "knowingly" done. This qualification is intended to protect persons who lose or mutilate draft cards accidentally. S.Rep. No. 589, 89th Cong., 1st Sess. (1965).

And the House Report explained:

Section 12 (b) (3) of the Universal Military Training and Service Act of 1951, as amended, provides that a person who forges, alters, or in any manner changes his draft registration card, or any notation duly and validly inscribed thereon, will be subject to a fine of $10,000 or imprisonment of not more than 5 years. H.R. 10306 would amend this provision to make it apply also to those persons who knowingly destroy or knowingly mutilate a draft registration card.

The House Committee on Armed Services is fully aware of, and shares in, the deep concern expressed throughout the Nation over the increasing incidences in which individuals and large groups of individuals openly defy and encourage others to defy the authority of their Government by destroying or mutilating their draft cards.

While the present provisions of the Criminal Code with respect to the destruction of Government property may appear broad enough to cover all acts having to do with the mistreatment of draft cards in the possession of individuals, the committee feels that in the present critical situation of the country, the acts of destroying or mutilating these cards are offenses which pose such a grave threat to the security of the Nation that no question whatsoever should be left as to the intention of the Congress that such wanton and irresponsible acts should be punished.

To this end, H.R. 10306 makes specific that knowingly mutilating or knowingly destroying a draft card constitutes a violation of the Universal Military Training and Service Act and is punishable thereunder; and that a person who does so destroy or mutilate a draft card will be subject to a fine of not more than $10,000 or imprisonment of not more than 5 years. H.R. Rep. No. 747, 89th Cong., 1st Sess. (1965).

MR. JUSTICE HARLAN, concurring.

The crux of the Court's opinion, which I join, is of course its general statement, *ante*, at 377, that

> ... a government regulation is sufficiently justified if it is within the constitutional power of the Government; if it furthers an important or substantial governmental interest; if the governmental interest is unrelated to the suppression of free expression; and if the incidental restriction on alleged First Amendment freedom is no greater than is essential to the furtherance of that interest.

I wish to make explicit my understanding that this passage does not foreclose consideration of First Amendment claims in those rare instances when an "incidental" restriction upon expression, imposed by a regulation which furthers an "important or substantial" governmental interest and satisfies the Court's other criteria, in practice has the effect of entirely preventing a "speaker" from reaching a significant audience with whom he could not otherwise lawfully communicate. This is not such a case, since O'Brien manifestly could have conveyed his message in many ways other than by burning his draft card.

MR. JUSTICE DOUGLAS, dissenting.

The Court states that the constitutional power of Congress to raise and support armies is "broad and sweeping" and that Congress' power "to classify and conscript manpower for military service is 'beyond question.' " This is undoubtedly true in times when, by declaration of Congress, the Nation is in a state of war. The underlying and basic problem in this case, however, is whether conscription is permissible in the absence of a declaration of war. That question has not been briefed nor was it presented in oral argument; but it is, I submit, a question upon which the litigants and the country are entitled to a ruling. I have discussed in *Holmes* v. *United States, post,* p. 936, the nature of the legal issue and it will be seen from my dissenting opinion in that case that this Court has never ruled on the question. It is time that we made a ruling. This case should be put down for reargument and heard with *Holmes* v. *United States* and with *Hart* v. *United States, post,* p. 956, in which the Court today denies certiorari.

The rule that this Court will not consider issues not raised by the parties is not inflexible and yields in "exceptional cases" (*Duignan* v. *United States,* 274 U.S. 195, 200) to the need correctly to decide the case before the Court. E.g., *Erie R. Co.* v. *Tompkins,* 304 U.S. 64; *Terminiello* v. *Chicago,* 337 U.S. 1.

In such a case it is not unusual to ask for reargument (*Sherman* v. *United States,* 356 U.S. 369, 379, n. 2, Frankfurter, J., concurring) even on a constitutional question not raised by the parties. In *Abel* v. *United States,* 362 U.S. 217, the petitioner had conceded that an administrative deportation arrest warrant would be valid for its limited purpose even though not supported by a sworn affidavit stating probable cause; but the Court ordered reargument on the question whether the warrant had been validly issued in petitioner's case. 362 U.S. at 219, n., par. 1; U.S. Sup. Ct. Journal, October Term, 1958, p. 193. In *Lustig* v. *United States,* 338 U.S. 74, the petitioner argued that an exclusionary rule should apply to the fruit of an unreasonable search by state officials solely because they acted in concert with federal officers (see *Weeks* v. *United States,* 232 U.S. 383; *Byars* v. *United States,* 273 U.S. 28). The Court ordered reargument on the question raised in a then pending case, *Wolf* v. *Colorado,* 338 U.S. 25: applicability of the Fourth Amendment to the States. Journal, October Term, 1947, p. 298. In *Donaldson* v. *Read Magazine,* 333 U.S. 178, the only issue presented, according to both parties, was whether the record contained sufficient evidence of fraud to uphold an order of the Postmaster General. Reargument was ordered on the constitutional issue of abridgment of First Amendment freedoms. 333 U.S., at 181–182; Journal, October Term, 1947, p. 70. Finally, in *Musser* v. *Utah,* 333 U.S. 95, 96, reargument was ordered on the question of unconstitutional vagueness of a criminal statute, an issue not raised by the parties but suggested at oral argument by Justice Jackson. Journal, October Term, 1947, p. 87.

These precedents demonstrate the appropriateness of restoring the instant case to the calendar for reargument on the question of constitutionality of a peacetime draft and having it heard with *Holmes* v. *United States* and *Hart* v. *United States.*

Obscene "Speech"

As the selections in this book demonstrate, the types of "speech" discussed by the courts are varied; "speech" may be oral discourse, written discourse, or nonverbal symbolic behavior. The classic *Schenck, Abrams,* and *Gitlow* cases all dealt with written "speech," pamphlets printed and distributed by the dissidents. The United States Supreme Court has grappled with the question of how much First Amendment protection should be accorded to another kind of written discourse, namely "obscene" literature and materials. The difficulty of reaching unanimity on the definition of "obscenity," has plagued the court for years. In *Roth,* for instance, Justice Brennan's majority opinion was accompanied by Justice Warren's concurring opinion, Justice Harlan's concurring and dissenting opinions, and Justice Douglas's and Blacks's dissenting opinion. In *Ginzburg,* the majority decision was accompanied by two dissenting opinions. *Roth* v. *the United States* (minus the Warren and Harlan opinions) and *Ginzburg* v. *United States* are reprinted here as two of the most important free-speech/obscenity cases to come before the Court.

Before the *Roth* decision in 1957, the definition of "obscene" was that which appeared in *Regina* v. *Hicklin,* an 1868 English court decision: "the test of obscenity is this, whether the tendency of the matter charged as obscenity is to deprave and corrupt those whose minds are open to such immoral influences, and into whose hands a publication of this sort may fall." The *Roth* decision held that the Government could impose general prohibitions on the dissemination of material on the ground of its "obscenity": "We hold that obscenity is not within the area of constitutionally protected speech or press." It rejected the Hicklin test and held that material is "obscene" only if "to the average person, applying contemporary community standards, the dominant theme of the material taken as a whole appeals to the prurient interest."

In *Ginzburg,* the United States Supreme Court held that where the obscenity of the material alone is in doubt under the Roth test, prohibition of the material is justified if it is produced, advertised, and sold in a "pandering" manner, because such pandering may "resolve all ambiguity and doubt" about its obscenity.

ROTH v. UNITED STATES

354 U.S. 476 (1957)*

ALBERTS v. CALIFORNIA

354 U.S. 476 (1957)*

Mr. Justice Brennan delivered the opinion of the Court.

The constitutionality of a criminal obscenity statute is the question in each of these cases. In *Roth*, the primary constitutional question is whether the federal obscenity statute violates the provision of the First Amendment that "Congress shall make no law . . . abridging the freedom of speech, or of the press. . . ." In *Alberts*, the primary constitutional question is whether the obscenity provisions of the California Penal Code invade the freedoms of speech and press as they may be incorporated in the liberty protected from state action by the Due Process Clause of the Fourteenth Amendment.

Other constitutional questions are: whether these statutes violate due process, because too vague to support conviction for crime; whether power to punish speech and press offensive to decency and morality is in the States alone, so that the federal obscenity statute violates the Ninth and Tenth Amendments (raised in *Roth*); and whether Congress, by enacting the federal obscenity statute, under the power delegated by Art. I, § 8, cl. 7, to establish post offices and post roads, pre-empted the regulation of the subject matter (raised in *Alberts*).

Roth conducted a business in New York in the publication and sale of books, photographs and magazines. He used circulars and advertising matter to solicit sales. He was convicted by a jury in the District Court for the Southern District of New York upon 4 counts of a 26-count indictment charging him with mailing obscene circulars and advertising, and an obscene book, in violation of the federal obscenity

* Footnotes and case citations have been deleted.

statute. His conviction was affirmed by the Court of Appeals for the Second Circuit. We granted certiorari.

Alberts conducted a mail-order business from Los Angeles. He was convicted by the Judge of the Municipal Court of the Beverly Hills Judicial District (having waived a jury trial) under a misdemeanor complaint which charged him with lewdly keeping for sale obscene and indecent books, and with writing, composing and publishing an obscene advertisement of them, in violation of the California Penal Code. The conviction was affirmed by the Appellate Department of the Superior Court of the State of California in and for the County of Los Angeles. We noted probable jurisdiction.

The dispositive question is whether obscenity is utterance within the area of protected speech and press. Although this is the first time the question has been squarely presented to this Court, either under the First Amendment or under the Fourteenth Amendment, expressions found in numerous opinions indicate that this Court has always assumed that obscenity is not protected by the freedoms of speech and press. *Ex parte Jackson*, 96 U.S. 727, 736–737; *United States* v. *Chase*, 135 U.S. 255, 261; *Robertson* v. *Baldwin*, 165 U.S. 275, 281; *Public Clearing House* v. *Coyne*, 194 U.S. 497, 508; *Hoke* v. *United States*, 227 U.S. 308, 322; *Near* v. *Minnesota*, 283 U.S. 697, 716; *Chaplinsky* v. *New Hampshire*, 315 U.S. 568, 571–572; *Hannegan* v. *Esquire, Inc.*, 327 U.S. 146, 158; *Winters* v. *New York*, 333 U.S. 507, 510; *Beauharnais* v. *Illinois*, 343 U.S. 250, 266.

The guarantees of freedom of expression in effect in 10 of the 14 States which by 1792 had ratified the Constitution gave no absolute protection for every utterance. Thirteen of the 14 States provided for the prosecution of libel, and all of those States made either blasphemy or profanity, or both, statutory crimes. As early as 1712, Massachusetts made it criminal to publish "any filthy, obscene, or profane song, pamphlet, libel or mock sermon" in imitation or mimicking of religious services. Acts and Laws of the Province of Mass. Bay, c. CV, § 8 (1712), Mass. Bay Colony Charters & Laws 399 (1814). Thus, profanity and obscenity were related offenses.

In light of this history, it is apparent that the unconditional phrasing of the First Amendment was not intended to protect every utterance. This phrasing did not prevent this Court from concluding that libelous utterances are not within the area of constitutionally protected speech. *Beauharnais* v. *Illinois*, 343 U.S. 250, 266. At the time of the adoption of the First Amendment, obscenity law was not as fully developed as libel law, but there is sufficiently contemporaneous evidence to show that obscenity, too, was outside the protection intended for speech and press.

The protection given speech and press was fashioned to assure unfettered interchange of ideas for the bringing about of political and social changes desired by the people. This objective was made explicit as early as 1774 in a letter of the Continental Congress to the inhabitants of Quebec:

> The last right we shall mention, regards the freedom of the press. The importance of this consists, besides the advancement of truth, science, morality, and arts in general, in its diffusion of liberal sentiments on the administration of Government, its ready communication of thoughts between subjects, and its consequential promotion of union among them, whereby oppressive officers are shamed or intimidated, into more honourable and just modes of conducting affairs. 1 Journals of the Continental Congress 108 (1774).

All ideas having even the slightest redeeming social importance — unorthodox ideas, controversial ideas, even ideas hateful to the prevailing climate of opinion — have the full protection of the guaranties, unless excludable because they encroach upon the limited area of more important interests. But implicit in the history of the First Amendment is the rejection of obscenity as utterly without redeeming social importance. This rejection for that reason is mirrored in the universal judgment that obscenity should be restrained, reflected in the international agreement of over 50 nations, in the obscenity laws of all of the 48 States, and in the 20 obscenity laws enacted by the Congress from 1842 to 1956. This is the same judgment expressed by this Court in *Chaplinsky* v. *New Hampshire,* 315 U.S. 568, 571–572:

> . . . There are certain well-defined and narrowly limited classes of speech, the prevention and punishment of which have never been thought to raise any Constitutional problem. *These include the lewd and obscene. . . . It has been well observed that such utterances are no essential part of any exposition of ideas, and are of such slight social value as a step to truth that any benefit that may be derived from them is clearly outweighed by the social interest in order and morality. . . .* (Emphasis added.)

We hold that obscenity is not within the area of constitutionally protected speech or press.

It is strenuously urged that these obscenity statutes offend the constitutional guaranties because they punish incitation to impure sexual *thoughts*, not shown to be related to any overt antisocial conduct which is or may be incited in the persons stimulated to such *thoughts*. In *Roth*, the trial judge instructed the jury: "The words 'obscene, lewd and lascivious' as used in the law, signify that form of immorality which has relation to sexual impurity and has a tendency to excite lustful *thoughts*." (Emphasis added.) In *Alberts*, the trial judge applied the test laid down in *People* v. *Wepplo*, 78 Cal. App. 2d Supp. 959, 178 P. 2d 853, namely, whether the material has "a substantial tendency to deprave or corrupt its readers by inciting lascivious *thoughts* or arousing lustful desires." (Emphasis added.) It is insisted that the constitutional guaranties are violated because convictions may be had without proof either that obscene material will perceptibly create a clear and present danger of anti-social conduct, or will probably induce its recipients to such conduct. But, in light of our holding that obscenity is not protected speech, the complete answer to this argument is in the holding of this Court in *Beauharnais* v. *Illinois, supra,* at 266:

> Libelous utterances not being within the area of constitutionally protected speech, it is unnecessary, either for us or for the State courts, to consider the issues behind the phrase 'clear and present danger.' Certainly no one would contend that obscene speech, for example, may be punished only upon a showing of such circumstances. Libel, as we have seen, is in the same class.

However, sex and obscenity are not synonymous. Obscene material is material which deals with sex in a manner appealing to prurient interest. The portrayal of sex, *e. g.,* in art, literature and scientific work, is not itself sufficient reason to deny material the constitutional protection of freedom of speech and press. Sex, a great and mysterious motive force in human life, has indisputably been a subject of absorbing interest to mankind through the ages; it is one of the vital problems of human interest and public concern. As to all such problems, this Court said in *Thornhill* v. *Alabama*, 310 U.S. 88, 101–102:

The freedom of speech and of the press guaranteed by the Constitution embraces at the least the liberty to discuss publicly and truthfully *all matters of public concern* without previous restraint or fear of subsequent punishment. The exigencies of the colonial period and the efforts to secure freedom from oppressive administration developed a broadened conception of these liberties as adequate to supply the public need for *information and education with respect to the significant issues of the times.* . . . Freedom of discussion, if it would fulfill its historic function in this nation, must embrace *all issues about which information is needed or appropriate to enable the members of society to cope with the exigencies of their period.* (Emphasis added.)

The fundamental freedoms of speech and press have contributed greatly to the development and well-being of our free society and are indispensable to its continued growth. Ceaseless vigilance is the watchword to prevent their erosion by Congress or by the States. The door barring federal and state intrusion into this area cannot be left ajar; it must be kept tightly closed and opened only the slightest crack necessary to prevent encroachment upon more important interests. It is therefore vital that the standards of judging obscenity safeguard the protection of freedom of speech and press for material which does not treat sex in a manner appealing to prurient interest.

The early leading standard of obscenity allowed material to be judged merely by the effect of an isolated excerpt upon particularly susceptible persons. *Regina* v. *Hicklin,* [1868] L. R. 3 Q. B. 360. Some American courts adopted this standard but later decisions have rejected it and substituted this test: whether to the average person, applying contemporary community standards, the dominant theme of the material taken as a whole appeals to prurient interest. The *Hicklin* test, judging obscenity by the effect of isolated passages upon the most susceptible persons, might well encompass material legitimately treating with sex, and so it must be rejected as unconstitutionally restrictive of the freedoms of speech and press. On the other hand, the substituted standard provides safeguards adequate to withstand the charge of constitutional infirmity.

Both trial courts below sufficiently followed the proper standard. Both courts used the proper definition of obscenity. In addition, in the *Alberts* case, in ruling on a motion to dismiss, the trial judge indicated that, as the trier of facts, he was judging each item as a whole as it would affect the normal person, and in *Roth,* the trial judge instructed the jury as follows:

> . . . The test is not whether it would arouse sexual desires or sexual impure thoughts in those comprising a particular segment of the community, the young, the immature or the highly prudish or would leave another segment, the scientific or highly educated or the so-called worldly-wise and sophisticated indifferent and unmoved. . . .
>
> The test in each case is the effect of the book, picture or publication considered as a whole, not upon any particular class, but upon all those whom it is likely to reach. In other words, you determine its impact upon the average person in the community. The books, pictures and circulars must be judged as a whole, in their entire context, and you are not to consider detached or separate portions in reaching a conclusion. You judge the circulars, pictures and publications which have been put in evidence by present-day standards of the community. You may ask yourselves does it offend the common conscience of the community by present-day standards.
>
> .   .   .   .
>
> In this case, ladies and gentlemen of the jury, you and you alone are the exclusive judges of what the common conscience of the community is, and in determining that conscience you are to consider the community as a whole, young and old, educated and uneducated, the religious and the irreligious — men, women and children.

It is argued that the statutes do not provide reasonably ascertainable standards of guilt and therefore violate the constitutional requirements of due process. *Winters* v. *New York,* 333 U.S. 507. The federal obscenity statute makes punishable the mailing of material that is "obscene, lewd, lascivious, or filthy . . . or other publication of an indecent character." The California statute makes punishable, *inter alia,* the keeping for sale or advertising material that is "obscene or indecent." The thrust of the argument is that these words are not sufficiently precise because they do not mean the same thing to all people, all the time, everywhere.

Many decisions have recognized that these terms of obscenity statutes are not precise. This Court, however, has consistently held that lack of precision is not itself offensive to the requirements of due process. ". . . [T]he Constitution does not require impossible

standards"; all that is required is that the language "conveys sufficiently definite warning as to the proscribed conduct when measured by common understanding and practices. . . ." *United States* v.
Petrillo, 332 U.S. 1, 7–8. These words, applied according to the proper
standard for juding obscenity, already discussed, give adequate
warning of the conduct proscribed and mark ". . . boundaries sufficiently distinct for judges and juries fairly to administer the law. . . .
That there may be marginal cases in which it is difficult to determine
the side of the line on which a particular fact situation falls is no sufficient reason to hold the language too ambiguous to define a criminal
offense. . . ." *Id.,* at 7. See also *United States* v. *Harriss,* 347 U.S.
612, 624, n. 15; *Boyce Motor Lines, Inc.* v. *United States,* 342 U.S.
337, 340; *United States* v. *Ragen,* 314 U.S. 513, 523–524; *United
States* v. *Wurzbach,* 280 U.S. 396; *Hygrade Provision Co.* v. *Sherman,*
266 U.S. 497; *Fox* v. *Washington,* 236 U.S. 273; *Nash* v. *United
States,* 229 U.S. 373.

In summary, then, we hold that these statutes, applied according to
the proper standard of judging obscenity, do not offend constitutional
safeguards against convictions based upon protected material, or fail
to give men in acting adequate notice of what is prohibited.

Roth's argument that the federal obscenity statute unconstitutionally encroaches upon the powers reserved by the Ninth and Tenth
Amendments to the States and to the people to punish speech and
press where offensive to decency and morality is hinged upon his
contention that obscenity is expression not excepted from the sweep
of the provision of the First Amendment that *"Congress* shall make
no law . . . abridging the freedom of speech, or of the press. . . ."
(Emphasis added.) That argument fails in light of our holding that
obscenity is not expression protected by the First Amendment. We
therefore hold that the federal obscenity statute punishing the use of
the mails for obscene material is a proper exercise of the postal power
delegated to Congress by Art. I, § 8, cl. 7. In *United Public Workers*
v. *Mitchell,* 330 U.S. 75, 95–96, this Court said:

> . . . The powers granted by the Constitution to the Federal Govern-
> ment are subtracted from the totality of sovereignty originally in the
> states and the people. Therefore, when objection is made that the
> exercise of a federal power infringes upon rights reserved by the
> Ninth and Tenth Amendments, the inquiry must be directed toward
> the granted power under which the action of the Union was taken.

If granted power is found, necessarily the objection of invasion of those rights, reserved by the Ninth and Tenth Amendments, must fail. . . .

Alberts argues that because his was a mail-order business, the California statute is repugnant to Art. I, § 8, cl. 7, under which the Congress allegedly pre-empted the regulatory field by enacting the federal obscenity statute punishing the mailing or advertising by mail of obscene material. The federal statute deals only with actual mailing; it does not eliminate the power of the state to punish "keeping for sale" or "advertising" obscene material. The state statute in no way imposes a burden or interferes with the federal postal functions. ". . . The decided cases which indicate the limits of state regulatory power in relation to the federal mail service involve situations where state regulation involved a direct, physical interference with federal activities under the postal power of some direct, immediate burden on the performance of the postal functions. . . ." *Railway Mail Assn.* v. *Corsi,* 326 U.S. 88, 96.

The judgments are

Affirmed.

Mr. Justice Douglas, with whom Mr. Justice Black concurs, dissenting.

When we sustain these convictions, we make the legality of a publication turn on the purity of thought which a book or tract instills in the mind of the reader. I do not think we can approve that standard and be faithful to the command of the First Amendment, which by its terms is a restraint on Congress and which by the Fourteenth is a restraint on the States.

In the *Roth* case the trial judge charged the jury that the statutory words "obscene, lewd and lascivious" describe "that form of immorality which has relation to sexual impurity and has a tendency to excite lustful thoughts." He stated that the term "filthy" in the statute pertains "to that sort of treatment of sexual matters in such a vulgar and indecent way, so that it tends to arouse a feeling of disgust and revulsion." He went on to say that the material "must be calculated to corrupt and debauch the minds and morals" of "the average person in the community," not those of any particular class. "You judge the circulars, pictures and publications which have been put in evidence by present-day standards of the community. You may ask yourselves does it offend the common conscience of the community by present-day standards."

The trial judge who, sitting without a jury, heard the *Alberts* case and the appellate court that sustained the judgment of conviction, took California's definition of "obscenity" from *People* v. *Wepplo,* 78 Cal. App. 2d Supp. 959, 961, 178 P. 2d 853, 855. That case held that a book is obscene "if it has a substantial tendency to deprave or corrupt its readers by inciting lascivious thoughts or arousing lustful desire."

By these standards punishment is inflicted for thoughts provoked, not for overt acts nor antisocial conduct. This test cannot be squared with our decisions under the First Amendment. Even the ill-starred *Dennis* case conceded that speech to be punishable must have some relation to action which could be penalized by government. *Dennis* v. *United States,* 341 U.S. 494, 502–511. Cf. Chafee, *The Blessings of Liberty* (1956), p. 69. This issue cannot be avoided by saying that obscenity is not protected by the First Amendment. The question remains, what is the constitutional test of obscenity?

The tests by which these convictions were obtained require only the arousing of sexual thoughts. Yet the arousing of sexual thoughts and desires happens every day in normal life in dozens of ways. Nearly 30 years ago a questionnaire sent to college and normal school women graduates asked what things were most stimulating sexually. Of 409 replies, 9 said "music"; 18 said "pictures"; 29 said "dancing"; 40 said "drama"; 95 said "books"; and 218 said "man." Alpert, Judicial Censorship of Obscene Literature, 52 Harv. L. Rev. 40, 73.

The test of obscenity the Court endorses today gives the censor free range over a vast domain. To allow the State to step in and punish mere speech or publication that the judge or the jury thinks has an *undesirable* impact on thoughts but that is not shown to be a part of unlawful action is drastically to curtail the First Amendment. As recently stated by two of our outstanding authorities on obscenity, "The danger of influencing a change in the current moral standards of the community, or of shocking or offending readers, or of stimulating sex thoughts or desires apart from objective conduct, can never justify the losses to society that result from interference with literary freedom." Lockhart & McClure, Literature, The Law of Obscenity, and the Constitution, 38 Minn. L. Rev. 295, 387.

If we were certain that impurity of sexual thoughts impelled to action, we would be on less dangerous ground in punishing the distributors of this sex literature. But it is by no means clear that obscene literature, as so defined, is a significant factor in influencing substantial deviations from the community standards.

There are a number of reasons for real and substantial doubts as to the soundness of that hypothesis. (1) Scientific studies of juvenile delinquency demonstrate that those who get into trouble, and are the greatest concern of the advocates of censorship, are far less inclined to read than those who do not become delinquent. The delinquents are generally the adventurous type, who have little use for reading and other non-active entertainment. Thus, even assuming that reading sometimes has an adverse effect upon moral conduct, the effect is not likely to be substantial, for those who are susceptible seldom read. (2) Sheldon and Eleanor Glueck, who are among the country's leading authorities on the treatment and causes of juvenile delinquency, have recently published the results of a ten-year study of its causes. They exhaustively studied approximately 90 factors and influences that might lead to or explain juvenile delinquency, but the Gluecks gave no consideration to the type of reading material, if any, read by the delinquents. This is, of course, consistent with their finding that delinquents read very little. When those who know so much about the problem of delinquency among youth—the very group about whom the advocates of censorship are most concerned—conclude that what delinquents read has so little effect upon their conduct that it is not worth investigating in an exhaustive study of causes, there is good reason for serious doubt concerning the basic hypothesis on which obscenity censorship is defended. (3) The many other influences in society that stimulate sexual desire are so much more frequent in their influence, and so much more potent in their effect, that the influence of reading is likely, at most, to be relatively insignificant in the composite of forces that lead an individual into conduct deviating from the community sex standards. The Kinsey studies show the minor degree to which literature serves as a potent sexual stimulant. And the studies demonstrating that sex knowledge seldom results from reading indicates [sic] the relative unimportance of literature in sex thoughts as compared with other factors in society. Lockhart & McClure, *op. cit. supra*, pp. 385–386.

The absence of dependable information on the effect of obscene literature on human conduct should make us wary. It should put us on the side of protecting society's interest in literature, except and unless it can be said that the particular publication has an impact on action that the government can control.

As noted, the trial judge in the *Roth* case charged the jury in the alternative that the federal obscenity statute outlaws literature dealing with sex which offends "the common conscience of the community." That standard is, in my view, more inimical still to freedom of expression.

The standard of what offends "the common conscience of the community" conflicts, in my judgment, with the command of the First Amendment that "Congress shall make no law . . . abridging the freedom of speech, or of the press." Certainly that standard would not be an acceptable one if religion, economics, politics or philosophy were involved. How does it become a constitutional standard when literature treating with sex is concerned?

Any test that turns on what is offensive to the community's standards is too loose, too capricious, too destructive of freedom of expression to be squared with the First Amendment. Under that test, juries can censor, suppress, and punish what they don't like, provided the matter relates to "sexual impurity" or has a tendency "to excite lustful thoughts." This is community censorship in one of its worst forms. It creates a regime where in the battle between the literati and the Philistines, the Philistines are certain to win. If experience in this field teaches anything, it is that "censorship of obscenity has almost always been both irrational and indiscriminate." Lockhart & McClure, *op. cit. supra*, at 371. The test adopted here accentuates that trend.

I assume there is nothing in the Constitution which forbids Congress from using its power over the mails to proscribe *conduct* on the grounds of good morals. No one would suggest that the First Amendment permits nudity in public places, adultery, and other phases of sexual misconduct.

I can understand (and at times even sympathize) with programs of civic groups and church groups to protect and defend the existing moral standards of the community. I can understand the motives of the Anthony Comstocks who would impose Victorian standards on the community. When speech alone is involved, I do not think that government, consistently with the First Amendment, can become the sponsor of any of these movements. I do not think that government, consistently with the First Amendment, can throw its weight behind one school or another. Government should be concerned with antisocial conduct, not with utterances. Thus, if the First Amendment guarantee of freedom of speech and press is to mean anything in this field, it must allow protests even against the moral code that the standard of the day sets for the community. In other words, literature should not be suppressed merely because it offends the moral code of the censor.

The legality of a publication in this country should never be allowed to turn either on the purity of thought which it instills in the mind of the reader or on the degree to which it offends the community conscience. By either test the role of the censor is exalted, and society's values in literary freedom are sacrificed.

The Court today suggests a third standard. It defines obscene material as that "which deals with sex in a manner appealing to prurient interest." Like the standards applied by the trial judges below, that standard does not require any nexus between the literature which is prohibited and action which the legislature can regulate or prohibit. Under the First Amendment, that standard is no more valid than those which the courts below adopted.

I do not think that the problem can be resolved by the Court's statement that "obscenity is not expression protected by the First Amendment." With the exception of *Beauharnais v. Illinois*, 343 U. S. 250, none of our cases has resolved problems of free speech and free press by placing any form of expression beyond the pale of the absolute prohibition of the First Amendment. Unlike the law of libel, wrongfully relied on in *Beauharnais*, there is no special historical evidence that literature dealing with sex was intended to be treated in a special manner by those who drafted the First Amendment. In fact, the first reported court decision in this country involving obscene literature was in 1821. Lockhart & McClure, *op. cit. supra*, at 324, n. 200. I reject too the implication that problems of freedom of speech and of the press are to be resolved by weighing against the values of free expression, the judgment of the Court that a particular form of that expression has "no redeeming social importance." The First Amendment, its prohibition in terms absolute, was designed to preclude courts as well as legislatures from weighing the values of speech against silence. The First Amendment puts free speech in the preferred position.

Freedom of expression can be suppressed if, and to the extent that, it is so closely brigaded with illegal action as to be an inseparable part of it. *Giboney* v. *Empire Storage Co.*, 336 U. S. 490, 498; *Labor Board* v. *Virginia Power Co.*, 314 U. S. 469, 477–478. As a people, we cannot afford to relax that standard. For the test that suppresses a cheap tract today can suppress a literary gem tomorrow. All it need do is to incite a lascivious thought or arouse a lustful desire. The list of books that judges or juries can place in that category is endless.

I would give the broad sweep of the First Amendment full support. I have the same confidence in the ability of our people to reject noxious literature as I have in their capacity to sort out the true from the false in theology, economics, politics, or any other field.

GINZBURG v. UNITED STATES

383 U.S. 463 (1966)*

Mr. Justice Brennan delivered the opinion of the Court.

A judge sitting without a jury in the District Court for the Eastern District of Pennsylvania convicted petitioner Ginzburg and three corporations controlled by him upon all 28 counts of an indictment charging violation of the federal obscenity statute, 18 U. S. C. § 1461 (1964 ed.) 224 F. Supp. 129. Each count alleged that a resident of the Eastern District received mailed matter, either one of three publications challenged as obscene, or advertising telling how and where the publications might be obtained. The Court of Appeals for the Third Circuit affirmed, 338 F. 2d 12. We granted certiorari, 380 U. S. 961. We affirm. Since petitioners do not argue that the trial judge misconceived or failed to apply the standards we first enunciated in *Roth* v. *United States,* 354 U.S. 476, the only serious question is whether those standards were correctly applied.

In the cases in which this Court has decided obscenity questions since *Roth,* it has regarded the materials as sufficient in themselves for the determination of the question. In the present case, however, the prosecution charged the offense in the context of the circumstances of production, sale, and publicity and assumed that, standing alone, the publications themselves might not be obscene. We agree that the question of obscenity may include consideration of the setting in which the publications were presented as an aid to determining the question of obscenity, and assume without deciding that the prosecution could not have succeeded otherwise. As in *Mishkin* v. *New York, post,* p. 502, and as did the courts below, 224 F. Supp., at 134, 338 F. 2d, at 14–15, we view the publications against a background of commercial exploitation of erotica solely for the sake of their prurient appeal. The record in that regard amply supports the decision of the trial judge that the mailing of all three publications offended the statute.

* Footnotes and case citations have been deleted.

The three publications were EROS, a hard-cover magazine of expensive format; Liaison, a bi-weekly newsletter; and *The Housewife's Handbook on Selective Promiscuity* (hereinafter the *Handbook*), a short book. The issue of EROS specified in the indictment, Vol. 1, No. 4, contains 15 articles and photo-essays on the subject of love, sex, and sexual relations The specified issue of Liaison, Vol. 1, No. 1, contains a prefatory "Letter from the Editors" announcing its dedication to "keeping sex an art and preventing it from becoming a science." The remainder of the issue consists of digests of two articles concerning sex and sexual relations which had earlier appeared in professional journals and a report of an interview with a psychotherapist who favors the broadest license in sexual relationships. As the trial judge noted, "[w]hile the treatment is largely superficial, it is presented entirely without restraint of any kind. According to defendants' own expert, it is entirely without literary merit." 224 F. Supp., at 134. The *Handbook* purports to be a sexual autobiography detailing with complete candor the author's sexual experiences from age 3 to age 36. The text includes, and prefatory and concluding sections of the book elaborate, her views on such subjects as sex education of children, laws regulating private consensual adult sexual practices, and the equality of women in sexual relationships. It was claimed at trial that women would find the book valuable, for example as a marriage manual or as an aid to the sex education of their children.

Besides testimony as to the merit of the material, there was abundant evidence to show that each of the accused publications was originated or sold as stock in trade of the sordid business of pandering —"the business of purveying textual or graphic matter openly advertised to appeal to the erotic interest of their customers." EROS early sought mailing privileges from the postmasters of Intercourse and Blue Ball, Pennsylvania. The trial court found the obvious, that these hamlets were chosen only for the value their names would have in furthering petitioners' efforts to sell their publications on the basis of salacious appeal; the facilities of the post offices were inadequate to handle the anticipated volume of mail, and the privileges were denied. Mailing privileges were then obtained from the postmaster of Middlesex, New Jersey. EROS and Liaison thereafter mailed several million circulars soliciting subscriptions from that post office; over 5,500 copies of *Handbook* were mailed.

The "leer of the sensualist" also permeates the advertising for the three publications. The circulars sent for EROS and Liaison stressed the sexual candor of the respective publications, and openly boasted that the publishers would take full advantage of what they regarded as an unrestricted license allowed by law in the expression of sex and sexual matters   The advertising for the *Handbook*, apparently mailed from New York, consisted almost entirely of a reproduction of the introduction of the book, written by one Dr. Albert Ellis. Although he alludes to the book's informational value and its putative therapeutic usefulness, his remarks are preoccupied with the book's sexual imagery. The solicitation was indiscriminate, not limited to those, such as physicians or psychiatrists, who might independently discern the book's therapeutic worth. Inserted in each advertisement was a slip labeled "GUARANTEE" and reading, "Documentary Books, Inc. unconditionally guarantees full refund of the price of THE HOUSE-WIFE'S HANDBOOK ON SELECTIVE PROMISCUITY if the book fails to reach you because of U. S. Post Office censorship interference." Similar slips appeared in the advertising from EROS and Liaison; they highlighted the gloss petitioners put on the publications, eliminating any doubt what the purchaser was being asked to buy.

This evidence, in our view, was relevant in determining the ultimate question of obscenity and, in the context of this record, serves to resolve all ambiguity and doubt. The deliberate representation of petitioners' publications as erotically arousing, for example, stimulated the reader to accept them as prurient; he looks for titillation, not for saving intellectual content. Similarly, such representation would tend to force public confrontation with the potentially offensive aspects of the work; the brazenness of such an appeal heightens the offensiveness of the publications to those who are offended by such material. And the circumstances of presentation and dissemination of material are equally relevant to determining whether social importance claimed for material in the courtroom was, in the circumstances, pretense or reality — whether it was the basis upon which it was traded in the marketplace or a spurious claim for litigation purposes. Where the purveyor's sole emphasis is on the sexually provocative aspects of his publications, that fact may be decisive in the determination of obscenity. Certainly in a prosecution which, as here, does not necessarily imply suppression of the materials involved, the fact that they originate or are used as a subject of pandering is relevant to the application of the *Roth* test.

A proposition argued as to EROS, for example, is that the trial judge improperly found the magazine to be obscene as a whole, since he concluded that only four of the 15 articles predominantly appealed to prurient interest and substantially exceeded community standards of candor, while the other articles were admittedly nonoffensive. But the trial judge found that "[t]he deliberate and studied arrangement of EROS is editorialized for the purpose of appealing predominantly to prurient interest and to insulate through the inclusion of nonoffensive material" 224 F. Supp., at 131. However erroneous such a conclusion might be if unsupported by the evidence of pandering, the record here supports it. EROS was created, represented and sold solely as a claimed instrument of the sexual stimulation it would bring. Like the other publications, its pervasive treatment of sex and sexual matters rendered it available to exploitation by those who would make a business of pandering to "the widespread weakness for titillation by pornography." Petitioners' own expert agreed, correctly we think, that "[i]f the object [of a work] is material gain for the creator through an appeal to the sexual curiosity and appetite," the work is pornographic. In other words, by animating sensual detail to give the publication a salacious cast, petitioners reinforced what is conceded by the Government to be an otherwise debatable conclusion.

A similar analysis applies to the judgment regarding the *Handbook*. The bulk of the proofs directed to social importance concerned this publication. Before selling publication rights to petitioners, its author had printed it privately; she sent circulars to persons whose names appeared on membership lists of medical and psychiatric associations, asserting its value as an adjunct to therapy. Over 12,000 sales resulted from this solicitation, and a number of witnesses testified that they found the work useful in their professional practice. The Government does not seriously contest the claim that the book has worth in such a controlled, or even neutral, environment. Petitioners, however, did not sell the book to such a limited audience, or focus their claims for it on its supposed therapeutic or educational value; rather, they deliberately emphasized the sexually provocative aspects of the work, in order to catch the salaciously disposed. They proclaimed its obscenity; and we cannot conclude that the court below erred in taking their own evaluation at its face value and declaring the book as a whole obscene despite the other evidence.

The decision in *United States* v. *Rebhuhn,* 109 F. 2d 512, is persuasive authority for our conclusion. That was a prosecution under the predecessor to § 1461, brought in the context of pandering of publications assumed useful to scholars and members of learned professions. The books involved were written by authors proved in many instances to have been men of scientific standing, as anthropologists or psychiatrists The Court of Appeals for the Second Circuit therefore assumed that many of the books were entitled to the protection of the First Amendment, and "could lawfully have passed through the mails, if directed to those who would be likely to use them for the purposes for which they were written. . . ." 109 F. 2d, at 514. But the evidence, as here, was that the defendants had not disseminated them for their "proper use, but . . . woefully misused them, and it was that misuse which constituted the gravamen of the crime." *Id.,* at 515. Speaking for the Court in affirming the conviction, Judge Learned Hand said:

> . . . [T]he works themselves had a place, though a limited one, in anthropology and in psychotherapy. They might also have been lawfully sold to laymen who wished seriously to study the sexual practices of savage or barbarous peoples, or sexual aberrations; in other words, most of them were not obscene per se. In several decisions we have held that the statute does not in all circumstances forbid the dissemination of such publications. . . . However, in the case at bar, the prosecution succeeded . . . when it showed that the defendants had indiscriminately flooded the mails with advertisements, plainly designed merely to catch the prurient, though under the guise of distributing works of scientific or literary merit. We do not mean that the distributor of such works is charged with a duty to insure that they shall reach only proper hands, nor need we say what care he must use, for these defendants exceeded any possible limit; the circulars were no more than appeals to the salaciously disposed, and no [fact finder] could have failed to pierce the fragile screen, set up to cover that purpose. 109 F. 2d, at 514–515.

We perceive no threat to First Amendment guarantees in thus holding that in close cases evidence of pandering may be probative with respect to the nature of the material in question and thus satisfy the *Roth* test. No weight is ascribed to the fact that petitioners have profited from the sale of publications which we have assumed but do not hold cannot themselves be adjudged obscene in the abstract; to sanction consideration of this fact might indeed induce self-censorship, and offend the frequently stated principle that commercial activity, in itself, is no justification for narrowing the protection of expression secured by the First Amendment. Rather, the fact that each of these publications was created or exploited entirely on the basis of its appeal to prurient interests strengthens the conclusion that the transactions here were sales of illicit merchandise, not sales of constitutionally protected matter. A conviction for mailing obscene publications, but explained in part by the presence of this element, does not necessarily suppress the materials in question, nor chill their proper distribution for a proper use Nor should it inhibit the enterprise of others seeking through serious endeavor to advance human knowledge or understanding in science, literature, or art. All that will have been determined is that questionable publications are obscene in a context which brands them as obscene as that term is defined in *Roth* — a use inconsistent with any claim to the shelter of the First Amendment. "The nature of the materials is, of course, relevant as an attribute of the defendant's conduct, but the materials are thus placed in context from which they draw color and character. A wholly different result might be reached in a different setting." *Roth v. United States*, 354 U. S., at 495 (WARREN, C. J., concurring).

It is important to stress that this analysis simply elaborates the test by which the obscenity vel non of the material must be judged. Where an exploitation of interests in titillation by pornography is shown with respect to material lending itself to such exploitation through pervasive treatment or description of sexual matters, such evidence may support the determination that the material is obscene even though in other contexts the material would escape such condemnation.

Petitioners raise several procedural objections, principally directed to the findings which accompanied the trial court's memorandum opinion, Fed. Rules Crim. Proc. 23. Even on the assumption that petitioners' objections are well taken, we perceive no error affecting their substantial rights.

Affirmed.

Mr. Justice Black, dissenting.

Only one stark fact emerges with clarity out of the confusing welter of opinions and thousands of words written in this and two other cases today. That fact is that Ginzburg, petitioner here, is now finally and authoritatively condemned to serve five years in prison for distributing printed matter about sex which neither Ginzburg nor anyone else could possibly have known to be criminal. Since, as I have said many times, I believe the Federal Government is without any power whatever under the Constitution to put any type of burden on speech and expression of ideas of any kind (as distinguished from conduct), I agree with Part II of the dissent of my Brother Douglas in this case, and I would reverse Ginzburg's conviction on this ground alone. Even assuming, however, that the Court is correct in holding today that Congress does have power to clamp official censorship on some subjects selected by the Court, in some ways approved by it, I believe that the federal obscenity statute as enacted by Congress and as enforced by the Court against Ginzburg in this case should be held invalid on two other grounds.

I

Criminal punishment by government, although universally recognized as a necessity in limited areas of conduct, is an exercise of one of government's most awesome and dangerous powers. Consequently, wise and good governments make all possible efforts to hedge this dangerous power by restricting it within easily identifiable boundaries. Experience, and wisdom flowing out of that experience, long ago led to the belief that agents of government should not be vested with power and discretion to define and punish as criminal past conduct which had not been clearly defined as a crime in advance. To this end, at least in part, written laws came into being, marking the boundaries of conduct for which public agents could thereafter impose punishment upon people. In contrast, bad governments either wrote no general rules of conduct at all, leaving that highly important task to the unbridled discretion of government agents at the moment of trial, or sometimes, history tells us, wrote their laws in an unknown tongue so that people could not understand them or else placed their written laws at such inaccessible spots that people could not read them. It seems to be that these harsh expedients used by bad governments to punish people for conduct not previously clearly marked as criminal are being used here to put Mr. Ginzburg in prison for five years.

I agree with my Brother HARLAN that the Court has in effect rewritten the federal obscenity statute and thereby imposed on Ginzburg standards and criteria that Congress never thought about; or if it did think about them, certainly it did not adopt them. Consequently, Ginzburg is, as I see it, having his conviction and sentence affirmed upon the basis of a statute amended by this Court for violation of which amended statute he was not charged in the courts below. Such an affirmance we have said violates due process. *Cole v. Arkansas*, 333 U. S. 196. Compare *Shuttlesworth v. Birmingham*, 382 U. S. 87. Quite apart from this vice in the affirmance, however, I think that the criteria declared by a majority of the Court today as guidelines for a court or jury to determine whether Ginzburg or anyone else can be punished as a common criminal for publishing or circulating obscene material are so vague and meaningless that they practically leave the fate of a person charged with violating censorship statutes to the unbridled discretion, whim and caprice of the judge or jury which tries him. I shall separately discuss the three elements which a majority of the Court seems to consider material in proving obscenity.

(a) The first element considered necessary for determining obscenity is that the dominant theme of the material taken as a whole must appeal to the prurient interest in sex. It seems quite apparent to me that human beings, serving either as judges or jurors, could not be expected to give any sort of decision on this element which would even remotely promise any kind of uniformity in the enforcement of this law. What conclusion an individual, be he judge or juror, would reach about whether the material appeals to "prurient interest in sex" would depend largely in the long run not upon testimony of witnesses such as can be given in ordinary criminal cases where conduct is under scrutiny, but would depend to a large extent upon the judge's or juror's personality, habits, inclinations, attitudes and other individual characteristics. In one community or in one courthouse a matter would be condemned as obscene under this so-called criterion but in another community, maybe only a few miles away, or in another courthouse in the same community, the material could be given a clean bill of health In the final analysis the submission of such an issue as this to a judge or jury amounts to practically nothing more than a request for the judge or juror to assert his own personal beliefs about whether the matter should be allowed to be legally distributed. Upon this subjective determination the law becomes certain for the first and last time.

(b) The second element for determining obscenity as it is described by my Brother BRENNAN is that the material must be "patently offensive because it affronts contemporary community standards relating to the description or representation of sexual matters. . . ." Nothing that I see in any position adopted by a majority of the Court today and nothing that has been said in previous opinions for the Court leaves me with any kind of certainty as to whether the "community standards" referred to are world-wide, nation-wide, section-wide, state-wide, country-wide, precinct-wide or township-wide. But even if some definite areas were mentioned, who is capable of assessing "community standards" on such a subject? Could one expect the same application of standards by jurors in Mississippi as in New York City, in Vermont as in California? So here again the guilt or innocence of a defendant charged with obscenity must depend in the final analysis upon the personal judgment and attitudes of particular individuals and the place where the trial is held. And one must remember that the Federal Government has the power to try a man for mailing obscene matter in a court 3,000 miles from his home.

(c) A third element which three of my Brethren think is required to establish obscenity is that the material must be "utterly without redeeming social value." This element seems to me to be as uncertain, if not even more uncertain, than is the unknown substance of the Milky Way. If we are to have a free society as contemplated by the Bill of Rights, then I can find little defense for leaving the liberty of American individuals subject to the judgment of a judge or jury as to whether material that provokes thought or stimulates desire is "utterly without redeeming social value. . . ." Whether a particular treatment of a particular subject is with or without social value in this evolving, dynamic society of ours is a question upon which no uniform agreement could possibly be reached among politicians, statesmen, professors, philosophers, scientists, religious groups or any other type of group A case-by-case assessment of social values by individual judges and jurors is, I think, a dangerous technique for government to utilize in determining whether a man stays in or out of the penitentiary.

My conclusion is that certainly after the fourteen separate opinions handed down in these three cases today no person, not even the most learned judge much less a layman, is capable of knowing in advance of an ultimate decision in his particular case by this Court whether certain material comes within the area of "obscenity" as that term is confused by the Court today. For this reason even if, as appears from the result of the three cases today, this country is far along the way to a censorship of the subjects about which the people can talk or write, we need not commit further constitutional transgressions by leaving people in the dark as to what literature or what words or what symbols if distributed through the mails make a man a criminal. As bad and obnoxious as I believe governmental censorship is in a Nation that has accepted the First Amendment as its basic ideal for freedom, I am compelled to say that censorship that would stamp certain books and literature as illegal in advance of publication or conviction would in some ways be preferable to the unpredictable book-by-book censorship into which we have now drifted.

I close this part of my dissent by saying once again that I think the First Amendment forbids any kind or type or nature of governmental censorship over views as distinguished from conduct.

II

It is obvious that the effect of the Court's decisions in the three obscenity cases handed down today is to make it exceedingly dangerous for people to discuss either orally or in writing anything about sex. Sex is a fact of life. Its pervasive influence is felt throughout the world and it cannot be ignored. Like all other facts of life it can lead to difficulty and trouble and sorrow and pain. But while it may lead to abuses, and has in many instances, no words need be spoken in order for people to know that the subject is one pleasantly interwoven in all human activities and involves the very substance of the creation of life itself. It is a subject which people are bound to consider and discuss whatever laws are passed by any government to try to suppress it. Though I do not suggest any way to solve the problems that may arise from sex or discussions about sex, of one thing I am confident, and that is that federal censorship is not the answer to these problems. I find it difficult to see how talk about sex can be placed under the kind of censorship the Court here approves without subjecting our society to more dangers than we can anticipate at the moment. It was to avoid exactly such dangers that the First Amendment was written and adopted. For myself I would follow the course which I believe is required by the First Amendment, that is, recognize that sex at least as much as any other aspect of life is so much a part of our society that its discussion should not be made a crime.

I would reverse this case.

Mr. Justice Douglas, dissenting.

Today's condemnation of the use of sex symbols to sell literature engrafts another exception on First Amendment rights that is as unwarranted as the judge-made exception concerning obscenity. This new exception condemns an advertising technique as old as history. The advertisements of our best magazines are chock-full of thighs, ankles, calves, bosoms, eyes, and hair, to draw the potential buyer's attention to lotions, tires, food, liquor, clothing, autos, and even insurance policies. The sexy advertisement neither adds to nor detracts from the quality of the merchandise being offered for sale. And I do not see how it adds to or detracts one whit from the legality of the book being distributed. A book should stand on its own, irrespective of the reasons why it was written or the wiles used in selling it. I cannot imagine any promotional effort that would make chapters 7 and 8 of the Song of Solomon any the less or any more worthy of First Amendment protection than does their unostentatious inclusion in the average edition of the Bible.

I

The Court has, in a variety of contexts, insisted that preservation of rights safeguarded by the First Amendment requires vigilance. We have recognized that a "criminal prosecution under a statute regulating expression usually involves imponderables and contingencies that themselves may inhibit the full exercise of First Amendment freedoms." *Dombrowski* v. *Pfister*, 380 U. S. 479, 486. Where uncertainty is the distinguishing characteristic of a legal principle — in this case the Court's "pandering" theory — "the free dissemination of ideas may be the loser." *Smith* v. *California*, 361 U. S. 147, 151. The Court today, however, takes the other course, despite the admonition in *Speiser* v. *Randall*, 357 U. S. 513, 525, that "[t]he separation of legitimate from illegitimate speech calls for . . . sensitive tools." Before today, due regard for the frailties of free expression led us to reject insensitive procedures and clumsy, vague, or overbroad substantive rules even in the realm of obscenity. For as the Court emphasized in *Roth* v. *United States*, 354 U. S. 476, 488, "[t]he door barring federal and state intrusion into this area cannot be left ajar; it must be kept tightly closed and opened only the slightest crack necessary to prevent encroachment upon more important interests."

Certainly without the aura of sex in the promotion of these publications their contents cannot be said to be "utterly without redeeming social importance." *Roth* v. *United States, supra,* at 484. One of the publications condemned today is *The Housewife's Handbook on Selective Promiscuity,* which a number of doctors and psychiatrists thought had clinical value. One clinical psychologist said: "I should like to recommend it, for example, to the people in my church to read, especially those who are having marital difficulties, in order to increase their tolerance and understanding for one another. Much of the book, I should think, would be very suitable reading for teen age people, especially teen age young women who could empathize strongly with the growing up period that Mrs. Rey [Anthony] relates, and could read on and be disabused of some of the unrealistic notions about marriage and sexual experiences. I should think this would make very good reading for the average man to help him gain a better appreciation of female sexuality."

The Rev. George Von Hilsheimer III, a Baptist minister, testified that he has used the book "insistently in my pastoral counseling and in my formal psychological counseling":

> The book is a history, a very unhappy history, of a series of sexual and psychological misadventures and the encounter of a quite typical and average American woman with quite typical and average American men. The fact that the book itself is the history of a woman who has had sexual adventures outside the normally accepted bounds of marriage which, of course for most Americans today, is a sort of serial polygamy, it does not teach or advocate this, but gives the women to

whom I give the book at least a sense that their own experiences are not unusual, that their sexual failures are not unusual, and that they themselves should not be guilty because they are, what they say, sexual failures.

I would think the Baptist minister's evaluation would be enough to satisfy the Court's test, unless the censor's word is to be final or unless the experts are to be weighed in the censor's scales, in which event one Anthony Comstock would too often prove more weighty than a dozen more detached scholars, or unless we, the ultimate Board of Censors, are to lay down standards for review that give the censor the benefit of the "any evidence" rule or the "substantial evidence" rule as in the administrative law field. Cf. *Universal Camera Corp.* v. *Labor Board,* 340 U.S. 474. Or perhaps we mean to let the courts sift and choose among conflicting versions of the "redeeming social importance" of a particular book, making sure that they keep their findings clear of doubt lest we reverse, as we do today in *Memoirs* v. *Massachusetts, ante,* p. 413, because the lower court in an effort to be fair showed how two-sided the argument was. Since the test is whether the publication is "utterly without redeeming social importance," then I think we should honor the opinion of the Baptist minister who testified as an expert in the field of counseling.

Then there is the newsletter *Liaison.* One of the defendants' own witnesses, critic Dwight Macdonald, testified that while, in his opinion, it did not go beyond the customary limits of candor tolerated by the community, it was "an extremely tasteless, vulgar and repulsive issue." This may, perhaps, overstate the case, but *Liaison* is admittedly little more than a collecton of "dirty" jokes and poems, with the possible exception of an interview with Dr. Albert Ellis. As to this material, I find wisdom in the words of the late Judge Jerome Frank:

> Those whose views most judges know best are other lawyers. Judges can and should take judicial notice that, at many gatherings of lawyers at Bar Association or of alumni of our leading law schools, tales are told fully as 'obscene' as many of those distributed by men . . . convicted for violation of the obscenity statute. . . . "One thinks of the lyrics sung . . . by a certain respected and conservative member of the faculty of a great law-school which considers itself the most distinguished and which is the Alma Mater of many judges sitting on᾿ upper courts."

Liaison's appeal is neither literary nor spiritual. But neither is its appeal to a "shameful or morbid interest in nudity, sex, or excretion." The appeal is to the ribald sense of humor which is — for better or worse — a part of our culture. A mature society would not suppress this newsletter as obscene but would simply ignore it.

Then there is EROS. The Court affirms the judgment of the lower court, which found only four of the many articles and essays to be obscene. One of the four articles consisted of numerous ribald limericks, to which the views expressed as to *Liaison* would apply with equal force. Another was a photo essay entitled "Black and White in Color" which dealt with interracial love: a subject undoubtedly offensive to some members of our society. Critic Dwight Macdonald testified.

I suppose if you object to the idea of a Negro and a white person having sex together, then, of course, you would be horrified by it. I don't. From the artistic point of view I thought it was very good. In fact, I thought it was done with great taste, and I don't know how to say it — I never heard of him before, but he is obviously an extremely competent and accomplished photographer.

Another defense witness, Professor Horst W. Janson, presently the Chairman of the Fine Arts Department at New York University, testified:

I think they are outstandingly beautiful and artistic photographs. I cannot imagine the theme being treated in a more lyrical and delicate manner than it has been done here.

.   .   .   .

I might add here that of course photography in appropriate hands is an artistic instrument and this particular photographer has shown a very great awareness of compositional devices and patterns that have a long and well-established history in western art.

.   .   .   .

The very contrast in the color of the two bodies of course has presented him with certain opportunities that he would not have had with two models of the same color, and he has taken rather extraordinary and very delicate advantage of these contrasts.

The third article found specifically by the trial judge to be obscene was a discussion by Drs. Eberhard W. and Phyllis C. Kronhausen of erotic writing by women, with illustrative quotations. The worth of the article was discussed by Dwight Macdonald, who stated:

> I thought [this was] an extremely interesting and important study with some remarkable quotations from the woman who had put down her sense of love-making, of sexual intercourse . . . in an extremely eloquent way. I have never seen this from the woman's point of view. I thought the point they made, the difference between the man's and the woman's approach to sexual intercourse was very well made and very important.

Still another article found obscene was a short introduction to and a lengthy excerpt from *My Life and Loves* by Frank Harris, about which there is little in the record. Suffice it to say that this seems to be a book of some literary stature. At least I find it difficult on this record to say that it is "utterly without redeeming social importance."

Some of the tracts for which these publishers go to prison concern normal sex, some homosexuality, some the masochistic yearning that is probably present in everyone and dominant in some. Masochism is a desire to be punished or subdued. In the broad frame of reference the desire may be expressed in the longing to be whipped and lashed, bound and gagged, and cruelly treated. Why is it unlawful to cater to the needs of this group? They are, to be sure, somewhat offbeat, nonconformist, and odd. But we are not in the realm of criminal conduct, only ideas and tastes. Some like Chopin, others like "rock and roll." Some are "normal," some are masochistic, some deviant in other respects, such as the homosexual. Another group also represented here translates mundane articles into sexual symbols. This group, like those embracing masochism, are anathema to the so-called stable majority. But why is freedom of the press and expression denied them? Are they to be barred from communicating in symbolisms important to them? When the Court today speaks of "social value," does it mean a "value" to the majority? Why is not a minority "value" cognizable? The masochistic group is one; the deviant group is another. Is it not important that members of those groups communicate with each other? Why is communication by the "written word" forbidden? If we were wise enough, we might know that communication may have greater therapeutical value than any sermon that those of the "normal" community can ever offer. But if the communication is of value to the masochistic community or to others of the deviant community, how can it be said to be "utterly without redeeming social importance"? "Redeeming" to whom? "Importance" to whom? We took quite a different stance in *One, Inc.* v. *Olesen*, 355 U. S. 371, where we unanimously reversed the decision of the Court of Appeals in 241 F. 2d 772 without opinion. Our holding was accurately described by Lockhart and McClure, Obscenity Censorship: The Core Constitutional Issue — What Is Obscene? 7 Utah L. Rev. 289, 293 (1961):

> [This] was a magazine for homosexuals entitled *One — The Homosexual Magazine*, which was definitely not a scientific or critical magazine, but appears to have been written to appeal to the tastes and interests of homosexuals.

Man was not made in a fixed mould. If a publication caters to the idiosyncrasies of a minority, why does it not have some "social importance"? Each of us is a very temporary transient with likes and dislikes that cover the spectrum. However plebeian my tastes may be, who am I to say that others' tastes must be so limited and that other tastes have no "social importance"? How can we know enough to probe the mysteries of the subconscious of our people and say that this is good for them and that is not? Catering to the most eccentric taste may have "social importance" in giving that minority an opportunity to express itself rather than to repress its inner desires, as I suggest in my separate opinion in *Memoirs* v. *Massachusetts*, *ante*, at 431–432. How can we know that this expression may not *prevent* antisocial conduct?

I find it difficult to say that a publication has no "social importance" because it caters to the taste of the most unorthodox amongst us. We members of this Court should be among the last to say what should be orthodox in literature. An omniscience would be required which few in our whole society possess.

II

This leads me to the conclusion, previously noted, that the First Amendment allows all ideas to be expressed — whether orthodox, popular, offbeat, or repulsive. I do not think it permissible to draw lines between the "good" and the "bad" and be true to the constitutional mandate to let all ideas alone. If our Constitution permitted "reasonable" regulation of freedom of expression, as do the constitutions of some nations, we would have much leeway. But under our charter all regulation or control of expression is barred. Government does not sit to reveal where the "truth" is. People are left to pick and choose between competing offerings. There is no compulsion to take and read what is repulsive any more than there is to spend one's time poring over government bulletins, political tracts, or theological treatises. The theory is that people are mature enough to pick and choose to recognize trash when they see it, to be attracted to the literature that satisfies their deepest need, and, hopefully, to move from plateau to plateau and finally reach the world of enduring ideas.

I think this is the ideal of the Free Society written into our Constitution. We have no business acting as censors or endowing any group with censorship powers. It is shocking to me for us to send to prison anyone for publishing anything, especially tracts so distant from any incitement to action as the ones before us.

[This opinion applies also to *Mishkin* v. *New York, post,* p. 502.]

Mr. Justice Harlan, dissenting.

I would reverse the convictions of Ginzburg and his three corporate co-defendants. The federal obscenity statute under which they were convicted, 18 U. S. C. § 1461 (1964 ed.), is concerned with unlawful shipment of "nonmailable" matter. In my opinion announcing the judgment of the Court in *Manual Enterprises, Inc.* v. *Day,* 370 U. S. 478, the background of the statute was assessed, and its focus was seen to be solely on the character of the material in question. That too has been the premise on which past cases in this Court arising under this statute, or its predecessors, have been decided. See, e. g., *Roth* v. *United States,* 354 U. S. 476. I believe that under this statute the Federal Government is constitutionally restricted to banning from the mails only "hardcore pornography," see my separate opinion in *Roth, supra,* at 507, and my dissenting opinion in *A Book Named "John Cleland's Memoirs"* v. *Attorney General of Massachusetts, ante,* p. 455. Because I do not think it can be maintained that the material in question here falls within that narrow class, I do not believe it can be excluded from the mails.

The Court recognizes the difficulty of justifying these convictions; the majority refuses to approve the trial judge's "exegesis of *Roth*" (note 3, *ante*, p. 465); it declines to approve the trial court's "characterizations" of the *Handbook* "outside" the "setting" which the majority for the first time announces to be crucial to this conviction (note 5, *ante*, p. 466). Moreover, the Court accepts the Government's concession that the *Handbook* has a certain "worth" when seen in something labeled a "controlled, or even neutral, environment" (*ante*, p. 472); the majority notes that these are "publications which we have assumed . . . cannot themselves be adjudged obscene in the abstract" (*ante*, p. 474). In fact, the Court in the last analysis sustains the convictions on the express assumption that the items held to be obscene are not, viewing them strictly, obscene at all (*ante*, p. 466).

This curious result is reached through the elaboration of a theory of obscenity entirely unrelated to the language, purposes, or history of the federal statute now being applied, and certainly different from the test used by the trial court to convict the defendants. While the precise holding of the Court is obscure, I take it that the objective test of *Roth*, which ultimately focuses on the material in question, is to be supplemented by another test that goes to the question whether the mailer's aim is to "pander" to or "titillate" those to whom he mails questionable matter.

Although it is not clear whether the majority views the panderer test as a statutory gloss or as constitutional doctrine, I read the opinion to be in the latter category. The First Amendment, in the obscenity area, no longer fully protects material on its face nonobscene, for such material must now also be examined in the light of the defendant's conduct, attitude, motives. This seems to me a mere euphemism for allowing punishment of a person who mails otherwise constitutionally protected material just because a jury or a judge may not find him or his business agreeable. Were a State to enact a "panderer" statute under its police power, I have little doubt that — subject to clear drafting to avoid attacks on vagueness and equal protection grounds — such a statute would be constitutional. Possibly the same might be true of the Federal Government acting under its postal or commerce powers. What I fear the Court has done today is in effect to write a new statute, but without the sharply focused definitions and standards necessary in such a sensitive area. Casting such a dubious gloss over a straightforward 101-year-old statute (see 13 Stat. 507) is for me an astonishing piece of judicial improvisation.

It seems perfectly clear that the theory on which these convictions are now sustained is quite different from the basis on which the case was tried and decided by the District Court and affirmed by the Court of Appeals. The District Court found the *Handbook* "patently offensive on its face" and without "the slightest redeeming social, artistic or literary importance or value"; it held that there was "no credible evidence that the *Handbook* has the slightest valid scientific importance for treatment of individuals in clinical psychiatry, psychology, or any field of medicine." 224 F. Supp. 129, 131. The trial court made similar findings as to EROS and *Liaison*. The majority's opinion, as I read it, casts doubts upon these explicit findings. As to the *Handbook*, the Court interprets an offhand remark by the government prosecutor at the sentencing hearing as a "concession," which the majority accepts, that the prosecution rested upon the conduct of the petitioner, and the Court explicitly refuses to accept the trial judge's "characterizations" of the book, which I take to be an implied rejection of the findings of fact upon which the conviction was in fact based (note 5, *ante*, p. 466). Similarly as to EROS, the Court implies that the finding of obscenity might be "erroneous" were it not supported "by the evidence of pandering" (*ante*, p. 471). The Court further characterizes the EROS decision, aside from pandering, as "an otherwise debatable conclusion" (*ante*, p. 471).

If there is anything to this new pandering dimension to the mailing statute, the Court should return the case for a new trial, for petitioners are at least entitled to a day in court on the question on which their guilt has ultimately come to depend. Compare the action of the Court in *Memoirs* v. *Massachusetts*, *ante*, p. 413, also decided today, where the Court affords the State an opportunity to prove in a subsequent prosecution that an accused purveyor of *Fanny Hill* in fact used pandering methods to secure distribution of the book.

If a new trial were given in the present case, as I read the Court's opinion, the burden would be on the Government to show that the motives of the defendants were to pander to "the widespread weakness for titillation by pornography" (*ante*, p. 471). I suppose that an analysis of the type of individuals receiving EROS and the *Handbook* would be relevant. If they were ordinary people, interested in purchasing EROS or the *Handbook* for one of a dozen personal reasons, this might be some evidence of pandering to the general public. On the other hand, as the Court suggests, the defendants could exonerate themselves by showing that they sent these works only or perhaps primarily (no standards are set) to psychiatrists and other serious-minded professional people. Also relevant would apparently be the nature of the mailer's advertisements or representations. Conceivably someone mailing to the public selective portions of a recognized classic with the avowed purpose of titillation would run the risk of conviction for mailing nonmailable matter. Presumably the Post Office under this theory might once again attempt to ban *Lady Chatterley's Lover*, which a lower court found not bannable in 1960 by an abstract application of *Roth*. *Grove Press, Inc.* v. *Christenberry*, 276 F. 2d 433. I would suppose that if the Government could show that Grove Press is pandering to people who are interested in the book's sexual passages and not in D. H. Lawrence's social theories or literary technique § 1461 could properly be invoked. Even the well-known opinions of Judge A. N. Hand in *United States* v. *One Book Entitled Ulysses*, 72 F. 2d 705, and of Judge Woolsey in the District Court, 5 F. Supp. 182, might be rendered nugatory if a mailer of *Ulysses* is found to be titillating readers with its "coarse, blasphemous, and obscene" portions, 72 F. 2d, at 707, rather than piloting them through the intricacies of Joyce's stream of consciousness.

In the past, as in the trial of these petitioners, evidence as to a defendant's conduct was admissible only to show relevant intent. Now evidence not only as to conduct, but also as to attitude and motive, is admissible on the primary question of whether the material mailed is obscene. I have difficulty seeing how these inquiries are logically related to the question whether a particular work is obscene. In addition, I think such a test for obscenity is impermissibly vague, and unwarranted by anything in the First Amendment or in 18 U. S. C. § 1461.

I would reverse the judgments below.

Mr. Justice Stewart, dissenting.

Ralph Ginzburg has been sentenced to five years in prison for sending through the mail copies of a magazine, a pamphlet, and a book. There was testimony at his trial that these publications possess artistic and social merit. Personally, I have a hard time discerning any. Most of the material strikes me as both vulgar and unedifying. But if the First Amendment means anything, it means that a man cannot be sent to prison merely for distributing publications which offend a judge's esthetic sensibilities, mine or any other's.

Censorship reflects a society's lack of confidence in itself. It is a hallmark of an authoritarian regime. Long ago those who wrote our First Amendment charted a different course. They believed a society can be truly strong only when it is truly free. In the realm of expression they put their faith, for better or for worse, in the enlightened choice of the people, free from the interference of a policeman's intrusive thumb or a judge's heavy hand. So it is that the Constitution protects coarse expression as well as refined, and vulgarity no less than elegance. A book worthless to me may convey something of value to my neighbor. In the free society to which our Constitution has committed us, it is for each to choose for himself.

Because such is the mandate of our Constitution, there is room for only the most restricted view of this Court's decision in *Roth* v. *United States*, 354 U. S. 476. In that case the Court held that "obscenity is not within the area of constitutionally protected speech or press." *Id.*, at 485. The Court there characterized obscenity as that which is "utterly without redeeming social importance," *id.*, at 484, "deals with sex in a manner appealing to prurient interest," *id.*, at 487, and "goes substantially beyond customary limits of candor in description or representation of such matters." *Id.*, at 487, n. 20. In *Manual Enterprises* v. *Day*, 370 U.S. 478, I joined Mr. Justice Harlan's opinion adding "patent indecency" as a further essential element of that which is not constitutionally protected.

There does exist a distinct and easily identifiable class of material in which all of these elements coalesce. It is that, and that alone, which I think government may constitutionally suppress, whether by criminal or civil sanctions. I have referred to such material before as hardcore pornography, without trying further to define it. *Jacobellis* v. *Ohio*, 378 U.S. 184, at 197 (concurring opinion). In order to prevent any possible misunderstanding, I have set out in the margin a description, borrowed from the the Solicitor General's brief, of the kind of thing to which I have reference. See also Lockhart and McClure, Censorship of Obscenity: The Developing Constitutional Standards, 45 Minn. L. Rev. 5, 63–64.

Although arguments can be made to the contrary, I accept the proposition that the general dissemination of matter of this description may be suppressed under valid laws. That has long been the almost universal judgment of our society. See *Roth* v. *United States*, 354 U.S., at 485. But material of this sort is wholly different from the publications mailed by Ginzburg in the present case, and different not in degree but in kind.

The Court today appears to concede that the materials Ginzburg mailed were themselves protected by the First Amendment. But, the Court says, Ginzburg can still be sentenced to five years in prison for mailing them. Why? Because, says the Court, he was guilty of "commercial exploitation," of "pandering," and of "titillation." But Ginzburg was not charged with "commercial exploitation"; he was not charged with "pandering"; he was not charged with "titillation." Therefore, to affirm his conviction now on any of those grounds, even if otherwise valid, is to deny him due process of law. *Cole* v. *Arkansas*, 333 U.S. 196. But those grounds are *not*, of course, otherwise valid. Neither the statute under which Ginzburg was convicted nor any other federal statute I know of makes "commercial exploitation" or "pandering" or "titillation" a criminal offense. And any criminal law that sought to do so in the terms so elusively defined by the Court would, of course, be unconstitutionally vague and therefore void. All of these matters are developed in the dissenting opinions of my Brethren, and I simply note here that I fully agree with them.

For me, however, there is another aspect of the Court's opinion in this case that is even more regrettable. Today the Court assumes the power to deny Ralph Ginzburg the protection of the First Amendment because it disapproves of his "sordid business." That is a power the Court does not possess. For the First Amendment protects us all with an even hand. It applies to Ralph Ginzburg with no less completeness and force than to G. P. Putnam's Sons. In upholding and enforcing the Bill of Rights, this Court has no power to pick or to choose. When we lose sight of that fixed star of constitutional adjudication, we lose our way. For then we forsake a government of law and are left with government by Big Brother.

I dissent.

PART

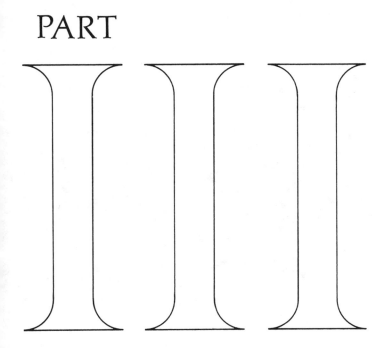

III

Contemporary Essays on
Freedom of Speech:
General Principles and
Specific Issues

THE RULERS AND THE RULED

Alexander Meiklejohn

The purpose of these lectures is to consider the freedom of speech which is guaranteed by the Constitution of the United States. The most general thesis of the argument is that, under the Constitution, there are two different freedoms of speech, and, hence, two different guarantees of freedom rather than only one.

More broadly, it may be asserted that our civil liberties, in general, are not all of one kind. They are of two kinds which, though radically different in constitutional status, are easily confused. And that confusion has been, and is, disastrous in its effect upon our understanding of the relations between an individual citizen and the government of the United States. The argument of these lectures is an attempt to clear away that confusion.

As an instance of the first kind of civil liberty I would offer that of religious or irreligious belief. In this country of ours, so far as the Constitution is effective, men are free to believe and to advocate or to disbelieve and to argue against, any creed. And the government is unqualifiedly forbidden to restrict that freedom. As an instance of the second kind, we may take the liberty of an individual to own, and to use the income from his labor or his property. It is agreed among us that every man has a right, a liberty, to such ownership and use. And yet it is also agreed that the government may take whatever part of a man's income it deems necessary for the promoting of the general welfare. The liberty of owning and using property is, then, as contrasted with that of religious belief, a limited one. It may be invaded by the government. And the Constitution authorizes such invasion. It requires only that the procedure shall be properly and impartially carried out and that it shall be justified by public need.

Our Constitution, then, recognizes and protects two different sets of freedoms. One of these is open to restriction by the government. The other is not open to such restriction. It would be of great value to our argument and, in fact, to all attempts at political thinking in the United States, if there were available two sharply defined terms by which to identify these two fundamentally different kinds of civil liberty. But, alas, no such accurate use of words has been established among us. Men speak of the freedom of belief and the freedom of property as if, in the Constitution, the word "freedom," as used in these two cases, had the same meaning. Because of that confusion we are in constant danger of giving to a man's possessions the same dignity, the same status, as we give to the man himself. From that confusion our national life has suffered disastrous effects in all its phases. But for this disease of our minds there is, so far as I know, no specific semantic cure. All that we can do at present is to remember that such terms as liberty, freedom, civil rights, etc., are ambiguous. We must, then, in each specific case, try to keep clear what meaning we are using.

1

We Americans think of ourselves as politically free. We believe in self-government. If men are to be governed, we say, then that governing must be done, not by others, but by themselves. So far, therefore, as our own affairs are concerned, we refuse to submit to alien control. That refusal, if need be, we will carry to the point of rebellion, of revolution. And if other men, within the jurisdiction of our laws, are denied their right to political freedom, we will, in the same spirit, rise to their defense. Governments, we insist, derive their just powers from the consent of the governed. If that consent be lacking, governments have no just powers.

Now, this political program of ours, though passionately advocated by us, is not — as we all recognize — fully worked out in practice. Over one hundred and seventy years have gone by since the Declaration of Independence was written. But, to an unforgivable degree, citizens of the United States are still subjected to decisions in the making of which they have had no effective share. So far as that is true, we are not self-governed; we are not politically free. We are governed by others. And, perhaps worse, we are, without their consent, the governors of others.

But a more important point — which we Americans do not so readily recognize — is that of the intellectual difficulties which are inherent in the making and administering of this political program of ours. We do not see how baffling, even to the point of desperation, is the task of using our minds, to which we are summoned by our plan of government. That plan is not intellectually simple. Its victories are chiefly won, not by the carnage of battle, but by the sweat and agony of the mind. By contrast with it, the idea of alien government which we reject — whatever its other merits or defects — is easy to understand. It is suited to simpleminded people who are unwilling or unable to question their own convictions, who would defend their principles by suppressing that hostile criticism which is necessary for their clarification.

The intellectual difficulty of which I am speaking is sharply indicated by Professor Edward Hallett Carr, in his recent book, *The Soviet Impact on the Western World.* Mr. Carr tells us that our American political program, as we formulate it, is not merely unclear. It is essentially self-contradictory and hence, nonsensical. "Confusion of thought," he says, "is often caused by the habit common among politicians and writers of the English-speaking world, of defining democracy in formal and conventional terms as 'self-government' or 'government by consent.'" What these terms define, he continues, "is not democracy, but anarchy. Government of some kind is necessary in the common interest precisely because men will not govern themselves. 'Government by consent' is a contradiction in terms; for the purpose of government is to compel people to do what they would not do of their own volition. In short, government is a process by which some people exercise compulsion on others."[1]

Those words of Mr. Carr seem to me radically false. And, whatever else these lectures may do or fail to do, I hope that they may, in some measure, serve as a refutation of his contention. And yet the challenge of so able and well-balanced a mind cannot be ignored. If we believe in our principles we must make clear to others and to ourselves that self-government is not anarchy. We must show in what sense a free man, a free society, does practice self-direction. What, then, is the difference between a political system in which men do govern themselves and a political system in which men, without their consent,

[1] Edward Hallett Carr, *The Soviet Impact on the Western World* (New York, Macmillan, 1947), p. 10.

are governed by others? Unless we can make clear that distinction, discussion of freedom of speech or of any other freedom is meaningless and futile.

Alien government, we have said, is simple in idea. It is easy to understand. When one man or some self-chosen group holds control, without consent, over others, the relation between them is one of force and counterforce, of compulsion on the one hand and submission or resistance on the other. That relation is external and mechanical. It can be expressed in numbers — numbers of guns or planes or dollars or machines or policemen. The only basic fact is that one group "has the power" and the other group has not. In such a despotism, a ruler, by some excess of strength or guile or both, without the consent of his subjects, forces them into obedience. And in order to understand what he does, what they do, we need only measure the strength or weakness of the control and the strength or weakness of the resistance to it.

But government by consent — self-government — is not thus simple. It is, in fact, so complicated, so confusing, that, not only to the scholarly judgment of Mr. Carr, but also to the simple-mindedness which we call "shrewd, practical, calculating, common sense," it tends to seem silly, unrealistic, romantic, or — to use a favorite term of reproach — "idealistic." And the crux of the difficulty lies in the fact that, in such a society, the governors and the governed are not two distinct groups of persons. There is only one group — the self-governing people. Rulers and ruled are the same individuals. We, the People, are our own masters, our own subjects. But that inner relationship of men to themselves is utterly different in kind from the external relationship of one man to another. It cannot be expressed in terms of forces and compulsions. If we attempt to think about the political procedures of self-government by means of the ideas which are useful in describing the external control of a hammer over a nail or of a master over his slaves, the meaning slips through the fingers of our minds. For thinking which is done merely in terms of forces, political freedom does not exist.

At this point, a protest must be entered against the oversimplified advice which tells us that we should introduce into the realms of economics, politics, and morals the "methods" of the "sciences." Insofar as the advice suggests to us that we keep our beliefs within the limits of the evidence which warrants them, insofar as it tells us that our thinking about human relationships must be as exact and tentative, as orderly and inclusive, as is the work done by students of physical or biological fact, no one may challenge either its validity or its importance. To believe what one has no reason for believing is a crime of the first order. But, on the other hand, it must be urged that the chief source of our blundering ineptness in dealing with moral and political problems is that we do not know how to think about them except by quantitative methods which are borrowed from non-moral, non-political, non-social sciences. In this sense we need to be, not more scientific, but less scientific, not more quantitative but other than quantitative. We must create and use methods of inquiry, methods of belief which are suitable to the study of men as self-governing persons but not suitable to the study of forces or of machines. In the understanding of a free society, scientific thinking has an essential part to play. But it is a secondary part. We shall not understand the Constitution of the United States if we think of men only as pushed around by forces. We must see them also as governing themselves.

But the statement just made must be guarded against two easy misinterpretations. First, when we say that self-government is hard to interpret, we are not saying that it is mysterious or magical or irrational. Quite the contrary is true. No idea which we have is more sane, more matter-of-fact, more immediately sensible, than that of self-government. Whether it be in the field of individual or of social activity, men are not recognizable as men unless, in any given situation, they are using their minds to give direction to their behavior. But the point which we are making is that the externalized measuring of the play of forces which serves the purposes of business or of science is wholly unsuited to our dealing with problems of moral or political freedom. And we Americans seem characteristically blind to the distinction. We are at the top of the world in engineering. We are experts in the knowledge and manipulation of measurable forces, whether physical or psychological. We invent and run machines of ever new and amazing power and intricacy. And we are tempted by that achievement to see if we can manipulate men with the same skill and ingenuity. But the manipulation of men is the destruction 'of self-government. Our skill, therefore, threatens our wisdom. In this respect the United States with its "know-how" is, today, the most dangerous nation in the world.

And, second, what we have said must not be allowed to obscure the fact that a free government, established by common consent, may and often must use force in compelling citizens to obey the laws. Every government, as such, must have external power. It must, in fact, be more powerful than any one of its citizens, than any group of them. Political freedom does not mean freedom from control. It means self-control. If, for example, a nation becomes involved in war, the government must decide who shall be drafted to leave his family and home, to risk his life, his health, his sanity, upon the battlefield. The government must also levy and collect and expend taxes. In general, it must determine how far and in what ways the customs and privileges of peace are to be swept aside. In all these cases it may be taken for granted that, in a self-governing society, minorities will disagree with the decisions which are made. May a minority man, then, by appeal to the principle of "consent," refuse to submit to military control? May he evade payment of taxes which he thinks unwise or unjust? May he say, "I did not approve of this measure; therefore, as a self-governing man, I claim the right to disobey it"?

Certainly not! At the bottom of every plan of self-government is a basic agreement, in which all the citizens have joined, that all matters of public policy shall be decided by corporate action, that such decisions shall be equally binding on all citizens, whether they agree with them or not, and that, if need be, they shall, by due legal procedure, be enforced upon anyone who refuses to conform to them. The man who rejects that agreement is not objecting to tyranny or despotism. He is objecting to political freedom. He is not a democrat. He is the anarchist of whom Mr. Carr speaks. Self-government is nonsense unless the "self" which governs is able and determined to make its will effective.

2

What, then, is this compact or agreement which underlies any plan for political freedom? It cannot be understood unless we distinguish sharply and persistently between the "submission" of a slave and the "consent" of a free citizen. In both cases it is agreed that obedience shall be required. Even when despotism is so extreme as to be practically indistinguishable from enslavement, a sort of pseudo consent is given by the subjects. When the ruling force is overwhelming, men are driven not only to submit, but also to agree to do so. For the time, at least, they decide to make the best of a bad situation rather than to struggle against hopeless odds. And, coordinate with this "submission" by the people, there are "concessions" by the ruler. For the avoiding of trouble, to establish his power, to manipulate one hostile force against another, he must take account of the desires and interests of his subjects, must manage to keep them from becoming too rebellious. The granting of such "concessions" and the accepting of them are, perhaps, the clearest evidence that a government is not democratic but is essentially despotic and alien.

But the "consent" of free citizens is radically different in kind from this "submission" of slaves. Free men talk about their government, not in terms of its "favors" but in terms of their "rights." They do not bargain. They reason. Every one of them is, of course, subject to the laws which are made.

But if the Declaration of Independence means what it says, if we mean what it says, then no man is called upon to obey a law unless he himself, equally with his fellows, has shared in making it. Under an agreement to which, in the closing words of the Declaration of Independence, "we mutually pledge to each other our Lives, our Fortunes, and our sacred Honor," the consent which we give is not forced upon us. It expresses a voluntary compact among political equals. We, the people, acting together, either directly or through our representatives, make and administer law. We, the People, acting in groups or separately, are subject to the law. If we could make that double agreement effective, we would have accomplished the American Revolution. If we could understand that agreement we would understand the Revolution, which is still in the making. But the agreement can have meaning for us only as we clarify the tenuous and elusive distinction between a political "submission" which we abhor and a political "consent" in which we glory. Upon the effectiveness of that distinction rests the entire enormous and intricate structure of those free political institutions which we have pledged ourselves to build. If we can think that distinction clearly, we can be self-governing. If we lose our grip upon it, if, rightly or wrongly, we fall back into the prerevolutionary attitudes which regard our chosen representatives as alien and hostile to ourselves, nothing can save us from the slavery which, in 1776, we set out to destroy.

3

I have been saying that, under the plan of political freedom, we maintain by common consent a government which, being stronger than any one of us, than any group of us, can take control over all of us. But the word "control" strikes terror into the hearts of many "free" men, especially if they are mechanically minded about their freedom. Out of that fear there arises the passionate demand that the government which controls us must itself be controlled. By whom, and in what ways?

In abstract principle, that question is easy to answer. A government of free men can properly be controlled only by itself. Who else could be trusted by us to hold our political institutions in check? Shall any single individual or any special group be allowed to take domination over the agencies of control? There is only one situation in which free men can answer "yes" to that question. If the government, as an institution, has broken down, if the basic agreement has collapsed, then both the right and the duty of rebellion are thrust upon the individual citizens. In that chaotic and desperate situation they must, for the sake of a new order, revolt and destroy, as the American colonies in 1776 revolted and destroyed. But, short of such violent lawlessness in the interest of a new law, there can be no doubt that a free government must be its own master. If We, the People are to be controlled, then We, the People must do the controlling. As a corporate body, we must exercise control over our separate members. That principle is a flat denial of the suggestion that we, acting as an unorganized and irresponsible mob, may drive into submission ourselves acting as an organized government. What it means is that the body politic, organized as a nation, must recognize its own limitations of wisdom and of temper and of circumstance, and must, therefore, make adequate provision for self-criticism and self-restraint. The government itself must limit the government, must determine what it may and may not do. It must make sure that its attempts to make men free do not result in making them slaves.

Our own American constitutional procedure gives striking illustration of the double principle that no free government can submit to control other than its own and that, therefore, it must limit and control itself. For example, our agencies of government do their work under a scheme of mutual checks and balances. The Bill of Rights, also, sharply and explicitly defines boundaries beyond which acts of governing may not go. "Congress shall make no law . . ." it says. And again, "No person shall be held to answer for a capital or otherwise infamous crime unless . . ." And again, "Excessive bail shall not be required, nor excessive fines imposed, nor cruel and unusual punishments inflicted." All these and many other limits are set to the powers of government. But in every case — let it be noted — these limits are set by government. These enactments were duly proposed, discussed, adopted, interpreted, and enforced by regular political procedure. And, as the years have gone by, We, the People, who, by explicit compact, are the government, have maintained and interpreted and extended them. In some cases, we have reinterpreted them or have even abolished them. They are expressions of our own corporate self-control. They tell us that, by compact, explicit or implicit, we are self-governed.

Here, then, is the thesis upon which the argument of these lectures is to rest. At the bottom of our American plan of government there is, as Thomas Jefferson has firmly told us, a "compact." To Jefferson it is clear that as fellow citizens we have made and are continually remaking an agreement with one another, and that, whatever the cost, we are in honor bound to keep that agreement. The nature of the compact to which we "consent" is suggested by the familiar story of the meeting of the Pilgrims in the cabin of the Mayflower. "We whose names are underwritten, . . ." they said, ". . . Do by these Presents solemnly and mutually, in the presence of God, and one another, Covenant and Combine ourselves together into a Civil Body Politick, for our better ordering and preservation, and furtherance of the ends aforesaid; and by virtue hereof do enact, constitute, and frame such just and equal Laws, Ordinances, Acts, Constitutions, and Offices, from time to time, as shall be thought most meet and convenient for the general good of the Colony; unto which we promise all due submission and obedience. . . ." This is the same pledge of comradeship, of responsible cooperation in a joint undertaking, which was given in the concluding words of the Declaration of Independence already quoted — "We mutually pledge to each other our Lives, our Fortunes, and our sacred Honor." And, some years later, as the national revolution moved on from its first step to its second, from the negative task of destroying alien government to the positive work of creating self-government, the Preamble of the Constitution announced the common purposes in the pursuit of which we had become united. "We, the People of the United States," it says, "in order to form a more perfect Union, establish justice, insure domestic tranquillity, provide for the common defense, promote the general welfare, and secure the blessings of liberty to ourselves and our posterity, do ordain and establish this Constitution of the United States of America."

In those words it is agreed, and with every passing moment it is reagreed, that the people of the United States shall be self-governed. To that fundamental enactment all other provisions of the Constitution, all statutes, all administrative decrees, are subsidiary and dependent. All other purposes, whether individual or social, can find their legitimate scope and meaning only as they conform to the one basic purpose that the citizens of this nation shall make and shall obey their own laws, shall be at once their own subjects and their own masters.

Our preliminary remarks about the Constitution of the United States may, then, be briefly summarized. That Constitution is based upon a twofold political agreement. It is ordained that all authority to exercise control, to determine common action, belongs to "We, the People." We, and we alone, are the rulers. But it is ordained also that We, the People, are, all alike, subject to control. Every one of us may be told what he is allowed to do, what he is not allowed to do, what he is required to do. But this agreed-upon requirement of obedience does not transform a ruler into a slave. Citizens do not become puppets of the state when, having created it by common consent, they pledge allegiance to it and keep their pledge. Control by a self-governing nation is utterly different in kind from control by an irresponsible despotism. And to confuse these two is to lose all understanding of what political freedom is. Under actual conditions, there is no freedom for men except by the authority of government. Free men are not non-governed. They are governed — by themselves.

And now, after this long introduction, we are, I hope, ready for the task of interpreting the First Amendment to the Constitution, of trying to clear away the confusions by which its meaning has been obscured and even lost.

4

"Congress shall make no law . . . abridging the freedom of speech . . ." says the First Amendment to the Constitution. As we turn now to the interpreting of those words, three preliminary remarks should be made.

First, let it be noted that, by those words, Congress is not debarred from all action upon freedom of speech. Legislation which abridges that freedom is forbidden, but not legislation to enlarge and enrich it. The freedom of mind which befits the members of a self-governing society is not a given and fixed part of human nature. It can be increased and established by learning, by teaching, by the unhindered flow of accurate information, by giving men health and vigor and security, by bringing them together in activities of communication and mutual understanding. And the federal legislature is not forbidden to engage in that positive enterprise of cultivating the general intelligence upon which the success of self-government so obviously depends. On the contrary, in that positive field the Congress of the United States has a heavy and basic responsibility to promote the freedom of speech.

And second, no one who reads with care the text of the First Amendment can fail to be startled by its absoluteness. The phrase, "Congress shall make no law . . . abridging the freedom of speech," is unqualified. It admits of no exceptions. To say that no laws of a given type shall be made means that no laws of that type shall, under any circumstances, be made. That prohibition holds good in war as in peace, in danger as in security. The men who adopted the Bill of Rights were not ignorant of the necessities of war or of national danger. It would, in fact, be nearer to the truth to say that it was exactly those necessities which they had in mind as they planned to defend freedom of discussion against them. Out of their own bitter experience they knew how terror and hatred, how war and strife, can drive men into acts of unreasoning suppression. They planned, therefore, both for the peace which they desired and for the wars which they feared. And in both cases they established an absolute, unqualified prohibition of the abridgment of the freedom of speech. That same requirement, for the same reasons, under the same Constitution, holds good today.

Against what has just been said it will be answered that twentieth-century America does not accept "absolutes" so readily as did the eighteenth century. But to this we must reply that the issue here involved cannot be dealt with by such twentieth-century a priori reasoning. It requires careful examination of the structure and functioning of our political system as a whole to see what part the principle of the freedom of speech plays, here and now, in that system. And when that examination is made, it seems to me clear that for our day and generation, the words of the First Amendment mean literally what they say. And what they say is that under no circumstances shall the freedom of speech be abridged. Whether or not that opinion can be justified is the primary issue with which this argument tries to deal.

But, third, this dictum which we rightly take to express the most vital wisdom which men have won in their striving for political freedom is yet — it must be admitted — strangely paradoxical. No one can doubt that, in any well-governed society, the legislature has both the right and the duty to prohibit certain forms of speech. Libellous assertions may be, and must be, forbidden and punished. So too must slander. Words which incite men to crime are themselves criminal and must be dealt with as such. Sedition and treason may be expressed by speech or writing.[2] And, in those cases, decisive repressive action by the government is imperative for the sake of the general welfare. All these necessities that speech be limited are recognized and provided for under the Constitution. They were not unknown to the writers of the First Amendment. That amendment, then, we may take it for granted, *does not forbid the abridging of speech*. But, at the same time, *it does forbid the abridging of the freedom of speech*. It is to the solving of that paradox, that apparent self-contradiction, that we are summoned if, as free men, we wish to know what the right of freedom of speech is.

5

As we proceed now to reflect upon the relations of a thinking and speaking individual to the government which guards his freedom, we may do well to turn back for a few moments to the analysis of those relations given by Plato. The Athenian philosopher of the fourth century B.C. was himself caught in our paradox. He saw the connec-

---

[2] I shall be grateful if the reader will eliminate from the sentence, "Sedition and treason may be expressed by speech or writing," the words "Sedition and." "Treason" is a genuine word, with an honest and carefully defined procedural meaning. But "sedition," as applied to belief or communication, is, for the most part, a tricky and misleading word. It is used chiefly to suggest that a "treasonable" crime has been committed in an area in which, under the Constitution, no such crime can exist. (Note added 1960.)

tion between self-government and intelligence with a clarity and wisdom and wit which have never been excelled. In his two short dialogues, the *Apology* and the *Crito*, he grapples with the problem which we are facing.

In both dialogues, Plato is considering the right which a government has to demand obedience from its citizens. And in both dialogues, Socrates, a thinker and teacher who had aroused Plato from dogmatic slumber, is the citizen whose relations are discussed. The question is whether or not Socrates is in duty bound to obey the government. In the *Apology* the answer is "No." In the *Crito* the answer is "Yes." Plato is obviously using one of the favorite devices of the teacher. He is seeming to contradict himself. He is thereby demanding of his pupils that they save themselves and him from contradiction by making clear a basic and elusive distinction.

In the *Apology*, Socrates is on trial for his life. The charge against him is that in his teaching he has "corrupted the youth" and has "denied the Gods." On the evidence presented by a kind of un-Athenian Subversive Activities Committee he is found guilty. His judges do not wish to put him to death, but they warn him that, unless he will agree to stop his teaching or to change its tenor, they must order his execution. And to this demand for obedience to a decree abridging his freedom of speech, Socrates replies with a flat and unequivocal declaration of disobedient independence. My teaching, he says, is not, in that sense, under the abridging control of the government. Athens is a free city. No official, no judge, he declares, may tell me what I shall, or shall not, teach or think. He recognizes that the government has the power and the legal right to put him to death. But so far as the content of his teaching is concerned, he claims unqualified independence. "Congress shall make no law abridging the freedom of speech," he seems to be saying. Present-day Americans who wish to understand the meaning, the human intention, expressed by the First Amendment, would do well to read and to ponder again Plato's *Apology*, written in Athens twenty-four centuries ago. It may well be argued that if the Apology had not been written — by Plato or by someone else — the First Amendment would not have been written. The relation here is one of trunk and branch.

But the argument of the *Crito* seems, at least, to contradict that of the *Apology*. Here Socrates, having been condemned to death, is in prison awaiting the carrying out of the sentence. His friend Crito urges him to escape, to evade the punishment. This he refuses to do. He has no right, he says, to disobey the decision of the government that he must drink the hemlock. That government has legal authority over the life and death of its citizens. Even though it is mistaken, and, therefore, unjust, they must, in this field, conform to its decisions. For Socrates, obedience to the laws which would abridge his life is here quite as imperative as was disobedience to laws which would abridge his belief and the expression of it. In passages of amazing beauty and insight, Socrates explains that duty to Crito. He represents himself as conversing with The Laws of Athens about the compact into which they and he have entered. The Laws, he says, remind him that for seventy years, he has "consented" to them, has accepted from them all the rights and privileges of an Athenian citizen. Will he now, they ask, because his own life is threatened, withdraw his consent, annul the compact? To do that would be a shameful thing, unworthy of a citizen of Athens.

Plato is too great a teacher to formulate for us, or for his more immediate pupils, the distinction which he is here drawing. He demands of us that we make it for ourselves. But that there is a distinction and that the understanding of it is essential for the practice of freedom, he asserts passionately and without equivocation. If the government attempts to limit the freedom of a man's opinions, he tells us, that man, and his fellows with him, has both the right and the duty of disobedience. But if, on the other hand, by regular legal procedure, his life or his property is required of him, he must submit; he must let them go willingly. In one phase of man's activities, the government may exercise control over him. In another phase, it may not. What, then, are those two phases? Only as we see clearly the distinction between them, Plato is saying, do we know what government by consent of the governed means.

6

The difficulties of the paradox of freedom as applied to speech may perhaps be lessened if we now examine the procedure of the traditional American town meeting. That institution is commonly, and rightly, regarded as a model by which free political procedures may be measured. It is self-government in its simplest, most obvious form.

In the town meeting the people of a community assemble to discuss and to act upon matters of public interest — roads, schools, poorhouses, health, external defense, and the like. Every man is free to come. They meet as political equals. Each has a right and a duty to think his own thoughts, to express them, and to listen to the arguments of others. The basic principle is that the freedom of speech shall be unabridged. And yet the meeting cannot even be opened unless, by common consent, speech is abridged. A chairman or moderator is, or has been, chosen. He "calls the meeting to order." And the hush which follows that call is a clear indication that restrictions upon speech have been set up. The moderator assumes, or arranges, that in the conduct of the business, certain rules of order will be observed. Except as he is overruled by the meeting as a whole, he will enforce those rules. His business on its negative side is to abridge speech. For example, it is usually agreed that no one shall speak unless "recognized by the chair." Also, debaters must confine their remarks to "the question before the house." If one man "has the floor," no one else may interrupt him except as provided by the rules. The meeting has assembled, not primarily to talk, but primarily by means of talking to get business done. And the talking must be regulated and abridged as the doing of the business under actual conditions may require. If a speaker wanders from the point at issue, if he is abusive or in other ways threatens to defeat the purpose of the meeting, he may be and should be declared "out of order." He must then stop speaking, at least in that way. And if he persists in breaking the rules, he may be "denied the floor" or, in the last resort, "thrown out" of the meeting. The town meeting, as it seeks for freedom of public discussion of public problems, would be wholly ineffectual unless speech were thus abridged. It is not a Hyde Park. It is a parliament or congress. It is a group of free and equal men, cooperating in a common enterprise, and using for that enterprise responsible and regulated discussion. It is not a dialectical free-for-all. It is self-government.

These speech-abridging activities of the town meeting indicate what the First Amendment to the Constitution does not forbid. When self-governing men demand freedom of speech they are not saying that every individual has an unalienable right to speak whenever, wherever, however he chooses. They do not declare that any man may talk as he pleases, when he pleases, about what he pleases, about whom he pleases, to whom he pleases. The common sense of any reasonable society would deny the existence of that unqualified right. No one, for example, may, without consent of nurse or doctor, rise up in a sickroom to argue for his principles or his candidate. In the sickroom, that question is not "before the house." The discussion is, therefore, "out of order." To you who now listen to my words, it is allowable to differ with me, but it is not allowable for you to state that difference in words until I have finished my reading. Anyone who would thus irresponsibly interrupt the activities of a lecture, a hospital, a concert hall, a church, a machine shop, a classroom, a football field, or a home, does not thereby exhibit his freedom. Rather, he shows himself to be a boor, a public nuisance, who must be abated, by force if necessary.

What, then, does the First Amendment forbid? Here again the town meeting suggests an answer. That meeting is called to discuss and, on the basis of such discussion, to decide matters of public policy. For example, shall there be a school? Where shall it be located? Who shall teach? What shall be taught? The community has agreed that such questions as these shall be freely discussed and that, when the discussion is ended, decision upon them will be made by vote of the citizens. Now, in that method of political self-government, the point of ultimate interest is not the words of the speakers, but the minds of the hearers. The final aim of the meeting is the voting of wise decisions. The voters, therefore, must be made as wise as possible. The welfare of the community requires that those who decide issues shall understand them. They must know what they are voting about. And this, in turn, requires that so far as time allows, all facts and interests relevant to the problem shall be fully and fairly presented to the meeting. Both facts and interests must be given in such a way that all the alternative lines of action can be wisely measured in relation to one another. As the self-governing community seeks, by the method of voting, to gain wisdom in action, it can find it only in the minds of its individual citizens. If they fail, it fails. That is why freedom of discussion for those minds may not be abridged.

The First Amendment, then, is not the guardian of unregulated talkativeness. It does not require that, on every occasion, every citizen shall take part in public debate. Nor can it even give assurance that everyone shall have opportunity to do so. If, for example, at a town meeting, twenty like-minded citizens have become a "party," and if one of them has read to the meeting an argument which they have all approved, it would be ludicrously out of order for each of the others to insist on reading it again. No competent moderator would tolerate that wasting of the time available for free discussion. What is essential is not that everyone shall speak, but that everything worth saying shall be said. To this end, for example, it may be arranged that each of the known conflicting points of view shall have, and shall be limited to, an assigned share of the time available. But however it be arranged, the vital point, as stated negatively, is that no suggestion of policy shall be denied a hearing because it is on one side of the issue rather than another. And this means that though citizens may, on other grounds, be barred from speaking, they may not be barred because their views are thought to be false or dangerous. No plan of action shall be outlawed because someone in control thinks it unwise, unfair, un-American. No speaker may be declared "out of order" because we disagree with what he intends to say. And the reason for this equality of status in the field of ideas lies deep in the very foundations of the self-governing process. When men govern themselves, it is they — and no one else — who must pass judgment upon unwisdom and unfairness and danger. And that means that unwise ideas must have a hearing as well as wise ones, unfair as well as fair, dangerous as well as safe, un-American as well as American. Just so far as, at any point, the citizens who are to decide an issue are denied acquaintance with information or opinion or doubt or disbelief or criticism which is relevant to that issue, just so far the result must be ill-considered, ill-balanced planning for the general good. *It is that mutilation of the thinking process of the community against which the First Amendment to the Constitution is directed.* The principle of the freedom of speech springs from the necessities of the program of self-government. It is not a Law of Nature or of Reason in the abstract. It is a deduction from the basic American agreement that public issues shall be decided by universal suffrage.

If, then, on any occasion in the United States it is allowable to say that the Constitution is a good document it is equally allowable, in that situation, to say that the Constitution is a bad document. If a public building may be used in which to say, in time of war, that the war is justified, then the same building may be used in which to say that it is not justified. If it be publicly argued that conscription for armed service is moral and necessary, it may likewise be publicly argued that it is immoral and unnecessary. If it may be said that American political institutions are superior to those of England or Russia or Germany, it may, with equal freedom, be said that those of England or Russia or Germany are superior to ours. These conflicting views may be expressed, must be expressed, not because they are valid, but because they are relevant. If they are responsibly entertained by anyone, we, the voters, need to hear them. When a question of policy is "before the house," free men choose to meet it not with their eyes shut, but with their eyes open. To be afraid of ideas, any idea, is to be unfit for self-government. Any such suppression of ideas about the common good, the First Amendment condemns with its absolute disapproval. The freedom of ideas shall not be abridged.

DOES FREEDOM OF SPEECH REALLY TEND TO PRODUCE TRUTH?*

Zechariah Chafee Jr.

> And though all the winds of doctrine were let loose to play upon the earth, so Truth be in the field, we do injuriously by licensing and prohibiting to misdoubt her strength. Let her and Falsehood grapple; who ever knew Truth put to the worse, in a free and open encounter? — MILTON, *Areopagitica*

Those of us who believe that no idea is so sacred as to be immune from inquiry ought not to shrink from trying in the fire of discussion our cherished faith in the inestimable value of discussion. Does truth really emerge from the conflict of ideas, as Milton said, or was he voicing an eloquent illusion?

The oldest and commonest attack on open discussion assumes that it is not needed to produce truth, because truth is already possessed by those in authority. Hence freedom to express other opinions would spread untruths. Thus Plato in his *Republic* was going to have all-wise Guardians who could punish writers for telling lies. An English law of 1401 which stayed in force for nearly three centuries ordered that anyone who taught or wrote anything "contrary to the decisions of Holy Church" should be burned before the people in some prominent place, so as to "prevent such erroneous opinions from being supported." The same view inspired our Sedition Act of 1798, through which the Federalists sent many editors of Jeffersonian newspapers to prison for "false, scandalous and malicious writings." Thomas Carlyle said that "it is the everlasting privilege of the foolish to be governed by the wise." The view that a few men are good enough to decide what is bad for a great many people has plenty of vitality today.

Not much will be said here about this authoritarian view because I have marshaled many arguments against it in my *Free Speech in the*

* Footnotes have been deleted.

United States and great writers have magnificently set forth the dangers to society when its rulers establish a monopoly of ideas. The whole of Milton's *Areopagitica* assails censorship of the press and Mill on *Liberty* opposes all the methods of suppressing thought and discussion. It will be enough for me to mention two of the weaknesses in the authoritarian view. First, it is almost impossible to find men with the wisdom and incorruptibility which are essential for the task of controlling the minds of everybody else and killing bad ideas *en masse.* Second, men in authority are tempted to identify their own policies with truth and to make opposing ideas criminal as a means of perpetuating those policies and their control of the government. Consequently, as Andrew Hamilton said in his defense of Peter Zenger:

> All freemen have a right publicly to remonstrate against the abuses of power in the strongest terms, to put their neighbors upon their guard against the craft or open violence of men in authority, and to assert with courage the sense they have of the blessings of liberty. . . .

The Sceptical Attack on Freedom of Speech

What I chiefly want to take up in this chapter is a recent and quite different attack on free speech, which in my opinion is much harder to repel than the authoritarian attack just described. Here discussion is attacked, not as false and evil, but as worthless. The supporters of this view deny the validity of Milton's assertion that truth emerges from the clash of ideas. According to them nothing emerges. An argument merely ends in a deadlock, with each side sticking obstinately to its own position.

This view forces us to re-examine the whole process of argument and counter-argument instead of taking its success for granted. A relentless prober of the process is Frank Knight, an economist at the University of Chicago, who likes Liberalism and wishes it could last, but reluctantly believes it doomed to disappear along with the pioneer conditions and the small communities in which political individualism flourished. Contrast the quotation from Milton at the head of this chapter with the following passages from Knight's essay:

> The settlement of issues by free general discussion is at best a costly process in time and mental effort and patience, even when the group is very small. . . . It is much simpler to have someone in charge.

Reflection on what happens in the simplest cases — say the discussion of presumably scientific problems by two social scientists — is hardly conducive to faith in the possibilities when larger groups and more tangible difficulties are involved.

In fact, "discussion" needs little formal suppression. There is little evidence that any large mass of people ever wanted to discuss or to attend to discussion, of serious issues, involving real intellectual effort.

Interest in winning [a game] and the interest in the game tend to run into conflict; too much interest in winning first spoils a game and then breaks it up altogether, converting it into a quarrel. . . . Discussion seems to manifest in an especial degree the tendency of games to deteriorate . . . first into ill-will, and ultimately into disruption or even violence. From this point of view, the history of intellectual activity . . . is surely far from encouraging. The specialized professional intellectuals have shown little enough capacity to maintain the spirit of discussion, even in small groups and under what should be extremely favorable conditions; and of their ability to settle issues and solve serious problems by discussion among themselves, it is more pleasant not to speak. . . . In the field of morals and politics — to say nothing of religion — it is questionable whether the net result has been progress toward consensus or the multiplication of controversy.

Are things quite so bad as all that, even though much of what Knight says is undoubtedly so? Each of us regrets his heated participation in many arguments which got nowhere. Yet is every argument fruitless? Before endeavoring to answer this question, I am going to consider what sort of fruit we expect a discussion to bring forth.

What Do We Mean by "Truth"?

Without presuming to answer Pontius Pilate's famous question: "What is truth?" I shall try to show that the "truth" which freedom of speech is said to promote is not a single unified concept. Instead of thinking just of the word "truth" it may be helpful to ask what Justice Holmes had in mind when he said "that *the ultimate good desired* is better reached by free trade in ideas." There are three rather different kinds of "ultimate good" which, we hope, will be produced by freedom of discussion.

First. When Milton spoke of Truth as victorious in a free and open encounter, he mainly referred to what Plato called the highest matters — the existence and nature of God, the purpose of the universe, our relations to God and the universe and our fellowmen, our reasons for living. Truth in this sense is especially furthered by freedom of religion. The persecutions and struggles of the past over freedom of expression were mostly in this area, and we can be happy that the victory of freedom has been so largely won. Let us trust that the search for truth in our understanding of the highest matters will continue to be untrammeled.

Second. The ultimate good desired from open discussion may be an accurate presentation of facts. Walter Lippmann in his *Public Opinion* showed the enormous importance, in the conduct of affairs, of having the pictures in our heads correspond to facts — those stubborn things in the external world, which are obvious to the five senses. The best argument I know for freedom of speech in order to attain this kind of truth is a story by Benjamin Constant:

> A sailor related that he was once on board a vessel with a passenger who had frequently made the same voyage. This passenger told the captain about a rock ahead which was hidden beneath the waves, but the captain would not listen to him. On his insisting on it, the captain had him thrown into the sea. This energetic measure put an end to all remonstrances, and nothing could be more touching than the unanimity which reigned on board. Suddenly the vessel hit the reef and was wrecked. They had got rid of the giver of the warning, but the rock remained.

Facts as such are rarely offered to the public. Occasionally a signed document just can't be denied. But all that is usually available is evidence, somebody's say-so, or inferences from other facts. The passenger could not show the submerged rock; he merely stated his recollection as evidence of the fact of the rock. Now, evidence may be mistaken or deliberately falsified. The public cannot be sure of the facts themselves till it has gone through a lengthy sifting of conflicting statements and inferences. Fortunately, the necessity of this process is pretty well realized in the United States, and there is widespread insistence that evidence may be given without serious risk of penalties. This is so even when the facts in issue are very disagreeable to the people in power, like corruption among federal tax-collecters. It is rare to have the situation before the Supreme Court in 1931, where the very district attorney whom a journal charged with being in league with houses of prostitution almost succeeded in putting the journal out of business on the ground that it was a scandal-sheet.

There is, however, an increasing tendency to discourage and perhaps penalize the disclosure of evidence on two types of facts. One is defense secrets, like the number of atomic bombs or the number of F.B.I. agents. Of these I say nothing now, except to point out that the area of facts subtracted by law or public opinion from open discussion is constantly growing larger.

The other type consists of issues of fact of unfamiliar sorts — not like charges of political corruption. When evidence on a particular side is distasteful to a considerable mass of Americans, it is becoming more and more perilous for anybody to offer it. Hence we are getting a lopsided presentation of information on issues of facts as to which the American people badly need to reach sound conclusions; for instance, the real size and fighting strength of Chinese troops at the disposal of Chiang Kai-shek or the real opinion of Spanish workers about the government of Franco.

Third. A very important result expected in much open discussion is what the Persian prince in Herodotus had in mind when he said:

> It is impossible, if no more than one opinion is uttered, to make choice of the best; . . . but if opposite speeches are delivered, then choice can be exercised.

For example, when a voter decides between two candidates for Congress, he is making a value-judgment. The issue is not "What exists?" but "What shall we do?" A sound decision is more probable if men can safely say what they believe or wish. Pericles told the Athenians in their black days that "we think discussion an indispensable preliminary to any wise action at all."

The value of open discussion is most frequently realized when it is preliminary to political action, but it is by no means confined to governmental controversies. As was pointed out in the preceding chapter, the same policy extends to the making of sound decisions and value-judgments in other matters of public interest, such as art, literature, education, and the relations between men and women. This wide scope of freedom of speech was recognized by the Supreme Court when it sustained artistic freedom against state censorship of the movies in the recent case of the *Miracle*.

Talking and writing on the heterodox side about political or social action and value-judgments raise more difficulties in our time as to the proper range of permissible discussion than does discussion about the other two kinds of truth. The bitterness which used to prevail in religious controversies has now been transferred to political and social disputes. Although nobody has yet been put to death in America for expressing non-religious ideas, a good many men in the last forty years have gone to prison or lost their jobs through legal proceedings because they presumed to differ from the opinions accepted by a majority of their fellow-citizens, and scores of aliens have been deported for speaking or even thinking heretically. Since 1945 the methods of enforcing intellectual uniformity by law have grown rapidly in variety and vigor.

Therefore, the problem of this chapter is whether freedom of speech really tends to produce a better understanding of the highest matters and more knowledge of facts and sounder decisions.

Some Obstacles to the Attainment of Truth in Open Discussion

After reading Frank Knight, I can no longer think of open discussion as operating like an electric mixer, which is the impression left by Milton and Jefferson — run it a little while and truth will rise to the top with the dregs of error going down to the bottom. There are at least three obstacles to the automatic emergence of truth from the contest.

The first is the increasing tendency for the most effective instrumentalities of communication to be owned and shaped by persons who are often on one side of many public questions. The Commission on the Freedom of the Press, of which Robert M. Hutchins was chairman, gave a great deal of thought to this matter and proper remedies for it.

For instance, we pointed out in our report on *A Free and Responsible Press* that when the First Amendment was adopted in 1791 anybody with anything to say had little difficulty in getting it published. A journeyman printer could set up a newspaper if he could borrow a few dollars. Each large town had many newspapers which, taken together, represented nearly all of the conflicting viewpoints on public issues. Contrast the press today, which has been transformed into an enormous and complicated machinery and consequently has become big business. There is a marked reduction in the number of newspapers relative to the total population. These facts led our report to state:

> The right of free public expression has therefore lost its earlier reality. Protection against government is now not enough to guarantee that a man who has something to say shall have a chance to say it. The owners and managers of the press determine which persons, which facts, which versions of the facts, and which ideas shall reach the public. . . .
>
> The press must be free from the menace of external compulsions from whatever sources. . . . The press must, if it is to be wholly free, know and overcome any biases incident to its own economic position, its concentration, and its pyramidal organization.

In other words, so far as law goes, freedom of the press is only the right to be let alone. The law itself does nothing affirmative. It leaves the whole task of promoting truth in the hands of authors, editors, reporters, publishers, broadcasters, motion-picture producers, and the rest of the communications people. Unless *they* do something worth while, not a mite of truth has been attained or communicated. All that has happened is that a bunch of outsiders with official titles and police badges has been reduced to inaction. The law is kept away, but is truth any farther ahead?

Thus the First Amendment and other parts of the law erect a fence inside which men can talk. The law-makers, legislators and officials stay on the outside of that fence. But what the men inside the fence say when they are let alone is no concern of the law.

It is, however, the concern of American citizens, and it ought to be the still greater concern of the men inside the fence. Freedom ought to be affirmative for the writers and newspaper publishers and motion-picture producers and operators of radio or television who are immune from legal interference. Nobody can blame the men who own and operate the instrumentalities of communication for seeking to make money. Neither publishers nor professors are called upon to serve God for naught. Yet the question remains: What are their other purposes, or have they no other purposes?

The defects found by the Commission on the Freedom of the Press would not be remedied, we said, by lessening the legal freedom of the press. What we did conclude was that this legal freedom ought to carry with it more moral responsibility to give the people of the United States what they need to get from the press. It is not enough to ask:

"Freedom *from* what?" A much bigger question, we insisted, is: "Freedom *for* what?"

The press must be free for the development of its own conceptions of service and achievement. It must be free for making its contribution to the maintenance and development of a free society. This implies that the press must also be accountable. It must be accountable to society for meeting the public need and for maintaining the rights of citizens and the almost forgotten rights of speakers who have no press.

Another obstacle to the attainment of truth is the multiplicity of issues and arguments which are thrown at any American all day long until he becomes satiated and the reasoning process which Milton and Jefferson presupposed begins to choke and stop. Is it any longer possible to discover truth amid the clashing blares of advertisements, loud-speakers, enormous headlines, gigantic billboards, television screens, party programs? To sift the truth from all these half-truths drenched with emotion seems to demand a calmness beyond human attainment and a statistical investigation beyond anybody's time and money.

The third obstacle is nothing new, and here we cannot throw the blame on inventors, propagandists, press magnates, or anybody except ourselves. Knight puts his finger on the weakness of each man of us:

[A man] set thinking . . . is as partial to his own ideas as he is to his own children. . . . There is in our field [of the social sciences] no objective test for separating either truth from opinion or the urge to promote an opinion "believed" to be true from the craving for personal aggrandizement. . . . Love of truth is humanly inseparable from the wish to spread the belief in what one believes to be true.

The older writers were not confronted with some of the causes of friction impeding the free flow of discussion, and they paid too little attention to those they did know about. The market for trading in ideas, of which Justice Holmes spoke, is not perfect any more than the market for goods. Yet we ought not to throw up the sponge, but we do have to recognize that the task of attaining truth through freedom is harder than we thought. Reason plays a smaller part in human affairs than we used to believe, but it still remains the best guide we have, better than our emotions, better than tradition, better than any few men in places of authority, however exalted.

Exploration of the Way Opinions Are Formed Out
of What Is Said During Discussion

A fuller understanding of the way discussion operates will keep us from being entirely discouraged about its outcome. The great writers did mislead us a little, because their inspiring words made us expect too much from discussion and too soon. Also I suspect we have gone astray by thinking of an argument between two sharply opposed antagonists, like the Lincoln-Douglas Debates, as characteristic of most discussion. After all, we say, Lincoln did not convince Douglas, and Douglas did not convince Lincoln, so neither of them was any closer to the truth than before. This pessimism is mistaken in stopping with the two chief participants. It ignores thousands of listeners and readers; many of them may have reshaped their half-formed views because of what Lincoln and Douglas said. A more important and more subtle mistake consists of overlooking the fact that discussion of a public issue is usually ever so much more unsystematic, informal, prolonged, fluid, far-flung, than this famous series of speeches by two men. Ordinarily the contest between truth and error bears no resemblance to a prize fight with a chance for bystanders to yell, "May the best man win!"

An utterly different metaphor is helpful to me in picturing what goes on while the conflicting statements of individuals are getting transformed into a satisfactory basis for public action: a bay with thousands of waves, piling up on the shore and then pulling back, sometimes higher, sometimes lower. We know that the tide is either coming in or going out, but we do not have a tide-table. The immeasurable motion appears aimless, but time will show the main course of the sea.

One thing I am sure of, that an alteration in our opinions very rarely comes right after an argument in which we have vigorously taken one side. Even so, perhaps two or three facts put forward by our opponent didn't quite fit into our own set-up. They stick in our minds. We observe other facts ourselves which re-enforce these. "A flying word from here and there" makes us uneasy about our conclusion. A friend we especially admire expresses a rather contrary opinion. Some extreme application of our own view occurs in real life and shocks us. In the end we may not go the whole way, but we have greatly shifted from our old position.

Not only does free discussion sometimes lead us to change our minds, but also it very often helps us to make up our minds on issues about which, previously, we did not care one way or the other. Suddenly we realize their importance and the necessity of taking sides.

All this shaping and reshaping takes time, and a good deal of it is not deliberate reasoning like solving an algebraic equation. What matters greatly is a willingness to receive impressions from many different sources and the opportunity for such impressions to reach us. "The wind bloweth where it listeth."

Now, if into this delicate process the government injects threats of penalties and perhaps actual suppression, the disastrous consequences are easily realized. The powerful emotion of fear impedes the process at every point. The multitudinous sources of our impressions begin to dry up; the impressions no longer come near us or if they do, their entrance into our minds is impeded by the barriers of anxiety. Everybody down the line, including you and me, tends to replace the vital question: "Do I believe this?" by asking, "Is this illegal or disloyal or liable to hurt me, perhaps a year of two hence in some way I can't now foresee?" As Kant says:

> It is absurd to expect to be enlightened by Reason, and at the same time to prescribe to her what side of the question she must adopt.

The foregoing survey of the complicated interchanging of facts and ideas shows, I hope, that a good deal of what is said one way and the other does eventually enter into the conclusions we accept as the basis for action or for the conduct of our lives.

Some of the Indirect Benefits of Freedom of Speech to Truth

The objection is often raised by the supporters of suppressing a given speech or pamphlet that what is said therein cannot possibly contribute anything to truth. It is all worthless. Nothing whatever is lost by junking it. Leaving out the possibility that an opponent is not the best judge of the merits of what his antagonist says, I do feel that a large portion of the output of radical extremists involved in the many free speech cases I have studied was so wordy, shopworn, and vituperative as to make reading it a complete waste of time. An example of this was the mass of material issued thirty or forty years ago by the Industrial Workers of the World.

Nevertheless, these I.W.W.s had grievances. They were homeless and uprooted, with their wages and working conditions largely determined by a succession of farmers who employed them for one crop here and another crop miles away. Their wild speeches and handbills called attention to their grievances. The remedies they proposed themselves were probably foolish, but they showed the need for *some* remedy. Eventually the Roosevelt Administration did a good deal about the problem of migratory agricultural labor.

Thus the voicing of a minority position is desirable even when stated with much error. "Those who are unhappy have no need for anything in the world except people capable of giving them their attention." Freedom increases the chances of attention. Thus it contributes indirectly to truth by hastening a sound decision on a public issue.

The educational value of free choices to the people is stressed by Milton in contrast with "a fugitive and cloistered virtue," and Mill ably shows how contact with error strengthens the presentation of truth. If, instead of silencing domestic Communists by mass prosecutions, we would engage in public debates with them, the noble gospel of American freedom would be enriched by fresh applications to current problems. As I said in Chapter II, we cannot make our tradition contagious for Europeans and Asiatics by merely repeating our great documents of the distant past. Into the old bottles must be put new wine.

The harm to truth from suppression does not come merely from the inability of the public to hear what the particular men would say, who are imprisoned or driven from their jobs. Very often they are loud-mouthed, unattractive men whose evidence and ideas are rather worthless. One of the evils of suppression is that such persistent trouble-makers are the only men with sufficient courage and energy to conflict with the law, so that freedom of speech becomes identified with unscrupulous pamphleteers and ranting soapbox orators. Consequently, it is widely assumed that the loss to the world of thought has been very small. But the governmental attack on the loud-mouthed few frightens a multitude of cautious and sensitive men, who do not dare to imperil their wives and children. It upsets their tranquility, which is essential to productive writing. We cannot know what is lost through the effect of repression on them, because it is not prosecuted but simply left unsaid. The agitator's contest is waged on behalf of these thoughtful men as well as for his own sake, and, if he wins, the gain to truth will usually come more from their writing than from his. Freedom creates an atmosphere of happiness and mastery of one's work of thinking and writing, which is very favorable to the attainment of truth. Suppression, as Spinoza says, is "paring down the state till it is too small to harbour men of talent." Since exile is not very feasible for American citizens, the best course is to write on safe subjects and keep away from problems which arouse hostility. Those happen to be the very problems on which the nation most needs light.

The Propriety of Legal Limitations on Speech

It follows from all I have been saying that the freer free speech is, the better the complicated process of discussion is going to work so as to discover and spread the truth. Because of inevitable elements of friction, truth comes with greater imperfections and delays than we used to think; but if freedom be lessened it comes still more imperfectly and slowly. The delicate machinery for the interchange of facts and ideas begins to slip gears and chatter and run wild.

Every sedition law or other novel restriction on speech seriously hinders the attainment of truth. Every individual case of suppression risks the loss of truth. Anybody who supports such measures is asserting in effect that something else is worth more than truth.

Nevertheless, the search for truth cannot be absolutely immune from legal interference. The settled recognition of damage-suits for slander and libel negatives such a doctrine. The seriousness of a tarnished reputation and the possibility of fights are thought to outweigh the risk that the jury will mistakenly penalize truth. Judges can punish newspapers for publishing evidence which has not been admitted at the trial, and thus influencing the jury; here the proper place for the contest between truth and error is the courtroom, and special rules apply. Plans of battleships and atomic energy formulas cannot be passed out to the public; the truer they are, the worse the disclosure. In short, the attainment of truth is not the only purpose for which the community exists. Truth may have to be sacrificed to some more important social need, just as the drafted soldier is required to sacrifice his right to personal liberty and perhaps to life for the sake of national safety.

Without trying to map out all the legitimate limitations on open discussion, I venture to state four guiding principles:

First. Those who are considering such measures should begin by reading and reflecting a good deal upon the importance to society of unrestricted talk, and be very sure that the nation will really be in great danger if the proposed limitation is rejected. The feasibility of alternative remedies for objectionable ideas ought to be carefully canvassed. It would be a good plan to have the relevant passages of Jefferson's First Inaugural read aloud in the Senate and the House of Representatives at the beginning of every debate on a sedition bill or a deportation bill. As Burke, who was no radical, cautioned:

> It ought to be the constant aim of every wise public counsel to find out by cautious experiments, and rational, cool endeavors, with how little, not how much restraint the community can subsist.

Second. Much attention ought to be paid to the capacity of a given tribunal to discriminate accurately between truth and error. Because twelve men from the street are trusted to apply standards of common sense in determining the falsity of a defamatory statement specific in nature, like a charge of stealing bank funds, it does not follow that jurymen are also suited to appraise the injuriousness of unfamiliar political and economic doctrines. And the fitness of a legislative committee of politicians with an eye on re-election to sift truth from error in such matters is far from plain.

Third. A restrictive law is especially objectionable when it has to be enforced through spies and informers. They are not needed in actions for libel or slander, because the plaintiff quickly finds out for himself that he has been defamed. But when political utterances are made crimes, secret police, spies, and eavesdroppers are necessary to discover that a crime has been committed at all. And, as I have already shown, spies have enormous power to imperil truth.

Fourth. Suppressions are much more questionable when the conceivable interference with truth will be extensive than when it will be slight. A law against profanity in public places hinders the communication of facts and ideas very little. A libel upon an individual may concern nobody else. See how obscenity laws illustrate this principle. Punishing the sale of gross pornography to school children does not block truth much; but the consequences are far more serious when such laws are used to ban *Strange Interlude* and *Strange Fruit,* and thus prevent the public from receiving new ideas about changes in marriage and interracial relations.

The conscription of truth should never be undertaken lightly. The men who propose suppressions, in Congress and elsewhere, speak much of the dangers against which they are guarding, but they rarely consider the new dangers which they are creating or the great value of what they are taking away.

THE FORMULATION OF LEGAL DOCTRINE: IN GENERAL*

Thomas I. Emerson

The attainment of freedom of expression is not the sole aim of the good society. As the private right of the individual, freedom of expression is an end in itself, but it is not the only end of man as an individual. In its social and political aspects, freedom of expression is primarily a process or a method for reaching other goals. It is a basic element in the democratic way of life, and as a vital process it shapes and determines the ends of democratic society. But it is not through this process alone that a democratic society will attain its ultimate ends. Any theory of freedom of expression must therefore take into account other values, such as public order, justice, equality and moral progress, and the need for substantive measures designed to promote those ideals. Hence there is a real problem of reconciling freedom of expression with the other values and objectives sought by the good society.

All institutions of society are necessarily involved in this process of reconciliation. We are concerned here, however, with the role of law and judicial institutions. And this requires that, to the extent the courts participate in the process, the principles of reconciliation must be expressed in the form of legal doctrine.

The major source of legal doctrine is, of course, the First Amendment. Other constitutional provisions — such as the requirement of due process, the privilege against self-incrimination, and the prohibition against unreasonable searches and seizures — are relevant and important; a workable system of free expression must rely upon the whole complex of legal rules designed for the protection of individual

* All but three footnotes have been deleted.

rights. But here we limit discussion to doctrines flowing from the First Amendment. Within that framework, however, proposals for acceptable doctrine will not be confined to those previously asserted as embodying the meaning of the First Amendment or those deduced from prior decisions of the Supreme Court.

The analysis assumes as its fundamental premise the proposition that the framers of the First Amendment intended that provision to serve as the legal basis for guaranteeing an effective system of freedom of expression, and that such fundamental constitutional provisions ought to be interpreted vitally to meet the requirements of the present day. In framing legal doctrine to carry out this basic purpose, the analysis necessarily incorporates by reference our previous discussion of the function of freedom of expression in a democratic society, the dynamics of limitation, and the role of law and legal institutions in supporting a system of freedom of expression. Each of these elements must be taken into account in formulating the basic principles of First Amendment doctrine and in constructing the specific rules to govern the various kinds of situations in which First Amendment problems are posed.

Before attempting these tasks, however, it is necessary to make a partial digression in order to examine the various theories which have from time to time been proposed for reconciling the right to freedom of expression with other social values and objectives.

A Critique of Existing Theories

At the outset certain general theories of reconciliation which have never received any substantial support as a proper interpretation of the First Amendment are rejected. The earliest, and one of the most common in previous periods, was simply to exclude certain groups altogether from the right to freedom of expression. Thus Milton would not have extended the freedom to Catholics, atheists, or non-Christians. Locke apparently would have denied political liberty to Catholics and would have punished those who "will not own and teach the duty of tolerating all men in matters of mere religion." Some of the earlier supporters of free expression seem to have contemplated that the right should be exercised only by a relatively small elitist group. Today this theory takes the form that freedom of expression should not be allowed to "anti-democratic" groups. The prevailing current view, however, is that freedom of expression should be extended to all groups, even those which seek to destroy it. This position is the only one consistent with the basic affirmative theory and compatible with successful administration of an effective system.

Likewise, some who support the affirmative theory have argued nevertheless that reconciliation should be framed generally in terms of the nature of the expression. Thus the old law of seditious libel, the suggestion that protection be extended to speech that is true but not to that which is false or misleading, limitations based on evil intent or motive, prohibition of abusive or vituperative communication, and the test of social utility, have all been urged as appropriate standards. These criteria are understandable as the product of an age when the theory was novel and could only be expected to make cautious headway against the long tradition of suppression. But they obviously cannot serve as useful standards for the present day. Some of them may be relevant, though not necessarily controlling, in particular types of situations. But as general standards they are clearly contrary to the affirmative theory, unworkable, and destructive of freedom of expression.

We come then to the major doctrines which have in recent times been enunciated by a majority or minority of the Supreme Court. It is possible to deal with them only in the briefest fashion.

Bad Tendency Test

In the earlier stages of the interpretation of the First Amendment, a majority of the Supreme Court accepted the so-called "bad tendency" test. According to this doctrine, expression which had a tendency, or which the legislature could reasonably believe had a tendency, to lead to substantial evil could be prohibited. The Court in the *Gitlow* case stated the doctrine broadly, "That a State in the exercise of its police power may punish those who abuse this freedom [of speech] by utterances inimical to the public welfare, tending to corrupt public morals, incite to crime, or disturb the public peace, is not open to question." With reference to the particular issue before it — speech thought to endanger the public peace and safety — the Court held that the legislature was entitled to "extinguish the spark without waiting until it has enkindled the flame or blazed into conflagration."

The bad tendency test offers virtually no protection to freedom of expression. In theory, achievement of all other social values or objectives is preferred to allowing expression where any apparent conflict between the two exists. In practice, the doctrine cuts off expression at a very early point on the road to action; significant opposition to the government or its policies, for instance, receives no legal protection. The test has now been abandoned.

Clear and Present Danger Test

In the development of Supreme Court doctrine, the bad tendency test came to be superseded by the "clear and present danger" test. As originally enunciated by Justice Holmes in the *Schenck* case the test was: "The question in every case is whether the words used are used in such circumstances and are of such a nature as to create a clear and present danger that they will bring about the substantive evils that Congress has a right to prevent." The doctrine was elaborated by Justice Brandeis in his *Whitney* opinion, and was extensively employed by the Court in various types of cases until the *Douds* and *Dennis* cases in the early 1950's.

The clear and present danger test represented a substantial advance over the bad tendency test and was welcomed by many supporters of freedom of expression. In theory, it protects some expression even though that expression interferes with the attainment of other social objectives, for the danger to the other interests must be immediate and clear. In practice, by drawing the line of allowable expression closer to the point of action, it opened up a wider area of protection. But there are serious objections to the test:

(1) The formula assumes that once expression immediately threatens the attainment of some valid social objective, the expression can be prohibited. But no very viable system of freedom of expression can exist under such limitations. The basic theory contemplates that conflict with other objectives must occur, and indeed the system can be said to operate only where such conflict does take place. To permit the state to cut off expression as soon as it comes close to being effective is essentially to allow only abstract or innocuous expression. In short, a legal formula framed solely in terms of effectiveness of the expression in influencing action is incompatible with the existence of free expression.

(2) The clear and present danger test is excessively vague. As experience has shown, its application by the Court leads to no one ascertainable result. And for the main participants in the system of freedom of expression — police, prosecutors, and other officials on the one hand and the individual seeking to exercise his rights on the other — the test furnishes little clarity in advance of a judicial decision.

(3) In all but the simplest situations the factual judgment demanded of the court is difficult or impossible to make through the use of judicial procedures. If the Supreme Court had taken the factual issue seriously in the *Dennis* case, for example, and attempted to assess whether the utterances of the Communist Party actually constituted a clear and present danger, it would have been plunged into consideration of a mass of historical, political, economic, psychological and social facts concerning the position and influence of the Communist Party in the United States and abroad. This judgment would have included both evaluation and prophecy of a sort no court is competent to give. In many situations, therefore, the test cannot be intelligently applied.[1]

(4) The doctrine grew out of cases where the restriction at issue was a direct prohibition of expression by criminal or similar sanctions, and is of doubtful application to other kinds of interference with freedom of expression. In a legislative investigating case, for example, a rule allowing the committee to inquire about expression that might create a clear and present danger of some substantive evil would seem to impose no limits whatever upon the scope of investigation into expression. And where the regulation in question is not aimed directly at punishing a particular utterance but affects freedom of expression in a more generalized or indirect way, as in a tax law or a disclosure requirement, the issues are not framed in terms of whether a specific utterance creates a specific danger. In any event, the clear and present danger test has not been applied in such cases.

(5) In the course of its development the clear and present danger test was expanded to include other factors than the immediate impact of expression in bringing about action. Thus such elements as the

---

[1] Mr. Justice Douglas, alone among the justices, did make a serious attempt to apply the clear and present danger test in *Dennis*, relying for his factual material on judicial notice. See *Dennis* v. *United States*, 341 U.S. at 585–87. Mr. Justice Douglas has since abandoned the test, at least for most purposes. See, e.g., *Scales* v. *United States*, 367 U.S. 203, 262–75 (1961).

nature and gravity of the evil sought to be prevented, the alternatives open to the government, and the value of the expression in relation to the harm feared were taken into account. When this is done, however, the clear and present danger test becomes indistinguishable from the ad hoc balancing test, discussed next, and is subject to the same infirmities.

The clear and present danger test was abandoned by a majority of the Supreme Court in the *Dennis* case. The substitute — the gravity of the evil, discounted by its improbability — excised the main features of the original test by eliminating or minimizing the requirement that the danger be immediate and clear. The present status of the clear and present danger test is thus in some doubt. There is still some blood remaining in the doctrine, and it has continued to be used in certain types of situations.[2] But as a general test of the limits of the First Amendment, the clear and present danger test must be regarded as unacceptable.

Ad Hoc Balancing

Whereas the bad tendency test accords no weight to the values of free expression, and the clear and present danger test gives them weight only in a limited area, the ad hoc balancing test purports to give them full weight. The formula is that the court must in each case balance the individual and social interest in freedom of expression against the social interest sought by the regulation which restricts expression. The test, first clearly enunciated in Chief Justice Vinson's opinion in the *Douds* case, has been employed by a majority of the Supreme Court in a number of subsequent decisions. It is not entirely clear whether the test is meant to be one of general application to all First Amendment issues, but it is fair to say that its supporters consider it the dominant theory.

The principal difficulty with the ad hoc balancing test is that it frames the issues in such a broad and undefined way, is in effect so unstructured, that it can hardly be described as a rule of law at all. As a legal doctrine for affording judicial protection to a system of freedom of expression, it is not tenable. More specifically:

---

[2] The clear and present danger test was recently applied to invalidate a conviction for contempt of court based upon utterances alleged to interfere with a grand jury proceeding. *Wood* v. *Georgia*, 370 U.S. 375 (1962). The decision was by a vote of 5 to 2, but all justices participating acquiesced in the use of the test.

(1) The ad hoc balancing test contains no hard core of doctrine to guide a court in reaching its decision.   Rather, a court is cast loose in a vast space, embracing the broadest possible range of issues, to strike a general balance in the light of its own best judgment.   Not only does the test allow a court to reach either conclusion in almost every case, but the lack of structure makes it realistically impossible for a court to perform its difficult function of applying accepted and impartial rules to hold in check the unruly forces that seek to destroy a system of free expression.

(2) If a court takes the test seriously, the factual determinations involved are enormously difficult and time-consuming, and quite unsuitable for the judicial process.   This is even more true here than in the application of the clear and present danger test.

(3) Actually, the test does not allow the judicial institution to exercise any real degree of independent judgment.   As applied to date, the test gives almost conclusive weight to the legislative judgment.   In the words of its chief exponent, Mr. Justice Frankfurter, the Court will not question the decision of the legislature unless that determination is "outside the pale of fair judgment."   It is true that the test does not necessarily compel this excessive deference to the legislature.   But the operation of the test tends strongly towards that result. For a court must rest its decision on the broadest considerations of policy, which are normally the grist of legislative determination.   A court is therefore in the difficult or impossible position of having either to acquiesce in the legislative judgment or to overrule the legislature on the latter's own ground.   In wholesale disregard of the fundamental difference between legislative and judicial functions, the decision is necessarily framed largely in terms of policy or wisdom, rather than in terms of limitation on power.

(4) The test gives no real meaning to the First Amendment.   As Mr. Justice Black has justifiably protested, it amounts to no more than a statement that the legislature may restrict expression whenever it finds it reasonable to do so, and that the courts will not restrain the legislature unless that judgment is itself unreasonable.   The same degree of protection could be obtained under the due process clause, without the First Amendment.   Surely the First Amendment was not intended and should not be applied to afford as little support as this for a system of free expression.

(5) The test cannot afford police, prosecutors, other government officials and the individual adequate advance notice of the rights es-

sential to be protected. Moreover, the test is unworkable from the viewpoint of judicial administration, requiring for ultimate decision an ad hoc resolution by the highest tribunal in each case. For these reasons the test is wholly incapable of coping with the dynamic forces evoked by governmental efforts at limitation of expression.

In sum, when examined in the light of our previous analysis of the elements essential to a system of freedom of expression, the ad hoc balancing test is, as a legal theory of reconciliation, illusory.

Absolute Test

The so-called "absolute" test is somewhat more unsettled in meaning than the other tests proposed, in part because its opponents have seemingly misunderstood it and in part because its supporters are not in full agreement among themselves. Two things are clear. The test is not that all words, writing and other communications are, at all times and under all circumstances, protected from all forms of government restraint. No advocate of the test, so far as this writer is aware, takes this extreme and obviously untenable position. Nor is the test necessarily one of the "literal meaning," in the sense that one need only look to the wording of the First Amendment to find immediately, on the face of the provision, the complete answer to every issue.

Actually, the absolute test involves two components:

(1) The command of the First Amendment is "absolute" in the sense that "no law" which "abridges" "the freedom of speech" is constitutionally valid. This proposition has been criticized as self-evident, though supporters of the ad hoc balancing test have at times used language which suggests disagreement with it. And the proposition may not appear to carry the decision maker very far, since it is still necessary to decide in each case the meaning of "abridge," of "the freedom of speech," and sometimes of "law." But the point being stressed is by no means inconsequential. For it insists on focusing the inquiry upon the definition of "abridge," "the freedom of speech," and if necessary "law," rather than on a general de novo balancing of interests in each case. And the text gives weight to the constitutional decision made in adopting the First Amendment by emphasizing that the entire question of reconciling social values and objectives is not reopened. This approach of "defining" rather than "balancing" narrows and structures the issue for the courts, bringing it more readily within

the bounds of judicial procedures. It is true that the process of "defining" requires a weighing of various considerations, but this is not the same as open-ended "balancing." On this aspect of the absolute test all proponents of the doctrine appear to be in agreement.

(2) The absolute test includes another component. It is intended to bring a broader area of expression within the protection of the First Amendment than the other tests do. It does this by including a wider sector of government activity within the definition of "abridge," a more extensive area of expression within "the freedom of speech," and at times a broader notion of state action within the term "law." It is perhaps misleading to apply the term "absolute" to this portion of the theory. As already noted, the process does not result in every communication being given unqualified immunity from restriction or regulation under the First Amendment. The characterization as "absolute" does serve the purpose, however, of emphasizing the positive features of the constitutional guarantee and limiting the area of restraint.

As to the first component of the absolute test — framing the issue as one of "defining" rather than "balancing" — the proponents of the doctrine are, in the opinion of this writer, entirely correct, though they may not have fully articulated the reasons in terms of the essential elements of a system of freedom of expression. As to the second component — the scope of the protected area of expression — the test remains in an unsatisfactory state, partly because the proponents are in disagreement over their conclusions, but primarily because they have never sufficiently defined the terms upon which its application rests. The reasons underlying a choice of definition have never been fully explored. Consequently, the test has remained not only vulnerable to attack as embodying merely "an unlimited license to talk," but as essentially undeveloped and inchoate. This state of affairs is no doubt explainable, at least in part, by the fact that the absolute test has never commanded a majority of the Supreme Court and hence its supporters have never been compelled to face the responsibility of formulating its scope with precision.

The upshot of this analysis of current legal doctrine attempting to reconcile competing values under the First Amendment is that the bad tendency test, the clear and present danger test, and the ad hoc balancing test do not afford adequate protection to a system of freedom of expression. Some better theory is urgently needed. The absolute test, while incorporating one basic principle of a satisfactory theory, has left a host of major issues unresolved and largely unexplored.

General Principles of First Amendment Interpretation

We come back, then, to the original problem: the formulation of a workable legal doctrine which will take into account the basic factors underlying a system of freedom of expression and which will give effect to the fundamental decision embodied in the First Amendment for reconciling freedom of expression with other social values and objectives. Upon the basis of the previous analysis, the essential principles of such a doctrine can be stated as follows:

(1) The root purpose of the First Amendment was to assure an effective system of freedom of expression in a democratic society. Its adoption and its continued acceptance imply that some fundamental decisions with respect to reconciliation have been made, that a certain major balancing of interests has already been performed. These judgments, these prior balancings, are those which necessarily flow from the decision to put into operation a system of free expression, with all the values that such a system is intended to secure, in the realistic context of the actual functioning of society and its legal institutions. It follows from our earlier analysis that the judgments made, stated in the most fundamental and general terms, were that expression must be freely allowed and encouraged; that it may not be restricted either for the direct purpose of controlling it or as a method of obtaining other social objectives; and that the attainment of such other objectives is to be achieved through regulation of action. A system of freedom of expression cannot exist on any other foundation, and a decision to maintain such a system necessarily implies a decision on these general propositions.

(2) The function of the courts is not to reopen this prior balancing but to construct the specific legal doctrines which, within the framework of the basic decision made in adopting the First Amendment, will govern the concrete issues presented in fitting an effective system of freedom of expression into the broader structure of modern society. This problem may appropriately be formalized, as the absolutists do, in terms of defining the key elements in the First Amendment: "freedom of expression," "abridge," and "law." These definitions must be functional in character, derived from the basic considerations under-

lying a system of freedom of expression which have previously been set forth.

This process does, of course, involve a weighing of considerations. But the task is narrower, taking place within better defined limits, than ad hoc balancing. And it results in more specific, more tightly structured doctrine than the ad hoc balancing approach permits. While the results may not be acceptable to all absolutists, in essence it seeks to accomplish their ultimate aims.

(3) The specific legal doctrines implementing the First Amendment must be framed in the light of the dynamics of a system of freedom of expression. It is not sufficient to formulate theory in the abstract, however refined. The rules must be workable in terms of the realities of maintaining a system in the everyday world. Thus the difficulty of framing precise regulations affecting expression, and the forces that tend to distort and overextend them, must be taken into account. The need of the individual to know with some assurance what his rights are, and of government officials to know with some certainty the limits of their power, require that the legal doctrine be constructed with this object as a major consideration. And the requirement of effective judicial administration, especially as concerns the functioning of the Supreme Court, is a critical factor.

(4) Construction of a definition of "freedom of expression" centers around two major problems:

(a) The first task is to formulate in detail the distinction between "expression" and "action." As we have seen, the whole theory and practice of freedom of expression — the realization of any of the values it attempts to secure — rests upon this distinction. Hence the starting point for any legal doctrine must be to fix this line of demarcation. The line in many situations is clear. But at many points it becomes obscure. Expression often takes place in a context of action, or is closely linked with it, or is equivalent in its impact. In these mixed cases it is necessary to decide, however artificial the distinction may appear to be, whether the conduct is to be classified as one or the other. This judgment must be guided by consideration of whether the conduct partakes of the essential qualities of expression or action. In the main this is a question of whether the harm attributable to the conduct is immediate and instantaneous, and whether it is irremediable except by punishing and thereby preventing the conduct. A second factor is also significant. This is whether the regulation of the conduct is, as a practical administrative matter, compatible with a workable system of free expression, a factor discussed above. In formulating the distinction between expression and action there is thus a certain leeway in which the process of reconciling freedom of expression with other values and objectives can remain flexible. But the crucial point is that the focus of inquiry must be directed toward ascertaining what is expression, and therefore to be given the protection of expression, and what is action, and thus subject to regulation as such.[3]

(b) The second task is to delineate those sectors of social activity which fall outside the area in which, under the basic theory, freedom of expression must be maintained. For reasons which will be elaborated later, these alien sectors include certain aspects of the operations of the military, of communication with foreign countries, and of the activities of children. The problem here is not only to ascertain the areas in which freedom of expression is not intended to operate, at least in its classic form, but to construct rules governing those situations where the area of free expression and the alien area interlock.

(5) Application of the term "abridge" is not difficult in many cases. But a problem arises in certain types of situations. The main ones are where a regulation is not a direct restriction of expression but is designed to accomplish another objective, and the impact upon expression is "secondary" or "indirect"; where the regulation is concerned not with reconciling freedom of expression with another social objective but operates within the framework of the system itself by attempting to allocate means of communication or facilitate the working of the system; and where the government itself participates in expression. In these situations the formulation of legal doctrine involves construction of a workable definition of "abridge."

(6) The interpretation of the First Amendment in protecting the right of expression against abridgment by private (non-governmental)

---

[3] In formulating the distinction between "expression" and "action" some of the concepts embodied in the clear and present danger test are utilized. But the approach here differs materially from the clear and present danger approach. It is designed to protect the whole general area of expression, regardless of whether that expression creates a danger of subsequent harm. In borderline cases, however, the determination of whether the conduct is to be treated as expression or action rests upon whether the harm is immediate, whether it is irremediable, and whether regulation of the conduct is administratively consistent with maintaining a system of freedom of expression.

centers of power revolves around the definition of "law." This problem is essentially the same as that of defining the scope of "state action."

These principles are necessarily general in character. They do not, of course, automatically solve difficult concrete problems in interpretation of the First Amendment. All that is suggested is that they furnish a method of approach which places the specific issues in a functional context, yet one within the capacity of judicial institutions to manage.

REPRESSIVE TOLERANCE

*Herbert Marcuse**

This essay examines the idea of tolerance in our advanced industrial society. The conclusion reached is that the realization of the objective of tolerance would call for intolerance toward prevailing policies, attitudes, opinions, and the extension of tolerance to policies, attitudes, and opinions which are outlawed or suppressed. In other words, today tolerance appears again as what it was in its origins, at the beginning of the modern period — a partisan goal, a subversive liberating notion and practice. Conversely, what is proclaimed and practiced as tolerance today, is in many of its most effective manifestations serving the cause of oppression.

The author is fully aware that, at present, no power, no authority, no government exists which would translate liberating tolerance into practice, but he believes that it is the task and duty of the intellectual to recall and preserve historical possibilities which seem to have become utopian possibilities — that it is his task to break the concreteness of oppression in order to open the mental space in which this society can be recognized as what it is and does.

Tolerance is an end in itself. The elimination of violence and the reduction of suppression to the extent required for protecting man and animals from cruelty and aggression are preconditions for the creation of a humane society. Such a society does not yet exist; progress toward it is perhaps more than before arrested by violence and suppression on a global scale. As deterrents against nuclear war, as police action against subversion, as technical aid in the fight against imperialism and communism, as methods of pacification in neo-colonial massacres, violence and suppression are promulgated, practiced, and

From Herbert Marcuse, *A Critique of Pure Tolerance* (pp. 81–123). Copyright © 1965 by Herbert Marcuse ("Repressive Tolerance"); copyright © 1969 by Herbert Marcuse ("Postscript 1968"). Reprinted by permission of the Beacon Press.

* This essay is dedicated to my students at Brandeis University.

defended by democratic and authoritarian governments alike, and the people subjected to these governments are educated to sustain such practices as necessary for the preservation of the status quo. Tolerance is extended to policies, conditions, and modes of behavior which should not be tolerated because they are impeding, if not destroying, the chances of creating an existence without fear and misery. This sort of tolerance strengthens the tyranny of the majority against which authentic liberals protested. The political locus of tolerance has changed: while it is more or less quietly and constitutionally withdrawn from the opposition, it is made compulsory behavior with respect to established policies. Tolerance is turned from an active into a passive state, from practice to nonpractice: laissez-faire the constituted authorities. It is the people who tolerate the government, which in turn tolerates opposition within the framework determined by the constituted authorities.

Tolerance toward that which is radically evil now appears as good because it serves the cohesion of the whole on the road to affluence or more affluence. The toleration of the systematic moronization of children and adults alike by publicity and propaganda, the release of destructiveness in aggressive driving, the recruitment for and training of special forces, the impotent and benevolent tolerance toward outright deception in merchandising, waste, and planned obsolescence are not distortions and aberrations, they are the essence of a system which fosters tolerance as a means for perpetuating the struggle for existence and suppressing the alternatives. The authorities in education, morals, and psychology are vociferous against the increase in juvenile delinquency; they are less vociferous against the proud presentation, in word and deed and pictures, of ever more powerful missiles, rockets, bombs — the mature delinquency of a whole civilization.

According to a dialectical proposition it is the whole which determines the truth — not in the sense that the whole is prior or superior to its parts, but in the sense that its structure and function determine every particular condition and relation. Thus, within a repressive society, even progressive movements threaten to turn into their opposite to the degree to which they accept the rules of the game. To take a most controversial case: the exercise of political rights (such as voting, letter-writing to the press, to Senators, etc., protest-demonstrations with a priori renunciation of counterviolence) in a society of total administration serves to strengthen this administration by testifying to the existence of democratic liberties which, in reality, have changed their content and lost their effectiveness. In such a case, freedom (of opinion, of assembly, of speech) becomes an instrument for absolving servitude. And yet (and only here the dialectical proposition shows its full intent) the existence and practice of these liberties remain a precondition for the restoration of their original oppositional function, provided that the effort to transcend their (often self-imposed) limitations is intensified. Generally, the function and value of tolerance depend on the equality prevalent in the society in which tolerance is practiced. Tolerance itself stands subject to overriding criteria: its range and its limits cannot be defined in terms of the respective society. In other words, tolerance is an end in itself only when it is truly universal, practiced by the rulers as well as by the ruled, by the lords as well as by the peasants, by the sheriffs as well as by their victims. And such universal tolerance is possible only when no real or alleged enemy requires in the national interest the education and training of people in military violence and destruction. As long as these conditions do not prevail, the conditions of tolerance are "loaded": they are determined and defined by the institutionalized inequality (which is certainly compatible with constitutional equality), i.e., by the class structure of society. In such a society, tolerance is *de facto* limited on the dual ground of legalized violence or suppression (police, armed forces, guards of all sorts) and of the privileged position held by the predominant interests and their "connections."

These background limitations of tolerance are normally prior to the explicit and judicial limitations as defined by the courts, custom, governments, etc. (for example, "clear and present danger," threat to national security, heresy). Within the framework of such a social structure, tolerance can be safely practiced and proclaimed. It is of two kinds: (1) the passive toleration of entrenched and established attitudes and ideas even if their damaging effect on man and nature is evident; and (2) the active, official tolerance granted to the Right as well as to the Left, to movements of aggression as well as to movements of peace, to the party of hate as well as to that of humanity. I call this non-partisan tolerance "abstract" or "pure" inasmuch as it refrains from taking sides — but in doing so it actually protects the already established machinery of discrimination.

The tolerance which enlarged the range and content of freedom was always partisan — intolerant toward the protagonists of the repressive status quo. The issue was only the degree and extent of intolerance. In the firmly established liberal society of England and the United States, freedom of speech and assembly was granted even to the radical enemies of society, provided they did not make the transition from word to deed, from speech to action.

Relying on the effective background limitations imposed by its class structure, the society seemed to practice general tolerance. But liberalist theory had already placed an important condition on tolerance: it was "to apply only to human beings in the maturity of their faculties." John Stuart Mill does not only speak of children and minors; he elaborates: "Liberty, as a principle, has no application to any state of things anterior to the time when mankind have become capable of being improved by free and equal discussion." Anterior to that time, men may still be barbarians, and "despotism is a legitimate mode of government in dealing with barbarians, provided the end be their improvement, and the means justified by actually effecting that end." Mill's often-quoted words have a less familiar implication on which their meaning depends: the internal connection between liberty and truth. There is a sense in which truth is the end of liberty, and liberty must be defined and confined by truth. Now in what sense can liberty be for the sake of truth? Liberty is self-determination, autonomy — this is almost a tautology, but a tautology which results from a whole series of synthetic judgments. It stipulates the ability to determine one's own life: to be able to determine what to do and what not to do, what to suffer and what not. But the subject of this autonomy is never the contingent, private individual as that which he actually is or happens to be; it is rather the individual as a human being who is capable of being free with the others. And the problem of making possible such a harmony between every individual liberty and the other is not that of finding a compromise between competitors, or between freedom and law, between general and individual interest, common and private welfare in an *established* society, but of *creating* the society in which man is no longer enslaved by institutions which vitiate self-determination from the beginning. In other words, freedom is still to be created even for the freest of the existing societies. And the direction in which it must be sought, and the institutional and cultural changes which may help to attain the goal are, at least in developed civilization, *comprehensible*, that is to say, they can be identified and projected, on the basis of experience, by human reason.

In the interplay of theory and practice, true and false solutions become distinguishable — never with the evidence of necessity, never as the positive, only with the certainty of a reasoned and reasonable chance, and with the persuasive force of the negative. For the true positive is the society of the future and therefore beyond definition and determination, while the existing positive is that which must be surmounted. But the experience and understanding of the existent society may well be capable of identifying what is *not* conducive to a free and rational society, what impedes and distorts the possibilities of its creation. Freedom is liberation, a specific historical process in theory and practice, and as such it has its right and wrong, its truth and falsehood.

The uncertainty of chance in this distinction does not cancel the historical objectivity, but it necessitates freedom of thought and expression as preconditions of finding the way to freedom — it necessitates *tolerance*. However, this tolerance cannot be indiscriminate and equal with respect to the contents of expression, neither in word nor in deed; it cannot protect false words and wrong deeds which demonstrate that they contradict and counteract the possibilities of liberation. Such indiscriminate tolerance is justified in harmless debates, in conversation, in academic discussion; it is indispensable in the scientific enterprise, in private religion. But society cannot be indiscriminate where the pacification of existence, where freedom and happiness themselves are at stake: here, certain things cannot be said, certain ideas cannot be expressed, certain policies cannot be proposed, certain behavior cannot be permitted without making tolerance an instrument for the continuation of servitude.

The danger of "destructive tolerance" (Baudelaire), of "benevolent neutrality" toward *art* has been recognized: the market, which absorbs equally well (although with often quite sudden fluctuations) art, anti-art, and non-art, all possible conflicting styles, schools, forms, provides a "complacent receptacle, a friendly abyss" (Edgar Wind, *Art and Anarchy* [New York: Knopf, 1964], p. 101) in which the radical impact of art, the protest of art against the established reality is swallowed up. However, censorship of art and literature is regressive under all circumstances. The authentic oeuvre is not and cannot be a prop of oppression, and pseudo-art (which can be such a prop) is not art. Art stands against history, withstands history which has been the history of oppression, for art subjects reality to laws other than the established ones: to the laws of the Form which creates a different reality — negation of the established one even where art depicts the established reality. But in its struggle with history, art subjects itself to history: history enters the definition of art and enters into the distinction between art and pseudo-art. Thus it happens that what was once art becomes pseudo-art. Previous forms, styles, and qualities, previous modes of protest and refusal cannot be recaptured in or against a different society. There are cases where an authentic oeuvre carries a regressive political message — Dostoevski is a case in point. But then, the message is canceled by the oeuvre itself: the regressive political content is absorbed, *aufeghoben* in the artistic form: in the work as literature.

Tolerance of free speech is the way of improvement, of progress in liberation, *not* because there is no objective truth, and improvement must necessarily be a compromise between a variety of opinions, but because there *is* an objective truth which can be discovered, ascertained only in learning and comprehending that which is and that which can be and ought to be done for the sake of improving the lot of mankind. This common and historical "ought" is not immediately evident, at hand: it has to be uncovered by "cutting through," "splitting," "breaking assunder" (*dis-cutio*) the given material — separating right and wrong, good and bad, correct and incorrect. The subject whose "improvement" depends on a progressive historical practice is each man as man, and this universality is reflected in that of the discussion, which a priori does not exclude any group or individual. But even the all-inclusive character of liberalist tolerance was, at least in theory, based on the proposition that men were (potential) *individuals* who could learn to hear and see and feel by themselves, to develop their own thoughts, to grasp their true interests and rights and capabilities, also against established authority and opinion. This was the rationale of free speech and assembly. Universal toleration becomes questionable when its rationale no longer prevails, when tolerance is administered to manipulated and indoctrinated individuals who parrot, as their own, the opinion of their masters, for whom heteronomy has become autonomy.

The telos of tolerance is truth. It is clear from the historical record that the authentic spokesmen of tolerance had more and other truth in mind than that of propositional logic and academic theory. John Stuart Mill speaks of the truth which is persecuted in history and which does *not* triumph over persecution by virtue of its "inherent power," which in fact has no inherent power "against the dungeon and the stake." And he enumerates the "truths" which were cruelly and successfully liquidated in the dungeons and at the stake: that of Arnold of Brescia, of Fra Dolcino, of Savonarola, of the Albigensians, Waldensians, Lollards, and Hussites. Tolerance is first and foremost for the sake of the heretics — the historical road toward *humanitas* appears as heresy: target of persecution by the powers that be. Heresy by itself, however, is no token of truth.

The criterion of progress in freedom according to which Mill judges these movements is the Reformation. The evaluation is *ex post*, and his list includes opposites (Savonarola too would have burned Fra Dolcino). Even the ex post evaluation is contestable as to its truth: history corrects the judgment — too late. The correction does not help the victims and does not absolve their executioners. However, the lesson is clear: intolerance has delayed progress and has prolonged the slaughter and torture of innocents for hundreds of years. Does this clinch the case for indiscriminate, "pure" tolerance? Are there historical conditions in which such toleration impedes liberation and multiplies the victims who are sacrificed to the status quo? Can the indiscriminate guaranty of political rights and liberties be repressive? Can such tolerance serve to contain qualitative social change?

I shall discuss this question only with reference to political movements, attitudes, schools of thought, philosophies which are "political" in the widest sense — affecting the society as a whole, demonstrably transcending the sphere of privacy. Moreover, I propose a shift in the focus of the discussion: it will be concerned not only, and not primarily, with tolerance toward radical extremes, minorities, subversives, etc., but rather with tolerance toward majorities, toward official and public opinion, toward the established protectors of freedom. In this case, the discussion can have as a frame of reference only a democratic society, in which the people, as individuals and as members of political and other organizations, participate in the making, sustaining, and changing policies. In an authoritarian system, the people do not tolerate — they suffer established policies.

Under a system of constitutionally guaranteed and (generally and without too many and too glaring exceptions) practiced civil rights and liberties, opposition and dissent are tolerated unless they issue in violence and/or in exhortation to and organization of violent subversion. The underlying assumption is that the established society is free, and that any improvement, even a change in the social structure and social values, would come about in the normal course of events, prepared, defined, and tested in free and equal discussion, on the open marketplace of ideas and goods.[1] Now in recalling John Stuart Mill's passage, I drew attention to the premise hidden in this assumption: free and equal discussion can fulfill the function attributed to it only if it is *rational* — expression and development of independent thinking, free from indoctrination, manipulation, extraneous authority. The notion of pluralism and countervailing powers is no substitute for this requirement. One might in theory construct a state in which a multitude of different pressures, interests, and authorities balance each other out and result in a truly general and rational interest. However, such a construct badly fits a society in which powers are and remain unequal and even increase their unequal weight when they run their own course. It fits even worse when the variety of pressures unifies and coagulates into an overwhelming whole, integrating the particular countervailing powers by virtue of an increasing standard of living and an increasing concentration of power. Then, the laborer, whose real interest conflicts with that of management, the common consumer whose real interest conflicts with that of the producer, the intellectual whose vocation conflicts with that of his employer find themselves submitting to a system against which they are powerless and appear unreasonable. The idea of the available alternatives evaporates into an utterly utopian dimension in which it is at home, for a free society is indeed unrealistically and undefinably different from the existing ones. Under these circumstances, whatever improvement may occur "in the normal course of events" and without subversion is likely to be improvement in the direction determined by the particular interests which control the whole.

[1] I wish to reiterate for the following discussion that, *de facto*, tolerance is *not* indiscriminate and "pure" even in the most democratic society. The "background limitations" stated on page 85 restrict tolerance before it begins to operate. The antagonistic structure of society rigs the rules of the game. Those who stand against the established system are a priori at a disadvantage, which is not removed by the toleration of their ideas, speeches, and newspapers.

By the same token, those minorities which strive for a change of the whole itself will, under optimal conditions which rarely prevail, be left free to deliberate and discuss, to speak and to assemble — and will be left harmless and helpless in the face of the overwhelming majority, which militates against qualitative social change. This majority is firmly grounded in the increasing satisfaction of needs, and technological and mental coordination, which testify to the general helplessness of radical groups in a well-functioning social system.

Within the affluent democracy, the affluent discussion prevails, and within the established framework, it is tolerant to a large extent. All points of view can be heard: the Communist and the Fascist, the Left and the Right, the white and the Negro, the crusaders for armament and for disarmament. Moreover, in endlessly dragging debates over the media, the stupid opinion is treated with the same respect as the intelligent one, the misinformed may talk as long as the informed, and propaganda rides along with education, truth with falsehood. This pure toleration of sense and nonsense is justified by the democratic argument that nobody, neither group nor individual, is in possession of the truth and capable of defining what is right and wrong, good and bad. Therefore, all contesting opinions must be submitted to "the people" for its deliberation and choice. But I have already suggested that the democratic argument implies a necessary condition, namely, that the people must be capable of deliberating and choosing on the basis of knowledge, that they must have access to authentic information, and that, on this basis, their evaluation must be the result of autonomous thought.

In the contemporary period, the democratic argument for abstract tolerance tends to be invalidated by the invalidation of the democratic process itself. The liberating force of democracy was the chance it gave to effective dissent, on the individual as well as social scale, its openness to qualitatively different forms of government, of culture, education, work — of the human existence in general. The toleration of free discussion and the equal right of opposites was to define and clarify the different forms of dissent: their direction, content, prospect. But with the concentration of economic and political power and the integration of opposites in a society which uses technology as an instrument of domination, effective dissent is blocked where it could freely emerge: in the formation of opinion, in information and communication, in speech and assembly. Under the rule of monopolistic media — themselves the mere instruments of economic and political power — a mentality is created for which right and wrong, true and false are predefined wherever they affect the vital interests of the society. This is, prior to all expression and communication, a matter of semantics: the blocking of effective dissent, of the recognition of that which is not of the Establishment, which begins in the language that is publicized and administered. The meaning of words is rigidly stabilized. Rational persuasion, persuasion to the opposite, is all but precluded. The avenues of entrance are closed to the meaning of words and ideas other than the established one — established by the publicity of the powers that be, and verified in their practices. Other words can be spoken and heard, other ideas can be expressed, but, at the massive scale of the conservative majority (outside such enclaves as the intelligentsia), they are immediately "evaluated" (i.e., automatically understood) in terms of the public language — a language which determines "a priori" the direction in which the thought process moves. Thus the process of reflection ends where it started: in the given conditions and relations. Self-validating, the argument of the discussion repels the contradiction because the antithesis is redefined in terms of the thesis. For example, thesis: we work for peace; antithesis: we prepare for war (or even: we wage war); unification of opposites: preparing for war *is* working for peace. Peace is redefined as necessarily, in the prevailing situation, including preparation for war (or even war) and in this Orwellian form, the meaning of the word "peace" is stabilized. Thus, the basic vocabulary of the Orwellian language operates as a priori categories of understanding: preforming all content. These conditions invalidate the logic of tolerance which involves the rational development of meaning and precludes the closing of meaning. Consequently, persuasion through discussion and the equal presentation of opposites (even where it is really equal) easily lose their liberating force as factors of understanding and learning; they are far more likely to strengthen the established thesis and to repel the alternatives.

Impartiality to the utmost, equal treatment of competing and conflicting issues is indeed a basic requirement for decision-making in the democratic process — it is an equally basic requirement for defining the limits of tolerance. But in a democracy with totalitarian organization, objectivity may fulfill a very different function, namely, to foster a mental attitude which tends to obliterate the difference between true and false, information and indoctrination, right and wrong. In fact, the decision between opposed opinions has been made before the presentation and discussion get under way — made, not by a conspiracy or a sponsor or a publisher, not by any dictatorship, but rather by the "normal course of events," which is the course of administered events, and by the mentality shaped in this course. Here, too, it is the whole which determines the truth. Then the decision asserts itself, without any open violation of objectivity, in such things as the make-up of a newspaper (with the breaking up of vital information into bits interspersed between extraneous material, irrelevant items, relegating of some radically negative news to an obscure place), in the juxtaposition of gorgeous ads with unmitigated horrors, in the introduction and interruption of the broadcasting of facts by overwhelming commercials. The result is a *neutralization* of opposites, a neutralization, however, which takes place on the firm grounds of the structural limitation of tolerance and within a preformed mentality. When a magazine prints side by side a negative and a positive report on the FBI, it fulfills honestly the requirements of objectivity: however, the chances are that the positive wins because the image of the institution is deeply engraved in the mind of the people. Or, if a newscaster reports the torture and murder of civil rights workers in the same unemotional tone he uses to describe the stockmarket or the weather, or with the same great emotion with which he says his commercials, then such objectivity is spurious — more, it offends against humanity and truth by being calm where one should be enraged, by refraining from accusation where accusation is in the facts themselves. The tolerance expressed in such impartiality serves to minimize or even absolve prevailing intolerance and suppression. If objectivity has anything to do with truth, and if truth is more than a matter of logic and science, then this kind of objectivity is false, and this kind of tolerance inhuman. And if it is necessary to break the established universe of meaning (and the practice enclosed in this universe) in order to enable man to find out what is true and false, this deceptive impartiality would have to be abandoned. The people exposed to this impartiality are no *tabulae rasae*, they are indoctrinated by the conditions under which they live and think and which they do not transcend. To enable them to become autonomous, to find by themselves what is true and what is false for man in the existing society, they would have to be freed from the prevailing indoctrination (which is no longer recognized as indoctrination). But this means that the trend would have to be reversed: they would have to get information slanted in the opposite direction. For the facts are never given immediately and never accessible immediately; they are established, "mediated" by those who made them; the truth, "the whole truth," surpasses these facts and requires the rupture with their appearance. This rupture — prerequisite and token of all freedom of thought and of speech — cannot be accomplished within the established framework of abstract tolerance and spurious objectivity because these are precisely the factors which precondition the mind *against* the rupture.

The factual barriers which totalitarian democracy erects against the efficacy of qualitative dissent are weak and pleasant enough compared with the practices of a dictatorship which claims to educate the people in the truth. With all its limitations and distortions, democratic tolerance is under all circumstances more humane than an institutionalized intolerance which sacrifices the rights and liberties of the living generations for the sake of future generations. The question is whether this is the only alternative. I shall presently try to suggest the direction in which an answer may be sought. In any case, the contrast is not between democracy in the abstract and dictatorship in the abstract.

Democracy is a form of government which fits very different types of society (this holds true even for a democracy with universal suffrage and equality before the law), and the human costs of a democracy are always and everywhere those exacted by the society whose government it is. Their range extends all the way from normal exploitation, poverty, and insecurity to the victims of wars, police actions, military aid, etc., in which the society is engaged — and not only to the victims within its own frontiers. These considerations can never justify the exacting of different sacrifices and different victims on behalf of a future better society, but they do allow weighing the costs involved in the perpetuation of an existing society against the risk of promoting alternatives which offer a reasonable chance of pacification and liberation. Surely, no government can be expected to foster its own subversion, but in a democracy such a right is vested in the people (i.e., in the majority of the people). This means that the ways should not be blocked on which a subversive majority could develop, and if they are blocked by organized repression and indoctrination, their reopening may require apparently undemocratic means.

They would include the withdrawal of toleration of speech and assembly from groups and movements which promote aggressive policies, armament, chauvinism, discrimination on the grounds of race and religion, or which oppose the extension of public services, social security, medical care, etc. Moreover, the restoration of freedom of thought may necessitate new and rigid restrictions on teachings and practices in the educational institutions which, by their very methods and concepts, serve to enclose the mind within the established universe of discourse and behavior — thereby precluding a priori a rational evaluation of the alternatives. And to the degree to which freedom of thought involves the struggle against inhumanity, restoration of such freedom would also imply intolerance toward scientific research in the interest of deadly "deterrents," of abnormal human endurance under inhuman conditions, etc. I shall presently discuss the question as to who is to decide on the distinction between liberating and repressive, human and inhuman teachings and practices; I have already suggested that this distinction is not a matter of value-preference but of rational criteria.

While the reversal of the trend in the educational enterprise at least could conceivably be enforced by the students and teachers themselves, and thus be self-imposed, the systematic withdrawal of tolerance toward regressive and repressive opinions and movements could only be envisaged as results of large-scale pressure which would amount to an upheaval. In other words, it would presuppose that which is still to be accomplished: the reversal of the trend. However, resistance at particular occasions, boycott, non-participation at the local and small-group level may perhaps prepare the ground. The subversive character of the restoration of freedom appears most clearly in that dimension of society where false tolerance and free enterprise do perhaps the most serious and lasting damage, namely, in business and publicity. Against the emphatic insistence on the part of spokesmen for labor, I maintain that practices such as planned obsolescence, collusion between union leadership and management, slanted publicity are not simply imposed from above on a powerless rank and file, but are *tolerated* by them — and by the consumer at large. However, it would be ridiculous to speak of a possible withdrawal of tolerance with respect to these practices and to the ideologies promoted by them. For they pertain to the basis on which the repressive affluent society rests and reproduces itself and its vital defenses — their removal would be that total revolution which this society so effectively repels.

To discuss tolerance in such a society means to re-examine the issue of violence and the traditional distinction between violent and non-violent action. The discussion should not, from the beginning, be clouded by ideologies which serve the perpetuation of violence. Even in the advanced centers of civilization, violence actually prevails: it is practiced by the police, in the prisons and mental institutions, in the fight against racial minorities; it is carried, by the defenders of metropolitan freedom, into the backward countries. This violence indeed breeds violence. But to refrain from violence in the face of vastly superior violence is one thing, to renounce a priori violence against violence, on ethical or psychological grounds (because it may antagonize sympathizers) is another. Non-violence is normally not only preached to but exacted from the weak — it is a necessity rather than a virtue, and normally it does not seriously harm the case of the strong. (Is the case of India an exception? There, passive resistance was carried through on a massive scale, which disrupted, or threatened to disrupt, the economic life of the country. Quantity turns into quality: on such a scale, passive resistance is no longer passive — it ceases to be non-violent. The same holds true for the General Strike.) Robespierre's distinction between the terror of liberty and the terror of despotism, and his moral glorification of the former belongs to the most convincingly condemned aberrations, even if the white terror was more bloody than the red terror. The comparative evaluation in terms of the number of victims is the quantifying approach which reveals the man-made horror throughout history that made violence a necessity. In terms of historical function, there is a difference between revolutionary and reactionary violence, between violence practiced by the oppressed and by the oppressors. In terms of ethics, both forms of violence are inhuman and evil — but since when is history made in accordance with ethical standards? To start applying them at the point where the oppressed rebel against the oppressors, the have-nots against the haves is serving the cause of actual violence by weakening the protest against it.

Comprenez enfin ceci: si la violence a commencé ce soir, si l'exploitation ni l'oppression n'ont jamais existé sur terre, peut-être la non-violence affichée peut apaiser la querelle. Mais si le régime tout entier et jusqu'à vos nonviolentes pensées sont conditionnées par une oppression millénaire, votre passivité ne sert qu'à vous ranger du côté des oppresseurs. (Sartre, Preface to Frantz Fanon, *Les Damnés de la Terre*, Paris: Maspéro, 1961, p. 22).

The very notion of false tolerance, and the distinction between right and wrong limitations on tolerance, between progressive and regressive indoctrination, revolutionary and reactionary violence demand the statement of criteria for its validity. These standards must be prior to whatever constitutional and legal criteria are set up and applied in an existing society (such as "clear and present danger," and other established definitions of civil rights and liberties), for such definitions themselves presuppose standards of freedom and repression as applicable or not applicable in the respective society: they are specifications of more general concepts. By whom, and according to what standards, can the political distinction between true and false, progressive and regressive (for in this sphere, these pairs are equivalent) be made and its validity be justified? At the outset, I propose that the question cannot be answered in terms of the alternative between democracy and dictatorship, according to which, in the latter, one individual or group, without any effective control from below, arrogate to themselves the decision. Historically, even in the most democratic democracies, the vital and final decisions affecting the society as a whole have been made, constitutionally or in fact, by one or several groups without effective control by the people themselves. The ironical question: who educates the educators (i.e., the political leaders) also applies to democracy. The only authentic alternative and negation of dictatorship (with respect to this question) would be a society in which "the people" have become autonomous individuals, freed from the repressive requirements of a struggle for existence in the interest of domination, and, as such, human beings choosing their government and determining their life. Such a society does not yet exist anywhere. In the meantime, the question must be treated *in abstracto* — abstraction, not from the historical possibilities, but from the realities of the prevailing societies.

I suggested that the distinction between true and false tolerance, between progress and regression, can be made rationally on empirical grounds. The real possibilities of human freedom are relative to the attained stage of civilization. They depend on the material and intellectual resources available at the respective stage, and they are quantifiable and calculable to a high degree. So are, at the stage of advanced industrial society, the most rational ways of using these resources and distributing the social product with priority on the satisfaction of vital needs and with a minimum of toil and injustice. In other words, it is possible to define the direction in which prevailing institutions, policies, opinions would have to be changed in order to improve the chance of a peace which is not identical with cold war and a little hot war, and a satisfaction of needs which does not feed on poverty, oppression, and exploitation. Consequently, it is also possible to identify policies, opinions, movements which would promote this chance, and those which would do the opposite. Suppression of the regressive ones is a prerequisite for the strengthening of the progressive ones.

The question, who is qualified to make all these distinctions, definitions, identifications for the society as a whole, has now one logical answer, namely, everyone "in the maturity of his faculties" as a human being, everyone who has learned to think rationally and autonomously. The answer to Plato's educational dictatorship is the democratic educational dictatorship of free men. John Stuart Mill's conception of the *res publica* is not the opposite of Plato's: the liberal too demands the authority of Reason not only as an intellectual but also as a political power. In Plato, rationality is confined to the small number of philosopher-kings; in Mill, every rational human being participates in the discussion and decision — but only as a rational being. Where society has entered the phase of total administration and indoctrination, this would be a small number indeed, and not necessarily that of the elected representatives of the people. The problem is not that of an educational dictatorship, but that of breaking the tyranny of public opinion and its makers in the closed society.

However, granted the empirical rationality of the distinction between progress and regression, and granted that it may be applicable to tolerance, and may justify strongly discriminatory tolerance on political grounds (cancellation of the liberal creed of free and equal discussion), another impossible consequence would follow. I said that, by virtue of its inner logic, withdrawal of tolerance from regressive movements, and discriminatory tolerance in favor of progressive tendencies would be tantamount to the "official" promotion of subversion. The historical calculus of progress (which is actually the calculus of the prospective reduction of cruelty, misery, suppression) seems to involve the calculated choice between two forms of political violence: that on the part of the legally constituted powers (by their legitimate action, or by their tacit consent, or by their inability to prevent violence), and that on the part of potentially subversive movements. Moreover, with respect to the latter, a policy of unequal treatment would protect radicalism on the Left against that on the Right. Can the historical calculus be reasonably extended to the justification of one form of violence as against another? Or better (since "justification" carries a moral connotation), is there historical evidence to the effect that the social origin and impetus of violence (from among the ruled or the ruling classes, the have or the have-nots, the Left or the Right) is in a demonstrable relation to progress (as defined above)?

With all the qualifications of a hypothesis based on an "open" historical record, it seems that the violence emanating from the rebellion of the oppressed classes broke the historical continuum of injustice, cruelty, and silence for a brief moment, brief but explosive enough to achieve an increase in the scope of freedom and justice, and a better and more equitable distribution of misery and oppression in a new social system — in one word: progress in civilization. The English civil wars, the French Revolution, the Chinese and the Cuban Revolutions may illustrate the hypothesis. In contrast, the one historical change from one social system to another, marking the beginning of a new period in civilization, which was *not* sparked and driven by an effective movement "from below," namely, the collapse of the Roman Empire in the West, brought about a long period of regression for long centuries, until a new, higher period of civilization was painfully born in the violence of the heretic revolts of the thirteenth century and in the peasant and laborer revolts of the fourteenth century.[2]

With respect to historical violence emanating from among ruling classes, no such relation to progress seems to obtain. The long series of dynastic and imperialist wars, the liquidation of Spartacus in Germany in 1919, Fascism and Nazism did not break but rather tightened and streamlined the continuum of suppression. I said emanating "from among ruling classes": to be sure, there is hardly any organized violence from above that does not mobilize and activate mass support from below; the decisive question is, on behalf of and in the interest of which groups and institutions is such violence released? And the answer is not necessarily ex post: in the historical examples just men-

---

[2] In modern times, fascism has been a consequence of the transition to industrial society *without* a revolution. See Barrington Moore's forthcoming book *Social Origins of Dictatorship and Democracy.*

tioned, it could be and was anticipated whether the movement would serve the revamping of the old order or the emergence of the new. Liberating tolerance, then, would mean intolerance against movements from the Right, and toleration of movements from the Left. As to the scope of this tolerance and intolerance: . . . it would extend to the stage of action as well as of discussion and propaganda, of deed as well as of word. The traditional criterion of clear and present danger seems no longer adequate to a stage where the whole society is in the situation of the theater audience when somebody cries: "fire." It is a situation in which the total catastrophe could be triggered off any moment, not only by a technical error, but also by a rational miscalculation of risks, or by a rash speech of one of the leaders. In past and different circumstances, the speeches of the Fascist and Nazi leaders were the immediate prologue to the massacre. The distance between the propaganda and the action, between the organization and its release on the people had become too short. But the spreading of the word could have been stopped before it was too late: if democratic tolerance had been withdrawn when the future leaders started their campaign, mankind would have had a chance of avoiding Auschwitz and a World War.

The whole post-fascist period is one of clear and present danger. Consequently, true pacification requires the withdrawal of tolerance before the deed, at the stage of communication in word, print, and picture. Such extreme suspension of the right of free speech and free assembly is indeed justified only if the whole of society is in extreme danger. I maintain that our society is in such an emergency situation, and that it has become the normal state of affairs. Different opinions and "philosophies" can no longer compete peacefully for adherence and persuasion on rational grounds: the "marketplace of ideas" is organized and delimited by those who determine the national and the individual interest. In this society, for which the ideologists have proclaimed the "end of ideology," the false consciousness has become the general consciousness — from the government down to its last objects. The small and powerless minorities which struggle against the false consciousness and its beneficiaries must be helped: their continued existence is more important than the preservation of abused rights and liberties which grant constitutional powers to those who oppress these minorities. It should be evident by now that the exercise of civil rights by those who don't have them presupposes the withdrawal of civil rights from those who prevent their exercise, and that liberation of the Damned of the Earth presupposes suppression not only of their old but also of their new masters.

Withdrawal of tolerance from regressive movements *before* they can become active; intolerance even toward thought, opinion, and word, and finally, intolerance in the opposite direction, that is, toward the self-styled conservatives, to the political Right — these anti-democratic notions respond to the actual development of the democratic society which has destroyed the basis for universal tolerance. The conditions under which tolerance can again become a liberating and humanizing force have still to be created. When tolerance mainly serves the protection and preservation of a repressive society, when it serves to neutralize opposition and to render men immune against other and better forms of life, then tolerance has been perverted. And when this perversion starts in the mind of the individual, in his consciousness, his needs, when heteronomous interests occupy him before he can experience his servitude, then the efforts to counteract his dehumanization must begin at the place of entrance, there where the false consciousness takes form (or rather: is systematically formed) — it must begin with stopping the words and images which feed this consciousness. To be sure, this is censorship, even precensorship, but openly directed against the more or less hidden censorship that permeates the free media. Where the false consciousness has become prevalent in national and popular behavior, it translates itself almost immediately into practice: the safe distance between ideology and reality, repressive thought and repressive action, between the word of destruction and the deed of destruction is dangerously shortened. Thus, the break through the false consciousness may provide the Archimedean point for a larger emancipation — at an infinitesimally small spot, to be sure, but it is on the enlargement of such small spots that the chance of change depends.

The forces of emancipation cannot be identified with any social class which, by virtue of its material condition, is free from false consciousness. Today, they are hopelessly dispersed throughout the society, and the fighting minorities and isolated groups are often in opposition to their own leadership. In the society at large, the mental space for denial and reflection must first be recreated. Repulsed by the concreteness of the administered society, the effort of emancipation becomes "abstract"; it is reduced to facilitating the recognition of what is going on, to freeing language from the tyranny of the

Orwellian syntax and logic, to developing the concepts that comprehend reality. More than ever, the proposition holds true that progress in freedom demands progress in the *consciousness* of freedom. Where the mind has been made into a subject-object of politics and policies, intellectual autonomy, the realm of "pure" thought has become a matter of *political education* (or rather: counter-education).

This means that previously neutral, value-free, formal aspects of learning and teaching now become, on their own grounds and in their own right, political: learning to know the facts, the whole truth, and to comprehend it is radical criticism throughout, intellectual subversion. In a world in which the human faculties and needs are arrested or perverted, autonomous thinking leads into a "perverted world": contradiction and counter-image of the established world of repression. And this contradiction is not simply stipulated, is not simply the product of confused thinking or phantasy, but is the logical development of the given, the existing world. To the degree to which this development is actually impeded by the sheer weight of a repressive society and the necessity of making a living in it, repression invades the academic enterprise itself, even prior to all restrictions on academic freedom. The pre-empting of the mind vitiates impartiality and objectivity: unless the student learns to think in the opposite direction, he will be inclined to place the facts into the predominant framework of values. Scholarship, i.e., the acquisition and communication of knowledge, prohibits the purification and isolation of facts from the context of the whole truth. An essential part of the latter is recognition of the frightening extent to which history was made and recorded by and for the victors, that is, the extent to which history was the development of oppression. And this oppression is in the facts themselves which it establishes; thus they themselves carry a negative value as part and aspect of their facticity. To treat the great crusades *against* humanity (like that against the Albigensians) with the same impartiality as the desperate struggles *for* humanity means neutralizing their opposite historical function, reconciling the executioners with their victims, distorting the record. Such spurious neutrality serves to reproduce acceptance of the dominion of the victors in the consciousness of man. Here, too, in the education of those who are not yet maturely integrated, in the mind of the young, the ground for liberating tolerance is still to be created.

Education offers still another example of spurious, abstract tolerance in the guise of concreteness and truth: it is epitomized in the concept of self-actualization. From the permissiveness of all sorts of license to the child, to the constant psychological concern with the personal problems of the student, a large-scale movement is under way against the evils of repression and the need for being oneself. Frequently brushed aside is the question as to what has to be repressed before one can be a self, oneself. The individual potential is first a negative one, a portion of the potential of his society: of aggression, guilt feeling, ignorance, resentment, cruelty which vitiate his life instincts. If the identity of the self is to be more than the immediate realization of this potential (undesirable for the individual as human being), then it requires repression and sublimation, conscious transformation. This process involves at each stage (to use the ridiculed terms which here reveal their succinct concreteness) the negation of the negation, mediation of the immediate, and identity is no more and no less than this process. "Alienation" is the constant and essential element of identity, the objective side of the subject — and not, as it is made to appear today, a disease, a psychological condition. Freud well knew the difference between progressive and regressive, liberating and destructive repression. The publicity of self-actualization promotes the removal of the one and the other, it promotes existence in that immediacy which, in a repressive society, is (to use another Hegelian term) bad immediacy (*schlechte Unmittelbarheit*). It isolates the individual from the one dimension where he could "find himself": from his political existence, which is at the core of his entire existence. Instead, it encourages non-conformity and letting-go in ways which leave the real engines of repression in the society entirely intact, which even strengthen these engines by substituting the satisfactions of private and personal rebellion for a more than private and personal, and therefore more authentic, opposition. The desublimation involved in this sort of self-actualization is itself repressive inasmuch as it weakens the necessity and the power of the intellect, the catalytic force of that unhappy consciousness which does not revel in the archetypal personal release of frustration — hopeless resurgence of the Id which will sooner or later succumb to the omnipresent rationality of the administered world — but which recognizes the horror of the whole in the most private frustration and actualizes itself in this recognition.

I have tried to show how the changes in advanced democratic societies, which have undermined the basis of economic and political liberalism, have also altered the liberal function of tolerance. The tolerance which was the great achievement of the liberal era is still professed and (with strong qualifications) practiced, while the economic and political process is subjected to an ubiquitous and effective administration in accordance with the predominant interests. The result is an objective contradiction between the economic and political structure on the one side, and the theory and practice of toleration on the other. The altered social structure tends to weaken the effectiveness of tolerance toward dissenting and oppositional movements and to strengthen conservative and reactionary forces. Equality of tolerance becomes abstract, spurious. With the actual decline of dissenting forces in the society, the opposition is insulated in small and frequently antagonistic groups who, even where tolerated within the narrow limits set by the hierarchical structure of society, are powerless while they keep within these limits. But the tolerance shown to them is deceptive and promotes coordination. And on the firm foundations of a coordinated society all but closed against qualitative change, tolerance itself serves to contain such change rather than to promote it.

These same conditions render the critique of such tolerance abstract and academic, and the proposition that the balance between tolerance toward the Right and toward the Left would have to be radically redressed in order to restore the liberating function of tolerance becomes only an unrealistic speculation. Indeed, such a redressing seems to be tantamount to the establishment of a "right of resistance" to the point of subversion. There is not, there cannot be any such right for any group or individual against a constitutional government sustained by a majority of the population. But I believe that there is a "natural right" of resistance for oppressed and overpowered minorities to use extralegal means if the legal ones have proved to be inadequate. Law and order are always and everywhere the law and order which protect the established hierarchy; it is nonsensical to invoke the absolute authority of this law and this order against those who suffer from it and struggle against it — not for personal advantages and revenge, but for their share of humanity. There is no other judge over them than the constituted authorities, the police, and their own conscience. If they use violence, they do not start a new chain of violence but try to break an established one. Since they will be punished, they know the risk, and when they are willing to take it, no third person, and least of all the educator and intellectual, has the right to preach them abstention.

POSTSCRIPT 1968

Herbert Marcuse

Under the conditions prevailing in this country, tolerance does not, and cannot, fulfill the civilizing function attributed to it by the liberal protagonists of democracy, namely, protection of dissent. The progressive historical force of tolerance lies in its extension to those modes and forms of dissent which are not committed to the status quo of society, and not confined to the institutional framework of the established society. Consequently, the idea of tolerance implies the necessity, for the dissenting group or individuals, to become illegitimate if and when the established legitimacy prevents and counteracts the development of dissent. This would be the case not only in a totalitarian society, under a dictatorship, in one-party states, but also in a democracy (representative, parliamentary, or "direct") where the majority does not result from the development of independent thought and opinion but rather from the monopolistic or oligopolistic administration of public opinion, without terror and (normally) without censorship. In such cases, the majority is self-perpetuating while perpetuating the vested interests which *made* it a majority. In its very structure this majority is "closed," petrified; it repels "a priori" any change other than changes within the system. But this means that the majority is no longer justified in claiming the democratic title of the best guardian of the common interest. And such a majority is all but the opposite of Rousseau's "general will": it is composed, not of individuals who, in their political functions, have made effective "abstraction" from their private interests, but, on the contrary, of individuals who have effectively identified their private interests with their political functions. And the representatives of this majority, in ascertaining and executing its will, ascertain and execute the will of the vested interests which have formed the majority. The ideology of democracy hides its lack of substance.

In the United States, this tendency goes hand in hand with the monopolistic or oligopolistic concentration of capital in the formation

338

of public opinion, i.e., of the majority. The chance of influencing, in any effective way, this majority is at a price, in dollars, totally out of reach of the radical opposition. Here too, free competition and exchange of ideas have become a farce. The Left has no equal voice, no equal access to the mass media and their public facilities — not because a conspiracy excludes it, but because, in good old capitalist fashion, it does not have the required purchasing power. And the Left does not have the purchasing power because it is the Left. These conditions impose upon the radical minorities a strategy which is in essence a refusal to allow the continuous functioning of allegedly indiscriminate but in fact discriminate tolerance, for example, a strategy of protesting against the alternate matching of a spokesman for the Right (or Center) with one for the Left. Not "equal" but *more* representation of the Left would be equalization of the prevailing inequality.

Within the solid framework of preestablished inequality and power, tolerance is practiced indeed. Even outrageous opinions are expressed, outrageous incidents are televised; and the critics of established policies are interrupted by the same number of commercials as the conservative advocates. Are these interludes supposed to counteract the sheer weight, magnitude, and continuity of system-publicity, indoctrination which operates playfully through the endless commercials as well as through the entertainment?

Given this situation, I suggested in "Repressive Tolerance" the practice of discriminating tolerance in an inverse direction, as a means of shifting the balance between Right and Left by restraining the liberty of the Right, thus counteracting the pervasive inequality of freedom (unequal opportunity of access to the means of democratic persuasion) and strengthening the oppressed against the oppressors. Tolerance would be restricted with respect to movements of a demonstrably aggressive or destructive character (destructive of the prospects for peace, justice, and freedom for all). Such discrimination would also be applied to movements opposing the extension of social legislation to the poor, weak, disabled. As against the virulent denunciations that such a policy would do away with the sacred liberalistic principle of equality for "the other side," I maintain that there are issues where either there is no "other side" in any more than a formalistic sense, or where "the other side" is demonstrably "regressive" and impedes possible improvement of the human condition. To tolerate propaganda for inhumanity vitiates the goals not only of liberalism but of every progressive political philosophy.

I presupposed the existence of demonstrable criteria for aggressive, regressive, destructive forces. If the final democratic criterion of the declared opinion of the majority no longer (or rather not yet) prevails, if vital ideas, values, and ends of human progress no longer (or rather not yet) enter, as competing equals, the formation of public opinion, if the people are no longer (or rather not yet) sovereign but "made" by the real sovereign powers — is there any alternative other than the dictatorship of an "elite" over the people? For the opinion of people (usually designated as The People) who are unfree in the very faculties in which liberalism saw the roots of freedom: independent thought and independent speech, can carry no overriding validity and authority — even if The People constitute the overwhelming majority.

If the choice were between genuine democracy and dictatorship, democracy would certainly be preferable. But democracy does not prevail. The radical critics of the existing political process are thus readily denounced as advocating an "elitism," a dictatorship of intellectuals as an alternative. What we have in fact is government, representative government by a non-intellectual minority of politicians, generals, and businessmen. The record of this "elite" is not very promising, and political prerogatives for the intelligentsia may not necessarily be worse for the society as a whole.

In any case, John Stuart Mill, not exactly an enemy of liberal and representative government, was not so allergic to the political leadership of the intelligentsia as the contemporary guardians of semi-democracy are. Mill believed that "individual mental superiority" justifies "reckoning one person's opinion as equivalent to more than one":

> Until there shall have been devised, and until opinion is willing to accept, some mode of plural voting which may assign to education as such the degree of superior influence due to it, and sufficient as a counterpoise to the numerical weight of the least educated class, for so long the benefits of completely universal suffrage cannot be obtained without bringing with them, as it appears to me, more than equivalent evils.[1]

[1] *Considerations on Representative Government* (Chicago: Gateway Edition, 1962), p. 183.

"Distinction in favor of education, right in itself," was also supposed to preserve "the educated from the class legislation of the uneducated," without enabling the former to practice a class legislation of their own.[2]

Today, these words have understandably an antidemocratic, "elitist" sound — understandably because of their dangerously radical implications. For if "education" is more and other than training, learning, preparing for the existing society, it means not only enabling man to know and understand the facts which make up reality but also to know and understand the factors that establish the facts so that he can change their inhuman reality. And such humanistic education would involve the "hard" sciences ("hard" as in the "hardware" bought by the Pentagon?), would free them from their destructive direction. In other words, such education would indeed badly serve the Establishment, and to give political prerogatives to the men and women thus educated would indeed be anti-democratic in the terms of the Establishment. But these are not the only terms.

However, the alternative to the established semi-democratic process is *not* a dictatorship or elite, no matter how intellectual and intelligent, but the struggle for a real democracy. Part of this struggle is the fight against an ideology of tolerance which, in reality, favors and fortifies the conservation of the status quo of inequality and discrimination. For this struggle, I proposed the practice of discriminating tolerance. To be sure, this practice already presupposes the radical goal which it seeks to achieve. I committed this *petitio principii* in order to combat the pernicious ideology that tolerance is already institutionalized in this society. The tolerance which is the life element, the token of a free society, will never be the gift of the powers that be; it can, under the prevailing conditions of tyranny by the majority, only be won in the sustained effort of radical minorities, willing to break this tyranny and to work for the emergence of a free and sovereign majority — minorities intolerant, militantly intolerant and disobedient to the rules of behavior which tolerate destruction and suppression.

2 *Ibid.*, p. 181.

BLACK POWER ADVOCACY:
CRIMINAL ANARCHY OR FREE SPEECH*

Paul Harris

[Black Power] is the capacity of black people to be and to become themselves, not only for their own good, but for the enrichment of the lives of all. White people are afraid of the term because they see in it a mirror of *white* power. And that spells abuse.[1]

The picture of black agitators traveling throughout the country, inciting ghettos to violence, is common in today's newspapers and television. This Comment will look closely at the picture, attempting to separate fact from distortion. The first question which presents itself is the nature of black power advocacy: Who are the speakers? What do they say? Why have they found so many willing ears? The first part of this Comment will examine black power advocacy and the use of criminal anarchy and syndicalism laws [hereinafter referred to as criminal anarchy] to silence that advocacy.

Some criminal anarchy statutes have been held unconstitutionally vague and overbroad. However, New York has recently enacted a criminal anarchy statute which, on its face, seems to avoid the problems of vagueness and overbreadth.[2] Yet, any statute which directly abridges speech must also meet the constitutional requirements of the clear and present danger test. There are two interpretations of the clear and present danger test; one is usually referred to as the Holmes-Brandeis formula, the other as the *Dennis* formula. The second section will analyze these two tests in light of recent black power advocacy and ghetto uprisings.

Paul Harris, "Black Power Advocacy: Criminal Anarchy or Free Speech," *California Law Review*, May 1968, pp. 702–755. Copyright © 1968 by Fred B. Rothman & Co. Reprinted by permission of the author and Fred B. Rothman & Co.

*This article as originally published contained 281 footnotes. To save space, most of them have been deleted. A few which the author considered "illuminating" have been retained and appear at the end of the selection.

After discussing these prevailing constitutional tests, the final part of the Comment will interpret the purposes of the first amendment's protection of freedom of speech and whether or not black power advocacy is consistent with those purposes. This discussion lays the groundwork for the suggestion of a different constitutional test of free speech. The Comment concludes with an argument that black power advocacy is within the scope of the first amendment and that it therefore should be protected from abridgment by criminal anarchy laws.

I. Free Speech Now

A. Failure of the Traditional Civil Rights Groups

For the first time in the twentieth century freedom of speech has entered the ghettos of black America in a meaningful way. It has previously lacked real meaning because the content of the speech has had little relationship to the problems of the listeners. Until recently white liberals and black leaders have not spoken to the issues which most concern the people in the northern ghettos, the issues of poverty and pride.

In the early 1960's, Martin Luther King, Jr. and the Southern Christian Leadership Conference (SCLC), James Farmer and the Congress of Racial Equality (CORE), and Bob Moses and the Student Non-violent Coordinating Committee (SNCC) all spoke of equality under the law. They struggled so that black men had the right to sit in the front of a bus, to go to the school of one's choice, to eat at a lunch counter, to gain employment according to one's skills, and to vote in elections. These are important rights, but translated into the world of reality they had little effect on the life of the black man in the northern ghettos. The right to sit in the front of the bus does not change the fact that the transportation system in Watts is hopelessly inadequate. The right to go to school with whites does not change the fact that in the north the proportion of black children going to schools which are in fact segregated has increased since 1954. The right to eat anywhere one chooses does not change the fact that food costs money and that "between 1949 and 1959, the income of Negro men relative to white men declined in every section of this country." The right to vote does not change the fact that Californians voted nearly 2–1 to repeal fair housing laws. The right to be employed according to one's abilities does not change the reality that in the major ghettos one out of three black men is either jobless or earning too little to live on. As a lady in Alabama said, "the food that Ralph Bunche eats doesn't fill my stomach." Poverty, not equality under the Civil Rights Act, is the issue for most black Americans.

Having a black skin not only means suffering economic and social discrimination, it means a lack of positive identity, a vague but decaying sense of shame, a hostility which vents itself on others in the community, and a frustration which explodes and destroys the self as well as others. Roy Wilkins and the National Association for the Advancement of Colored People (NAACP) and Whitney Young and the National Urban League did not speak to the problem of pride; they spoke of integration. The philosophy of integration encouraged the black person to get rid of his ghetto accent, to speak like white people, to dress like them and to accept their values and their aspirations. Hopefully the white society would then accept the black person, and the end result would be a world of equality and brotherhood. But the means to that goal did not work; in fact, the means never were accepted by the majority of black people. Blackness, not integration, is the issue for the man in the ghetto.

B. *Malcolm X and the Beginning of Black Power*

While these civil rights organizations were involved in a dialogue with the white society, an organization called the Black Muslims had opened a dialogue with the people of the black ghetto. In the early 1960's their membership was over 100,000 and they were considered a genuine mass movement. Malcolm X was their major advocate; he spoke to the black man as no one had before. He told them that the white man had beaten their fathers and raped their mothers, that the white man's police harassed them, his merchants cheated them, and his politicians lied to them. These were things every black person had known, but had never heard anyone say in public or outside of quiet private conversations. Malcolm told them that there had been a great civilization in Africa, that Tarzan was the savage, not the black native. He told them that the wealth of the United States has been built on the backs of their ancestors. He told them that curly hair was beautiful, that black skin was beautiful, that a black man was as good or better than a white man. He told them that the majority of the world was colored, not white, and that the future was black — bright, beautiful black. Thus, black people were finally articulating ideas which had been lying dormant deep inside many ghetto dwellers. Now the feelings of pride in one's ancestors, one's appearance, and one's future began to come alive throughout the ghetto.

During the last year of his life Malcolm X split from the Muslims, rejecting the notion of black superiority and separation and began to develop a theory of black power. He discussed the necessity for political unity of black people, the development of an Afro-American culture, and the role of sympathetic whites in the struggle for freedom. Malcolm X was shot and killed in 1965, but the concept of black power did not die with him; it is now being developed and advocated in every ghetto of America. Black men such as Stokely Carmichael, Bill Epton, John Harris and Rap Brown are speaking to the problems of the ghetto, and they are speaking the thoughts of millions of black people.

II. Nature of Black Power

A. Black Power Advocacy

The words "black power" often refer to a political philosophy which analyzes the position of black people in American society. Its major thrust is into the area of political power, advocating the need for an independent political party which would represent the needs of the black masses. Black power philosophy also explores the relationship of black people to the job market, the law enforcement agencies, the educational system and to other black people. It stresses the need for black people to control their own communities and to run their own lives without interference from white people.

The law has not concerned itself with black power advocacy in general; rather it has attempted to prosecute the advocacy only during times of ghetto unrest. Although most speeches during racially tense periods have not resulted in criminal anarchy indictments, there have been two cases in which recognized black power advocates have spoken or passed out leaflets and were subsequently charged with criminal anarchy. An analysis of these two cases and Rap Brown's infamous speech in Cambridge will enable one to examine the notion of black power advocacy and its relationship to criminally punishable speech.

The speeches and leaflets for which the black power spokesmen are being prosecuted have three major themes. First, and foremost, is a criticism of police and their policies. The most common cry of the ghetto is that black people must suffer daily harassment by the police. When an incident occurs in which a policeman shoots a black person as happened in Harlem and Watts, black power advocates articulate the cries of police brutality. These advocates argue that the police have continually brutalized black people; they call for the arrest of the officer involved in the specific shooting, and they warn the people of the ghetto to arm and defend themselves against attack by the police.

The second common thread running through the prosecuted advocacy is the intolerable conditions in which black people live. The spokesmen point out the realities of the ghetto and then blame the white society for those conditions and for profiting from their continuance.

The third theme of black power advocates is the need for black people to control their community. They argue that three types of control are necessary: First, the ownership of the business in the ghetto; second, the control of welfare agencies, ghetto school boards, and law enforcement within their community; third, the election of black men who truly represent the ghetto poor.

The speeches and leafleting of Brown, Carmichael, Epton, and Harris are clearly distinguishable from specific calls to violence made by black persons during times of ghetto uproar. For example, shortly before the Newark uprising began, a black man who was part of the demonstration protesting the police beating of a black cab-driver took the speaker's bullhorn and said, "Come down the street, we got some shit." This statement was an exhortation to pick up bottles and to begin throwing them at the police precinct station. The man's statement was comparable to a leader of a gang urging others to effect immediate harm. He stated no philosophy, analyzed no power relationships, and demanded no political changes. It was solely a call to specific violence, and thus was not within the scope of the first amendment's protection.

The Newark example is not atypical. Often during the uprisings or immediately preceding them, someone, upon drawing the attention of a volatile crowd, will say something to the effect of "Burn, baby burn" or "let's get whitey." The men, or boys, making these spontaneous speeches have sometimes been referred to as agitators. Black power advocates also are often described as "agitators." However, the difference between them is essential and ought not to be confused in the eyes of the law. Black power advocacy is political speech; it describes life in the ghetto, analyzes the cause and effects of that life, demands social and economic changes, and often advocates revolution. Certainly there are violent statements and threats in the advocacy. But advocating violent revolution is not enough by itself to take speech outside of the protection of the first amendment.

The key in examining the advocacy is to recognize that the violent statements are part of a totality. That totality is a speech or leaflet in the traditional form of revolutionary political advocacy. Sentences should not be read out of context, and the most violent words of the black power spokesmen are an integral part of their general, not violent, advocacy. In each of the four instances under examination, a general statement of political analysis or philosophy immediately precedes or follows the threat of violence. The leaflet distributed by John Harris, which is the basis of a criminal syndicalism indictment, states in part:

> Bring Parker, Yorty, and Bova to trial for murder — in a court of the people. Disarm the guards in the concentration camp. If 80% of us don't work in the factories, *you* don't produce! ! !

Taken alone, these words can be viewed as a threat of violence to take place in the future. However, the sentences immediately preceding these words are in the tradition of classic political protest as they state the failure of the present system and point to the oppressed people's right of revolution:

> Murder by cops and death by unemployment are methods of systematic extermination. This extermination isn't going to be stopped by going to the court of the exterminator as advised by some "Negro" politicians and preachers.

> George Washington and the American revolutionaries never went to King George's court. The Jews never asked to go to Hitler's court.

> The concentration camp must develop its own court and its own method of trial.

Bill Epton's speech in Harlem is another example of the nature of black power advocacy and its difference from the call to specific violence. The New York Court of Appeals quotes Epton as saying: "They [the police] declared war on us and we should declare war on them and every time they kill one of us damn it, we'll kill one of them and we should start thinking that way right now. . . ." Taken alone these words might be interpreted to be a call to immediate violence. But the words were part of a larger speech, and later in that speech Epton had more to say about the police:

> To my left is a Puerto Rican policeman in plain clothes . . . I tell him now, and I tell my black brother on my right, that they had better choose their sides. Because when the deal goes down . . . he will have to go too unless he chooses the right side. There is only one right side. That's our side. That's the cause of the people and what we demand and what we get.

It is clear from these words and the speech as a whole that Epton was not suggesting that those in the crowd pick up a bottle or brick and attack the plainclothesman. If he had, there is no doubt he would be guilty of inciting a crime; he would be in the position of a gang leader directing criminal actions. But neither Epton, nor any of the other black power advocates were prosecuted for directing attacks on police or property. Their indictments were based on the speeches and leaflets which were expositions of their political philosophy and which included general advocacy of revolution and armed defense.

The attention of the press and the public has not been focused on anonymous street leaders and "agitators" such as the man in the Newark example. Rather the attention has been on the black power spokesmen, who are held responsible for the violence which has so shaken America in the past four years. In a *Newsweek* survey to find out what white adults thought were the basic causes of the uprisings, 45 per cent of those questioned blamed "outside agitation;" the next most frequent reply, "prejudice-bad treatment," was mentioned by only 16 per cent. In the examples of Brown, Harris, and Epton, local law enforcement agencies have responded like the general public to the ghetto uprisings and indicted outspoken black leaders under rarely used criminal anarchy statutes. The Congress has had a similar response as it passed an antiriot bill, which makes it a crime to travel or use any facility in interstate commerce with intent to incite a riot. In order to appraise correctly black power advocacy it is worthwhile to delve into the nature of ghetto "riots."

B. Race Riots in American History

Race riots are not new in America, and those people who are surprised by the present turmoil have forgotten their history. On July 3 and 4, 1916, East St. Louis was torn by rioting in which thirty-nine blacks and nine whites were killed. From July 27 to August 2, 1919, an ugly race riot in Chicago left twenty-three blacks and fifteen whites dead. In Detroit, on June 20, 1943, a fight started between a couple of black youths and a white man; soon white sailors joined in and within hours a major race riot was in progress. White mobs, estimated at over 1,000 people, attempted to march into the black ghetto, but were turned back. When it ended two days later, twenty-four blacks and nine whites had been killed. These were three of the worst of the many riots between blacks and whites in the first half of the twentieth century. They were marked by intensive fighting between black people and white people, rather than the recent pattern of black people against the police and national guard. They were usually touched off by an interracial clash, not by a law enforcement incident. This pattern of racial confrontation and violence was broken twice; once by the Harlem violence of 1935, and again by the Harlem uprising of 1943.

In Harlem the violence was touched off by police incidents, and the objects of the people's fury were mainly the police and the commercial establishments. In the Harlem uprising of 1935 only two blacks and two whites were killed. During the violence of 1943, five blacks were killed. It is not surprising that the Harlem experience was one with political as well as racial consciousness. Harlem is where the poor black man first began to organize on the issues of poverty and blackness. In the 1920's it was the center of Marcus Garvey's Universal Negro Improvement Association, the largest mass movement in the history of black Americans. His teachings were the precursor of today's concept of black power, and they gave Harlem residents an awareness that the enemy was not a white skin, but a white system.

While blacks and whites in East St. Louis and Chicago were tearing at each other's skins, the black people of Harlem were attacking the most visible signs of their oppression — the police and the merchants. Harlem was not a race riot; it was an unstructured uprising of the black ghetto dwellers against a political and social system controlled by whites for the benefit of whites. The difference between the two types of violence is important. It is impossible to deal rationally with a race riot, whose object is to destroy a people of a different color. But one can deal in a rational way with an uprising, for its demands are a change of political relationships and an alteration of social conditions.

C. Uprisings of the 1960's

The last four years of ghetto violence reveal a movement away from race rioting to a form of rebellion. The Harlem uprising of 1964 followed the pattern of earlier Harlem explosions. There were definite political demands, such as the suspension of the police officer who had shot a black teenager; to a significant degree, however, the uprising was colored by racial hatred.

One year after Harlem, the ghetto of Watts exploded to the cry of "Burn, baby, burn." Watts, as Harlem, was a mixture of racial hatred and political awareness. After Watts, a serious debate began in political and civil rights circles as to the character of the Watts violence. Some believed it was basically a race riot; others saw it as the beginnings of a revolution; the majority characterized the Watts violence as an uprising, an unorganized rebellion.

In July, 1967, the ghetto of Newark broke loose. The Governor of New Jersey called it an "open rebellion" and later described it as a "criminal insurrection." With the remains of Newark's fires still smoldering, the first national black power conference was held, attempting to translate the fury of the rebellion into political alternatives.

One month after Newark, a ghetto holocaust hit Detroit. In many sections of Detroit, poor whites and poor blacks looted side by side. *Time* called it an "uprising." The *Berkeley Barb* described it as "revolution." Whatever the word one chooses, it is clear that the identity of the enemy is no longer seen as a white face; rather it is viewed as a white power structure which oppresses all blacks and many whites.[4] Some of the "establishment" news magazines have recognized this change. *Newsweek* observed: "In the view from the street corners of Harlem or Watts or Detroit's West Side, the riots are rebellions, the rioters not criminals at all but the freedom fighters of an oppressed, beleaguered, powerless colony of the white world downtown."

There has been no sign that ghetto rebellions will cease in the next few years. On the contrary, the growth of all black organizations, the development of ghetto political awareness, and the continued militancy of indigenous leaders point to many more summers of strife and turbulence. There is similarly no evidence to suggest that states will stop arresting those who during times of tension raise the cry of black power. Given these two patterns, it is likely that criminal anarchy and criminal syndicalism statutes will continue to be used to attempt to quiet the violent voice of the ghetto. The remainder of this Comment will attempt to analyze the constitutionality of criminal anarchy and criminal syndicalism laws.

III. Criminal Anarchy

A. Differing Tests of Free Speech

Criminal anarchy statutes grew out of the labor turmoil and anarchist political activities of the late 1800's and early 1900's. A few months after an alleged anarchist assassinated President McKinley in 1901, the New York legislature enacted the first criminal anarchy law. Fifteen years later against the background of three thousand arrests of suspected communists and radicals by the Justice Department, California passed, as an emergency measure, the first criminal syndicalist statute. By 1922, nineteen states, as well as Hawaii and Alaska, had passed similar laws.

The New York criminal anarchy statute, the prototype for most other state anarchy statutes, was held constitutional by the United States Supreme Court in *Gitlow* v. *New York*. The Court's test of the first amendment's protection of free speech was whether or not the words in question had a tendency to lead to an evil which the state constitutionally could prohibit. This test, often referred to as the "bad tendency" test, was broadly stated in *Gitlow*:

> That a State in the exercise of its police power may punish those who abuse this freedom [of speech] by utterances inimical to the public welfare, tending to corrupt public morals, incite to crime, or disturb the public peace, is not open to question.

In 1927, the Court also used the "bad tendency" test in *Whitney* v. *California* to uphold the constitutionality of the California criminal syndicalism statute. In a concurring opinion, Justice Brandeis argued that the correct test was the clear and present danger formula which the Court had used in six cases from 1919 through 1920.

Justice Holmes first enunciated the clear and present danger formula in *Schenck* v. *United States*:

> The question in every case is whether the words used are used in such circumstances and are of such a nature as to create a clear and present danger that they will bring about the substantive evils that Congress has a right to prevent.

Unlike the bad tendency test, the Holmes-Brandeis formula allows speech even though there is a threat to public interests. It offers more protection to speech than the bad tendency test by allowing speech unless there is an immediate threat of grave danger. In actual practice the Court used the clear and present danger test to uphold six convictions of advocacy which in retrospect do not seem to have presented an imminent danger to the state. In these cases the "nub of the evidence held sufficient to meet the 'clear and present danger' " test was as follows: publication of twelve newspaper articles attacking World War I, one speech attacking United States' participation in the war; circulation of copies of two different socialist circulars attacking the war; publication of a German-language newspaper with allegedly false articles, critical of capitalism and the war, circulation of copies of a small pamphlet written by a clergyman, attacking the purposes of the war and United States' participation; mailing of circulars to draftees advocating that conscription was involuntary servitude.

During the 1920's, the Court refused to apply the clear and present danger test, although Justice Holmes' dissent in *Gitlow* and Justice Brandeis' concurrence in *Whitney* were eloquent testimonials to free speech and were influential in the Court's return to the clear and present danger formula. Starting with *Herndon* v. *Lowry* in 1937, the Court for twelve years protected the first amendment right in question through the use of the clear and present danger rule.

In 1950, the Court in *Feiner* v. *New York* used the test to find that the speech did constitute an imminent threat of a breach of the peace, affirming a conviction for disorderly conduct. A year later in *Dennis* v. *United States* the Court reformulated the clear and present danger test, accepting the words of Judge Learned Hand who had written the majority decision for the court of appeals: "In each case [courts] must ask whether the gravity of the 'evil,' discounted by its improbalility, justifies such invasion of free speech as is necessary to avoid the danger."[5] Under this interpretation the Court balances the right of free speech against the gravity of the evil. As the gravity of evil increases, the necessity to show an immediate danger decreases. This reinterpretation in effect strikes out the requirement of immediate danger, and stresses the importance of the state's interest.

The Court used the *Dennis* interpretation in *Yates v. United States,* in which fourteen members of the Communist Party had been convicted for advocacy of overthrow of the government by force and violence. The Court modified the *Dennis* test by requiring strict evidentiary proof of the criminal nature of the advocacy in question, proof which the government was unable to acquire. Since *Yates* in 1957, the Supreme Court has not used the *Dennis* test. It seems to have limited the Holmes-Brandeis test to cases where the state has held an individual in contempt of court because of his out-of-court publication.

In 1967, the New York Court of Appeals used the *Dennis* formula in affirming the conviction of William Epton under New York's criminal anarchy statute. This was the first time the New York criminal anarchy law had been invoked since *Gitlow* in 1925. The court admitted that *Gitlow* and the bad tendency test were no longer good law. To preserve the constitutionality of the anarchy law, however, they read the following requirement into the statute: "There must be a 'clear and present danger' that the advocated overthrow may be attempted or accomplished." The court cited *Dennis* as authority for the clear and present danger test and did not require a showing that Epton's advocacy produced an imminent danger. The Supreme Court denied certiorari and dismissed the appeal "for want of a substantial federal question." The concurrence by Justice Stewart suggests the Court's reasoning in denying certiorari. Stewart points out that Epton had been convicted of conspiring to riot, as well as advocating criminal anarchy and conspiring to advocate criminal anarchy. He argues that since the riot conviction raises no substantial federal question, and since the three one-year sentences run concurrently, there is no necessity for the Court to consider the two criminal anarchy charges. He goes on to state that if the constitutionality of New York's criminal anarchy laws were properly before the Court, he would have voted to grant certiorari and not probable jurisdiction of the appeal "to reconsider the Court's decision in *Gitlow* v. *United States . . .* and to decide whether the New York anarchy statutes, either on their face or as applied in this case, violate the First and Fourteenth Amendments." The only other written opinion was by Justice Douglas, who dissented on both the conspiracy to riot conviction and the criminal anarchy convictions.

It is likely that the rest of the Court based its denial of certiorari on the validity of the conspiracy to riot count, which along with the concurrent sentences made it unnecessary to review the other counts of the indictment. Regardless of the reason for the Court's abstention, the result is that an important state court decision, which used the *Dennis* clear and present danger test to sustain a conviction for black power advocacy, has been allowed to stand. However, this result does not mean that the Court has expressly, or even impliedly, sanctioned the use of criminal anarchy statutes to silence black power advocacy such as Epton's. Three factors indicate that the Court was not deciding the constitutionality of criminal anarchy statutes, or the use of the *Dennis* clear and present danger formula as a test of the first amendment's protection of black power advocacy.

The first factor is Justice Stewart's reliance on the conspiracy to riot charge. His action is similar to that of the one judge in the New York Court of Appeals who dissented as to the criminal anarchy counts but accepted the conviction for conspiracy to riot. It may be that the facts in this case persuaded the justices that there was enough evidence of overt acts unrelated to advocacy so as to substantiate a conviction for conspiracy to riot. The second factor suggesting the Court's sidestepping of the criminal anarchy conviction is that Justice Black, traditional guardian of free speech, did not dissent from the per curiam opinion. The third factor, which strongly suggests that if the criminal anarchy law had been properly before the Court it would have been declared unconstitutional on its face, is the court's decision in *Keyishian* v. *Board of Regents of New York.*

B. Attacking the Statute on its Face

Early in 1967, the Supreme Court in *Keyishian* held as unconstitutionally vague New York statutes which disqualified persons from employment in the Civil Service and the educational system on the grounds of "the utterance of any treasonable or seditious word or words or the doing of any treasonable or seditious act or acts." The statutes equated the word "seditious" with "criminal anarchy" as defined in the New York criminal anarchy statute. The Supreme Court did not have to reach the clear and present danger issue, because it held that the definition, on its face, was unconstitutionally vague.

Recently there have been four important federal court decisions in the field of criminal anarchy. In February, 1967, a three-judge district court in the Fifth Circuit, relying on *Keyishian*, held that the Mississippi Syndicalism Act, on its face, was unconstitutionally vague and overbroad. A month later, another three-judge district court held that the Georgia criminal insurrection statute was, on its face, unconstitutionally vague and overbroad. In September, 1967, a three-judge district court in the Sixth Circuit held that the Kentucky criminal syndicalism and sedition statute was, on its face, unconstiutionally vague. In March 1968, a three-judge district court in the Ninth Circuit held that the California criminal syndicalism statute was, on its face, unconstitutionally vague and overbroad.

For a criminal anarchy statute to be constitutional it must clear two hurdles: First, the statute, on its face, must not suffer from vagueness or overbreadth. Second, the statute, as applied to the defendant, must require a showing of a clear and present danger of an evil which the state can legitimately prohibit. The recent development of the convening of three-judge federal courts to determine the constitutionality of criminal anarchy statutes on their face will force state legislatures to rewrite their statutes in narrow and specific terms. Already the New York legislature has redrafted the criminal anarchy law, reducing five paragraphs into three phrases. However, regardless of how narrowly a state draws its statute, a law which attempts to prosecute advocacy must still clear the second constitutional hurdle — the clear and present danger test.

C. Clear and Present Danger

The constitutional protection which the clear and present danger test affords is in a somewhat confused state. Although it seems that the Supreme Court will use the *Dennis* formula, the Holmes-Brandeis test is not yet dead, as evidenced by *Wood* v. *Georgia* and its persistent use in significant lower court decisions. A comparison of the Holmes-Brandeis version of the clear and present danger test with the *Dennis* interpretation is a fruitful method of analyzing when, if ever, black power advocacy should be punishable. Therefore, if one assumes that a narrowly drawn criminal anarchy statute is not unconstitutionally vague or overbroad, then the question is whether black power advocacy in times of ghetto tension creates a clear and present danger under either the Holmes-Brandeis formulation or the *Dennis* standard.

1. *The Holmes-Brandeis Formula*   The clear and present danger test as expounded by Holmes and Brandeis involves four requirements which must be satisfied before advocacy can be constitutionally punished: First, the circumstances must be potentially dangerous in fact. Second, the feared evil must be "extremely serious." Third, there must be "reasonable ground to fear that the serious evil will result if free speech is practiced." Fourth, the "degree of imminence" of the danger must be "extremely high."

The first and second requirements seem to be easily satisfied in most tense ghetto situations. The large number of violent upheavals caused by small incidents point to the conclusion that the ghettos are black social dynamite and that in times of unrest circumstances are in fact potentially dangerous. The requirement that the evil must be "very serious" is also applicable to the uprisings whether one defines the evil as attempted overthrow of the government or as the destruction of lives, homes, and businesses.

The requirement that the danger is highly imminent is more difficult to apply. Given the explosive nature of the ghetto it seems on first glance that in almost all situations serious violence is imminent. Yet, the incidents which have ignited the uprisings occur almost daily in the ghetto, and in the vast majority of instances there is no violence. The case of John Harris is a good example of how the imminence of danger requirement is incorrectly confused with the potentially dangerous circumstances requirement. Harris was leafleting outside the inquest into the shooting of Leonard Deadwyler. The courtroom was filled with angry black people, and in general the atmosphere was one of tense excitement. The shadow of the Watts uprising of the previous summer cast itself darkly over the courtroom. Clearly the requirement of potential danger was satisfied. However, there were other factors which pointed to the lack of an imminent danger. The inquest was being held downtown, not in the ghetto. The courthouse and surrounding area were filled with a majority of white people. The number of policemen present was high. Finally, the response of the people receiving the leaflets from Harris did not evidence an immediate attempt to act violently. Thus, the evidence indicates that the district attorney was in error when he concluded that there was an "extremely high" likelihood of immediate violence. Moreover, the fact that he did reach that conclusion and then acted on it by prosecuting Harris, illustrates the danger in using such a test at all. It is at best a vague notion susceptible to abuse, at worst a meaningless phrase which allows the silencing of advocacy whenever the circumstances are potentially dangerous.

The final requirement that there must be reasonable ground to fear that the speech will produce a serious evil is a requirement of causation. The underlying assumption is that it is advocacy which causes people to revolt, an assumption which results from superficial and simplistic analysis. Vice-President Humphrey offered some insight into the problems of causation when he said:

> I'd hate to be stuck in a fourth floor in a tenement with the rats nibbling on the kids' toes — and they do — with the garbage uncollected — and it is — with the streets filthy, with no swimming pools, with little or no recreation.
>
> I'd hate to be put in those conditions, and I want to tell you if I were in those conditions and that should happen to have been my situation, I think you'd have had a little more trouble than you've had already because I've got enough spark left in me to lead a mighty good revolt under those conditions.

The Vice-President is pointing out that it is the basic conditions in which people live that are the root causes of rebellions. This is a basic rule of human behavior which white people can and do understand. A *Newsweek* survey asked whites the following question: "As an individual, what do you think it feels like to be discriminated against as a Negro?" The largest number of whites, 26 per cent, felt it might incite them to fight back, even to riot.

It is difficult for a middle-class white person to understand the conditions of the ghetto and probably impossible to empathize with those who live day to day on the outside of our plentiful society.

Without attempting a comprehensive documentation of ghetto conditions, a few specifics are necessary. De facto segregation of northern urban schools has increased in the past years. Education within the ghetto has in general failed to fulfill its purpose. A recent study has shown that scores on I.Q. tests of Harlem school children actually declined between the third and sixth grade. The campaign to keep black people in school is based on the theory that a high-school graduate will find a job easier than a drop-out. However, unemployment among black high-school graduates is 16.1 per cent while the rate for black drop-outs is 16.3 per cent.

Between 1960 and 1965, unemployment among nonwhites was twice as high as whites. The black person makes up only 3.5 per cent of the nation's professional and technical pool, while he constitutes 26 per cent of the unskilled laborers. Of all those engaged in apprentice training programs he makes up only 3.1 per cent. In Cleveland's ghetto of Hough, where a four-day uprising took place in 1966, the unemployment rate is 15.6 per cent. In other major cities, black unemployment is from two to four times higher than white unemployment.

One complaint of black power advocates is that merchants in the ghetto charge more for goods than in wealthier areas. *Time* magazine substantiates this practice, stating that:

> In Detroit's slums, a 5-lb. bag of flour costs 14 cents more than in fashionable Grosse Pointe, Michigan, peas 12 cents more per can, eggs up to 25 cents more per dozen. A television set selling for $124.95 in downtown Detroit costs $189 in a ghetto shop.

Housing is one of the ugliest realities of ghetto life. About 29 per cent of the Negro population live in housing which is substandard and overcrowded. A committee on the Illinois General Assembly, after touring slum housing in 1965, stated, "It is hardly possible to believe that human beings live in a modern city in the conditions which the Committee observed." Although there has been a good deal of legislation on slum housing, in general the law has given little or no help to the tenant. Public housing, instead of solving the problem, has created cities within the city where black children grow up isolated and unstimulated by their environment.

The law has also failed to protect the rights of the poor black man. In the North the failure seems to result from neglect and the inherent inequities of our legal system. In the South the guarantees of the law have been subverted by "the failure of local officials in several Southern states to adhere to their oath of office to support the Federal Constitution," and by the absence of federal prosecutions.

No statistics, no matter how dramatic, can bring the ghetto to life. The life and cry of the ghetto can best be understood through the artist, the musician and the poet. However, the law has created the phrase "clear and present danger" which it uses as a tool to dissect the ghetto and to analyze whether black power advocacy should be treated as criminal anarchy or free speech.

It may be argued that the clear and present danger formula is not concerned with the basic conditions which cause frustration and hate. The issue as viewed by Holmes and Brandeis is whether there is a reasonable ground to fear that the advocacy is the triggering device, the specific agent which touches off the explosion.[6] This test does not require that violence has actually occurred, only that reasonable men could agree that in the tense circumstances there was a high likelihood of imminent danger. This requirement of reasonable fear forces one to develop some criteria of reasonableness.

In order to determine whether it is reasonable to conclude that advocacy will produce violence in crisis circumstances, one must look to a survey of crisis situations and analyze the causes of the explosions. If one could show that in most tense situations an outbreak of violence immediately followed a black power speech, this would be strong evidence that it was reasonable to expect that the speech would cause the violence. However, the studies of ghetto uprisings reveal that the opposite is true; that is, in 93 per cent of the cases there was no such advocacy.

The President's Commission on Law Enforcement and Administration of Justice found that the seven uprisings in the summer of 1964 were all touched off by police incidents. The following year the uprisings grew worse. On August 11, 1965, a black ghetto called Watts broke loose with a fury and intensity that caused the white residents of Los Angeles, many of whom had never heard of Watts, to lock their doors in fear. Although the McCone Commission found that "the Los Angeles riot started with the arrest of Marquette Frye" this statement tells little of the relations between the black community and the Los Angeles Police Department which helped to precipitate the uprising.

In Los Angeles the police often refer to their night sticks as "nigger-knockers," and some police stations had posted on their bulletin boards a picture of Eleanor Roosevelt, with the caption "Nigger Lover." On the other side, some black men had little respect for the law; as one said, "Whitey talks about law and order — it's his law and order! Not mine!" Every day, black citizens and white policemen passed each other on the streets of Los Angeles as enemies. When relations between police and the ghetto become this warped it is not surprising that it was a police incident, rather than black power advocacy, which sparked the destruction of 175 million dollars worth of property and the death of thirty-six persons.

In July and August of 1967, there were more uprisings than there were summer days, with Detroit being the worst in this country's history. The Detroit rebellion started after a police raid on an after-hours club. As the squad cars and a paddy wagon carried away the seventy-four black people arrested, a crowd gathered and then, as in Watts, a bottle smashed against a squad car window; within minutes the rebellion was in progress. In Detroit, as in the overwhelming majority of the uprisings, there was no black power advocacy.

Even in situations where black community leaders have advocated peaceful protest, other members of the community have taken matters into their own hands. The events surrounding the beginning of the Newark rebellion shed light on the spontaneous outbreak of violence. In Newark on the evening of July 12, 1967, a black cab driver was arrested after he had "tailgated" a police car and had entered into a "short scuffle" with the police. At the bail hearing the cab driver testified that the police "caved in my ribs, busted a hernia, and put a hole in my head." Within a few hours, the story of the beating had circulated through Newark's shadowy slum. A large crowd began to converge on the Fourth Precinct where the driver was being held. Leaders of the local poverty program, the Legal Services Project, and the Congress of Racial Equality, with police permission and bull-horns, spoke to the crowd; they militantly criticized the police and pledged their resources to the defense of the cab driver. A peaceful protest march was attempted, but gained little support. Soon rocks and bottles were crashing through the precinct windows, and the Newark rebellion had begun.

If a black power spokesman had stood up in front of the precinct and had given a speech advocating violence, there is no doubt that the mass media would have reported that he had instigated the violence. Furthermore, it is quite likely that he could have been convicted under a criminal anarchy statute. However, the facts show that the people had decided to act and did not need an "agitator" to spark their violence. Speech, any speech, in this situation would not have been the factor which produced the action.

Examining the 7 per cent of the cases which did involve both advocacy and violence, it can be shown that in almost half of them speaking or leafleting did not ignite the violence. The example of Bill Epton in Harlem is a good illustration of a situation where there was militant advocacy but no triggering of an uprising. In a highly tense situation Epton spoke to a crowd on a Harlem street corner advocating the necessity of smashing the state and declaring war on the police. After the speech the crowd peacefully broke up. That night the Harlem uprising began. Though it is possible that Epton's speech helped to create a mood of hostility, other factors also contributed to that mood. The poor relations between the police and the community, the recent police shooting of a black teenager, the news coverage, even the sweltering heat of the night might have been factors which combined to create the violent mood. The New York Court of Appeals recognized that there was no immediate causal chain between the speech and the violence when it stated that there was "no evidence here that the defendant . . . had any hand in causing the riots that began on the evening of July 18." It is likely that many of those involved in the fighting and looting had been in the crowd that listened to Epton's speech. However, at the time of the speech they were not ready to act, and even though Epton's advocacy was provoking and explosive there was no explosion, no violence.

In the remaining 4 per cent of the cases it is difficult, if not impossible, to prove that advocacy caused the uprisings. An illustration of this type of situation is the Atlanta rebellion of September, 1966. A few hours after a police officer shot a black man, Stokely Carmichael released a protest statement to a local radio station. An hour later there was a demonstration started by local members of SNCC, at which Carmichael was not present. Two people in the crowd got up and talked about the shooting incident. The police considered the statements inflammatory and ordered George Ware of SNCC to remove the sound truck. When he refused, he was arrested. Another member of SNCC, Bobby Walton, tried to speak, but he too was arrested. The district court stated that "The arrest of these two men stirred up additional excitement and resentment, resulting in the first physical interference with the work of the police." The crowd began to shake the patrol wagon but the police were able to drive it away from the crowd. However, the patrol wagon hit a pregnant woman, and with that people began throwing rocks and bottles at the police.

From these facts one could not fairly conclude that Carmichael's statement which had been broadcast over the radio was the triggering agent. It is possible that these words helped to create a mood of anger, but other factors, such as the shooting itself, may have contributed equally and probably more to the mood than Carmichael's statement. When there is a time lag between the speech and the action, the causal connection becomes almost impossible to define. In the Epton case there was a two or three hour time lag, and the court had no difficulty stating there was no causal connection. In a case such as this where the time lag was one hour, it would seem that sixty minutes is sufficient for the volition of the individual to become primary. It seems that the Solicitor General of the Atlanta Judicial Circuit was in agreement with this analysis, as he stated to reporters that he did not have sufficient evidence to indict Carmichael for insurrection or incitement to insurrection. However, unknown to the Solicitor General, Carmichael was arrested for violation of the State Riot Statute and the city disorderly conduct ordinance.

The speeches of the two SNCC members during the demonstration are more difficult to analyze. In the situation presented above, there were three events occurring within the space of ten to fifteen minutes. First, there were the speeches by the black protestors; at this point there had been no action by the listeners. Second, there was the stopping of the speeches by the police and the arrest of the SNCC workers who tried to speak; at this point the crowd began to act. Third, there was the patrol wagon accident; at this point the uprising began. It would be difficult to conclude that the speeches were any more responsible for the violence than the other two events. In fact, it may be more reasonable to conclude that the stopping of the speech triggered the hostility of the crowd. Another possible conclusion is that if the patrol wagon had not hit the woman, the angry crowd would have dispersed. A fourth conclusion is that the three events were so close in time and so interrelated that they must be viewed as one event. Given these possible conclusions and the difficulty in choosing between them, singling out the advocacy for criminal penalty would not seem justified; this is especially true in light of the Holmes and Brandeis opinions which stress the importance of free speech and imply that advocacy can be punished only when it is a primary cause of the evil. In this situation the Solicitor General did not give in to the public hysteria, as he refrained from indicting the SNCC spokesmen for inciting insurrection.

In each of the cases where speech and violence are closely related in time and space there are significant independent factors intervening between the advocacy and the action. The only proof of a causal relationship between black power advocacy and the forcible action is the time and space relationship itself. Since it has been shown that in 93 per cent of the cases speech was not necessary to the violence, there is little basis to infer that in the few other situations the speech was an essential causative factor of the violence.

The clear and present danger test sidesteps the question whether or not there was a real causal connection by requiring only that reasonable men agree that the advocacy could have caused the violence. But this sidestepping only restates the problem of what is the standard of reasonableness. If there is no proof that the advocacy was the cause of the violence, there is no concrete basis upon which one can state that it is reasonable to believe that the advocacy produced the uprising. Without a concrete basis, vague notions of fiery speeches causing mob action become the standard of reasonable fear.

A further difficulty caused by the use of the standard of reasonable fear, instead of requiring proof that the speaker caused the action, is that there have been many tense situations where there was black power advocacy but no violence. Unfortunately, these cases are rarely reported; yet, from this author's study it seems that there may be more of the advocacy-no-violence-type of situation than any other. However, for purposes of analysis this survey is limited to the situation where there is violence. The conclusion one draws is that in 93 per cent of the cases advocacy was not present; in 3 per cent advocacy was not a primary factor, and in the remaining 4 per cent it is difficult, if not impossible, to prove that the advocacy caused the violence. Based on this evidence, it does not seem reasonable to believe that in times of ghetto tension black power advocacy will produce an uprising.

There is one seemingly strong argument for using a reasonable belief test instead of a results test. This argument points out that in order to protect the state and its citizens from harm it is necessary to be able to stop a speech which is likely to create violence. If the police must wait to arrest a person until the violence has taken place, then the prevention of harm is impossible. Regardless of the merits of this argument in other situations, it is irrelevant to most criminal anarchy prosecutions. Criminal anarchy arrests usually take place days, even weeks, after the advocacy. Criminal anarchy cases are not like the "insulting or fighting words" cases in which a speaker infuriates a hostile crowd. In the situation of a black power advocate speaking to a black audience there is no danger of fights between the listeners, nor is there danger that the crowd will attack the speaker. The only possible danger is that the crowd will attack police and property. This danger cannot be avoided by arresting the advocate during his speech because the other factors which contribute to the violence are still present. The ghetto crowd listening to the speech and already hostile to the police would be more likely to act violently if the police tried to arrest the black spokesman. Criminal anarchy arrests, both historically and practically, are not a means for preventing the imminent danger. Of course the argument can be made that although criminal anarchy prosecutions will not stop the violence caused by that particular instance of advocacy, they will act as a deterrent to future black power advocacy. While this argument may be persuasive in theory, the last four years of increasing black power advocacy have shown that arrests and even convictions for advocacy do not deter other black power speakers.

The Court has never made a full empirical analysis of the advocate's relationship to the expected danger. It may be that the judicial process is not adequate to make these kinds of factual determinations. But if the Court is committed to a formula which requires determinations as to when there is an actual danger and as to the likelihood of speech causing action, then its refusal to attempt empirical answers to these issues results in vague notions of danger and causality determining the scope of free speech. If one allows the constitutional test of free speech to be a vague requirement of a reasonable belief of clear and imminent danger, then every time there is a ghetto crisis militant black power advocacy will be open to prosecution.

2. *The Dennis Test of Clear and Present Danger*   The Supreme Court, in *Dennis* v. *United States*, gave a new interpretation to the clear and present danger test in an effort to deal with the advocacy of

members of the American Communist Party. This test not only emasculates the concept of present danger as meaning imminent or immediate, it also makes the probability necessary for limiting free speech dependent on the seriousness of the evil; that is when an evil is very grave, then a lesser degree of probability is necessary. Applying this formula, the Court viewed the evil as an attempt to overthrow the government, which it classified as an extremely grave evil. However, it did not try to find that there was a "present" danger of this evil occurring. The time when this attempt to overthrow the government would take place was seen as being sometime in the indefinite, possibly remote future. The Court accepted the trial judge's instructions to the jury which stated the time element in the following words: "[O]verthrow . . . by force and violence as speedily as circumstances would permit."

It is important to note that when the danger is imminent, the *Dennis* test produces the same result as the Holmes-Brandeis test. Therefore in the case where someone advocates violent change during a ghetto crisis, both tests allow for punishment of that speech. However, there are frequent situations in which the two tests produce different results. In circumstances such as Harris spreading leaflets during the Deadwyler inquest or Carmichael making a statement over the radio after a police incident, a court might well decide that there had been no immediate danger. Therefore, according to the Holmes-Brandeis test, the advocacy would be constitutionally protected. However, using the *Dennis* test where there is no requirement of imminent danger, the advocacy is punishable.

In *Yates* v. *United States,* the Supreme Court read *Dennis* to mean that advocacy of action was punishable but that advocacy of abstract doctrine was within the traditional protection of the first amendment. The Court accepted the *Dennis* reformulation of the clear and present danger test, balancing the requirement of immediate danger against the gravity of the evil. However, it stressed that the punishable advocacy must be present advocacy of immediate or future forcible action. This question then arises: If the violent action is to occur at some time in the future, what is the rationale for viewing the present advocacy as constituting a danger? The Court in *Dennis* rested its answer on the then prevailing notion of the Communist Party of the United States. It stressed the high degree of organization, the intricate chain of command which linked every individual cell, and the rigidly disciplined members who were conditioned to respond immediately to their leaders' commands almost as Pavlov's dogs were conditioned to respond to the bell. The Court in *Yates* stated:

> The essence of the *Dennis* holding was that indoctrination of a group in preparation for future violent action, as well as exhortation to immediate action, by advocacy found to be directed to "action for the accomplishment" of forcible overthrow, to violence as a "rule or principle of action," and employing "language of incitement," . . . is not constitutionally protected when the group is of sufficient size and cohesiveness, is sufficiently oriented toward action, and other circumstances are such as reasonably to justify apprehension that action will occur.

If black power organizations do not fit the model of a dangerous group as described in *Dennis* and *Yates*, it is arguable that this more restrictive test should not apply to them.

Black power organizations fall into several classifications. There are four general categories of groups whose members are likely to give speeches or pass out literature during periods of ghetto tension. The first consists of national organizations which adhere to Marxist revolutionary theory, such as the Progressive Labor Movement and the W. E. B. Du Bois Clubs. The second category consists of local ghetto groups not tied to any particular political-economic philosophy, such as the Black Panther Party for Self-Defense in Oakland, California. The third grouping includes the college based Afro-American organizations such as the Afro-American Student Union at the University of California Berkeley campus, the Black Student Union at San Francisco State College, and the Student's Afro-American Society at Columbia University. The fourth category is made up of those groups, such as SNCC and CORE, which carry on both traditional civil rights activities and nationwide black power organizing.

None of the above mentioned groups has a network of highly organized and intricately related local units. In two of the categories the groups have only local membership. None of the organizations maintains a high degree of discipline over its members. The most publicized and seemingly dangerous group, SNCC, is not even a membership organization. It is a loose collection of people with no national directives; nor does it require those working on a SNCC project to agree with every policy of SNCC. The other groups are also distinguished by their local autonomy, and their lack of discipline. Even the two traditional revolutionary groups, Progressive Labor and the Du Bois Clubs, have rejected the rigidity of the leader-member relationship of the Communist Party of the 1940's and 1950's. They stress local autonomy and do not require their members to forsake dissenting views. Thus, none of those groups fit the dangerous group model fashioned in *Dennis* and *Yates*.

A reading of the best in-depth study of a major uprising, The Los Angeles Riot Study (LARS), suggests that Watts violence was produced not by a preestablished plan, but by a spontaneous community catharsis. The study testifies to the facts that (1) up to 15 per cent of the Negro adult population, or about 22,000 persons, were active at some point during the rioting, and in more than a spectator role; (2) an additional 35 or 40 per cent of the Negro adult population, or at least an additional 51,000 persons, were active spectators to the disturbance; (3) support for the riot was as great among the relatively well educated and economically advantaged as among the poorly educated and economically disadvantaged in the curfew area.

Although there have been accusations of a conspiracy behind the uprisings, the evidence strongly points to the conclusion that there was no conspiracy, no preestablished plan, no group of subversives. The report of the FBI on the uprisings of the summer of 1964 testifies to the spontaneous nature of the violence. The McCone Commission concluded:

> . . . There is no reliable evidence of outside leadership or pre-established plans for the rioting. . . . The Attorney General, the District Attorney, and the Los Angeles Police have all reached the conclusion that there is no evidence of a pre-plan or a pre-established central direction of the rioting activities.

The Detroit Police Commissioner stated that there was "no evidence of any conspiracy involved in the riots." The Governor's Select Commission on Civil Disorder issued a comprehensive report on the Newark uprising in which it found that "[t]he evidence presented to the Commission does not support the thesis of a conspiracy or plan to initiate the Newark riot." The National Advisory Commission on Civil Disorders concluded that "the urban disorders of the summer of 1967 were not caused by, nor were they the consequence of, any organized plan or "conspiracy." The Commission also stated that it had "found no evidence that all or any of the disorders or the incidents that led to them were planned or directed by any organization or group, international, national or local."

Although this evidence strongly rejects the conspiracy theory, a court might focus on the fact that it was dealing with a black power group and ignore the group's indirect relationship to the uprising. It might disregard the rationale of *Dennis* and *Yates* and look solely to the literal test used in those cases. The evil would be seen as an attempt to overthrow the government as quickly as circumstances would permit, and thus as dangerous as that presented in the Communist cases. The advocacy would be present advocacy of forcible action. The group might be falsely described as disciplined, organized and dangerous. The result of mechanically using the *Dennis* test would be that a court could easily find black power advocacy punishable under a criminal anarchy statute.

The Court in *Yates* held the Government to very strict evidentiary requirements. The Government had to show that the defendants had been engaging in present advocacy of forcible action, which meant a present call to violence to take place at some future time. Five defendants were acquitted because of the weakness of the evidence, and new trials were ordered for the remaining nine. However, the others were never tried because the Government asked the district court to dismiss the case as they had been unable to satisfy the Supreme Court's evidentiary requirements.

There are two reasons why, in most instances, the *Yates* restriction on the *Dennis* test will not result in protecting black power advocacy. First, most advocacy takes place where there is a situation of imminent danger, and is thus punishable under any formulation of the clear and present danger test. Second, in the instances where there is no immediate danger, the advocacy is still phrased in terms of a present call to forcible action and not in terms of abstract doctrine.

After the *Yates* decision it was observed that the Government would have to use informers and undercover agents in order to acquire the necessary evidence. This is exactly what was done in the *Epton* case. An undercover agent was planted in the Harlem Progressive Labor group. The agent, wired with a "minifon," taped a conversation in which Epton said the demonstration to protest police brutality would lead to violence. Two "police cadets" were infiltrated into the Cleveland Du Bois Club and their reports on the activities of members of the Du Bois Club, the Jomo Kenyatta Freedom House, and the John F. Kennedy House were used extensively in the hearings on the antiriot bill. If federal and state police agencies continue to use undercover agents, they will have little trouble acquiring the evidence necessary to convict under the *Dennis-Yates* formula.

This formula, which stresses the grave evil of an international conspiracy to overthrow the government, was developed during the height of McCarthyism and was based on the then prevailing notion that the American Communist Party was merely a cog in a tightly intertwined, monolithic, international communist conspiracy directed by Moscow. It is questionable whether this vast, robot-like conspiratorial model is applicable to black power groups. Now that the cold war has in some ways subsided, the Court should feel free to reevaluate its reasoning in *Dennis*, or stated in another manner, the Court should determine whether they will treat blacks as they have treated reds.

3. The Abridgment of Advocacy Only in Times of Tension This Comment has argued that both the Holmes-Brandeis test and the Dennis formulation are vague and uncertain. Therefore the courts are defining statutes which punish speech by uncertain formulas. In actual practice, the vague formula is filled with the subtle prejudices and hidden fears of the white society.

Those who favor the clear and present danger test state that in some situations advocacy is so closely linked with action that to protect society advocacy must be punished. They could point out that Carmichael is free to publish his ideas; after all, his book on black power is sold in bookstores around the country. They might argue that Harris and Epton are free to advocate these ideas except when a community is on the verge of a riot. This argument in its theoretical form states that all views will be expressed, with the exception that during relatively short periods of tension, speech may be silenced.

In practice, the above theory has been used to silence speech not only during brief periods of crisis, but to silence certain speech altogether.[7] Even when speech is limited for brief periods, the effect is to create an atmosphere of caution if not fear. The general public reacts to the branding of certain speech as illegal by identifying the content of that speech with criminal activity. Those people who agree with the speech are wary of voicing their ideas, feeling unwilling to suffer public disapproval, or possibly the loss of a job, or other recriminations. Many will not speak, for they know that police and lower courts often have a more restricted notion of the first amendment than the Supreme Court, and that challenging them would involve long and costly court battles.[8] It is in these ways that limiting speech in one situation produces a chilling effect on freedom of speech in general.

The second difficulty with the theory which allows the limiting of speech only during times of immediate crisis is that it seriously limits the effectiveness of speech. People are most responsive to ideas when their interests are clearly at stake. When a policeman shoots a black man in the ghetto, it creates a potentially violent situation. At the same time, if black spokesmen are free to speak, it forces white people to open their eyes and ears to police activity in the ghetto. The shooting also motivates black people to express their views and to join together to pressure for change. It is in this type of situation that people want to exercise the right to speak and want to hear others express their ideas for change. It is in this situation that society can benefit from hearing all voices, not just those of the black politicians and respectable spokesmen. To allow speech only after a crisis has calmed down means allowing speech after the community is no longer actively concerned.

It is precisely in the crisis situation where the black community watches to see if "whitey" will allow the deepest feelings of the ghetto to be heard. If national and state governments are concerned about creating a new atmosphere in which the black community will trust the white society, then it must allow the angry voice of the ghetto to speak.

Those who favor the temporary limiting of advocacy say that speech is not limited during all crisis situations but only in those during which there is a likelihood of imminent danger. However, this argument is irrelevant to the ghetto because the authorities have treated "crisis" and "imminent danger" as synonymous in the ghetto context. If one agrees that the ghetto is black social dynamite, then it is true that any crisis creates a general clear and present danger of violence as long as that crisis exists. Therefore, the result of accepting the clear and present danger test is that speech is suppressed in the very instances when it plays its most meaningful role. This inhibiting of speaking and organizing in the community makes peaceful change more difficult to achieve. It may, in a specific ghetto, temporarily maintain the present order; but this restriction of community action allows conditions to continue which will cause, in a week, a month or a year, that very ghetto to explode with even greater violence. A different test of the first amendment is needed to protect freedom of speech against the political and social turmoil of the times. Two obstacles stand in the path of accepting a more protective test. First, it is difficult for lawyers, professors and judges to comprehend the ghetto and thereby see the value of black power advocacy. Second, there is a lack of understanding of the role which the first amendment was designed to play in America's political system. An understanding of the purposes of the first amendment makes it possible to decide whether or not black power advocacy is consistent with those purposes and thus whether it should be protected as an expression of freedom of speech.

IV. Purposes of Free Speech

There are four basic purposes of free speech which consistently run through the writings of the founding fathers, the court decisions and the writings of the classic free speech theorists. These purposes, generally stated, are: self-government; search for truth; ensuring societal change; dignity of the individual.

A. Self-Government

The participation of citizens in the political decisions which affect their lives is at the heart of a democratic system of government. The American revolution was a protest against the limitation of that right of self-government. The concept of self-government means that elected officials should be responsive to the will of the people, and not vice versa. Free speech is one of the primary constitutional mechanisms which ensures the continuation of this relationship between the people and their government, for it is through public debate that the government is made aware of the criticisms and suggestions of the people. As Justice Douglas has said: "[O]ne main function of the First Amendment is to ensure ample opportunity for the people to determine and resolve public issues." In order to make those decisions, all relevant views must be heard and analyzed. Free speech is then the tool by which the building of a democratic society continues; it is the essence of self-government.

Black power advocates argue that in order for self-government to become a reality to the ghetto dweller there must be a break with the two party system. They argue that most black elected officials do not represent the interests of the poor black man. They point out that even in cities where blacks are in a majority or a near majority black people do not run the city government. Believing that the political system of America is unresponsive to the voice of the ghetto, they advocate the organizing of power blocs. These black power blocs could then exert economic, social, and political pressure so that black people could affect the decisions which control their lives and thereby make self-government a reality.

B. Search for Truth

The quest for truth has been one of the strongest justifications for protecting speech. What is truth to one man is blasphemy to another. A doctrine which at one moment in time is regarded as obviously true, in another time is shown to be false. Galileo was prosecuted for believing what today any schoolboy takes for granted. Justice Frankfurter expressed the relationship between speech and truth in the following manner:

> The history of civilization is in considerable measure the displacement of error which once held sway as official truth by beliefs which in turn have yielded to other truths. Therefore the liberty of man to search for truth ought not to be fettered, no matter what orthodoxies he may challenge. Liberty of thought soon shrivels without freedom of expression.

Truth is difficult to perceive when there is little or no communication. The truth about life in the ghetto, the inner feelings of ghetto dwellers, and the relationship between the ghetto and the rest of society is hidden beneath years of fear and prejudice. Fear is one of the most disabling of emotions. The fear with which the black man has grown up makes it difficult for him to see the white man as he really is. The fear results in half-truths and distortions, often leading black people to see oppression where there is a genuine interest by white society in bettering conditions. For example, many ghetto families feel that special school classes for slightly retarded children are dumping grounds for black children who act up in class, and that children are put in these classes on the basis of unfair, biased tests and arbitrary decisions over which the parents have no control. School authorities are often unaware of these feelings or how to deal with them, and they mistake the parents' negative attitude toward the special help as a sign of their ignorance or lack of concern for the child.

Black power advocates have directed much of their criticism at the schools.[9] The fact that these speeches attack the schools in generalized and often unfair terms does not detract from the fact that they are exposing the relationship between a white school system and a black community. This exposure allows the distortions and half-truths to be aired publicly. In this way, hidden feelings can be dealt with, and half-truths will eventually give way to whole truths.

C. Ensuring Positive Change

The third purpose of freedom of speech is to ensure positive change in society. Free speech is necessary to maintain a balance between order and chaos. The voicing of new ideas and demands puts those in power on notice of the weaknesses within the established system. Sometimes these weaknesses can be cured by better communication between the representatives of the status quo and the dissenters. At other times the weaknesses are so ingrained in the status quo that structural changes are necessary. In both instances, freedom of speech combats the tendency of established authority to become isolated from the needs of the people and to resist change.

One of the characteristics of a governing body is to resist change and disruption of the status quo, to look with disfavor upon new ideas and new methods of treating old problems. If the voices of the protestors are effectively silenced, one of two results may occur. The first is that others holding the same dissenting views will be afraid to speak. Controversial subjects will not be taught in schools, suspect books will be taken off library shelves, and the demands for change will die unheard in a thousand private souls. Soon the people, having heard only one view, begin to accept it. The society becomes stultified and the ideas of those in positions of power become all-pervasive. In our age of material comfort and the incredible potential of mass media to influence and control thoughts and opinions, the society which George Orwell envisioned may no longer be merely a science fiction nightmare.

The alternative result of silencing open dissent in a society is to eliminate speaking above ground and force dissenters underground to speak and organize. When the conditions demanding change are so extreme that they effect millions, then the silencing of the dissent does not produce the death of that dissent. This Comment has implied that the need for comprehensive changes in the lives of black Americans is an absolute necessity. It has put forth evidence that a sizeable portion of the black population was active in the uprisings and about half the population of the ghetto was sympathetic to the uprisings. It has argued that the demands of black power advocates, although phrased in exaggerated, "shock-effect" statements, are the demands of a large segment of the black community. These arguments suggest that it will be impossible to stop black power advocacy by limiting their ability to speak in the open.

When courts silence black power advocacy they endow black power ideas with a fascination that an oppressed doctrine has for an oppressed people. An alternative to making martyrs of black power advocates is to allow full freedom of speech so that their doctrine can be met above ground, and stripped of its claim that "whitey" is afraid to let these ideas be heard.

Black power advocacy has not yet been completely suppressed and consequently its ideas are being fiercely debated in black communities throughout the country. Martin Luther King argued on the issue of violence versus nonviolence:

> It is unfortunately true that however the Negro acts, his struggle will not be free of violence initiated by his enemies, and he will need ample courage and willingness to sacrifice to defeat this manifestation of violence. But if he seeks it and organizes it, he cannot win.

The debate is joined by Huey Newton of the Black Panther Party for Self-Defense who argues, "The racist dog policemen must withdraw immediately from our communities, cease their wanton murder and brutality and torture of black people, or face the wrath of the armed people."

The black man hears both sides; he then can enter into the debate, and eventually make his own choice. He is experiencing a real dialogue, and faces a real choice. If speech is silenced, then the choice is made in dark tenement basements which have been transformed from prisons to fortresses. At that point the choice will almost certainly be violence; the result is almost guaranteed to be chaos, not order.

Another loud and often vicious debate in the ghetto concerns the responsibility of the black middle class to help the black lower class. In militant speeches black power advocates have charged that many successful black men have turned their backs on their brothers in the ghetto after moving into positions of influence and status within the white world. They have warned the "black bourgeoisie" that some day soon they would suffer the wrath of the mass of poor blacks. One of the many positive results of this verbal attack has been the gradual realization and acceptance by the black middle and upper classes that:

> the [black] middle class owes a debt to Negro progress in this country. That debt can be paid partially by educated men taking their acquired skills to the ghetto and offering them at a fair and honest rate. . . . Black Americans of all walks of life must pull together or face the possibility of slipping back.

Freedom of speech in this situation has created an awareness in the black middle class which may produce constructive change and avoid a violent "clash between classes."

D. Dignity of the Individual

The dignity of a human being is something very precious. To an American it means that he has certain rights which must be respected by all, by friends and strangers, by police and government. If those rights are violated, he can seek vindication before an impartial body of his peers. The average white American has the protection of the law, and, knowing that he has that protection, goes through his daily life acting and speaking as he feels. These feelings of security and respect create pride, and encourage expression of one's ideas. But the black man's most familiar feelings have been those of fear and caution. These feelings create shame and silence. The black actor and playwright Ossie Davis, in his eulogy to Malcolm X, described those feelings:

> White folks do not need anybody to remind them that they are men. We do! . . . Protocol and common sense require that Negroes stand back and let the white man speak up for us, defend us, and lead us from behind the scene in our fight. . . . But Malcolm said to hell with

that! Get up off your knees and fight your own battles. That's the
way to win back your self-respect. That's the way to make the white
man respect you. And if he won't let you live like a man, he certainly
can't keep you from dying like one!

Malcolm . . . scared hell out of the rest of us, bred as we are to
caution, to hypocrisy in the presence of white folks, to the smile that
never fades.

Free speech means that people can say aloud what they are thinking. For many years the threats and pressure put on the black man
by the white society has kept him from speaking his thoughts. The
example of black power advocates speaking in public the hidden feelings of the black person has begun to break through the emotional
block resulting from years of subservience and silence. It is only when
the black man can freely speak his mind that he will feel the dignity
enjoyed by white Americans.

Black power advocacy, especially in times of crisis, creates the pre-
requisites for peaceful change by waking whites out of their ignorance and shaking blacks out of their fear. Black power advocacy
enhances the black man's drive for dignity and self-government. It
can partially overcome the barriers to communication between black
and white. Silencing that advocacy, even if only in times of an alleged
clear and present danger, will not stop violence; rather it will increase
the intensity and professionalism of that violence.[10] Strictly drawn
criminal anarchy statutes under present constitutional standards of
clear and present danger can be used to punish black power advocacy,
thereby producing harmful results for both black and white Americans. A constitutional test of the first amendment which protects
black power advocacy is necessary to help create a society where black
and white can live together in real equality.

V. The Scope of the First Amendment

The test this Comment proposes is not new; it is based on the words
of the first amendment and concentrates on interpreting the phrase,
"freedom of speech." If the speech in question comes within the
scope of this phrase, then the words of the first amendment take their
literal effect: "Congress shall make no law . . . abridging the freedom
of speech." The fourteenth amendment makes this prohibition
equally applicable to the states.

A. *Freedom of Speech Includes Political Speech*

For the purposes of this Comment, "freedom of speech" is interpreted to include "political" speech. This does not imply that the term excludes other kinds of speech; it only means that within the minimum scope of the first amendment's protection of speech is the protection of political speech. Two questions present themselves: What evidence supports the statement that freedom of speech includes political speech? Is black power advocacy within the traditional understanding of political speech?

The evidence that political speech cannot be abridged lies in the theory of the state on which our Constitution is based. The *Federalist Papers* are the finest expression of this theory. The state is seen as the force which dominates the life of society. The greatest amount of power within the society is concentrated in the governing body. Power feeds on itself; powerful forces in a country, if allowed to go unchecked, will consume all opposing forces, resulting in an "absolute tyranny." The builders of our nation created three mechanisms by which the tyranny of unlimited power could be avoided: The federal system, the separation of powers, and the Bill of Rights.

Within a federal system the national government did not have all the power. The states were given some power in the belief that they would be a strong check upon the national government. However, with the geographic expansion and economic development of the United States, the states' power has diminished in many areas. Thus, an effective check upon the growth of an "absolute tyranny" must be found elsewhere.

Within the scheme of the separation of powers James Madison aptly expressed the role of the judiciary:

> If they [the first ten amendments] are incorporated into the Constitution, independent tribunals of justice will consider themselves in a peculiar manner the guardians of those rights; they will be an impenetrable bulwark against *every* assumption of power in the Legislative or Executive; they will be naturally led to resist *every* encroachment upon rights expressly stipulated for in the Constitution by the declaration of rights.

The legislature was viewed as the primary check on the executive, and a necessary weapon of the legislature was the right of its members to speak freely on all matters pertaining to the governing of the society. This right of free speech for legislators was recently affirmed in *Bond* v. *Floyd*, where the Court stated: "The manifest function of the First Amendment in a representative government requires that legislators be given the widest latitude to express their views on issues of policy." A representative government by definition is responsive to the will of the people. Therefore, if the first amendment protects the legislator's right to discuss local or national policy, it must also protect the right of the people to discuss those policies.

The right of the people to discuss freely government policy is inherent in a democracy. Yet the men who wrote the Constitution specifically expressed that right in the language of the first amendment. The first amendment and the other amendments which make up the Bill of Rights were to be the third formal check on the possible abuse of power. Since these rights resided in the people, they were the only one of the three checks of power outside the formal governmental structure. The right of the people to discuss and criticize government officials and policy was seen as the best means of protecting the democratic system.

In order to determine whether or not black power advocacy is political speech it is necessary to decide upon a meaning of political speech. The dictionary definition of "political" is "pertaining to . . . the conduct of government, referring in the widest application to the judicial, executive, and legislative branches. . . ." "Public" is defined as "pertaining to the people; or affecting a nation, state, or community, at large." In common usage, "political" refers to activities of the government and actions of citizens, such as voting and running for office, or taking part in organizations which try to influence local, state, or national government.

A third definition can be drawn from political theory. Political speech is that speech which concerns itself with the relationship between man and state. The state is viewed as a hierarchy of power units, each unit capable of control over the activities of man, and each unit is related in some way to other units. For example, a single police precinct is part of the hierarchy of power. The police precinct is intimately tied up with the city police department, which is related to numerous local, state, and federal agencies. An obvious illustration would be an emergency situation where the police must work along with state highway patrol, the national guard, and sometimes federal troops. The police are also interrelated with nonlaw enforcement agencies such as welfare departments, colleges and universities, and even the bar examiners.

The local school is also part of the hierarchy. It receives money from the federal government. Its curriculum is to some degree determined by the state legislature. Some of its practices, such as opening class with a prayer, or restricting its students to one color, are profoundly affected by decisions of the Supreme Court. There are many more examples of the relationship between elected governmental bodies and other units of power within society. In our present day of mass media, it is possible to argue that political speech is speech relating to the policies of major newspapers or even to the advertising practices of municipal buses. However, the narrowest definition of political speech is still broad enough to encompass black power advocacy.

B. *Black Power Advocacy Is Political Speech*

Most black power advocacy consists of three major themes, all of which are definitely political. First, criticism of the police, which in most cases is the prime object of the advocacy, is an expression of the people's right to protest actions of the executive arm of the state. Second, analyzing the relationship between the ghetto and the rest of society is an indictment of the structure and functioning of the state. And third, urging of community power is in the classic American tradition of minority groups such as the Jews, Italians, and Irish, who organized their ghettos in order to establish political and economic power blocs.

The two other themes which often run through the advocacy are the theory of violent revolution, and the psychology of the black American. Advocating the necessity of overthrowing the state is advocacy of the right of revolution, an age-old political demand, and one which is written into our own Declaration of Independence. The rhetoric which revolves around racial pride is also intimately tied to political demands, as shown by the following excerpt from a speech by Stokely Carmichael:

> Don't be afraid, 'cause you're black and nappy-headed and got a broad nose, that you can't handle power. Don't you let 'em shame you! . . . We look at another Negro and say, "Now he is somebody!" I want a black sheriff in this county so our kids can look at him and say, "Some day I'm gonna be sheriff!"

An examination of black power speeches and leaflets makes it clear that the advocacy falls within any generally accepted definition of political speech. The test of free speech suggested above confines itself to an interpretation of the phrase "freedom of speech" and therefore offers more protection to black power advocacy than either of the clear and present danger formulas. The scope of inquiry is not into a myriad of social and psychological factors inherent in determining the degree of imminent danger and the causal relation between speech and action. Using the proposed test the only inquiry of the law is whether or not black power advocacy is political advocacy. Although this test is not completely independent of public hysteria and political pressure, it is far less susceptible to misuse than the present test in that it closely circumscribes the area of judicial inquiry and avoids the vagueness of the clear and present danger notions.

The major criticism of the preceding test of the first amendment is that it allows for speech in situations where that speech may create a danger to society. No argument can prove conclusively that advocacy never has, or never will produce ghetto violence. However, the risk, based on empirical evidence, that advocacy will produce an uprising is quite small. Those who believe that risk must be avoided regardless of its degree do not solve the problem, for even if violence is stopped one day by punishing advocacy, the ghetto is just as likely to erupt the next week or the next month. Rap Brown recognized this independence and spontaneity of the ghetto when he said, "No one person, no black person in America could have stopped Detroit from burning."

Black power advocacy has been used as a scapegoat. As the National Advisory Commission on Civil Disorders said: "What white Americans have never fully understood — but what the Negro can never forget — is that white society is deeply implicated in the ghetto. White institutions created it, white institutions maintain it, and white society condones it." As long as the scapegoating continues, the basic causes of the uprisings will not be adequately met.

Conclusion

The method used in this Comment allows one to see in concrete terms the need to protect black power advocacy. All too often people accept the statement that free speech should be protected, without understanding why it is important to protect. If questioned, they reply that advocacy should be protected because the first amendment says so. They are unable to take their justification any further than a general approval of the freedom of the individual to speak his mind. The result of this superficial understanding is that in politically tense situations they fail to persuade others of the value of allowing dissent to be heard, and often lose their own faith in free speech. Hopefully, the analysis undertaken in this Comment will give some substance to the vague notions of what freedom of speech is all about, for free speech is a theory which is strengthened when its assumptions and arguments are vigorously tested.

Footnotes

[1] Dr. Nathan Wright, chairman of the Newark Black Power Conference, quoted in *Newark: Post-riot summit for Black Power*, Life, Aug. 4, 1967, at 28.

[2] "A person is guilty of criminal anarchy when (a) he advocates the overthrow of the existing form of government of this state by violence, or (b) with knowledge of its contents, he publishes, sells or distributes any document which advocates such violent overthrow, or (c) with knowledge of its purpose, he becomes a member of any organization which advocates such violent overthrow." N.Y. Pen. Law § 240.15 (McKinney 1967).
This Comment will deal only with the advocacy provisions of (a) and (b).

[3] "Babies die. 500 people die a year for lack of food and nourishment. And yet we got enough money to go to the moon. . . . People in New York and Harlem die from fire and bites to death. Big old rats bite them to death and you tell the man about it and the honkey say: 'Hell, man, we can't do nothing about them rats.' Do you realize this is the same man who exterminated the buffalo? He killed the buffalo. Hell, if he wanted to kill the rats he could do it." Speech by Rap Brown to a crowd at Cambridge, Md., quoted in testimony of B. Kinnamon, Chief of Police of Cambridge in *Antiriot Bill Hearings, supra* note 29, at 32–33.

[4] "The white man is irrelevant to blacks, except as an oppressive force. Blacks want to be in his place, yes, but not in order to terrorize and lynch and starve him. They want to be in his place because that is where a decent life can be had." Carmichael, *supra* note 14, at 8.
"While the civil disorders of 1967 were racial in character, they were not *inter*racial. The 1967 disorders, as well as earlier disorders of the recent period, involved action within Negro neighborhoods against symbols of

white American society — authority and property — rather than against white persons." RIOT COMMISSION REPORT, *supra* note 31, at 110.

⁵ *Dennis* v. *United States*, 341 U.S. 494, 510 (1951). Learned Hand's formula is strikingly similar to that which he used to determine the standard of care in a negligence case. *United States* v. *Carroll Towing Co.*, 159 F.2d 169 (2d Cir. 1947). In that case Hand was attempting to solve the problem of whether "absence of a bargee . . . will make the owner of the barge liable for injuries . . . if she breaks loose from her moorings." *Id.* at 173. The formula he created stated that there is liability if the burden of adequate precautions is less than the gravity of the injury multiplied by the probability of the accident occurring. The formula in *Dennis* could be similarly stated: Speech can be abridged when the interest of free expression is less than the gravity of the evil times the probability (the probability being a less important factor when the seriousness of the evil is high). Although Hand's formula may be an excellent tool by which the liability of barge owners is determined, one must have serious doubts about its application to the totally different area of first amendment law.

⁶ *Whitney* v. *California*, 274 U.S. 357, 376 (1927) (concurring opinion). With regard to ghetto uprisings it may be that there is no triggering event upon which responsibility can be fixed. The National Advisory Commission on Civil Disorders reported that "[d]isorder did not typically erupt without preexisting causes, as a result of a single 'triggering' or 'precipitating' incident. Instead, it developed out of an increasingly disturbed social atmosphere, in which typically a series of tension-heightening incidents over a period of weeks or months became linked in the minds of many in the Negro community with a shared network of underlying grievances." RIOT COMMISSION REPORT, *supra* note 31, at 111.

⁷ Between 1919 and 1920, the Supreme Court upheld convictions of antiwar advocates in six separate cases. See note 69 *supra*. It is important to a consideration of free speech issues of today to realize that the indictment against antiwar advocates Dr. Benjamin Spock, Rev. William Coffin, and three other dissenters is based on the same law used to convict the antiwar advocates of World War I. The Christian Science Monitor, Jan. 16, 1968, at 1, col. 2.

⁸ Ann Fagan Ginger, unpublished manuscript (on file with the Alexander Meiklejohn Civil Liberties Library in Berkeley, Cal.). Mrs. Ginger argues persuasively that a decision by the Supreme Court vindicating an individual's right to speak years after the actual event does not adequately protect the freedom of the individual. She points out that by the time of the decision the political situation is different, the parties to the action are often significantly changed and the individual is exhausted financially and emotionally.

In order for freedom of speech to be meaningful to citizens, it must be protected at the time and place it occurs. This protection can best be achieved by educating the public, the news media, the schools, the law enforcement agencies and the lower courts to the benefits enjoyed by a society which strictly adheres to the first amendment.

[9] "Public education is a weapon. Cause they're teaching people how to hate black. They're teaching little children how to hate black. They're putting in their old stinky history books that Columbus discovered America. How in the world is some dumb honkey going to discover a country with people living there? The Indian was here, but he was saying . . . he was saying that the Indian ain't human cause he ain't white." Speech by Rap Brown quoted in *Antiriot Bill Hearings, supra* note 29, at 34–35.

[10] Prosecuting advocacy does not prevent the evil which the State is attempting to avoid. The speeches in public may be stopped, but this only forces the groups underground, where they continue their dangerous activities in secret. For example in 1951 the Supreme Court upheld the conviction of leaders of the Communist Party for what essentially amounted to advocacy or teaching. *Dennis v. United States*, 341 U.S. 494 (1951). In 1953 Attorney General Brownell stated that the Communist Party was a "greater menace now than at any time" because "the Communists have gone underground since the Smith Act trials started." Quoted in Chase, *The Libertarian Case for Making it a Crime to be a Communist*, 29 TEMP. L.Q. 121, 132–33 (1956). As long as black power advocates are allowed to speak, the Government is put on notice of any threat of violent attack upon the state. However, if prosecutions continue, so that they cannot continue to advocate publicly, the black power movement will be forced to move underground, to the vast concrete jungles of the urban ghettos.

"FLAMBOYANT PROTEST," THE FIRST AMENDMENT AND THE BOSTON TEA PARTY*

James E. Leahy

The Supreme Court has made many eloquent statements concerning the place that the right of free speech occupies in our system of constitutional government. Among its recent pronouncements one finds the following:

> Under our Constitution, free speech is not a right that is given only to be so circumscribed that it exists in principle but not in fact. Freedom of expression would not truly exist if the right could be exercised only in an area that a benevolent government has provided as a safe haven for crackpots. The Constitution says that Congress (and the States) may not abridge the right to free speech. This provision means what it says. We properly read it to permit reasonable regulation of speech-connected activities in carefully restricted circumstances. But we do not confine the permissible exercise of First Amendment rights to a telephone booth or the four corners of a pamphlet, or to supervised and ordained discussion in a school classroom.

Justice Black, a champion of free speech, has written in terms of the absoluteness of the free speech guarantee:

> As I have indicated many times before, I do not subscribe to that doctrine [balancing] for I believe that the First Amendment's unequivocal command that there shall be no abridgement of the rights of free speech and assembly shows that the men who drafted our Bill of Rights did all the "balancing" that was to be done in this field.

James E. Leahy, " 'Flamboyant Protest,' the First Amendment and the Boston Tea Party," *Brooklyn Law Review*, Winter 1970, pp. 185–211. Reprinted by permission of the author and the *Brooklyn Law Review*.

* Footnotes and case citations have been deleted.

While it cannot be doubted that speech has a high place in the hierarchy of values in our society, the freedom to speak is not absolute. This is particularly true with regard to speech-related activities. For example, in *Cox* v. *Louisiana,* Justice Goldberg wrote:

> The rights of free speech and assembly, while fundamental in our democratic society, still do not mean that everyone with opinions or beliefs to express may address a group at any public place and at any time.

More recently Chief Justice Warren wrote:

> We cannot accept the view that an apparently limitless variety of conduct can be labeled "speech" whenever the person engaging in the conduct intends thereby to express an idea.

As these statements indicate, free speech is a cherished right which belongs to a free people; but it is a right that can be restricted and even prohibited by governmental action under some circumstances, especially where the expression is a speech-related activity.

In trying to delineate those areas of speech which can be regulated or prohibited, the Court has devised several tests, the use of which depends upon its characterization of the speech problem at hand.

Justice Holmes wrote in *Schenck* v. *United States:*

> The question in every case is whether the words used are used in such circumstances and are of such a nature as to create a clear and present danger that they will bring about the substantive evils that Congress has a right to prevent.

This test has generally been applied where that which is being tested was the effect of the verbal (or written) expression of the speaker. If the speaker's words present a clear and present danger of the occurrence of some substantive evil which the government can prevent, then the speech can be prohibited before the evil occurs.

This test has been the subject of some criticism by Justices Douglas and Black in *Brandenburg* v. *Ohio.* Justice Douglas would confine its use only to those instances in which "speech is brigaded with action."

The Court has also used a "balancing" test at times. This test requires the Court to balance the governmental interests in the restriction of speech against the interest of the individual in the free exercise of his right to speak freely. There has been some dispute on the

Court, however, as to the type of case to which this test applies. It has been applied where the government seeks to force disclosure of membership in certain organizations. Justice Black has objected to the use of the test in this type of case, contending that the balancing test applies only to "cases in which the power of municipalities to keep their streets open for normal traffic was attacked by groups wishing to use those streets for religious or political purposes."

In recent years the Court has developed a test which it refers to as "overbreadth." This test has been used to hold unconstitutional statutes restricting the first amendment right of freedom of association when the Court determines that the statutes are so broad that they not only prohibit that which can be prohibited, but also infringe upon protected association. This test was applied in the case of *United States* v. *Robel*, where the statute made it unlawful to belong to a communist-action organization under an order to register with the government as such, and at the same time be employed in a defense facility. The Court held that the statute was so broad that it infringed upon the protected right of freedom of association, and therefore was unconstitutional. In *Brandenburg* v. *Ohio* the Court used this test to strike down the Ohio Criminal Syndicalism Act, which the Court said, "purports to punish mere advocacy and to forbid, on pain of criminal punishment, assembly with others merely to advocate the described type of action." Mere advocacy, not coupled with incitement to imminent action, is protected by the first amendment, and therefore the statute was too broad.

There have been in existence for many years two other tests used by the Court in analyzing restrictions imposed upon first amendment rights. One states that, as a general rule, prior judicial restraint upon the exercise of free speech is unconstitutional. The Court used this test in the recent case of *Carroll* v. *President and Commissioners of Princess Anne*, where it struck down an ex parte court order which prohibited a racist organization from holding a meeting and presenting its views on segregation.

The other test relates to restrictions upon expression-related activities on streets and other public property. It requires that restrictions upon such activities be narrowly drawn, with definite guidelines (such as time, place and manner) to any licensing authority. These guidelines must eliminate any possible discriminatory application as to who can use such public areas for the exercise of their right of expression.

In *Shuttlesworth* v. *City of Birmingham*, the Court had before it a municipal ordinance regulating parades, processions and demonstrations, which gave the license-issuing authority power to withhold the license if "in its judgment the public welfare, peace, safety, health, decency, good order, morals, or convenience require that it be refused." In discussing this ordinance, Justice Stewart, writing for the majority, stated:

> This ordinance as it was written, therefore, fell squarely within the ambit of the many decisions of this Court over the last 30 years, holding that a law subjecting the exercise of First Amendment freedoms to the prior restraint of a license, without narrow, objective, and definite standards to guide the licensing authority, is unconstitutional.

While narrowly drawn statutes which control the conduct aspect of soliciting, parading, picketing, etc., are permissible, such statutes may also meet constitutional requirements when aimed at controlling the time and place of pure speech. In *Niemotko* v. *Maryland* the Court reversed a conviction of disorderly conduct of one who was giving a speech in a public park without permission from the City Council. In so doing, the Court noted that there did not exist narrowly drawn, reasonable and definite statutory standards to guide the permit-issuing authority. Two years later the Court upheld the conviction of one who proceeded to hold a meeting in a park after being denied a permit under such a valid ordinance.

It would appear that the tests set forth above ought to provide the Court with a sufficient number of methods by which it can resolve any and all first amendment issues, including those involving speech-related activities. The exercise of the right to protest, however, by students on campuses, anti-war demonstrators and proponents and opponents of integration raise questions as to which of the above tests ought the Court to use in testing whether the right of protest can be restricted, prohibited or punished. And even though we now have a number of approaches to these first amendment issues, some questions are still unanswered. In *United States* v. *O'Brien*, the Court said:

> We cannot accept the view that an apparently limitless variety of conduct can be labeled "speech" whenever the person engaging in the conduct intends thereby to express an idea.

If that statement is intended to mean that the *person* engaging in the conduct cannot label it expression, but that there is some conduct which is expressive and thus protected by the first amendment, what determines when the conduct is an expression and thereby entitled to some protection? What is there about parading, picketing, soliciting, demonstrating, distributing pamphlets, sit-ins, burning draft cards, wearing armbands, displaying a red flag, burning an American flag, hanging clothes on a front lawn, sitting on a sidewalk, or wearing a vest made out of a flag, that characterizes some of these acts as expressive and others as just plain conduct?

If a statute punishes conduct and satisfies the due process requirements of not being vague and uncertain, nor arbitrary and unreasonable, it suffers no constitutional infirmity. And as long as the activity in question is conduct pure and simple, convictions under statutes prohibiting it are valid. Further, under the test used in *O'Brien* (about which more will be said later), even if there is some measure of expression in the conduct, it can be punished "if the governmental interest is unrelated to the suppression of free expression . . . ." But how is one to determine whether the governmental interest is unrelated to the suppression of free expression? Is this to be determined only by reference to the statute itself? The zoning ordinance in *People* v. *Stover* would seem to be clearly unrelated to the suppression of free expression, and the same might be said of the statutes prohibiting the desecration of the American flag, as in *Street* v. *New York* and *People* v. *Cowgill*. On its face this is also true of the statute against the mutilation of draft cards. Does this mean that as long as the legislature frames the statute in such a way that on its face it punishes conduct, the statute not only is constitutional, but that it can in every case be applied against one using the prohibited conduct to express an opinion?

If the individual is then subject to punishment for violating the statute, is he to be punished without any consideration being given at all to the fact that his conduct may have been for the purpose of conveying a message? If the Court stops at this point in its analysis of the problem, without considering the communicative aspect of the conduct, does not that give legislative bodies considerable opportunity to stifle expression, as long as their enactments, on their face, are aimed solely at conduct?

It will be the purpose of this article to examine speech-related activities to which the Court has given first amendment protection to determine why such activity commands such protection. Further, an attempt will be made to determine whether there is something characteristic about those speech-related activities which can serve as a guide to determine which other speech-related activities should be protected. A third inquiry will be made to determine whether or not there are speech-conduct situations which do not have the characteristic that entitles them to first amendment protection, but nevertheless are an expression of an idea, and therefore ought to be tested under one of the first amendment tests, rather than merely classified as conduct and therefore punishable as such.

Protected Activities

Distribution of Literature

That freedom of the press includes freedom of distribution was decided in *Ex parte Jackson*, where the Court held that "[l]iberty of circulating is as essential to that freedom as liberty of publishing . . . ." The Court cited *Ex parte Jackson* with approval in *Lowell v. City of Griffin*, without indicating that there was anything about distribution of literature that was anything other than a part of the exercise of freedom of the press. In *Schneider v. State*, however, the Court did recognize that distribution of information was more than just the exercise of a first amendment freedom, and therefore could be regulated.

> So long as legislation to this end does not abridge the constitutional liberty of one rightfully upon the street to impart information through speech or the distribution of literature, it may lawfully regulate the conduct of those using the streets.

Even though regulation is permitted, it is clear that what the Court is saying is that inherent in the concept of free expression is the right to distribute literature. Distribution, even though a part of expression itself, is conduct, and as such can be regulated. Justice Black in referring to freedom of speech and the press in *Martin v. City of Struthers*, stated the proposition this way: "This freedom embraces the right to distribute literature . . . ."

Soliciting

The first amendment also protects solicitation. In *Cantwell v. Connecticut* the solicitation was by those exercising their religious freedom. The Court in referring to this freedom stated:

Thus the Amendment embraces two concepts, — freedom to believe and freedom to act. The first is absolute but, in the nature of things, the second cannot be. Conduct remains subject to regulation for the protection of society. . . . In every case the power to regulate must be so exercised as not, in attaining a permissible end, unduly to infringe the protected freedom.

That the conduct phase of the right is subject to regulation can also be seen by the statement of the Court in *Thomas* v. *Collins:*

Once the speaker goes further, however, and engages in conduct which amounts to more than the right free discussion comprehends, as when he undertakes the collection of funds or securing subscriptions, he enters a realm where a reasonable registration or identification requirement may be imposed.

Parading

While statutes regulating parading have been before the Court in several cases dating back to 1939, *Shuttlesworth* v. *City of Birmingham* is the most explicit in answering the question whether parading is an activity protected by the first amendment. In answer to the contention that what was involved in that case was not pure speech, but the use of streets and sidewalks, the Court stated:

But our decisions have also made clear that picketing and parading may none the less constitute methods of expression, entitled to First Amendment protection.

Upon affirming the position that parading is entitled to first amendment protection, the Court acknowledged that statutes may be enacted to regulate the use of streets for parades, providing that the regulations relate to time, place and manner of holding the parade, and do not give the official who grants the permit discretionary power which he can use to discriminate in the selection of those given parade permits.

Picketing

In striking down a statute which prohibited all picketing, the Court, in *Thornhill* v. *Alabama*, brought peaceful picketing within the protection of the first amendment. The statute under consideration in that case

> embrace[d] nearly every practicable, effective means whereby those interested—including the employees directly affected—may enlighten the public on the nature and causes of a labor dispute. The safeguarding of these means is essential to the securing of an informed and educated public opinion with respect to a matter which is of public concern.

Peaceful picketing, in the words of Justice Frankfurter, "is the workingman's means of communication."

But peaceful picketing, too, is subject to reasonable regulation and even to being absolutely prohibited in certain instances. Insofar as it being subject to complete prohibition at the whim of the legislature, Justice Douglas, in *International Brotherhood of Teamsters* v. *Vogt, Inc.*, called this a "retreat" and "formal surrender." He argued that "this form of expression can be regulated or prohibited only to the extent that it forms an essential part of a course of conduct which the State can regulate or prohibit."

Picketing has taken on a new dimension in recent years. While the older cases have generally dealt with labor picketing, picketing is now being used by those who desire to communicate opinions with regard to segregation, war policies, welfare rules, etc. In such cases, however, it is also subject to regulation. In *Cox* v. *Louisiana* the Court upheld a statute which prohibited picketing or parading in or near a courthouse.

> The conduct which is the subject of this statute — picketing and parading — is subject to regulation even though intertwined with expression and association.

Sit-ins

Whether a sit-in is an activity that enjoys first amendment protection is somewhat in doubt. Although the Court has been called upon to consider a number of sit-in cases, it has usually been able to resolve them by referring to constitutional requirements other than the first amendment.

In *Garner* v. *Louisiana* the Court was able to resolve the matter by finding that the convictions were devoid of evidence to support them and therefore violated due process. Justice Harlan, although concurring in the result, was unwilling to let the matter stand on this ground. He was of the opinion that "petitioners' conduct . . . was a form of expression within the range of protections afforded by the Fourteenth Amendment which could in no event be punished by the State under a *general* breach of the peace statute . . . ." He also wrote that:

> There was more to the conduct of those petitioners than a bare desire to remain at the "white" lunch counter and their refusal of a police request to move from the counter. We would surely have to be blind not to recognize that petitioners were sitting at these counters, where they knew they would not be served, in order to demonstrate that their race was being segregated in dining facilities in this part of the country.
>
> Such a demonstration, in the circumstances of these two cases, is as much a part of the "free trade in ideas," . . . as is verbal expression, more commonly thought of as "speech." It, like speech, appeals to good sense and to "the power of reason, as applied through public discussion," . . . just as much as, if not more than, a public oration delivered from a soapbox at a street corner. This Court has never limited the right to speak, a protected "liberty" under the Fourteenth Amendment, . . . to mere verbal expression.

The Court was again confronted with the sit-in situation in two cases decided the same day, *Peterson* v. *City of Greenville* and *Lombard* v. *Louisiana*. The convictions in those cases were reversed upon the basis that there was state action in bringing about segregated lunch counters, which violated the equal protection clause of the fourteenth amendment. Although the Court did not consider these sit-ins as being a first amendment activity, Justice Harlan, concurring in part and dissenting in part, once again alluded to the sit-in as being "in the realm of expression."

A sit-in as a first amendment activity received somewhat more support in *Brown* v. *Louisiana*. Justice Fortas, in an opinion concurred in by Chief Justice Warren and Justice Douglas, concluded that the Court was "dealing with an aspect of a basic constitutional right — the right under the First and Fourteenth Amendments guaranteeing freedom of speech and assembly, and freedom to petition the Government for redress of grievances." Justices Brennan and White, concurring in the *Brown* reversal, did not decide the issue of whether petitioners' conduct was constitutionally protected.

Justice Harlan joined the dissenting opinion of Justice Black which was to the effect that Louisiana could apply its breach of peace statute to this sit-in, particularly in view of the fact that the statute was aimed at trespasses on government property. Justice Black, however, did not let the matter rest there. He was critical of Justice Fortas' opinion because it relied upon the first amendment. He referred to it as establishing "a completely new constitutional doctrine." Justice Black's position seems to be that the first amendment "does not guarantee to any person the right to use someone else's property, even that owned by government and dedicated to other purposes, as a stage to express dissident ideas."

Justice Harlan's position, however, must be that sit-ins are a legitimate form of protest, but that the government can by appropriate statutes regulate or prohibit them. In *Garner* he wrote that "a state legislature may enact a trespass statute, or a disturbance of the peace statute which either lists in detail the acts condemned by legitimate state policy or proscribes breaches of the peace generally, thus relating the offense to the already developed body of common law defining that crime." It cannot, however, make freedom of expression subject to criminal sanctions by means of a general and all inclusive breach of the peace prohibition.

This leaves us then without a clear determination that a sit-in is an activity entitled to first amendment protection.

Group Legal Services

When the State of Virginia attempted to apply certain of its statutes regulating the conduct of lawyers to the NAACP, the Court was first confronted with the problem of determining the extent to which a state may regulate group legal services. In *NAACP v. Button* it held that, "[i]n the context of NAACP objectives, litigation" is "a form of political expression" and therefore is protected under the first amendment. Being a first amendment freedom, the Court said it "need[s] breathing space to survive, [and] government may regulate in the area only with narrow specificity." Not finding the regulations specific enough, the Court held that they could not be applied to the activities of the NAACP.

The Court also brought the balancing test into the case. The argument was made that the statutes were a justified regulation of the legal profession, which, of course, has long been subject to state regulation. The Court reviewed the dangers from the traditionally illegal practices of barratry, maintenance, and champerty, but concluded that "[t]here has been no showing of a serious danger here of professionally reprehensible conflicts of interest which rules against solicitation frequently seek to prevent." The Court then balanced in favor of the exercise of freedom of association as against the state's interest in preventing unethical conduct by attorneys.

In dissenting, Justice Harlan argued that "litigation, whether or not associated with the attempt to vindicate constitutional rights, is *conduct;* it is speech *plus.*" For him the question was simply one of balancing.

> So here, the question is whether the particular regulation of conduct concerning litigation has a reasonable relation to the furtherance of a proper state interest, and whether that interest outweighs any foreseeable harm to the furtherance of protected freedoms.

Applying this test led him to conclude that the interest of the state was greater and therefore he would have upheld the application of the Virginia statutes to the activities of the NAACP.

The question of the extent of the regulation of group legal services passed through two more cases before its characteristics were clearly outlined. In *Brotherhood of Railroad Trainmen* v. *Virginia State Bar,* the BRT maintained a legal department which recommended to its members lawyers whom they believed to be honest and competent. In overturning an injunction prohibiting the BRT from continuing such activities, the Court, through Justice Black, held "that the First and Fourteenth Amendments protect the right of the members through their Brotherhood to maintain and carry out their plan for advising workers who are injured to obtain legal advice and for recommending specific lawyers." For Justice Black and the majority it was clear that what was at issue here was the exercise of a first amendment freedom, pure and simple.

Justices Clark and Harlan disagreed. To them "[p]ersonal injury litigation is not a form of political expression, but rather a procedure for the settlement of damage claims. No guaranteed civil right is involved." This was not even "speech plus." It was just the regulation of the legal profession, which had long been recognized as within the power of the state.

But Justice Black and the majority would have nothing to do with this approach. In *United Mine Workers* v. *Illinois Bar Ass'n*, again writing for the majority, Justice Black reiterated their position. In this case the union employed a licensed attorney to represent any member who desired his services to prosecute workmen's compensation claims. The Illinois Supreme Court, looking back at *Button*, concluded that this kind of activity was protected only when the litigation was a form of political expression. Justice Black responded:

> We do not think our decisions in *Trainmen* and *Button* can be so narrowly limited. We hold that freedom of speech, assembly, and petition guaranteed by the First and Fourteenth Amendments gives petitioner the right to hire attorneys on a salary basis to assist its members in the assertion of their legal rights.

Before taking a look at the more recent speech-conduct cases, it would seem appropriate to bring into focus the Court's approach to cases of this kind. As the above review indicates the Court has concluded that certain kinds of conduct are expressive and therefore included within the first amendment guarantee.

Distributing literature, soliciting, parading, and picketing are examples of such conduct. It is not clear whether sit-ins also enjoy this characteristic, but the trend seems to be in that direction. On the other hand, the activity involved in the group legal services turns out to be first amendment pure and simple, *i.e.*, speech and assembly, according to the majority. This, of course, does not mean that it is absolute. Certainly the practice of law part of the group legal services can be regulated, and possibly the group activity itself if the regulation is narrowly drawn.

In the speech-conduct cases reviewed above, although recognizing that there is a legitimate state interest in regulating the conduct aspect of the matter, the Court has required that the state do so through a narrowly drawn statute which clearly defines the limits of the regulation and eliminates the possibility of any censorship by the exercise of discretion on the part of any permit-granting official. In those cases where there was a complete ban on the activity in question, the Court held such ban unconstitutional. In some of the labor picketing cases, however, injunctions which banned all picketing, in the context of the facts then before the Court, were approved.

Draft Cards — Armbands — Burning Flags — and Vests

Turning to recent speech-conduct cases, we note that the Court has recently decided three such cases, *United States* v. *O'Brien, Tinker* v. *Des Moines Independent Community School District* and *Street* v. *New York,* and dismissed an appeal in one, *People* v. *Cowgill.*

O'Brien

David O'Brien burned his draft card on the steps of the South Boston Courthouse. For this he was indicted, tried and convicted as one "who forges, alters, knowingly destroys, knowingly mutilates, or in any manner changes any such . . . [draft card]." On its face this is clearly a statute which punishes conduct. On its face it punishes conduct in the same manner that breach of peace and disorderly conduct statutes do, and as do a great variety of other statutes. This statute does not regulate any activity that, on is face, is in any way related to a first amendment activity. It differs from soliciting, picketing, parading, etc., which, as pointed out above, are expression-related to the extent that they enjoy first amendment protection. Upon doing the act, the doer is guilty, and one should not even have to ask, as Chief Justice Warren does in this case, whether "the governmental interest is unrelated to the suppression of free expression; and if the incidental restriction on alleged first amendment freedoms is no greater than is essential to the furtherance of that interest." As long as "an apparently limitless variety of conduct can [*not*] be labelled 'speech' whenever the person engaging in the conduct intends thereby to express an idea" no reference to the first amendment, or to any of the first amendment tests set forth above, are needed.

Although seemingly making this position quite clear, Chief Justice Warren then turned to the first amendment claim asserted by O'Brien, and, making an assumption that it was applicable, proceeded to discuss the issue as if the problem was simply one of balancing governmental interests in the nonmutilation of the draft card against O'Brien's interest in freely expressing his opposition to the war and the draft. After discussing the interest of the government and finding it legitimate and substantial, Chief Justice Warren concluded that "a sufficient governmental interest has been shown to justify O'Brien's conviction."

This disposition of the *O'Brien* case makes it clear that (1) conduct, unless it is conduct which is inherently part of expression, can be punished simply by the enactment of a statute punishing the conduct, even though that conduct may be of the type that the doer has chosen to express an idea, and (2) even if the Court will assume that the conduct was used to express an idea, it can be punished as conduct where there is a legitimate and substantial governmental interest to be protected by the enactment of the statute.

In the process of "balancing," Chief Justice Warren lists four things that if found to exist will tip the scales in favor of the government. He states that:

[A] government regulation is sufficiently justified if it is within the constitutional power of the government; if it furthers an important or substantial government interest; if the governmental interest is unrelated to the suppression of free expression; and if the incidental restriction on alleged First Amendment freedom is no greater than is essential to the furtherance of that interest.

The opinion then goes on to find that the first three of the above are satisfied. The Court finds governmental power, legitimate and substantial interest, and that the statute is unrelated to free expression. Nowhere does the Court even discuss the fourth part of this "balancing" test. There is no evaluation whatsoever of whether this enactment is only an incidental restriction on freedom of expression.

In any event, the use of the first amendment balancing test to justify legislation affecting pure conduct is inappropriate. Such statutes need not be measured by the first amendment to be constitutional. They need only to be measured by due process standards.

The first amendment balancing test has been used when there is governmental action directed against first amendment rights. In *NAACP v. Alabama*, the right was freedom of association, as was the case in *Konigsberg v. State Bar*. Even in those cases in which Justice Black agrees that balancing should be used, *e.g.*, where municipalities need to keep streets open, a *first amendment right*, such as soliciting, parading, or distributing literature, was involved.

Cases such as *O'Brien* offer the Court several alternative methods of reaching a solution. One alternative would be to hold that only conduct is involved, and as such it is punishable as long as the statute meets due process standards. This is about what the Court did in

O'Brien, for the Court said that it was "[f]or this non-communicative impact of his conduct, and nothing else, he was convicted."

Justice Harlan was concerned that the majority's absolutist approach might stifle legitimate protest under some circumstances. He wanted it understood that, as far as he was concerned, this approach would not "foreclose consideration of first amendment claims in those rare instances [when the test used by the majority] has the effect of entirely preventing a 'speaker' from reaching a significant audience with whom he could not otherwise lawfully communicate."

The majority approach leaves legislative bodies free to enact any type of statute governing conduct which in their opinion is necessary to protect the public safety, convenience and welfare. That legislative bodies can, and will, use this freedom to prohibit the use of certain kinds of conduct as a means of expression is clear from enactment of the non-mutilation statute used to convict O'Brien.

Another alternative would be to examine the conduct prohibited to see if it has within it any first amendment characteristic such as the Court has found in parading, etc. If the conduct is of this type, then the test applicable thereto ought to be applied. This would require the legislature to narrowly draft the statute so as not to abridge the first amendment right any more than is reasonably necessary to protect a legitimate governmental interest. It would seem that a sit-in, for example, should be tested this way. Sit-ins certainly are conduct. They are very expressive conduct. However, there are also governmental interests to be protected, such as the non-disruption of the activity being protested, whether it be the induction of men into the armed forces or the undisturbed operation of a university. But to prohibit *all* sit-ins would be as onerous as to prohibit all peaceful picketing. A narrowly drawn statute, therefore, could set forth the ground rules of when and under what circumstances sit-ins would be permitted. As long as the statute met the test heretofore used by the Court in such speech-conduct cases, conviction thereunder would be constitutional.

Not all conduct so easily lends itself to this kind of classification. Draft card burning, and hanging clothes on front lawn are not inherently expressive, nor is the mere wearing of a flag as a vest. The third alternative, then, is to recognize that under some circumstances these activities, although conduct, can be extremely expressive. There can be little doubt that the circumstances under which O'Brien burned his draft card told a story to many thousands of people, far more effectively than simply making a speech at that particular time and place.

If the Court is to recognize that under some circumstances such acts are expressive and should enjoy first amendment protection, it will then need to determine the extent to which they can be prohibited or restricted. This will require the application of one of the first amendment tests set forth above.

The Court might use either the clear and present danger test, or the first amendment balancing of interests test. In applying the clear and present danger test the Court, although recognizing that what is involved is conduct which is prohibited by a statute, might ask whether the action of the individual sought to be punished really did present a clear and present danger to the happening of the event that the government sought to prevent by the enactment of the statute. In *O'Brien* the Court would have had to ask whether O'Brien's burning his draft card, under the circumstances which he did, really did present a clear and present danger to the draft system. If the Court were to find that it did, then the conviction would stand.

On the other hand, the Court might adopt the balancing test, which it has used in other first amendment cases. It could set forth the government's interest in the prohibition of the conduct and the individual's interest in the exercise of the right of free expression, under the circumstances of the case. This, of course, would require the Court to accept the fact that the conduct chosen by the "speaker" was for the purpose of expressing a point of view. If the Court found that the governmental interests outweighed the individual's interest, the statute could be applied and the conviction stand.

It is clear that in *O'Brien* the Court did not adopt this kind of a balancing test. The Court only assumed that O'Brien's conduct had in it a communicative element. Further, after adopting a four-part test, as set forth above, the Court never decided whether "the incidental restriction on [O'Brien's] alleged First Amendment freedoms . . . [might have been] greater than is essential to the furtherance of [the governmental] interest." The Court discusses at length why the non-mutilation statute was necessary to protect a governmental interest, and concluded that what O'Brien had done frustrated this interest.

The Court then reverted back to its original premise that what was involved here was conduct pure and simple and it was for this and nothing more that O'Brien was punished.

That the Court made no real attempt to balance any first amendment rights which O'Brien may have had is confirmed by an examination of the dissent in *Street*, written by Chief Justice Warren who wrote the *O'Brien* opinion. In that dissent, the Chief Justice argued that flag burning is conduct, and as such punishable even though the person doing the burning claims that he is doing so as a method of protest.

Tinker

Three teenage students desiring to publicize their objections to the war in Vietnam decided to wear black armbands to school. The school officials, upon learning of the plan, adopted a policy that any student wearing an armband to school would be suspended until he removed it. The students wore the armbands and were immediately suspended.

When the matter reached the Supreme Court, the wearing of an armband was characterized as "closely akin to 'pure speech' which . . . is entitled to comprehensive protection under the First Amendment." Having characterized this as "pure speech" and noting that as such it was entitled to greater protection than expressive conduct, the Court concluded that in the absence of any interference with school activities, or of any disorder on the school grounds, wearing armbands could not be prohibited:

> Clearly, the prohibition of expression of one particular opinion, at least without evidence that it is necessary to avoid material and substantial interference with school work or discipline is not constitutionally permissible.

The fact that the speech in question was taking place on school grounds was no reason for prohibiting it. School grounds, the Court held, is a place where the expression of opinions must be allowed:

> A student's rights therefore, do not embrace merely the classroom hours. When he is in the cafeteria, or on the playing field, or on the campus during the authorized hours, he may express his opinions, even on controversial subjects like the conflict in Vietnam, if he does so "without materially and substantially interfering with . . . appro-

priate discipline in the operation of the school" and without colliding with the rights of others.

The students in *Tinker* were exercising a first amendment right in the wearing of the armbands. Their right to continue to do so was subject to those limitations on first amendment rights which the Court has heretofore found constitutionally permissible.

The school officials had attempted to ban the wearing of armbands at all times and at all places on the campus. Only in unusual circumstances has the Court permitted prior restraints on the exercise of first amendment rights. In *Carroll* the Court reviewed this area of the law, and noted that "[o]rdinarily, the State's constitutionally permissible interests are adequately served by criminal penalities imposed after freedom to speak has been so grossly abused that its immunity is breached." Although the Court did not decide whether a properly granted injunction would have been upheld in *Carroll v. President and Commissioners of Princess Anne,* the implication from that case is that there may be a time when the facts are such that a prior restraint in the form of an injunction will be permitted in order to prevent violence. It seems unlikely that just the wearing of an armband, in the fact situation of *Tinker,* would be such as to allow a complete prior restraint.

If the school officials had adopted regulations specifying the time and place for wearing armbands, such regulations would have been constitutionally permissible if narrowly drawn, reasonable, and containing definite standards. Further, even the requirement of securing a permit to wear the armbands would have been permissible, if the standards which guided the permit issuer related to time and place, and did not give the permit issuer discretionary authority over those seeking permits, which he could exercise in a discriminatory manner.

Determining then that the campus is a permissible place for the exercise of free speech, and there being no justification for a complete ban upon the wearing of the armbands, and there being no specific regulations as to time and place of the wearing thereof, how should the action of the school officials be tested? Referring back to the first amendment tests heretofore used by the Court, it is apparent that the clear and present danger test should apply in this case.

What is sought to be prevented here is disorder on the campus and substantial interference with school work. This is a substantive evil which the school officials have a right to prevent. The wearing of the armbands should therefore be permissible until there is a clear and present danger that the evil will occur. In the absence thereof, no disciplinary action should be permitted.

Street   Upon learning that a civil rights leader had been shot in Mississippi by a sniper, Street took his United States flag to a nearby intersection and burned it. He was heard to say: "We don't need no damn flag." and "Yes; that is my flag, I burned it. If they let that happen to Meredith; we don't need an American flag." Street was convicted of malicious mischief under a penal statute which makes it a misdemeanor "publicly [to] mutilate, deface, defile or defy, trample upon, or cast contempt either by words or act [upon any flag of the United States]." Because there was the possibility that Street's conviction may have rested in part upon his casting contempt upon the flag *by words*, which could not constitutionally be punished, the Court reversed and sent the case back for further consideration. The Court did not reach the question of whether Street could constitutionally be punished for the act of publicly destroying the flag as a means of protest on the ground that such an act constitutes expression protected by the first amendment.

The four dissenters, Chief Justice Warren, Justices Black, White and Fortas, would have reached this issue, and all would have held that the defendant could constitutionally be convicted for burning his flag, even though he did so as a form of protest. To these Justices the case was simply one of punishing conduct which was prohibited by a valid criminal statute.

This case presents the Court with the same alternatives discussed in connection with *O'Brien*. Four of the Justices were willing to adopt the first alternative and eliminate from their consideration any alleged first amendment claim. In the words of Justice Fortas, "[p]rotest does not exonerate lawlessness." The statute made it unlawful to mutilate the flag, "[a]nd the prohibition against flag burning on the public thoroughfare being valid, the misdemeanor is not excused merely because it is an act of flamboyant protest." To go further and give consideration to a first amendment claim would require the Court to accept the view that at least some conduct can be labelled "speech" when the person engaging in the conduct intends thereby to express an idea. Once the Court accepts the position that there is a valid first amendment issue it will be faced with the question of testing the conduct to determine whether it can be prohibited or restricted. Again, as pointed out above, if the activity has within it a first amendment characteristic, as found in parading, etc., the Court could apply the test generally used in those cases.

The use of the flag as a means of protest, including flag burning, might fall into this category. Recently the use of the flag as a means of expression has been considered by the courts of Delaware (display of a flag in a subordinate position to the flag of the United Nations), Georgia (tearing of a flag in the process of lowering it to half mast as symbolic of a state of mourning by those protesting segregation), New York (use of flags in an art gallery display in form of a dead human body being hanged by the neck), and California (flag cut and sewn into a vest and worn on a public street). And, of course, the flag was the basis of the protest in *Street.*

If the Court were to acknowledge that the flag can be a vehicle for "flamboyant protest," it could require that statutes punishing desecration thereof be carefully drawn so as to punish only the most loathsome and flagrant acts of desecration, leaving some "unusual" uses of the flag available as a means for the exercise of free expression. This, of course, would not be an easy task. But what is at issue here is the preservation of the right of free expression, while acknowledging that there are governmental interests which require protection.

If the Court is unwilling to characterize the use of the flag as expression-related conduct, it might still accord such use first amendment protection by applying either the clear and present danger test or the balancing of interests test to the conduct sought to be punished, on a case by case basis.

The motivation for the enactment of statutes punishing desecration of the flag seems to be to prevent breaches of the peace. If the facts surrounding the "illegal" use of the flag indicate that the user chose it as a tool to express an idea, the Court might ask whether in the context of that use there existed a clear and present danger of a breach of the peace. If no such danger actually existed, there should be no punishment.

It may be that the prevention of breaches of the peace is not the only purpose served by anti-desecration statutes. In *Halter v. Nebraska* the Court had before it a Nebraska statute making it a misdemeanor to sell any article of merchandise which had printed or placed thereon a flag for the purpose of advertisement. In discussing the use of flags as national symbols the Court wrote:

> From the earliest periods in the history of the human race, banners, standards and ensigns have been adopted as symbols of the power and history of the peoples who bore them. . . . For [the American] flag every true American has not simply an appreciation but a deep affection. No American, nor any foreign born person who enjoys the privileges of American citizenship, ever looks upon it without taking pride in the fact that he lives under this free government.

In view of the fact that the flag is a symbol of this free government and does instill a deep sense of pride in our people, the Court could use the first amendment balancing test to adjudicate cases involving "illegal" use thereof. The Court would have to weigh the interests of the state in the preservation of the flag, undefiled as our national symbol, against the interests of the individual (and of society too) in the free exercise of the right of free expression. By doing so, at least some consideration is then given to the right of free speech, which consideration was not given in any of the recent flag desecration cases referred to above, and would not be accorded under the approach taken by the dissenters in *Street*.

People v. *Radich* is a case in point. A proprietor of an art gallery was charged with and convicted of violating the New York flag desecration statute by putting on display various art exhibits in which the flag was displayed:

> 1 — in the form of a male sexual organ, protruding from the body of form, in the anterior portion of the body of the form and depicting the erected male penis, protruding from a form of a cross. 2 — The flag of the United States of America, wrapped in a chained bundle. 3 — The standard of the United States on the form of an alleged elephant. 4 — The Union of the flag of the United States of America, depicted in the form of an octopus (sic). 5 — The American flag attached to a gas meter. 6 — The American flag wrapped around a bundle attached to a two wheeled vehicle. 7 — The American flag in the form of a body, hanging from a yellow noose.

In affirming the conviction, Judge Gibson of the New York Court of Appeals framed the issue as if he were going to give some recognition to the defendant's first amendment claim:

While it seems well established that a clear violation of a valid statute may not be saved on First Amendment grounds, it is necessary in this case eventually to reach a somewhat different question, which is, whether or not the act said to constitute the violation is tempered by the application of the First Amendment.

Just how a violation of a valid statute cannot be saved by the first amendment, but a violation may be tempered by the first amendment, is not clear. But because Judge Gibson framed the issue the way that he did, it is assumed that he did intend to consider the defendant's first amendment claim.

It is clear, however, that the first amendment claim was not tested by any of the first amendment tests heretofore discussed. What the court did was to decide the case on the basis that conduct, under a valid conduct statute, is punishable as such even though the actor-speaker is expressing an opinion by his conduct.

After citing cases that have sustained convictions under flag desecration statutes to support the conclusion that the New York statute was constitutional, the court noted

that a person with the purest of intentions may freely proceed to disseminate the ideas in which he profoundly believes, but he may not break a valid law to do it.

And further:

The defendant may have a sincere ideological viewpoint, but he must find other ways to express it.

The only recognition the court gives to a first amendment claim is to note that, in the "balancing" test used by the Supreme Court in *O'Brien*, there is the requirement that "the governmental interest . . . [be] unrelated to the suppression of free expression . . . ." But the court of appeals concludes that "a flag desecration statute is aimed at keeping the public peace" and thus not aimed at expression, and therefore the *O'Brien* requirement is satisfied.

From this, according to the court, it follows that the conviction must be affirmed — thus all the discussion concerning the application of the first amendment turns out to be just so much rhetoric. Radich was found guilty of violating a conduct statute, and his conviction was not "tempered by the application of the First Amendment."

This approach leads to a wrong result in this case. The flag was being used as part of a medium of expression, *i.e.*, as art. Art is a form of expression — paintings, sculptures, and other artistic constructions are intended by their creator to convey a message to the viewer. As such they are entitled to first amendment protection.

The use of a flag in an art display is not the same as burning a draft card or a flag, which acts in themselves are not expressive. Thus, what is being judged here is not abstract conduct; it is a medium of expression in which the creator has chosen the flag as a vehicle. Because it is a form of expression it is entitled to first amendment protection. As a medium of expression, infringement upon it ought to be tested by one of the first amendment tests heretofore discussed. And if the court had applied the clear and present danger test, this conviction should have been set aside.

As set forth above, and as acknowledged by the court of appeals, one of the reasons for the existence of flag desecration statutes is to prevent breaches of the peace. There is nothing in this case, the court to the contrary notwithstanding, to indicate that there was a clear and present danger of any breach of the peace from this art display. As Chief Judge Fuld wrote in dissent.

> [I]n the absence of a showing that the public health, safety or well being of the community is threatened, the State may not act to suppress symbolic speech or conduct having a clearly communicative aspect, no matter how obnoxious it may be to the prevailing views of the majority.

He concludes by stating:

> In sum, I do not understand how it may reasonably be said that the mere display of Morrel's constructions in an art gallery, distasteful though they may be, poses the type of threat to public order necessary to render such an act criminal.

While these statements do not indicate that Judge Fuld was thinking in terms of the clear and present danger test, clearly that test leads to the same conclusion that he reached, and would have given the same kind of consideration to the defendant's first amendment claim as did Judge Fuld.

Even if the court had given full consideration to the first amendment claim by applying the first amendment balancing test, a strong argument can be made for balancing in favor of the artist. Because art by its very creation becomes a medium of expression, the artist has a substantial interest in his freedom to express his opinion by his art. But society too has a great interest here in protecting the artist's freedom to create.

As Judge Basel pointed out in a dissenting opinion when the case was before the Criminal Court of the City of New York, there are many loyal dissenters protesting the war in Vietnam. The artist in this instance has chosen to "voice" his protest by using the flag as part of his protest art.

> We may quarrel with his theme, disagree with his method, condemn his goal. We cannot dispute his right to express dissent even though the means be loathsome to us. "Laws must, to be consistent with the First Amendment, permit the widest toleration of conflicting viewpoints consistent with a society of free men."

Cowgill

People v. *Cowgill* is another flag desecration case. The defendant cut up an American flag and had it made into a vest which he then wore in public. This case differs from *Street* because the California flag desecration statute does not contain any reference to casting contempt upon the flag by words, as does the New York statute. In affirming Cowgill's conviction, the California District Court of Appeal adopted the view of the dissenters in *Street* that states "have the power to protect the flag from *acts* of desecration and disgrace."

There can be no question that this position is correct as long as courts are unwilling to consider the fact that the act may be an expression of an opinion. As pointed out above, what this approach overlooks is that some acts which are punishable as such may actually be a very effective method of expressing a viewpoint. Were the courts to recognize this, then the first amendment tests ought to be used to test the infringement upon the individual's right to freely express himself in this manner.

The Supreme Court of the United States dismissed an appeal in this case; not, however, without Justices Harlan and Brennan expressing their concern for the Court's apparent insensitivity to the first amendment issues in cases of this kind. While concurring in the dismissal, these Justices do so on the narrow ground that the record in the case was not sufficient to justify consideration of the broader first amendment constitutional issue. But, Justice Harlan points out, the issue "is one that . . . [he] cannot regard as insubstantial."

What courts ought not to overlook in flag desecration cases is that in recent years the mere display of a flag has come to signify more than just one's patriotism. Under certain circumstances today, just hanging the flag outside one's home may be an indication that the occupant believes in the correctness of certain actions of the government, such as the conduct of the war in Vietnam.

The Boston Tea Party

Our history books tell us that on the night of December 16, 1773, a group of men masquerading as Indians boarded three ships in Boston Harbor which were loaded with tea. These "Indians" broke open the chests and dumped the tea into the water. While this was done as a protest against the English Tea Act of 1773, it formed a part of a greater protest by the people living in the colonies against the rule of the British Government. That this was conduct, and was illegal, there is no doubt. Nor can there be any doubt that the "Indians" would have been punished if caught. But neither can there be any doubt that this was conduct with a message. It was indeed "flamboyant protest."

What is true of the Boston Tea Party is also true of draft card burning, flag burning, and the use of flags as part of art displays or wearing them as clothing. Not to recognize this and not to give them some first amendment consideration is to greatly narrow the field of effective protest. If the view is to prevail that is suggested by the four dissenters in *Street*, free expression will be confined to verbal expression, to those speech-conduct situations in which the Court will find an inherent first amendment characteristic, and to those types of conduct not yet made illegal by those bodies having legislative powers. And that legislative bodies are subject to pressure to enact statues punishing conduct which the public dislikes is evidenced by the draft card anti-mutilation statute in *O'Brien* and the number of bills which have been dropped in hoppers of the various state legislatures and Congress concerning campus unrest.

If the right to free expression is as precious as the quotations at the beginning of this article indicate, legitimate expressive-conduct should not be cut off simply by classifying it as conduct and allowing the government to punish it as such. The Court should accept the view that an apparently limitless variety of conduct *can* be labelled "speech" when the "speaker" in good faith intends to express an idea by his conduct.

Once it acknowledges that the actor has a good faith first amendment claim, the Court should then apply to the infringement thereon the appropriate first amendment test. In some instances the Court ought to treat the conduct as having an inherent first amendment characteristic, and accord to it the same kind of protection as is given to parading, picketing, etc.; that is, to require that the statute regulating it be narrowly drawn so as not to unnecessarily infringe upon the first amendment right. The flag cases fall into this category. The use of a flag, as the Court noted in *Halter*, conveys a message; today that message may be more than just a message of patriotism.

In the absence of a narrowly drawn statute, and for those kinds of conduct which have no inherent first amendment characteristic, except insofar as the actor in good faith claims to be expressing an opinion, the clear and present danger test should be used. This approach would not justify "breaking windows in government buildings," as Justice Fortas implies in *Street*. The clear and present danger test can be used to punish a speaker when, by using "pure speech," he has created a clear and present danger of a riot. It can also be used to punish an actor for using expressive conduct to destroy property. As "pure speech" is not absolute, neither would expressive conduct be absolute.

What is needed in approaching cases involving freedom of expression (including expression-related conduct) is for courts to have a strong commitment to the preservation of the ideals set forth at the beginning of this article. As pointed out by Professor Emerson:

> A system of free expression can be successful only when it rests upon the strongest possible commitment to the positive right and the narrowest possible basis for exceptions. And any such exceptions must be clear-cut, precise and readily controlled. Otherwise the forces that press toward restriction will break through the openings, and freedom of expression will become the exception and suppression the rule.